Kill Devil Hill

Kill Devil Hill

Discovering the Secret of the Wright Brothers

Harry Combs

with Martin Caidin

Foreword by Neil Armstrong

Illustrated with Photographs and Drawings

Houghton Mifflin Company
Boston 1979

Library of Congress Cataloging in Publication Data
Combs, Harry.
  Kill Devil Hill.

  Bibliography: p.
  Includes index.
  1. Wright, Orville, 1871–1948. 2. Wright,
Wilbur, 1867–1912. 3. Aeronautics — United States
— Biography. I. Caidin, Martin, date   joint
author.   II. Title.
TL540.W7C65   629.13′0092′4   [B]   79-9362
ISBN 0-395-28216-0

Printed in the United States of America
W 10 9 8 7 6 5 4 3 2 1

Drawings by Jess Smithback

To Ginney

Neither could have mastered the problem alone. As inseparable as twins, they are indispensable to each other.

Bishop Milton Wright, father
of Wilbur and Orville,
January 16, 1904.

Acknowledgments

WHEN JOHN DONNE WROTE his now familiar "No man is an island," his metaphysical philosophies must have anticipated the tribulations of aviation historical writers. Few endeavors more clearly illustrate the principle of man's dependence on man. Indeed, when I undertook this work, assistance came from every direction. I am eternally grateful for the kind help so generously and enthusiastically given by many wonderful people.

I am particularly indebted to Paul Edward Garber, historian emeritus of the National Air and Space Museum, a principal advocate of American aviation's heritage, a friend of Orville Wright and a witness of his Signal Corps trial flights in 1909 at Fort Myer. His encouragement, his knowledge of the problems of flight, and his personal insight into the character and warm personality of the Wright brothers were invaluable.

I am grateful to Charles Dollfus, pioneer balloonist and co-founder of the French Air Museum of 1918 and curator of the Musée de l'Air, who not only put the significance of the Wright brothers in proper perspective but, above all, arranged a meeting with that fascinating French gentleman, Henri Delgove — eyewitness of Wilbur Wright's first public earth-shattering flight of August 8, 1908, at Le Mans — when the true brilliance of the Wrights first burst upon a skeptical world and kindled a flame that lighted the pathway to the stars; a flame that Henri personally kept burning in his own way, in his own time and in his own place.

To Mrs. Ivonette Wright Miller, niece of Orville and Wilbur, whose delightful reminiscence and personal observations provided invaluable family insights. To Harold Miller for his great contribution as an executor of the Wright estate, and his monumental decision to provide the Wright papers to the Library of Congress, without access to which any writer would flounder.

To Bernie Whelan, one of the earliest flying students of the Wrights at Simms Station, who recalls the colorful instruction techniques of Orville Wright with affection.

To Jerome Fanciulli, who as a newsman covered the 1908 flight trials at Fort Myer, and who as an intimate of the Wrights supplied many insights into the characters of Orville, Katharine, and Wilbur, and some of their immediate associates.

To my longtime dear friend and mentor, Billy Parker, a veritable walking encyclopedia of aviation, who built and flew his own airplane in the latter days of the Wrights and who so clearly explained the control differences between the Wright and Curtiss airplanes.

To Charles Gibbs-Smith, brilliant historian, Honorary Companion of the Royal Aeronautical Society, great authority on the Wrights, who in the short time available in a visit to the Science Museum of South Kensington, London, so accurately and clearly defined the significance of the Wrights' accomplishments.

To Mike Collins, former astronaut and veteran moon voyager, now Undersecretary of the Smithsonian Institution, who placed his fine staff of experts and treasured resources at the disposal of all those wonderful people who aided me in this work.

To Elvie Smith of Pratt & Whitney, Canada, for sources of information on the Wrights' English connections.

To Don Keeley, NCR Corporation director of flight operations, who made the many visits to Dayton memorable and productive experiences.

To Capt. Ralph S. Barnaby, veteran flier and friend of the brothers, respected authority on the earliest days of flight, a valued source for many hitherto hidden facts.

To George Hardie, Jr., of the Experimental Aircraft Association, who opened a window into the past by bringing to life an exact replica of the Wright engine so that I could hear how it sounded. It was a clattering roar of history I shall never forget — it sounded like hell! Anyone would have to be brave to fly behind, in front of, or beside such a powerplant.

To Mickey Roth, former National Aeronautic Association executive who generously opened doors to hidden archives when this pilgrimage first began.

To Marvin W. McFarland, whose dedication and effective compilation and definition of the correspondence, and other personal records of the Wrights, have contributed enormously to the body of aeronautical knowledge.

To Frances L. Apt, whose command of the English language and depth of knowledge helped fine-tune the finished product.

To James Thompson for his keen editorial insight and guidance, for his personal commitment and enthusiasm, and for the sensitive touch he brought to this effort.

To Martin Caidin, prolific storyteller and brave comrade, one of the roughest-speaking, kindest-hearted, gentlest souls on earth, and to Bill Ficks who picked up the ball and ran.

To Barbara Bishop and Treva Stamps for their untiring efforts and assistance.

To Maxine Greenwood, proofreader, typist par excellence, for her persevering insistence on accuracy, and to Lee Hayes, friend and associate of many years, whose patience and support and endless typing contributed immeasurably.

And to Jim Greenwood — noble gentleman and friend — whose staunch support in adversity and whose steady hand and cool head carried us through many ups and downs. His knowledge of sources, his organization of our research, and his long intimate association with the aviation world made this book possible.

Finally, there are all those who through organizations helped so much, and can only be recognized through those institutions — the National Air and Space Museum of the Smithsonian Institution, the Library of Congress and the National Archives, in Washington, D.C.; the Air Force Museum, Wright State University, Carillon Park, and the NCR Corporation of Dayton, Ohio; the Franklin Institute, Philadelphia; the Science Museum of

South Kensington, London; the Musêe de l'Air of Paris; the Royal Scottish Museum, Edinburgh; and the Deutsches Museum of Munich.

To all of you, named and unnamed, who helped return the full heritage to that nation where the fires of flight were kindled. Thank you.

— Harry Combs

Foreword

IT WAS a convivial bunch of riders. Dismounting to let their horses graze, they joked of the events of the morning ride through the Wyoming hills. It was warm and bright, and the grassy bank along the crystal-clear tributary of the North Platte was a perfect spot for lunch and relaxed conversation.

Inevitably, the talk turned to airplanes. Inevitably, because these men were drawn together by a common interest in progress aeronautical. Each had dedicated his career to aviation, and each had made his mark.

It was not clear how or why talk turned to Wilbur and Orville Wright; nor was it surprising, considering the nature of the group. It was surprising that they were unable to agree on certain major facts relating to the brothers' lives.

To one of those assembled, Harry Combs, the point was not insignificant: everyone knew of the Wrights; few recalled the essence of their lives and achievements. This spark of interest continued to glow. In *Kill Devil Hill*, Harry Combs relates how, in time and circumstance, it kindled a flame that grew into a consuming blaze of fascination. He became addicted to discovering the key to the Wrights' success. He retraced their path, both technically and geographically, and, along the way, he grew to know them as people.

The brothers were not easy to know, in person or in retrospect. But their ability and their integrity were impressive by the standards of their day or our own. They were both imaginative and pragmatic. They were doers with dreams.

Throughout all of human history, men have envied the flight of the birds. Perhaps no desire better exemplifies our natural predilection toward freedom. The Wrights, too, admired and studied the gull and hawk. Although their inspiration probably stemmed more from the accomplishments of men, they acknowledged the importance of the contributions of the feathered fliers. Five years after his first powered flight, when receiving an award from a French aviation society, Wilbur said, "I sometimes think that the desire to fly after the fashion of birds is an ideal handed down to us by our ancestors who, in their grueling travels across trackless lands in prehistoric times, looked enviously on the birds soaring freely through space, at full speed, above all obstacles, on the infinite highway of the air."

Their access ramp to that "highway of the air" was Kill Devil Hill, a sandy knoll on the lonely windswept Carolina beach. And it was at Kill Devil Hill that Harry Combs began his quest to unravel the mystery of the birth of flight.

The author is an airman. He writes from the vantage point of one who has known the exhilaration and the terror of flight.

Harry Combs also has a deep respect for, and broad knowledge of, history. By historians' standards, the written records of the Wright activities are excellent. Additionally, some of the relatives, friends, and observers of the brothers were available to personally confirm (or deny) the accuracy of the various accounts of their lives and work.

It is said that history is like a mirror; it can only look back. Undoubtedly true, but there is great value in pausing to look back, for only with an appreciation of where we've been can we hope to understand where we are heading.

Kill Devil Hill is a story of synergism and serendipity, of sense and sensitivity. More important, it is an airman's careful analysis of one of the most dramatic achievements in the human experience.

— *Neil Armstrong*

Contents

Illustrations

Kill Devil Hill

Prologue

JUST OVER the nose cone: a sharp line easing barely higher along the center, the sides softening and gently falling away. I am suspended along the top of an enormous globe, drifting mote-like, high enough to see the planet's curvature as the rolling surface falls away with distance.

Incredible. I shift my body in the seat; it's an old trick to dismiss sensations so compelling they push aside reality. So I shift my weight to change the body pressure and I blink several times and I tell the sightseeing part of my mind to knock it off and . . .

It is still there — the magic carpet and the beauty, this suspension, a rendezvous of time and distance and space. Directly before me, snapping into focus as I concentrate, are the instruments that speak of raging fires I have kindled a short time before — kindled, caged, controlled, and directed — flame that in an instant would vaporize lead and in a few moments more would turn solid aluminum into wispy gas. The fire scream comes to me only as a low hum, a sound of comfort, although this same flame shrieks away from two gleaming exhausts mounted to the flanks of the sleek metal shape that encompasses me.

Legerdemain has its price, and my levitation across the higher edges of a planet 8000 miles in diameter is paid in the coin of the technological realm. The instruments tell the story at a glance: the pressures and flow and electrical resistance and the sleekly contoured fanjets behind me functioning with all the

precision and reliability necessary for this gleaming magic carpet.
Everything's in the green.

The instruments talk to you. It is right where it all belongs, with no surprises — solid, functional, continuing, and predictable. That's the stuff from which magic carpets are woven, and I know at a glance that all is well. I hold my gaze another moment on the instruments so sharply defined in the brilliant sunshine at 45,000 feet above the North Atlantic.

My eyes move the barest fraction of an inch to present me with the magnificent blue sky along the bending horizon. It's that rarest of all blues, such as we find only in the depths of Crater Lake or at the very rim of space itself. The blue arcs upward in a constantly deepening hue until, directly overhead, it has become the inky black of space velvet. The thought brings a reflective smile, for astronaut friends have told me of this color. Looking back at the Earth they saw the blue wonder of our world suspended against a backdrop of utterly black, black, black velvet. Those are their words.

I look down, away from black, from the deepest of blues, and far below me is the white misty canopy that covers the cold waters of the sea. From up here, it is a layer of the purest white cotton. To the people on the surface, it appears as high, thin cirrus clouds, a blanket between them and the glory of the sun.

I take a deep breath. I have never been one to tire of wonder or miracles, and there is much to absorb. For there is no Earth where I am. No Earth, no world as most of us have shared a planetary home know it. There is only the capsule of this Learjet 35, the knowledge of its purity of strength and performance, the soothing hum of the turbines.

I study the instrument panel again. The flick of eyes from heavenly canvased wonder to technology. The right engine shows an exhaust-gas temperature of 730 degrees centigrade, and the left engine is barely 5 degrees higher in its reading. Both are well within peace-of-mind limits. Turbine speed indicates 91.8 percent, which is about as close as you can get to the fan-speed reading of 92. We're on long-range cruise control, so the twin jet engines are burning fuel at the rate of 955 pounds per hour. Through the little window of the altimeter, we see that the instrument is set at 29.92 (the variable settings compensate for changes in barometric pressure). Reading that dial another way is to accept that we're rushing over a world with its surface nearly nine miles below us.

There is the mach indicator. The very term — mach indicator — is an understatement. The needle shows a specific point seven four, Mach 0.74: long-range cruise; at our altitude it means we're rushing from the continent of North America, eastward to Europe, at a velocity three-fourths the speed of sound.

Shirt-sleeve comfort, coffee no more than an extended hand away, the mighty power of a thousand genies working for us and — let's look at it another way. Right now our speed over the surface of the earth, our ground speed, computes at 547 miles an hour. That's right — computes. The electronic oracles that tell us this have been compressed in size until they fit neatly into the palm of a man's hand, and that means you can fit into an airplane as many as you need. And they translate and compute and deduce and predict and whatever else electronic oracles are supposed to do. They translate airspeed into ground speed, and it's the latter that really counts, because it means our speed over the planet far below. The number comes out to 476 knots, which is another way of saying that we are traveling faster than a pistol bullet.

It's more than speed, because we're in what pilots call "light country." Sunlight, starlight, moonlight — it doesn't matter. This is a jet that can knife a course through air as high as 51,000 feet. That means we're above the tropopause and therefore above all but the most exceptional outrages of weather.

Below is the troposphere, where we live our daily lives. It's filled with surging air, booming pressure changes, lightning and thunder, dust storms, fog, rain, snow, ice, smog, and feathered creatures and spiders riding the winds higher than the highest mountain. It is where the weather lives. You start out at sea level and climb. For every thousand feet of altitude, the temperature drops, on the average, 3 degrees Fahrenheit. But climb into the serenity of the stratosphere, and the temperature is almost always constant, at 70 degrees below zero. You're in the midst of a friendly phenomenon. There's a stratification to the air that offers a startling crystal clarity.

Inside this capsule the temperature is a comfortable 72 degrees, but just beyond the windowpanes the temperature is 142 degrees lower; the wind rushes past with the force of a hurricane multiplied *more than seven times.* The air is so thin out there that no human lungs could keep their bearer alive for longer than a few brief and convulsive seconds.

I think again of magic; it has taken me a lifetime to understand that we truly possess magic about us in every element of our lives. What witch doctor, what Merlin of old would have dared prophesy the giants we capture in small black boxes, who do our bidding with only the nudge of a fingertip and a hum of current.

I look down at the global navset on the pedestal. So ordinary a name, so commonplace the initials. GNS. Yet it is a black box that is a constantly moving hub of a myriad of forces, the center of an enormous phantom spider web around the globe, from which it draws out for us the secrets of time and distance so that we can know at any given moment our exact place in the physical world. We ask for longitude and latitude and minutes and hours and seconds, and refer to chart coordinates; but when it all boils down, we are turning to our electronic sorcery with questing eyes, and the genie nods, points his finger, and says, "You are here."

GNS does that for us. It is in electronic touch with a network of very low frequency communication and navigation stations strategically located around the world. It extracts motion from that contact as it bisects time, and it muddles it all together in some potpourri of humming and weaving, and then it talks to us. It is well that we know its language.

Course is zero four one degrees. Digital numbers glow at me in the same heading: 041. Our speed over the surface of the earth is just about 550 miles an hour. The wind blows at us from the west; specifically, it says from 271 degrees with a velocity of 73 knots, or just about 84 miles an hour. The time remaining for us to reach our destination is 1 hour, 38 minutes, 15 seconds. Let's see now; we've been airborne — wheels off the departure runway at Goose Bay — for precisely 1 hour, 43 minutes, 12 seconds.

Position check. I switch the selector on the black box. The GNS offers the numbers to me almost as a sacrifice, a justification of all else I have learned. Here we are. North latitude 60 degrees, 40.3 seconds; and west longitude 46 degrees, 38.2 seconds. It flickers changes as we progress.

We're coming up on Checkpoint Charlie — Prince Christian Beacon. Just before us is the southern tip of Greenland. I think about that cloud layer beneath us. If it were not there, then the view of Greenland would open wide for our eyes, and I never tire of looking at that awesome landscape. Beautiful, mysterious, easily the most shockingly terrifying island on the face of this planet.

At our present ground speed we're scheduled to make the hop from Goose Bay to Reykjavik in just over 3 hours and 15 minutes. But there's got to be reality in flight, especially an item called "approach pattern delays." We may or may not be slowed or "vectored about" in time- and fuel-consuming positioning before we can land, but anybody who's warmed a pilot seat for more than a few hours will always fatten high flight time by expecting delays.

I nod to Pinky, old Learjet captain turned co-pilot for this trip. "Let's get the Prince Christian Beacon on the ADF [automatic direction finder]." He turns the crank on the frequency selector dial until the kilocycles window reads 239. He flips the audio switch, and we listen to the station broadcasting its specific Morse code identification — OZN.

Dah Dah Dah
Dah Dah Dit Dit
Dah Dit
OZN

And again, and again, and forever if need be.

The number one remote compass in the cockpit presents its information with a needle, and as we watch, the needle swings 15 degrees to the left of our heading. We study it for several moments and are satisfied to see it moving slowly from right to left. Everything in an airplane that has a pointer or a needle or an indicator always has its special message, and this one tells us we're close in to Cape Farewell and we'll slide by perhaps 20 miles to the south. Very good.

Reflecting on cloud layers, as I do now, prompts old memories, and a renewed chuckle, this time at the myopia through which so many pilots once labored, as I did. The years ghost through my mind to when I first trespassed in the blue, when my wings were still glistening-wet with the touch of the fledgling.

It was 50 years ago this morning, but I can still smell that green June grass of the pasture and sense the warm slipstream of the idling OX-5 engine. We sat on a corner of the field in an old Standard, a cousin of the Curtiss Jenny. I had just made 10 successful circuits of the field with three-point landings that satisfied the god in the cockpit in front of me.

The god wore a helmet and goggles and a long brown overall flying suit; he was a god because he was my instructor.

He reached up and grabbed the inner bay struts and pulled himself up out of the cockpit and swung out to the ground. Then he turned to me — lean hawk face, with piercing eyes from which his goggles had been lifted to his forehead.

"Well, you can handle it," he said. "She'll be a little lighter with me out of it, but don't let that fool you. Keep your nose down on the turns, and when you come in to land, keep your glide speed up and don't forget to flare out in time. Just hold her off steady and you'll do all right. Okay, kid — you're ready to go."

My heart was pounding, for I knew this was an invitation to Valhalla. He stepped away from the slipstream, I pulled my goggles down from my helmeted forehead to shield my eyes, looked out one side of the cockpit to see ahead, and slowly opened the throttle. The engine's idling broke into a roar. The slipstream became a hurricane, and the old Standard trundled forward, bouncing and banging over the turf. A little forward pressure on the stick, and the tail came up, and through the haze of the revolving propeller I could see the end of the field approaching.

Soon the ship had life, controlled life. The ailerons were taut; the elevator equalized with the stabilizer and began relieving the stick pressure; and as I eased back a little on the stick, the banging and bouncing ceased and the smooth joy of flight was mine. It was my first solo! I, too, would soon be in the company of the immortals. It was 1928 and I was fifteen.

I remember so well the dropping away of the trees and fields and farmhouses around me and the view of the toylike railroad tracks and the passing trains, the unreal playland of buildings and streets a few miles to my right — the city of St. Louis. I was delirious with joy. The world was mine. The sky was mine — and unlimited. And below me lay the playground of Earth whose bonds I had just escaped. Less than five minutes were used in the circuit of that field. When I throttled back and glided down toward the green postage stamp of a cow pasture, my real life had just begun.

I was enthralled. I was taken. I was gone. There was no other way. Nothing else would ever satisfy me. I knew then and there that flying was my life and that the promise was boundless. This has come true; for 50 years I have spent my life in the sky or with thoughts of the sky. It has been my home, and it seemed that those periods I spent on Earth were only for purposes of planning better ways and better machinery for touring the ocean of the air.

From the very nature of things it seemed self-evident. Didn't the air surround both the land and the sea, and if the airman lived and navigated in the air, would he not live and see and love more things than other men?

It is such a simple doctrine — and so true. I have tested it for half a century — always with a sense of wonder — always with a sense of awe, that those wings that stretch out beneath me, crafted by the hand of man and wrung from the resources of the earth, supply the means of sailing with ease over mountains and forests, seas and icecaps, highways and congested cities.

In those early years — less than 25 years after the era of flight had begun — I used to scour the books on meteorology. The textbooks that proclaimed their wisdom of the air. But how ignorant we were!

No one knew that vertical winds howled through the thunderheads with energies of 200 and 300 miles an hour. No one had ever heard of jetstreams, either high or low. Wind shear, a storm-related phenomenon that can be hazardous to landing jets, didn't exist as far as we knew, nor did anyone even dream of such violence. Vortices would show only in tornadoes; they didn't hide in clouds to snare unwary aviators. We had never heard of ice-crystal clouds or sun dogs or moon dogs.

To a great extent we even believed the stratosphere was utterly and eternally still, and the times of stratospheric flight or looking down from orbit were beyond not only our grasp but also our fears or imagination. So we could not possibly conceive that those mighty thunderheads actually reared to 75,000 feet, not 25,000, as we had been told. Nor did we ever dream that those high thin cirrus clouds our meteorologists had proclaimed to be at about 20,000 feet actually hover at 40,000.

The appearance in the middle and late thirties of the great new machines of the sky, like the fabled DC-3, failed to break our barriers of ignorance. The DC-3 was a quantum jump ahead in air transportation, but still it plowed through the thicker, lower air. It wasn't until we got our hands on the pressurized Constellations and the DC-6s, and made the higher altitudes a crossway of *everyday* flying, that we began to remain long enough at the levels of around 20,000 to 23,000 feet to find, despite our new mechanical lungs and great power and reach into the higher levels, that far, far above us were still those thin arcing canopies of clouds — the "high thin scattered" for which men always groped and which we still called "cirrus."

Not until the jets appeared on the scene and made everyday flying an affair of touching the stratosphere, not until we doubled the altitudes of those grand DC-6 airliners and their brethren, did we skim the wispy underbelly of the unattainable cirrus and know the first trembling wonder of true high flight. The magical touch was now upon us, and, with exultation pounding through our veins, with this new magic always at our fingertips, we punched up and up. We troped out and broke into the stratosphere, and for the first time gave to *all* men the miracle of sweeping the *true* wild blue yonder — the open range of the higher skies. That's how it went!

I look down at the white canopy below, lift my eyes to the almost painful brightness of the horizon, lift them still higher to the dark domain of ships that fly by centrifugal force, and wonder at my own thoughts. Have I been enthralled so many times, for so many years, that I walk apart from my fellow man?

No, for there are too many links; I know because a wise old man told me so. That history teacher of mine, who said, "The ancient Greeks probably had the best concept of man and his position in the infinite." He told us that they saw man as a heroic figure, fighting against impossible odds, because he was mortal, because there must come the day of his death, when all his achievements would be for naught.

The ancient Greeks were consistently aware of this reality, and thus they referred always to the mortal man and the immortal gods; and these gods had human qualities and felt jealousy, anger, envy, hatred, love — and were in competition with men.

Yet these very vulnerable, pitifully mortal men, at some time during the brief apogee of their lives, if they were true heroes like Theseus or Hercules, would manage to touch the hands of the immortal — to walk in the company of such as Zeus and Apollo for only brief moments of glory, not very unlike the soaring wonder of a jet touching the world above that of mortal men. Ours is a brief enough traverse of what we call life, and it is worth remembering only for the heights a life may attain. It is here, in this isolation and serenity, the suspension of hurtling speed, far above even the thin, high scattered cirrus, where we may touch the fingertips of the gods, who for a moment may smile upon us.

Perhaps they smile now — for directly below us is the end of the overcast. Somewhere, in these heavens we have been sharing with invisible beings, a great knife has sliced the skies, and the high thin cirrus ends abruptly below us — as far as we can see from north to south. Beyond the edge of that thin cliff layer waits all the glory of Greenland, seen by us as only the great Norse gods, Thor and Wotan, might have looked down upon it.

As the gossamer canopy slides away beneath us, there, far below, to our left, lie the icy fingers of Cape Farewell, jutting into the sea. The massive mountains seem to be struggling, as they have for thousands upon thousands of years, to contain the staggering mass of the great icecap.

In the great distance along the west coast of Greenland are peaks lofting eight and nine thousand feet into frigid air. It increases our range of sight to 400 miles, and yet we can barely see one-fourth the distance to the northern edge of this island. It's better than 1600 miles from Cape Farewell beneath us to the frozen ramparts in the north!

And most of it as cold as the heart of its icebergs, as lifeless as the floes choking the fjords, as free from green and warmth as dead stone. Bleak, barren, frozen, lifeless, disheartening. Except for those fjords down there. Life nestles in *those* high-walled reaches.

There's the big western one: Brede Fjord. Next along the line is Eric's Fjord, with its long and unpronounceable Eskimo name. To me it has always been, always will be, Eric's Fjord. That is the fingering touch of the sea into dark rock where Eric the Red — the Viking, the Norseman — took his longship when he explored Greenland.

In the year 986.

How must that fjord have looked to Eric and his crew a thousand years ago? Then the time was midsummer and the hills were green on up to the snowline. It was also warmer and more hospitable, but even then the great ice peaks pierced the sky, as they still do at this very moment.

I whetted the appetite of my imagination as a youth on the mighty Vikings. I read the translations of the old Norse sagas, excerpts from the Icelandic *Landnámabók,* and the epic stories of Eric the Red, his son Leif the Lucky, and Bjarni Herjolfsson, and all the rest. Every one of them sailed into and along Eric's Fjord, which I see below me now. They all shared the exultation of the sea mists rolling aside before them and looked up at the awesome frozen cataracts of the mountains.

I remember an earlier trip to Greenland when I flew up that Tunugdliarfik Fjord and landed at Narsarssuak.

I persuaded an Eskimo to sled us across the frozen fjord's left arm to the ruins of Eric the Red's old homestead. From there I could see it all in my mind's eye — the towering ice mountains, the green hills of summer, the placid waters of the fjord churned by the glistening oars of the Viking longships.

In Greenland those ancient Norse had prospered and their numbers multiplied. By the twelfth century, some say, 10,000 of them lived on the edges of this enormous island. Greenland bears the marks of their stay for over three centuries. The ruins of hundreds of homesteads and churches and monasteries litter the long shorelines of the fjords. But by the year 1450 they were all gone. So we are left with only this rubble of history and the still great unsolved mystery: What happened to the Greenland Norse, where did they go, and why did they leave?

I recall rocketing out of our base the next morning, over walled waters, with the Learjet's roar echoing among the ice mountains. I had looked for old Norse longships and found none, but from where a glacier spilled its blue-white ice into the fjord's side arm, a flock of white Arctic terns had risen in wheeling circles. They knew the spirit of flight, and I kept their memory in a poem — because that is what it is really like to fly:

> *Like free spirits*
> *From the polar snows*
> *They soar on shining wings*
> *And climb to dizzy heights above*
> *And lose the little sordid earthly things*
> *Up where there is wind and space*
> *And stars and time to love.*

Now, today, as we fly 45,000 feet over Greenland's ice tip, I know that any noise generated by a jet aircraft drifts down nine miles to Earth as a whisper of thunder, a hollow drifting of sound. Will it disturb creatures far below? Hardly. I believe its whisper-thunder is accepted, is known and understood, is *familiar* to creatures on the surface. Sometimes, if the sun is warm and the wind calm, the sound will bring eyes lifted upward and initiate an instinctive wheeling of the terns, but free and without fright.

Is it a strange thing I do, bridging the vertical gulf between my own solid wings and the hollow-boned Arctic terns I know wheel over snows and cold water so far below? Not really, for we are all bound — bird and man and iron machine — in a single purpose between us. *Flight.* We have taken different paths to dizzying heights, but we have all sought the same goals, more instinctive than measured, perhaps, but known to all of us. It's a way of life, a way of love.

Perhaps, too, the ghosts of ancient Norse warriors look up and nod their helmeted horned heads to one another knowingly, for surely that thunder passing is the sound of the hammer of old Thor.

Again I shift in my seat, a reminder to climb down from whatever lofty perch I had found in the recesses of memory and return at once to the real world. I look down at the fjords drifting by, and there is that now familiar shimmering in my imagination.

Think of a time when man could *not* fly. It seems so long, long ago, smoldering in its own ashes of antiquity.

Not to fly is to be chained to the ground, and not merely in the physical sense; it is to be outraged by this heaviness of both body and spirit, to feel that our world was bigger than the entire solar system, that our vision was limited, our grasp feeble, our tomorrow creakingly ancient and wheezing no matter *what* our accomplishments.

Not to know flight, not to soar and glide and to grace the heavens with our wings and embrace within them an entire planet, is to be *caged*. And that is not for men.

This sleek jet with which I cruise the upper atmosphere emerged from the earth, fashioned by the *hands* of men — hands *and brains.* And from all this came metals and alloys and ceramics and wires and glass and plastics and electronics and fabric and the squeezed and flame-lashed remnants of fossil fuels that drive this magic carpet.

I fly at 550 miles an hour nine miles above the earth.

What in the hell holds us up?

What makes this mass of metal *fly?*

How did we capture this miracle? Who gave it to us? Where did it all start?

I think back to the day not long ago when I experienced an awful shock — the realization that I had spent 50 years flying through the skies above the Earth without really knowing the true story of how flying all began.

This was a staggering blow, but I discovered that I was not alone and that my lack of knowledge was shared by most people, even those who fly. We have taken flight for granted. And I, like so many others, had pictured the Wright brothers as a couple of boys who ran a bicycle shop in Dayton, Ohio, and who kept fiddling around with the idea of a flying machine until finally they staggered into the air. Nothing could be further from the truth.

My awakening was brought about by the kindness and interest of a great friend who one day walked into my office with two books under his arm.

He is a man of sensitivity and depth. He knew of my concern, and having considerable knowledge of the Wrights' accomplishments, he had obtained copies of *The Papers of Wilbur and Orville Wright*, which were originally published in 1953* under the editorial direction of Marvin W. McFarland of the Library of Congress, and these were the volumes he now presented to me. He said that he was giving me the books to aid me in the future when I discussed the Wright brothers. The fact that he had been an accomplished test pilot and a professor of aeronautical engineering, as well as the first man to set foot on another celestial body in this galaxy, did not detract from the authority of his opinion.

He might as well have placed a time bomb on my desk. I began to read — first, with mild interest; and then, for a time, I knew no other world. Between the lines there arose an image of high drama, and a bitter struggle to overcome almost impossible odds.

I learned, to my surprise, that when the Wrights finally succeeded in flight, their accomplishment was shrouded, through an incredible series of circumstances, in almost total obscurity. This may account for the phenomenal American ignorance of the Wrights. Real news of their achievement did not burst upon the world for five long years.

Few Americans know the story of that recognition, which included processionals of presidents and kings, princes and prime ministers, financiers and scientists, jeweled and beautiful women — all a seemingly endless and tumultuous acclaim for the wonder that had been wrought.

I was determined to tell this story, and in order to tell it properly I would travel all over America and Europe and back — visiting the shrines of flight, from Kitty Hawk and Simms Station to Le Mans and Pau, from Stanford Hall to Hawthorn Hill, from Fort Myer, Virginia, to Camp d'Auvours, France — searching for and dreaming in my mind's eye about what had really happened there. I wanted to walk in the footsteps of those

* McGraw-Hill Book Company, Inc.

incredible brothers, to picture their historic flights, and to hear the popping clatter of those rickety old homemade, four-cylinder engines and the whir of fragile, fledgling wings.

And before it was done, I would visit many museums and study all kinds of ancient flying contraptions. I would race against time to talk with men and women still living who had known the Wrights personally — before their recollections were lost forever.

Interestingly, in recent years a number of highly trained and experienced airplane designers and builders have attempted to construct and fly "authentic" replicas of the original *Kitty Hawk Flyer*. None of the reproductions ever flew successfully. Missing were the precise conditions at Kill Devil Hill that chilly December day in 1903, but so was the most essential factor of all: the unique genius of the Wright brothers themselves.

It is my purpose to share my delight in discovering the fascinating drama of a decade when the energy and the intellect of two remarkable brothers burned their brightest. Perhaps parts of this story will illuminate some aspects of what these men did and how they did it. To my knowledge, many of the physical reasons for the success of some of their flights, and the failure of others, have never before been fully explained or even explored.

Some questions have remained unanswered for more than three quarters of a century:

How did the Wrights achieve in just four and a half short years what the best minds of the world had failed to accomplish in centuries?

What was the real significance of that quantum jump in developing their own body of empirical data — a jewel beyond price, without which flight was impossible?

What was the happy accident of design that enabled them to learn to fly without killing themselves?

Why did they court the press at first, then retreat into a secrecy that masked their work in later years?

Why did they abandon flying for two and a half crucial years, from November 1905 until May 1908?

And why were the great flights of the brothers in France and at Fort Myer, Virginia, far more important than their first flights at Kitty Hawk?

And now, flying along the edges of space, I marvel at the achievement of these two great minds . . . at the strength of their courage and determination that appears in every page of their letters and diaries . . . and I am ashamed of my own ignorance, and, being an American and a flier, I realize that I had almost missed my own heritage — almost, but not quite.

This is a pilgrimage, a search for the truth about that great adventure. There remains much to tell about the brothers, and there is more to be discovered, but right now this pilgrimage itself seems like high flight: beautiful, exciting, and, in the terms of the airman, "way out in the wild blue yonder."

CHAPTER 1

The Dunes

THIS IS WHERE it all came true.

This is Big Kill Devil Hill, one of the four hills of Kill Devil, near the village of Kitty Hawk, sandwiched in the Outer Banks of North Carolina between Albemarle Sound and the Atlantic Ocean.

It is an expanse of yellow sand, so windblown that the four hills often changed their shape over the years, heaving sluggishly in slow motion, but shifting enough in a few days of hard winds to confuse the infrequent visitor.

It is here that two brothers came in the summer and autumn months of 1900 to 1903. They traveled by train, by wagon, by flat-bottomed boat, and smoke-belching steamer; and always there was a great deal of manpower expended, as well.

Here they set upon a task that had defied the greatest minds of science and engineering, a mystery that had been lethal in the defense of its secrets and proclaimed by both philosophers and fools to be beyond the reach of man. Yet Orville and Wilbur Wright came here across the Outer Banks and watched the flight of birds, marveled at their sweeping delight in the air, studied their skills, their tiny movements and flexing of feathers and bodies. Here they made their camp, built their tents and sheds, set up their sleeping quarters and their workshops, and assembled a series of unusual structures of wood, metal, fine fabric, and wires.

They assembled their own fragile, motorless wings, and flew

them like kites, first ballasted with chains and then with their own bodies. Then they attempted free gliding, probing tentatively into the realm that had forever eluded man, slowly turning their wings into the wind and coming to understand its capriciousness and to gain confidence in its soft strength and support. The clumsy stumbles became gentle glides and then sweeping runs above the surface, across the yellow sands, not touching them for seconds, which continued to mount, one on the other, until the brothers knew they were gliding as none had ever done before. Then they knew it was time to commit their minds and their bodies to the ultimate test: to build a machine with fixed wings, controls, a place for a man, an engine, a tank for fuel and another for oil, a place for the engine to connect to chains and these in turn to great curving wooden blades, and then, when the whole thing was arranged as well as possible and balanced on a launching rail, and the wind was right, and the integrity of the structure seemed assured, and the frailty of the human occupant with his appalling lack of experience never more in evidence, then and only then was it time to commit to madness — to attempt what no man had ever done.

The first powered and controlled aerodynamic flight of man — that was the miracle of the morning of December 17, 1903.

It was the first in all the history of the world, a feat that ranks with man's discovery of the use of fire. It rattled the planet and shook dust from history, and it is just now beginning to have its greatest effect on the course of our lives. Scarcely noticed at the time, it was clouded by geographical isolation and later by deliberate secrecy.

If one stands at Kitty Hawk as a pilgrim, he sees many things, and what he sees depends on contemplation as much as on the scene that stretches before him. It is worth remembering that one can no longer see it as it was in those years, except in the photographs the Wrights took. They flew here with gliders for years, but flew here in true flight with a powered aircraft for only a few precious moments of a single day — and then did not come back for almost five years.

Their campsite, where they dragged their tents, lumber, food, and equipment summer after summer, was four miles south of Kitty Hawk. A thousand feet away reared Big Kill Devil Hill, 100 feet high, its yellowish sand covering an area of some 26 acres. Nearby, there rose above the flat and sandy wastes three other dunes, constantly reshaped by the shifting winds. They were all lumped under the collective name of Kill Devil Hills, and they were perfect for experiments by men still pursuing the lofty privilege of the birds. Through the period of 1900 to 1903, three of the four hills served as launch platforms for unpowered gliding flights of Wilbur and Orville Wright — Big Kill Devil Hill, the West Hill, and the Little Hill.

This ground is now called the Wright Brothers National Memorial, but only since 1953 — a strange carry-over of a national habit that seemed almost intentionally to relegate the names and deeds of the Wrights to obscurity.

Here I have stood, and walked slowly, feeling the wind tugging my clothes, savoring the gentle sting of blowing sand across these 425 acres of the land. The wind and sand are not much different from what they must have been. The clouds are the same, and the skies, whether blue or gray.

History masks these moments. We look upon frozen mementos, and it is not easy to imagine clouds of mosquitoes or sand in your food or the fear that wind-lashed rain will splinter your thin boards and destroy the fragile linen-covered creature within; but perhaps we can imagine some of it as we walk over these hills.

The one view commanding all: I begin here, and the panorama flows before me. In one long, sweeping glance I see the 1903 camp — the painstakingly authentic reproduction of the original — where Wilbur and Orville had made their commitment. Then there are the stone markers to identify the takeoff and landing points of the first four powered flights. At last there is the great memorial to the Wright brothers, directly atop Kill Devil Hill. It is 60 feet of soaring gray granite in the form of a triangular pylon, its sides bearing outspread wings in bas-relief; and its resemblance to an enormous bird about to hurl itself into the air is uncanny. Yet it is a product of the present, and I turn instead to Kill Devil Hill.

Strange and unsettling stirrings of history affect me as my feet tread these sands, and for a moment there is no staying my feet, which move as if they now command my senses. I run suddenly, as the Wrights must have run, as their assistants ran with them, and my feet kick up spurts of sand as I run into the wind, feeling its life and freshness, imagining the sigh and song of wind through wires, the snapping of linen pulled taut by the same wind, the scuffing of feet in sand . . . here on the north slope of Kill Devil Hill.

I walk slowly now to a point barely a hundred feet west of the reconstructed camp of 1903, and before me looms an enormous boulder, a madman's paperweight of ten tons, placed here in 1928, a quarter-century after the fact, to mark the site of *the* flight. The boulder marks the exact point where the first four flights of all our lives began, and a single-rail launching track leads away from the boulder. To the north, there are four numbered markers, each designating precisely where one of the first four flights skidded to a halt.

Anyone who comes here, as so many thousands do, can see the markers, monuments, launching rails, and reconstructions. But there is a photograph that was taken long afterward, and at this moment it adds a new dimension. It shows a scene looking across a level plain of dust and rocks. No sand here, but a gritty dust that kicked weirdly upward from booted feet and fell even more strangely back to the surface. Not a sign of life. Nothing above the ground, really. Nothing to break the horizon. Silence, except for the picture-taker and the man with him. A flat and bleak surface.

I look away from the photograph. I must move. My positioning must be perfect. The track was . . . right over *there.* Sixty feet of wooden starting track, laid in a south-to-north direction where the level ground stretched away smoothly. The site is less than 100 feet from the camp hangar, more than 1000 feet north of Kill Devil Hill. I close my eyes for a moment. The wind blowing across my face is a gentle breeze of some 10 miles an hour. On one morning in 1903, the winds gusted at more than twice this speed. But the ground was level and bleak, and that was important, for it was here that the clattering roar rose in volume and a restraining wire was released and a machine rushed forward and bit into the wind.

I move back to take in the entire scene. The emptiness, the fairly level ground except for depressions and sandy hummocks of small but unmistakable size. It is stark here, and except that I *know* what had happened here, this could well be the surface of an uninhabited planet.

So I look again at the photo taken on the Sea of Tranquility, where astronaut Neil Armstrong spoke his heart-gripping words: *"The Eagle has landed . . ."*

The similarity between the surfaces of the two worlds is absolutely astonishing.

The yellow sands of Kitty Hawk.

The gritty dust of a lunar mare.

They are connected forever.

There is another photograph that shows Wilbur in the glider the brothers flew that year. He had just launched from West Hill, and the photographer was almost directly behind him as, lying prone on his machine, Wilbur had eased into a turn to the right. Well beyond the glider, Kill Devil Hill looms in the background. The gently sloping hills of the moon are almost indistinguishable from the dunes of Kill Devil Hill.

There is yet another photograph of a glider, a side view with Wilbur on the machine, as he is launched from the upper slopes of Kill Devil Hill; a helper is in the background, his arm upraised after just releasing his grip on the left wing. In the foreground, one arm also raised, still running, is Orville, with his feet kicking up the sand of the great dune.

There are dozens of photographs of astronauts on the moon, moving quickly down similar slopes, with their booted feet kicking up dust in spurts so like the photographs at Kitty Hawk that one marvels at this coincidence.

It is only coincidence, of course, but there is something wonderful in this similarity of terrain and movement that marks the moments of man's first flights on this planet and his first free steps on another body.

So it was and it remains a source of wonder to turn back the clock to an archaic time, so long ago — nearly 80 years — so far away that man was still chained to the surface of his planet.

When on several occasions I returned to this historic shrine, I would stand on Kill Devil Hill and contemplate the remarkable events that happened here. And I would think of the first man to set foot on the moon; for it was Neil Armstrong who really stirred my curiosity about the Wrights. Here, with this sweeping view of Kitty Hawk sands and the photographic imprint of the Sea of Tranquility fresh in mind, I would reflect on a letter I had written him on the 30th of July, 1975:

Dear Neil:

I am having a hard time finding words to express to you how much the two volumes of the Wright brothers *Papers* have meant to me.

I have not only read both books from cover to cover, but I have really studied both books from cover to cover — all 1217 pages . . . And to top it off, I made a special trip to Kitty Hawk just to get the real feel of the fantastic miracle that took place there on that December day in 1903.

It was a spiritual experience — not only because one could see clearly and definitely the astonishing twist of the airplane's lateral control, but also one could grasp the feel in the design . . . how closely the Wright boys tried to imitate nature in the cathedral angle of the stable soaring birds, and still couple the fore and aft balance by a mechanical means of their own.

I studied the aircraft for a couple of hours, and then went out to the pylon rock that marks the starting place and paced off the various flights, imagining them in my mind. When I went out to the fourth position, Wilbur's last flight of 852 feet, I looked at that marker and looked back at the starting place with its sixty feet of track. I saw in my mind's eye what the aircraft must have looked like sitting there — what the engine must have sounded like to an observer who stood at the finishing point. (Probably he couldn't have heard it with that 21-mile-an-hour wind blowing until it got quite close.) I took out my stopwatch and counted off 59 seconds, imagining the aircraft coming toward me to finally end up where I stood. *It was a long, long flight.*

It must have been totally and completely clear to not only the two Wright boys, but to those people from the life saving station, that man had at long, long last on that day really flown.

I came away from the whole experience with a sense

of humility and awe. Humility first, because I cannot understand how I could have been so uninformed regarding the Wright brothers and that marvelous accomplishment.

I knew, of course, a few things about them, but as you will recall, not very accurately. I was sure that their time must have been exciting, but I had no feel of it and didn't know how it went.

Secondly, there remains with me a sense of great awe at the kind of minds that these men had, and the way they grappled with the problems which truly seemed insoluble. Certainly those men had brains the equivalent of any of the great brains in history. It is a stirring thought that they came from such apparently ordinary, average, everyday American backgrounds. There was nothing ordinary about them — they were tremendous scientists, highly competent mechanics, possessed of an incredible determination and integrity of logic.

I am forever indebted to you for giving me the opportunity, while browsing through those "papers," to live for a few hours in the company of the great . . .

CHAPTER 2

Charmed by the How and Why

IT IS LIKE a miller's wheel, this thing we call gravity. Ponderous, overwhelming, a yoke on our collective necks from time immemorial, chaining us to a two-dimensional planet, grinding us into the soil. To fight gravity is to fight against the fundamental physical force that holds the planets and the stars of the universe together.

It is with an effort that we try to imagine what for most of us is unimaginable — that time when man lacked the magic grasp of the air and *could not fly.* Can we bend our imagination back to such a time? When we were imprisoned on the surface of this world? When *all* travel was two-dimensional? When the idea of man moving through thin air was as insane as the notion of going to the moon? At that time, the greatest minds of science had established, by theory and cruel, practical failure, that flight with a heavier-than-air machine was beyond the grasp of man.

The attainment of human flight has been called a miracle, but the real miracle was that at one critical period in history, from all the world, from all the tumultuous growth in engineering and invention and science, from all the bubbling cauldrons of curiosity, there came these two men with just the proper mechanical background, with just the right scientific turn of mind, and above all with an overwhelming dedication to the conviction that somehow it was possible for man to fly.

Orville and Wilbur Wright were two men possessed of an innovative genius that was so rare, available on such a narrow spectrum of human intelligence and experience, that a miracle truly *was* wrought. That is the fact that has escaped us, that has been misplaced in our national ledger of credit and accomplishment, where it is long overdue.

And just as absent from our rich heritage is the true nature, the real cut, of these two marvelous men, Wilbur and Orville. We have another miracle in that these two men, extraordinarily young at the time they carved their way in the skies, worked so closely, fitted their minds so intimately, formed so total a rapport with one another, that history properly records their accomplishments as the work and efforts of a single entity.

Those who knew these brothers best brushed aside all notion that one contributed more than the other. Their father, for instance, emphasized again and again the remarkable intimacy of thought between his sons. Even the brothers themselves did everything they could to clarify the matter. Wilbur wrote fondly of that wonderful meeting of mind and creativity he and Orville had shared. "From the time we were little children," wrote Wilbur, "my brother Orville and myself lived together, played together, worked together and, in fact, thought together. We usually owned all of our toys in common, talked over our thoughts and aspirations so that nearly everything that was done in our lives has been the result of conversations, suggestions and discussions between us."

That has been perhaps the greatest reward of this pilgrimage to seek out the Wright brothers: discovering the intense humanity of these people as individuals, and that star-struck brotherhood, in family and in mind, of Orville and Wilbur. And I found myself asking questions. What kind of men were these two brothers? What motivated their lives? How did they act? What was their disposition? How did they work? At what were they successful? Where, if at all, did they fail, and if they failed, how did this experience set them onto newer and more successful paths? How did they play? What were their loves?

They were athletes, these two. They were fun-loving and curious about almost all things. Each had a marvelous sense of humor. How different from the dimensionless characters often found in the words written on these two men! That they were honest, decent, humble men has been said about them often enough.

But that they loved a good joke, that they were inventive in almost all things, that they dedicated themselves fiercely to family love and care, that their respect for others was so unbending that it tugged the edge of imagination — all this, and more, lay buried behind newspaper copy and their photographs.

The older, Wilbur, showed to the world a face of hawklike determination, so often unsmiling, he became identified with excessive seriousness and a tenacity that forbade the presence of humor. How should we know that he was as tender and warm as he really was behind that hawkish look — that he could retain a gentle dignity with steel behind it, a sense of humor dry and deep, that he could throw off frustrations and continue to strive when all odds were against him, and never, through all this, change from the warm soul his family and friends had always known? Where is *this* Wilbur Wright, the real human being? Not in our archives; but I found him, as I did Orville, through others who had known these men and talked with them and even flown with them. It had to be done in a rush, for the sands of time were draining and would soon take from us the last remaining members of a generation who could speak to me on a first-person basis of the Wright brothers.

Four years the younger, bearer of a mustache that hid an impish curling of the lip, was Orville. In him one could see at once the sensitive and inquiring expression that reflected an agile mind, darting swiftly from one grand idea to another.

To the public, Orville Wright showed an impassive countenance, but it was deliberate, and it was there to serve his purpose. Beyond initial contact, when he had come to know a new acquaintance, he changed, and the warmth within became visible to those who knew how to seek out its presence.

We know that their lives were filled with small inventions, that they had marvelous hands that shaped and constructed; and we know that on West Third Street in Dayton, Ohio, they built and serviced and sold bicycles, and thus became known to their countrymen and even the world as bicycle mechanics. This was to become a source of bitter controversy in the years following their efforts with their cycles, for what they did in that shop with these wheeled machines represented only a sliver of their engineering ability, and yet it has obscured the staggering genius and magnitude of their accomplishment.

Like many Middle American families, the brothers were fortunate in their ancestry and their upbringing. Their maternal grandfather was John G. Koerner, a German bitterly opposed to the militarism and autocracy of his native land. In 1818 he had migrated from a village near Schleiz, Thuringia, to the United States, where he settled in Virginia. A man of wisdom and curiosity, he married Catherine Fry, an American girl of German-Swiss stock. Their daughter Susan Catherine, mother of the Wright brothers, was born at Hillsboro, Virginia, on April 30, 1831.

On the paternal side, their great-great-grandmother, Catharine Benham Van Cleve, would become the first white woman to live in the Dayton area. In 1790 she and her husband, John, moved from New Jersey to the roaring frontier wilderness of the Ohio, locating in Losantiville — later renamed Cincinnati. Frontier life took its toll, for less than two years after establishing a new home there, John Van Cleve was killed by Indians. His widow married again, and in 1796 traveled by flat-bottomed boat up the Miami River some 50 miles to the north, to a place called Dayton, named for Jonathan Dayton, a soldier of the Revolutionary War.

One of Catharine's children by her first husband, Benjamin Van Cleve, was subsequently appointed the first postmaster, the first county clerk, and the first schoolmaster of Dayton. The maternal line was already planting its roots in the city the Wrights would make famous a century later.

Benjamin's sister, Margaret, married George Reeder, an innkeeper. In 1818 at Centerville, Ohio, their daughter Catharine married Dan Wright, a descendant of Samuel Wright, who had come to American in 1636, settling in Springfield, Massachusetts. Dan's lineage can be traced back to a John Wright who became the owner of Kelvedon Hall in Essex County, England, in 1538.

On November 17, 1828, in Rush County, Indiana, a son, Milton, was born to Dan and Catharine Wright, who were reportedly very strict with their offspring. Milton attended county schools in Rush County and for a short time was a student at Hartsville

College, Indiana. In 1853 he received a license to preach from the White River Conference of the Church of the United Brethren in Christ, which had been founded around 1767 by the Reverend P. W. Otterbein and Martin Boehm, a former Mennonite.

Becoming an itinerant minister, Milton, like many young men, soon turned his face westward and in 1857 traveled by steamer to Panama, thence across the isthmus by the newly constructed Panama Railway, from there by steamer to San Francisco, and on to Willamette Valley, Oregon, where he arrived in August. There he taught in a small denominational school run by the United Brethren. Returning to Hartsville in 1859, Milton Wright married his lifetime sweetheart, Susan Catherine Koerner, on November 24 of the same year. He had just turned thirty-one. Of this union were born Reuchlin (1861), Lorin (1863), Wilbur (1867), Orville (1871), and Katharine (1874), whose name took still another spelling in a family of "Catharines" and "Catherines." There were also twins, who died in infancy.

There is no question that Susan Koerner Wright was a powerful influence on her youngest sons, Wilbur and Orville. She had perhaps inherited certain mechanical abilities from her father, a designer of fine carriages and farm wagons, and, in addition to designing and making her own clothes, as many women of that day did, she performed work around the home traditionally reserved for men, such as fixing things in the house and making sleds for the children.

Because of his calling, Milton Wright frequently traveled and occasionally had to move the entire family. It was while the Wrights were living in Cedar Rapids, Iowa, that Milton returned from a trip with the Alphonse Pénaud *"hélicoptère,"* a toy flying machine constructed of bamboo, cork, and paper. It was powered, as some model airplanes still are, by tightly wound rubber bands. Apparently the boys were fascinated by the toy and even built several models of their own. Wilbur was thirteen and Orville nine at the time.

Next, the family moved to Richmond, Indiana; then, in June 1884, re-established residence at 7 Hawthorn Street in Dayton, where Orville and Katharine had been born.

Wilbur, who had just completed his high school term in Richmond but shunned the formalities of an "official" graduation, decided to take extra courses in Greek and trigonometry. Orville, the more spirited of the two, also showed great promise in arithmetic, algebra and, later, in Latin. Both brothers were fond of serious reading, including such heavy fare as Plutarch's *Lives,* Boswell's *Life of Johnson,* Gibbon, Scott, Hawthorne, Green's *History of England,* Marey's *Animal Mechanism,* and two encyclopedias, the *Britannica* and *Chambers.* Years later, the brothers were to appreciate how fortunate they were to have been raised in the house of their father, a man of letters.

The bishop was a man of kindly disposition with a sense of wonder at creativity, and with a deep sense of honor, integrity, dignity, and, above all, respect for others, which he gave to his sons. These principles were not inflicted or forced upon them, but given lovingly, and daily, as a facet of their lives, until it shaped the character of Orville and Wilbur. Bishop Milton Wright taught by the leadership of his own life instead of preaching his disciplines. Because the bishop was an eminent recorder of events, there come to us those moments we might otherwise never have known.

Although they had this background in common, it is said that in those days, unless a stranger knew beforehand that Wilbur and Orville were brothers, no one would have assumed kinship between them. Orville in particular had a touch of the imp in him. He darted from one interest to another, hurled himself into projects with a happy abandon, went on social outings, and, in his challenges to the tried-and-true forms of society, generally tended to drive his schoolteachers frantic, although they did their best to contain his high spirits. While the family was still living in Richmond, Indiana, too much mischief was traceable to Orville in the sixth grade, and his teacher had dismissed him. Orville decided simply to keep the matter largely to himself and away from his overworked parents; he never bothered to return to school for the remainder of the year. In Dayton, the local school authorities determined that, since he lacked documents to prove his academic studies, he must repeat the sixth grade in full. No one anticipated his angry reaction, nor was anyone prepared to deal with his adamant refusal, no matter who said what, to face a dreary repetition of any part of the sixth grade. He was at last told that he could have his chance at the seventh grade, but that he would remain there only if his efforts and results met the school's standards.

At the year's end, Orville was the outstanding student in mathematics for the entire city of Dayton. When he encountered situations where he felt his spirit being muzzled, he often reacted in this fashion, flaring out angrily against those who tried to control him, and proving them wrong by his subsequent performance, whatever the field or the demand.

In addition to possessing the maternal virtues one would expect of a woman in a devoted family, and in addition to being handy — often by necessity — about the house, Susan Koerner Wright was one of those women, rare especially in her time, with an innate grasp of physical principles. She understood how things worked, and had acquired, particularly from her father, a fascination with and a respect for the wonders of the mechanical world. To Orville and Wilbur she not only gave this secret — to be charmed by the how and why of working things — but also encouraged them to satisfy their curiosity whenever it arose. If the boys could not discover why something worked the way it did, they did not hesitate to dismember the object or device and then return it to its original state, often with improvements. Even before his teens, Orville's hands, which seemed never to be quite free of mischief, were seeking more useful outlets.

In Indiana, when Orville was twelve, wood engravings had struck his fancy. He threw himself into learning the craft, and immediately left his playgrounds and surprised his friends by going to the local library to study methods and material. He made an engraving tool from the spring of a broken pocketknife and worked laboriously through his first woodcuts.

In March 1885, Wilbur had completed the necessary steps to attend Yale Divinity School, intending eventually to enter the ministry.

CHAPTER 3

"To Get at Something That Interested Us"

IT CAME WHISTLING through the air, an angled shaft of hardwood swung with desperate strength and carrying with it a brutal impact.

And so it happened while he was playing a game of "shinny" on skates, this March day of 1885 when the moving wood was seen only as a striking blur. Flung from his feet by the blow, Wilbur tumbled to the ground and writhed in terrible pain, his mouth now a savaged pulp. In an instant Wilbur's lips were shredded, his gums torn, and many of his teeth shattered. The accident occurred on a frozen lake beside a Dayton veteran soldiers' home, and an army surgeon was there at once to attend him. His face heavily bandaged, Wilbur later that day went home to confront years of pain — emotional as well as physical. He was in his eighteenth year when the world that he had planned crashed to a heartbreaking halt.

A good student and an avid reader, he excelled in athletics of almost all kinds, including — despite his spare and wiry frame of five feet ten inches and 140 pounds — the physically punishing game of football in which youngsters battered one another without the heavy protective gear of modern times. Every day his future had looked brighter, as he saw himself profiting from his hard studies and his eagerness to meet great intellectual challenges.

Wilbur Wright closeted himself at home, rocking with the pain that stayed with him for months and eased slowly, recurring each time the doctors examined his knitting bones and worked on his mouth to prepare it for false teeth. When he could, he retreated to his books, his only way out of the prison in which he found himself, and which, in truth, he was reluctant to leave. He abandoned his plans to enter the ministry.

It was not simply what had happened to his mouth, teeth, and jaw; complications had set in. A few weeks after the accident he experienced nervous palpitations of the heart, and doctors later pronounced that his heart had been weakened. He developed an unexplained intestinal disorder that defied virtually all treatment. Wilbur, sunk in melancholy, became convinced that his heart would fail soon. With this in store for him, he felt there was no reason to waste the time or the effort or the finances of his family on pursuing any new endeavors.

So went his logical mind. Still, he considered a new direction; behind the battered face and the other disorders, the magnificent mind remained, even though depressed. As Wilbur later recalled, he had harbored "thoughts of a scientific career, but the lack of a suitable opening, and the knowledge that I had no special preparation in any particular line, kept me from entertaining the idea very seriously."

His mother attended Wilbur with all her own time and strength, for she considered him truly handicapped and in need of whatever aid and comfort she could bring. It seemed more and more fruitless, and the family concern came close to alarm as Wilbur's withdrawal from reality lasted months, then years. The long silences of the wan and ghostlike figure in their midst became not only difficult to endure, but impossible for them to understand. Wilbur would either dabble in household chores or bury himself in a book. He made virtually no contribution to his own life and, for some time, added only sparingly to the lives of others. His seclusion was to last more than four years.

Orville's interest in printing grew from his early experience with wood engraving. He turned to his father's old-fashioned letter press, which he had used before as a vise to hold other objects he was working on. This interest changed from hobby to serious business, despite Orville's youth, and in time gave rise to several newspaper publications that had some financial success. Newspapers, circulars, handbills, posters, pamphlets — all began to flow from the steadily modified printing systems on which Orville labored.

The extensive printing activity of young Orville took place without Wilbur, who was still in a deep state of depression. No one who knew the brothers at this time would have been able, without benefit of foresight, to assess the extraordinary rapport of these two minds in the future. Orville stormed along, four years the junior, and still free in body and spirit to pursue whatever star shone brightest for him. Within the same house, as Wilbur wrapped himself in melancholy, Orville transformed a room his mother had set aside for this purpose into a printing office — both a headquarters and a workshop. Orville's rush of enthusiasm appeared unending, recognizing no stopping time of day or night; and as fast as he completed one concept or modified a piece of equipment, he hurled himself into the next project. He was always improving, enlarging, seeking greater efficiency. When he sought a bed for a new press he wanted, he went, rather than to a printing supply house, to a supplier of mausoleum materials — where a marble dealer sold him, for comparatively little, an old gravestone that suited his printing requirements.

If Orville lacked knowledge, he dug into encyclopedias and other library reference works to find what he wanted, and then adapted that information to his needs. If nothing could be found, Orville was discovered with a deep frown until his fine geometrical imagination came into play, and he began to *create*. Printing seemed his hobby, his pleasure, and his future. When he was a teen-ager, he spent his summer vacations working 60 hours a week in a printing shop, and as many hours after work as he could find in his own shop at home.

By the late 1880s, Susan Wright had too long borne both Wilbur's pain and her own, and pulmonary complications steadily drained her strength to the point where she could barely walk. As consumption reduced his mother more and more to a feeble shadow of herself, Wilbur stirred from his own lethargy. His mother by 1887 was a bedridden invalid. With Bishop Wright now absent much of the time because of his church duties, the family hired a girl, Carrie Kayler, to attend to cooking and household chores, and Wilbur, who had been sustained by his mother's strength, now gave in kind. For two years, despite his physical handicap, he threw himself, with warmth and love, into the care of his mother. Each morning he lifted her wasting body from its bed and brought her downstairs to the parlor so that she might be with the world rather than be shut in as a recluse. At night, no matter how difficult he found it to move even his own body, he found the strength to carry the frail woman back upstairs for the night.

Bishop Wright said several times that the last two years of Susan Koerner Wright's life were a loving gift from her son Wilbur; that had it not been for this man rising from his own pain and despair, she would have died shortly after her confinement to bed. As it was, she struggled on to July 1889, and at fifty-eight, she closed her eyes forever.

On December 17, 1929, the ladies of the Rivanna Garden Club of Charlottesville erected a memorial marker in Hillsboro, Virginia. It reads:

THIS IS THE BIRTHPLACE OF
SUSAN KOERNER WRIGHT
April 30, 1831–July 4, 1889
Mother Of
WILBUR AND ORVILLE WRIGHT
Inventors Of The Airplane
A Notable Woman Who Largely Guided and Wisely
Inspired Her Sons To Their
IMMORTAL DISCOVERY
She Was The Mother Also Of
KATHARINE WRIGHT HASKELL
August 19, 1874–March 3, 1929
Whose Sisterly Devotion Aided In Giving
Mankind Access To The
UNLIMITED AERIAL HIGHWAY

Their "Immortal Discovery" — has it ever been better said?

Katharine, the younger sister of Orville and Wilbur, was very close to both brothers. When Susan Wright died, she assumed the task of running the household and its family. The Wright home on Hawthorn Street became her responsibility, and in the years following her mother's death, her devotion to Orville and

Wilbur grew. Bishop Wright was more and more on the move with his duties, and Katharine came to assume all responsibilities for the family and hearth, acting as mother, sister, cook, seamstress, friend, confidante and scold, and later as an unsuccessful matchmaker. She held this role for eight years, until 1897, when she left for two years to attend Oberlin College to get her credentials as a teacher. Except for this interruption, the family remained a tightly knit group, and even brief intervals of separation were filled with almost constant letters between them.

We search back through years and study broad events and look for the smaller critical moments, and we find one of the great turning points in the spring of 1888. Not an event planned, but a small event, a part of larger moments that later we come to recognize as so intimately revealing of mood and mind and purpose and ability. Orville was nearly seventeen years old, and his mother had been taken critically ill the year before.

Wilbur at that time had already spent three years suffering the lingering effects of his accident; although glum and morose, for the past twelve months he had devoted himself to the care of his mother. There had been many projects before now, building things and tinkering, doing carpentry to alter the Wright household, but in the spring of 1888, Orville determined to build a press bigger than anything else he had created to date, and better.

He threw himself into the task and showed his brilliant performance as a scrounger. He could not afford lumber for the press framework, but firewood did as well. Orville poked through various junkyards and scrap heaps in Dayton, searching out odds and ends of metal.

He lacked the means of applying the exact pressure needed to force his type against the surface to be printed. If there was too much pressure, the result would be smearing; if too little, the reproduction would be inadequate. The system also would have to apply the exact pressure on a consistent basis, rather than on one derived from guesswork. He couldn't solve the issue no matter how hard he racked his mind. After searching junkyards and stores, he browsed through the family barn and toolshed. Resting on the barn floor was an object that suddenly caused his mind to assemble a scene, a picture of pieces coming together and performing as he wanted them to do.

Not many minutes later, Orville had disassembled an old family buggy. He eagerly removed joining pieces and bolts, and when he had what he wanted, he dragged into his printing room the folding top. He had run through his mind the exact procedure by which the buggy top functioned. It folded down in the manner of an accordion pleat so that it would be out of the way. When it was to be in an upraised position, because of sun or rain, steel bars hinged in the center of the folding system locked it precisely in place. Orville assembled the buggy top with his printing equipment in his workroom and then made his first test. That "geometrical imagination" had again proved its worth — the top moved to an exact distance that was always repeated, always exerting the same force, and Orville was almost ready to go to work with his new mechanical contraption.

Problems beyond his grasp stumped the teen-ager. Wilbur, now twenty-one years old, and, having spent the years of his isolation in reading, came forward with useful ideas. He studied the balked press and made suggestions to Orville. He also began to emerge from his gloom, and his hands went to work in concert with his brother's. What astonished everyone was that Wilbur's recommendations, and the work he did, appeared to be in stark violation of the rules of how such machinery worked. No matter. The press was a rousing success; how much so was best described by a newspaper-pressroom foreman who visited the printing shop. He slipped off his jacket, lay flat on the floor, and worked his way under the press. For some minutes, while the brothers watched, the foreman remained on the shop floor. Finally he emerged, dusted off his clothes, picked up his jacket, and stared at the brothers. "I still don't understand *why* it works," he muttered as he left.

By 1889, Orville, eighteen years old, had rented larger quarters, was printing on a full-time basis, and was also publishing his own newspaper. Three months later Susan Wright died, and Wilbur was freed of this last commitment to remain at home to care for the dying woman. The year following, Orville expanded his printing business, and now Wilbur was working as one of his editors.

Perhaps now we can understand more clearly the peculiar and brilliant strokes of imagination that even a teen-age boy would show, when his older brother stepped into the scene to add his own imagination and solution to a problem, and how, from this event, repeated in other forms from time to time, the two brothers slowly came into the mental harmony that would be all-important later on.

The two brothers were now working as partners, but the several years of effort with their own press designs, although outstanding for their time, were overshadowed by the new commercial equipment that had been rushed into use by the major newspapers of the city. Slowly but surely they were being squeezed from competition, and they turned to a new interest.

The new "safety bicycle," with both wheels of the same size, was just making its appearance in the United States, and in 1892 Orville spent $160 to buy one of the new machines. The Columbia bicycle had pneumatic tires and, to Orville, was a marvelous device, which totally absorbed his attention. He lost interest in printing and was found at almost every bicycle race and track competition in the city. Wilbur also owned a new machine and often accompanied his younger brother to the meets, but only as a spectator. No matter that he had been a dazzling performer in gymnastics and on ice skates and in other athletics. His stomach still stabbed him almost daily, and he felt more pain from his heart; he was, if not content, at least willing to watch Orville.

Then came another step in the process of brotherly cooperation. Late in 1892 the printing business was slack. Bicycles were by now the rage. Orville and Wilbur were excellent riders, and, even better, they were superlative mechanics. They had many friends; they had enough money to start their own business. That fall they joined in their first adventure as a team — opening a bicycle sales shop on West Third Street in Dayton.

By December of 1892, they were in a full-time business, selling bicycles. Very quickly they discovered that those who bought bicycles also wanted service and repairs, and several months later they moved into new and larger quarters. They achieved success and expanding business so quickly, they moved their shop several times to accommodate the work pouring in, and decided that, as rewarding as was selling, servicing, and repairing, the demand for bicycles was so great that they had to design, build, and sell their own product.

The team was born.

In the next years they continued their success. Ever inquisitive, they took full advantage of the seasonal nature of their business. Dayton was snowy and bitterly cold in the winter, and there was little activity in the salesroom. But they made improvements on their machines, including the first full-pressure balloon tires with widened forks and frames. Sales increased correspondingly.

While engaged in the office work for their firm, Orville discovered his distaste for the limited capacity of the accounting machines of the day. His nimble fingers created a wholly new calculating machine, one that enabled him to multiply as well as add and subtract. The petty delays of office work annoyed him; typewriters were clumsy, clattering, and generally inefficient. Orville took an existing model and built a greatly simplified and improved machine.

Another clue as to their character emerges from their business practice as it carried over into their personal lives. The Wright Cycle Company was doing well, and they worked so closely together, functioning as the superb intellectual team the world would eventually come to know, that it never occurred to them to separate the financial matters of their business and their personal lives. As soon as they began producing income, they opened a joint bank account. Either could deposit or draw, which each did, without bothering to account to one another. They were coming closer and closer together, and Wilbur, still chained by the melancholy that had so long affected him, was at last beginning to accept that he must live with what had happened to him.

Wilbur was happy in his home life, enjoying his nephews and nieces, but was still plagued by the inability to slow his drifting in almost an aimless fashion. Indeed, it was Orville's success in business, as well as his excitement with the challenges of each succeeding day, that not only raised Wilbur's spirits but also turned his intrinsic brilliance to creative pursuits. The change in Wilbur's attitude was enhanced by an extraordinary piece of news.

In September 1894, *McClure's* magazine published the story of

Otto Lilienthal and his man-carrying gliders, including stirring photographs of his adventures and experiments, and his long glides from hilltops in Germany. The two brothers looked with awe at the pictures of the rigid-winged gliders, from which Lilienthal suspended himself by his arms and ran into the wind, finally to hurl himself into the air. And not to tumble or crash to the ground, but to glide startling distances. It was hang-gliding, as we know today, but it was rudimentary. The wings were barely efficient enough for brief glides, but the German engineer regarded this as only a beginning.

Wilbur had been accepting self-isolation for years. When reminded that he had abandoned his pursuit of a career in the ministry or any further education, he would return to his doldrums. But by the end of 1894 his health had improved so greatly that his theological ambitions seemed again within reach. Bishop Wright had offered to provide a loan for college, but Wilbur wrote to him:

> I have been thinking for some time of the advisability of my taking a college course. I have thought about it more or less for a number of years but my health has been such that I was afraid that it might be time and money wasted to do so, but I have felt so much better for a year or so that I have thought more seriously of it and have decided to see what you think of it and would advise.
>
> I do not think I am specially fitted for success in any commercial pursuit even if I had the proper personal and business influences to assist me. I might make a living but I doubt whether I would ever do much more than this. Intellectual effort is a pleasure to me and I think I would be better fitted for reasonable success in some of the professions than in business.
>
> I have always thought I would like to be a teacher . . .

Wilbur contented himself with the cycle shop, with a men's club in which he shared membership with his brother Lorin, and in idle contemplation of man's being able to fly. For there remains no question but that the spark struck by Lilienthal was still smoldering, even if dimly, in the minds of both brothers. Years would pass between the news of Lilienthal's experiments and the first active moves of the Wrights, but much of this time the brothers spent in intense, if sporadic, conversation about the new challenges. Orville especially was always ready to leap at even the suggestion of a new idea or concept. "Wilbur and I could hardly wait for morning to come," he reflected later, "to get at something that interested us. *That's* happiness!"

Wilbur, who agreed but with less exuberance, spent much of his effort in deep thought, especially about flying. He was drawn to an area beyond Dayton, a tumbled small wilderness known locally as the Pinnacles. Here, the wind was tossed about as it flowed across the surface of the land, and those same winds lifted suddenly, invisibly, to form great waves in the sky. Wilbur Wright could not see or understand this force, but birds instinctively used it. They came to the Pinnacles in vast numbers and all types, and they wheeled and soared effortlessly upward. Far below, binoculars held to his eyes, Wilbur looked at these feathered wonders, watching, studying, looking for signs or indications of how they were able to perform so freely and brilliantly. He had been a proficient gymnast, and he tried to associate his own feelings and former athletic freedom with what he saw in the sky.

CHAPTER 4

"Man and Machine Fell to the Ground"

IN AUGUST 1896, Otto Lilienthal kicked himself free of his starting hilltop at Rhinow, in Germany, and hurled himself into the wind. The frail wings of his glider took him along an unusually high path. The lifting power of the wings was at best minimal, and altitude, for Lilienthal's apparatus, was a dangerous enemy to be avoided at all costs. It was his final moment of flight. The glider nosed down suddenly and plunged into the ground, snapping Lilienthal's neck. He died the next day.

When news of the accident reached Dayton, Orville Wright was in no condition to care about such matters. He lay in his bedroom in a delirium, a victim of typhoid fever.

Wilbur must have felt the strange sensation of having endured this before. Only a few years earlier, he had sat at the bedside of his dying mother; now Orville lay racked by fever, with no better than an even chance, for typhoid in 1896 was a killer and no doctor could predict the outcome. But he was strong, and his care was excellent; and the Wrights were at last relieved to learn that the fever had broken and Orville would recover.

Sitting alongside the trembling form of Orville, Wilbur had time to ponder the details of what had happened to Otto Lilienthal. He read further newspaper accounts of how the German pioneer had died, and perhaps suspected even then that newspaper accounts of subjects poorly known to the reporter were apt to be misleading. *The New York Times*, allegedly a paragon of accuracy, wrote, "The apparatus worked well for a few minutes."

This was ridiculous, for had any man flown in a winged craft "for a few minutes," the story would have been headlined sensationally throughout the world. Wilbur groaned and then read that "Lilienthal flew quite a distance, when suddenly the machinery of the apparatus got out of order, and man and machine fell to the ground."

With Orville out of his fever and convalescing in bed, the brothers could discuss at length what had gone wrong with Lilienthal's flight.

These weeks did a great deal to direct the brothers toward eventual experiments in flying. They discussed and argued and probed, often deliberately reversing their roles in order to clarify a subject, and in these long talks they began to define for themselves the problems and the possible solutions of manned flight.

A mechanical object always obeys mechanical laws. It was clear to the Wrights that sometimes those laws were hidden, but when answers were not attainable it did *not* mean that the laws were nonexistent; it meant only that men were still seeking the truth about them.

Lilienthal was an investigative scientist of the highest order, and the Wright brothers, as they probed deeper into his background, reading articles by and about him in various periodicals, were astonished to learn that the German had spent twenty years in meticulous, exhaustive studies of the art of flight. Many men had observed birds flying and dreamed of emulating their flight, but Lilienthal had *studied* birds. From that study and his many years of calculations had evolved his design of a wing differing from almost all others that had been used unsuccessfully. Lilienthal built his wing with a "gentle parabolic curve" across its upper surface, and it was this subtle bulge on the upper side of the wing, stated Lilienthal, that gave the wing its lifting power. Since Lilienthal had made glides of a thousand feet, he had established that this idea was correct — but he didn't know *why* the wing produced lift.

Lilienthal took the criticisms of his research poorly; his critics called him a "flying squirrel" and other, less pleasant things. Writing of his detractors, scientists and newsmen alike, that "there are still prominent investigators who will not see that the arched or vaulted wing includes the secret of flight," Lilienthal explained that the parabola of the wing, the gentle curve bulging upward higher at the front of the wing and receding gradually to its rear, was a clear imitation of a bird. He had calculated what he believed to be just the curve that would provide him the greatest lift. The maximum depth of this curve, wrote the German, must be one-twelfth the measurement of the wing from front to back.

Wilbur mused that Otto Lilienthal had been following several dead ends. He offered his ideas to Orville, who often took an argumentative position with his brother in order to explore a question, and together they were able to discover where Lilienthal had been wrong.

First, the curving wing was not new to experimenters; if one knew where to search, then one would find recognition of the need of the curved wing in ancient times. Ovid in the first century had shown that he was aware of the need for curvature in his story of the wings fashioned by Daedalus for his son — who succumbed not to a faulty wing curvature but to material failure when he flew too near the sun.

Yet curvature was still debatable in its practical application. Otto Lilienthal, like so many others before him, believed that the secret of flight lay not only in building curved wings, but also in flapping those wings — making an ornithopter.

Another wrong avenue Lilienthal had pursued was his method of control. A glider, as we know it today, is simply a powerless airplane, its broad, thin wings designed to produce maximum lift at minimum weight. It has wings sufficient to provide lift, and it has the proper controls — rudder, elevator, and ailerons — to make it respond immediately and properly to the pilot.

Lilienthal's glider was only the barest trace of what lay in the future. His wings were lacking in width (they spanned barely more than 20 feet) and were proportionately lacking in lifting ability. His control surfaces were practically nonexistent — they were fixed, and offered only the stability imparted to an arrow or a finned missile, which was Lilienthal's goal. He knew that sudden wind gusts could unbalance his flimsy craft, and he had worked out a system in which the shifting of his body weight from side to side, or forward and backward, would alter the center of gravity and thus maintain equilibrium. He could even manage a very shallow bank and a hazardous slipping or skidding movement that would change his path from a straight line.

Lilienthal had recognized that he faced great obstacles, and, with his great intellect and engineering ability, he was sufficiently objective to admit that he was still "far from supposing that my wings possess all the delicate and subtle qualities necessary to the perfection of the art of flight. But my researches show that it is well worthwhile to prosecute the investigations further."

Recovered from his bout with typhoid, Orville joined Wilbur in a search for more information on flight. They were struck with the possibilities, and the mechanical difficulties seemed more of a challenge than an obstacle. After Orville was well enough to get about, the brothers searched the libraries in Dayton for whatever else they could find on man's attempts to fly, but they were poorly rewarded; little of any consequence existed on the subject. Wilbur had read several books on the locomotion of birds, but these had been published before the magazine stories about Lilienthal. Unable to learn from the experience of others, except Lilienthal, they were forced to think for themselves.

The Wrights were intrigued at this point with the idea of manned flight, but their own ideas on the subject were barely forming; for the next four years their interest would grow as they argued back and forth.

There were later to be moments of great — though cooperative — contention between Orville and Wilbur in their discussions about the possibility of flight, but their greatest contests at this point often took place in the kitchen. At various times before 1900, and permanently after that, there was either Katharine or the family helper, Carrie Kayler, in the house to attend to chores. If neither was there, the brothers, who — like many bachelors — enjoyed cooking, prepared the meals, although each did not always relish the other's culinary habits. During one period when Katharine was away from home, Wilbur wrote to her that "Orville cooks one week and I cook the next. Orville's week we have bread and butter and meat and gravy and coffee three times a day. My week I give him more variety. You see that by the end of his week there is a big lot of cold meat stored up, so the first half of my week we have bread and butter and 'hash' and coffee, and the last half we have bread and butter and eggs and sweet potatoes and coffee. We don't fuss a bit about whose week it is to cook. Perhaps the reason is evident. If Mrs. Jack Spratt had undertaken to cook all fat, I guess Jack wouldn't have kicked on cooking every other week either."

When Katharine was there, she was frequently a referee during the brothers' more intensely argumentative moments.

Few have ever stated it better than J. G. Crowther, in *Six Great Inventors*:

> The unique bond of intellectual collaboration was not based on similarity of temperament, but rather on contrast. They were complementary to each other. Apart from their passionate interest in the same thing, almost the only characteristic they had in common was greyblue eyes. Orville resembled his mother, and was meticulous over his clothes. Wilbur was more like his father, and perfunctory about his appearance. The extraordinary collaboration between the two brothers, unparalleled in the history of science, seemed to some extent to be a repetition in the realm of intellectual understanding of the deep affection that had united their father and mother . . . They formed a family group of exceptional understanding . . . Their affections were deeply engaged among themselves. They had an extraordinary cohesion, which continued through all the great affairs in which they were subsequently involved.

Their bachelorhood might suggest an austere family life, without the sounds and sights of what most of us would envision as a happy family — children laughing and playing and bringing their own brand of warmth into a household. However, Lorin, raising his own family of four children, lived only three blocks away, and the youngsters often visited their uncles. All four children found huge delight in Orville, who, with his impish turn of mind, would play familiar games, make up new ones when the occasion demanded, and when the games palled, would hie everyone off to the kitchen to make all manner of strange and delicious candies. In Wilbur they did not find quite the devilment and playfulness of Orville; Wilbur was an elder uncle who loved them dearly and could capture his young and worshipful audience with his splendid ability to weave enchanting stories.

Mrs. Ivonette Wright Miller, Lorin's daughter, recalled that her uncles "baby sat with us many times." Perhaps the best moments of all were when one of the brothers would have the children in a group, seated in chairs or lying on the floor. Orville or Wilbur would then read wonderful stories, particularly verses from the "Goop Book." (A goop was a child who had misbehaved.) When one of the children got out of hand, Mrs. Miller recalled, Aunt Katharine would say, "I believe we have a goop with us today."

Speculation and discussion continued, along with the daily round of business, social occasions, and family affairs. Then somehow out of the mist of doubt and wonder came that moment — that instant — that great fraction of a second in history, perhaps after a long evening discussion when Orville and Wilbur, who were dreamers, but dreamers of great practical capability, simultaneously became convinced that human flight was not only possible but that they must somehow devote themselves to its realization. They would begin by making formal inquiries to the Smithsonian Institution. And Wilbur would write a letter.

It was never planned or intended. It was the result of one thing leading to another — upbringing, home life, thwarted dreams in other areas, inherent genius that was as yet barely tested, and the times in which they lived.

CHAPTER 5

"I Wish to Avail Myself of All That Is Already Known"

WHEN WILBUR took pen in hand to write the Smithsonian in May of 1899, the state of Ohio was a fine place to live. Few areas on earth enjoyed more peace and stability than the towns and cities, and the beautiful rolling farmland, of this part of Middle America.

The frontier had passed over the wilderness of the Ohio Valley almost a hundred years before, leaving behind it the materials and pattern for a new way of life. Now, at the dawn of the twentieth century, it was a land reaching for that great promise of a new kind of life.

The countryside was checkered with farms; networks of railroads crisscrossed the land, and the distant enchanting whistle of the steam locomotive was as familiar and romantic to every child as the sound of the river steamer had been in earlier years to Mark Twain.

The picturesque gingerbread houses, clean and prim as matrons, lined the elm-shaded town streets, and stately mansions with the awkward grace of Victorian dowagers looked out across their pillared verandas at the green lawns of every square.

Ohio's solid, stable prosperity came from its bountiful agriculture and the bustling trade of its rivers, canals, and railroads, built by the hands of hard-working immigrants, mostly from northern Europe, a race of stolid, stubborn farmers and industrious and inventive mechanics.

Even the shadow of the terrible War Between the States was

nearly two generations past; the devastation and heartbreak of Shiloh, the crashing cannonade of Gettysburg lived on only in the memory of men in their advancing years. The wavering lines of gray and blue were seen in the Decoration Day parades, and not in the smoke of battle.

The Indian Wars of a quarter-century ago had faded into the mists; the wild Comanche yells at the Battle of Adobe Walls, and the thunder of the Sioux drums at Custer's Last Stand on the Little Big Horn, had long since passed with the prairie wind, leaving only a faint echo. But just nine years before, there had been the abomination called Wounded Knee. Indeed, in the long nights, while Ohio slept, the cattle and mining towns of the Rocky Mountains — Walden and Cripple Creek, Deadwood and Virginia City — danced to the sound of the honky-tonk pianos of the bordellos or the roar of guns in the streets. Butch Cassidy and the Sundance Kid still rode with the "Wild Bunch" out of their Wyoming "Hole in the Wall" hideout in the summer of 1899.

All of this faraway clamor Ohio largely ignored, and moved on with industrious, peaceful intent. The world was relatively calm, although there were distant wars and rumors of wars. Only the year before, the battleship *Maine* had blown up in Havana harbor. There had been a flurry of excitement and patriotism when an American hero named Teddy Roosevelt rode into battle at the head of his Rough Riders, but that was all over now; throughout the valley of the Ohio it was again business as usual. Times were changing, though, and there were signs of things to come and hints of great promise.

For most of the latter half of the nineteenth century, the telegraph had been the standard means of rapid communication. The transcontinental wire had gone through in the summer of 1867; messages could be transmitted with the speed of light from coast to coast and, since the laying of the new Atlantic cable in 1866, to Europe, as well.

There were other signs of new ways and new methods. Only 23 years before, Alexander Graham Bell had discovered a way of transmitting the human voice over wires by electrical impulses. Yet the telephone was slow in coming into general use. Few houses had them in the decade of the 1890s, and by 1899 the distribution was still so scarce that the Wrights had little occasion to use one.

Only about ten years before, a great new device had begun to clatter and rattle along dusty roads. The automobile appeared, plagued with a host of mechanical troubles of all kinds, including hand-cranked, balky, unreliable engines that were the terror of carriage horses and old ladies alike. Tires shredded after only a few miles over impossible roads, and gears jammed and ground to a halt in awkward places, but it was the beginning of great things.

In 1899 there were fewer than 8000 cars in the entire United States. Most of them, of course, were concentrated in the northeast portion of the country, but Ohio, with its population of inquisitive and innovative mechanics, certainly had more than its share of the automobiles that were available.

The Wrights saw them from time to time but had little occasion to use them. They were expensive, noisy, and unreliable. The bicycle and the interurban trolley served the Wrights' purposes to a greater advantage.

Still more important were the steam railway trains, the incredible, fascinating triumph of the nineteenth century and, in a sense, its embodiment. With the railroads' ribbons of steel laid across the country, through tunnels, and over trestles, thundering locomotives roared by at speeds of 60 to 70 miles an hour, towing everything from coaches to the luxurious private cars of the great moguls of industry. The railroad had not only changed travel enormously from the slow, dusty, bone-jarring horsedrawn vehicle, but also, with its nervous system, the telegraph, had affected the entire organization of life.

For the first time, all civilization was keyed to trains that left at specific times and arrived at specific times. The world had shrunk mightily, and it had learned to operate on schedule.

The greatest triumph of all were the transatlantic steamships. They were the product of almost a hundred years of steam-propelled floating transportation, which had begun with Robert Fulton's voyage up the Hudson in 1807.

The passenger steamships of that time were in many ways the apex of technological achievement. They were floating palaces,

with luxurious cabins, baths, great dining halls, and salons —
enormous giants, 500 to 600 feet long, that plowed through the
great rollers of the North Atlantic, with very reasonable, reliable
schedules for carrying their passengers, who looked out from
upper decks at a sea that swirled by 40 feet below.

Twenty years before, Edison had contributed to their magic by
the invention of the electric light bulb; now the steamships'
generators lit thousands of lights, in the cabins, on deck, and in
the salons. These great ships moved over the waves, glittering in
the depths of the night. Many steamship companies vied for the
trade, and literally hundreds of liners made their way between
ports like New York and Southhampton, Le Havre and Boston,
Baltimore and Liverpool. The North Atlantic was a veritable
highway, and seldom at night, in good weather, was it possible
to go out onto the deck of a great ocean liner, scan the horizon,
and not see the lights of another ship. The most glorious of sights
was that of two of the liners passing one another closely at night,
the decks filled with waving and cheering passengers, bands playing, and thousands of lights burning like floating beacons in the
void between the blackness of the sky and sea.

One could travel from San Francisco to New York in five and
a half days by train, take a ship the following day, and six days
later be in London. This did indeed represent a great step toward
man's domination of the planet, and gave most people the feeling
that the age of progress had arrived — that anything could be
accomplished, if only the minds of men were set to the problem
— anything, perhaps, but flying.

An education was an important thing in those days, taught in
no-nonsense grammar and high schools throughout the land. In
many ways, a boy or girl completing high school got as good an
education as some college graduates gain today. Learning was a
privilege, and, in most cases, students applied themselves diligently. The reluctant ones were, more often than not, convinced
by the tune of the hickory stick.

Customs were straight-laced and purposeful. There was a
meaning and a pattern to all life, influenced — in fact, almost
dictated — by the prejudiced opinion of an elderly, widowed
queen sitting on the British throne, 4000 miles away. That awe-

some woman, Victoria, the great-grandmother of most of the princes and princesses of modern Europe, cast a strong shadow from India westward, all the way around the world to the Pacific shores of the American continent. So great was her influence that respectable life throughout most of the English-speaking world was patterned on her opinions and molded to her concept of virtue.

Gentlemen wore stiff collars, coats, and ties every day, and women bound their charms in stiff whale-boned corsets, long skirts, and button shoes. Morality in sexual behavior was strict — monitored by a system of chaperones under whose watchful eyes conformity to Victorian virtues was enforced. The only relationship that could exist between a young man and a young woman prior to marriage was that of companionship.

But matrimony was the furthest thing from the brothers' minds at this point.

On May 30, 1899, Wilbur wrote to the Smithsonian Institution. His letter expressed very clearly, as his writings always would, the point their thinking had reached:

I believe that simple flight at least is possible to man and that the experiments and investigations of a large number of independent workers will result in the accumulation of information and knowledge and skill which will finally lead to accomplished flight . . . I am about to begin a systematic study of the subject in preparation for practical work to which I expect to devote what time I can spare from my regular business. I wish to obtain such papers as the Smithsonian Institution has published on this subject, and if possible a list of other works in print in the English language. I am an enthusiast, but not a crank in the sense that I have some pet theories as to the proper construction of a flying machine. I wish to avail myself of all that is already known and then if possible add my mite to help on the future worker who will attain final success. I do not know the terms on which you send out your publications but if you will inform me of the cost I will remit the price.

Government bureaucracy of that time being somewhat less convoluted than it is today, and the mails considerably faster, the reply from the Smithsonian was sent on June 2, from the assistant secretary of the Institution, Richard Rathbun. He forwarded to the Wrights a list of works relating to aerial navigation which included *Progress in Flying Machines,* by Octave Chanute (1894, New York); *Experiments in Aerodynamics,* by Samuel P. Langley (1891, Washington); and *The Aeronautical Annual* for 1895, 1896, 1897, edited by James Means (1895–1897, Boston). Rathbun included in his packet four pamphlets from the Smithsonian: *Empire of the Air,* by Louis-Pierre Mouillard (No. 903); *The Problem of Flying* and *Practical Experiments in Soaring,* by Otto Lilienthal (No. 938); *Story of Experiments in Mechanical Flight,* by Samuel P. Langley (No. 1134); and *On Soaring Flight,* by E. C. Huffaker (No. 1135).

With these publications as a beginning, the Wrights began a systematic study and correlation of all they could find on the subject of the struggle for human flight, taking all past efforts in turn and examining them to see what had been accomplished. Leonardo da Vinci's speculations on form and structure they recognized immediately as just that — speculations that led to a dead end. They dismissed this effort.

The papers caused a mixture of reactions. The writings of Mouillard, a Frenchman who in the 1870s had studied the flights of buzzards in the Egyptian desert, gave the brothers special encouragement; for despite his own failures in attempting to soar successfully, the French engineer was filled with a stirring wonder of the skies, and cast aside all restraint in his heart-stirring desire for the heavens. "If there be a domineering, tyrant thought," he wrote, "it is the conception that the problem of flight may be solved by man. When once this idea has invaded the brain it possesses it exclusively. It is then a haunting thought, a walking nightmare, impossible to cast off."

In the remainder of the works the brothers studied, there was less cause for enthusiasm. On examining the tribulations of the men who had preceded them, they were struck with the enormous complexity of the task they had set for themselves. Orville later would recall his and Wilbur's awe at the realization that some of the greatest minds in history had been applied to the subject of flight without tangible results.

The first man to have made significant headway in the theory of successful flight was, in their judgment, Sir George Cayley, a wealthy Englishman who perceived, early in the nineteenth century, that adopting the wing-flapping method of flight used by birds *might* be a fruitless avenue. Cayley suggested that there were really two separate problems of flight: to sustain a machine in the air, and to propel it. If Cayley's ideas were sound, then pursuit of a flapping-wing machine was destined to fail. What surprised Orville and Wilbur was that, despite these conjectures, Cayley had expended his energies in trying to develop a machine that would fly by flapping its manmade wings.

Then, in the 1840s, William S. Henson had advanced the concept of a machine powered by a steam engine driving large propellers and designed with a fixed wing to sustain its movement through the air. The propeller concept of this Englishman intrigued the Wrights, but it did not take them long to determine that these were the same type of propellers with which others were trying to drive balloons.

They read of other experiments, tests, ideas, conjectures, proposals, actual machines — and their failures. Alexander Graham Bell had tried to capture controlled movement through the air and had failed as thoroughly as all the others.

The roster went on. The Wrights read of the efforts of Sir Hiram Maxim, an experienced, respected engineer and inventor, who had produced the successful and lucrative Maxim rapid-fire machine gun. Maxim spent a small fortune in constructing a monstrosity of a flying vehicle that, although impressive in its great size and complexity, proved as incapable of flight as anything built before.

What about Thomas Edison? He had produced a vast number of splendid inventions, and, at the insistence of James Gordon Bennett, the explorer, publisher, and sportsman, had begun his own preliminary experiments in flight research. He brought his work to a halt when he concluded that flight would not be possible without an engine that could produce at least 50 horsepower and weighed less than 40 pounds. At that stage of engine development, although gasoline engines were being improved, this was a technology many years in the future. Edison had quit while he was still ahead.*

The Wrights came quickly to accept that, despite the mass of material before them, there existed no data on flight that could be considered conclusive; flight was neither an art nor a science. There were few facts and an overwhelming mass of almost useless theory.

They had no idea that so much work had been done and had resulted in so much failure and disaster. This realization sobered Orville and Wilbur and more than once brought them to wonder whether they were foolhardy in attempting what so many brilliant men had failed to achieve. Critically objective of their own abilities, they were humbled by their lack of background in this subject, to which they were able to accord more enthusiasm than technical knowledge. As Wilbur had implied in his first letter to the Smithsonian, *they may not have intended, at that time, to perfect a flying machine of their own, but only to carry out an intellectual and mechanical exercise that might add another rung on the ladder to ultimate success in flight.*

Most of what is written about their experiments comes from Wilbur. He and Orville agreed that the older brother, with his superior command of language, should record their efforts. Wilbur in later years would look back on that summer of 1899 with disbelief at what he and Orville were to attempt.

> At that time [wrote Wilbur], there was no flying art in the proper sense of the word, but only a flying problem. Thousands of men had thought about flying machines, and a few had even built machines which they called flying machines, but these machines were guilty of almost everything except flying. Thousands of pages had been written on the so-called science of flying, but for the most part the ideas set forth, like the designs for machines, were mere speculations and probably ninety percent was false. Consequently, those who tried to study the science of aerodynamics knew not what to believe and what not to believe. Things which seemed reasonable

---

* Edison had been interested in aeronautics since childhood; he had once fed birdseed to a friend and encouraged him to jump from an upper-story window to see if his friend could fly.

were very often found to be untrue, and things which
seemed unreasonable were sometimes true . . . things
which we at first supposed to be true were really untrue
. . . other things were partly true and partly untrue . . . a
few things were really true . . ."

After reading every document at hand, they obtained many
more in the next few months, and they studied them with the
intensity and thoroughness that were to be characteristic of their
efforts in the years to come. They concluded that it was Otto
Lilienthal, above all others, who had attacked flight most successfully. Lilienthal, with his brother Gustav, had worked on the
problem for more than two decades, and his papers and reports
on their experiments were the best data available.

There was material that went far beyond the magazine and
newspaper articles they had read more than four years earlier. In
1889 the Lilienthals had begun their aerial tests in a fashion the
Wrights found astonishing because of the dangers involved. Leap-
ing off towers, low or high, has a built-in disaster factor, and this
is how Otto had first spread his fragile wings. Four years later
the Germans wisely moved to the Rhinow Hills near Berlin,
which offered terrain and other conditions more suited to their
gliding experiments. The hills were a series of heather-covered
knolls, where experience showed wind conditions to be perfect
for their needs.

In all, Otto Lilienthal had made more than 2000 glides. At
times he soared to 65 feet above the ground, and many of his
flights were hundreds of feet long, including his record glide of
a thousand feet from his starting point. On his highest ascent,
Otto Lilienthal had felt the extraordinary thrill of soaring, and
had commented on the marvel of gliding "over ravines and
crowds of people who looked up in wonder."

Wonder it was, indeed, and wonder that he managed to survive
his perilous glides from the Rhinow Hills until August 9, 1896,
when he crashed. He died of his injuries the next day. To the
last, Lilienthal had remained dedicated to his dream. His final
words could be an epitaph for all pioneers everywhere:

"Opfer müssen gebracht werden!" (Sacrifices must be made!)

The brothers were now familiar with Lilienthal's work and agreed that his single ·most important contribution was the curved wing surface. They also recognized that the fragility of the Lilienthal glider resulted from his determination to build a craft of the lightest possible weight, rather than from flaws of design or construction. Indeed, Lilienthal's gliders were beautifully put together, shaped in the sweeping feathery lines of a great bird, except for his addition of a horizontal tail stabilizer and the fixed vertical rudder to the rear of the wings. He had gotten the greatest possible strength for such a light craft.

In an important paper in the growth of aviation, "The Carrying Capacity of Arched Surfaces in Sailing Flight," written in 1893 for the German publication *Zeitschrift für Luftschiffahrt und Physik der Atmosphäre,* Lilienthal had lamented that his predecessors had used a flat wing surface and that most experimenters were *still* using it. He was disturbed particularly by Professor Samuel P. Langley's stubbornness in this regard. Langley occupied an important and highly influential position as secretary of the Smithsonian Institution, had spent many thousands of dollars on his experiments, and for a long time refused to budge from a position favoring the flat surface. Even at this late date, noted Lilienthal, when tests proved the superiority of the curved wing, Langley continued to maintain that flat surfaces were the form that would make the airplane successful.

In Lilienthal's own words, which the Wrights would find to be prophetic: "It is also to be greatly regretted that the extended experiments of Professor Langley, carried out with so much care and expense, were limited to the resistance of plane surfaces, as for such surfaces data have long been on record sufficient for computing all cases occurring in practice."

The Wrights found themselves on the horns of a dilemma. The painstaking care exhibited by Lilienthal commended his efforts to them, for their own mechanical turn of mind and their mechanical skills enabled them to distinguish between nonsense and good engineering. Lilienthal was brilliant, innovative, shrewd, and courageous, *and yet he was still wrong.*

Could this really be so? If Orville and Wilbur were correct in their studies of the material now spread through their sitting

room and on their study tables, it meant that everyone else who
had ever pioneered the study of flight had been following dead
ends.

Could the Wrights be in step and the rest of the army be
stumbling along? That they even entertained doubts was discom-
forting, for they held aviation's pioneers in respect, and not in
little awe, chiefly for their staggering accomplishments in other
fields. Through this labyrinth of doubts they moved on, intent
and seeking.

Even when Katharine would bring a girl friend home, it was
simply no contest as to which would receive their attention, the
young lady or the skies. Wilbur and Orville were not to be dis-
tracted. Seated on opposite sides of the fireplace, each sifted and
sorted his own ideas and then criticized the other's. It was a sight
that would be long remembered by those in the Wright household. Orville had a habit of assuming a certain posture when he
was deep in thought. He sat staring into the fire, seated erect on
a straight chair, his arms folded, his manner determined. Not his
brother, for Wilbur was the angular sort; he sat with the small
of his back hard against the chair, his hands clasped behind his
head, his legs jutting straight ahead.

One would remain silent for minutes after the other spoke,
and then declare, "'Tisn't, either." The other would accept the
statement, swirl it about in his own imagination, weigh it carefully, and then calmly reply, "'Tis, too." Quiet at first, then
growing in volume, their "'Tis"'s and "'Tisn't"'s became the battle cries of the arguments they so thoroughly enjoyed, for their
sessions produced results.

It did not take them long, despite their reservations about
declaring the great men of science to be wrong, to know that
there was a fundamental deficiency in Lilienthal's glider designs.
It was the result of his decision to maintain the lateral stability
of the glider — that is, to keep his wings level — by shifting his
body weight. If a sudden gust of air lifted the left wing of the
glider, then the aeronaut, hanging beneath the machine, would
find that his feet naturally swung toward the right, or that wing
tilted toward the earth's surface. Yet this had to be avoided at all
costs, since it was critical for him to swing his weight "upwing"

— to reach the higher wing in order to rebalance the glider.

It was impossible to ask this of any man hanging under a glider, and the Wrights came to believe that Lilienthal's inability to accomplish this acrobatic feat in gusty air had been his undoing.

Other inventors offered almost as many solutions as problems. It had occurred to many of them that the proper thing to do was to place the center of gravity well below the wings of a machine. It was then obvious that the wings, always seeking that center of gravity, would gain a built-in stability. This is a fine idea in theory, but in practice it's a killer: the entire machine not only seeks this deep center of gravity, but seeks it constantly, and at once an oscillation builds up, destroying stability rather than maintaining it.

Still others had reasoned that the only way a winged machine could fly was to have its surfaces produce lift. No matter what oscillations or twisting or movement is produced by a bird, the result is lift. Well, then, reasoned the Wrights, if we build our wings in the shape of a *V*, with a strong positive dihedral, each wing will be contributing lift toward a common center. If the machine is unbalanced by gusty air, the wing that drops down is now level with the horizon, and its upward lift operates most effectively against gravity. Dihedral works; it is used today in many aircraft. *But without other control systems* it defeats itself. If the air is perfectly calm, dihedral without other balancing systems can be effective temporarily. However, the moment the air becomes turbulent, or there is a major shifting of weight within the machine, the craft begins rocking severely from side to side in an oscillation almost impossible to stop without another control force.

Then there had been Alphonse Pénaud, in the 1870s. Here was a model builder of extraordinary ability. No matter that he had worked with toys — those toys *flew*. Pénaud had used the energy of elastic bands to spin small propellers. He also used a wing design with positive dihedral, but he later introduced another factor, the details of which were not yet known to the Wrights — a rear stabilizer. This was not placed in any random fashion; it was so contrived that the forward edge of the horizontal tail was lower than the trailing edge. The arrangement was intended

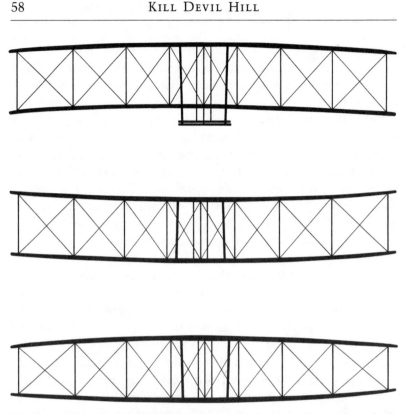

Wing configuration: Wright designs featured the cathedral angle on both upper and lower surfaces (top), structure with dihedral only (center), and both cathedral and dihedral angles (bottom).

to give lateral stability — keeping the wings level — and also to provide an inherent longitudinal stability — preventing the nose from pitching up or down.

Yet Pénaud went no further than his models. It seemed to the brothers that he was traveling along a road he knew to be the one leading to his destination but had come to an insuperable barrier.

Any man who creates something new owes much to those who have gone before. So it was with the Wright brothers. But what must be kept in mind is that little of the earlier work was truly useful. Indeed, the Wrights had to overcome obstacles created by the errors of other experimenters.

Because these experimenters were legion, historians have assumed that enough of their work was correct so that all the Wrights had to add was the finishing touch — and take off into the skies. This thesis has been propounded so often that I have chosen to risk the reader's patience by repeating that what the Wrights found, when they examined papers written by others, was a morass of disorganized data, mistaken conclusions, and circular arguments based on previous errors. After they had slogged their way through this swamp, they knew they had no choice but to return to Lilienthal.

Now, having already determined that Lilienthal's method of flight control was faulty, they began to suspect an associated flaw. Lilienthal had insisted that a glider of limited size — one with no more than around 155 square feet of wing surface — could be properly controlled by a man. This principle, which led Lilienthal to curtail the length of his glider, was based on the same fatal system for controlling his glide — the shifting of the pilot's body weight.

Thus, Lilienthal had been caught on the horns of a dilemma: if he had stayed with the same size glider, he would never have had sufficient lifting surface to really fly; but if he had attempted a larger one with a greater lifting surface, the effect of the man's weight in counteracting gusts against the wings would have been negligible. It would have had virtually no effect on an airborne machine. The effect would have been somewhat like that of a surfer attempting to control a huge, heavy, and ungainly surfboard. Lilienthal had, therefore, compromised by using a wing with excessive curve to obtain greater lift from the small surface. What he had not known — nor did the Wrights know it at this stage — was that such a high airfoil curvature produced a dangerously unstable aircraft.

The brothers were aware that a contemporary of Lilienthal, the Scottish engineer Percy Pilcher, had also been conducting gliding experiments — first from a farm hill in Scotland on the banks of the Clyde and later in England in a sheep pasture at Stanford Hall, near Market Harborough. There, Pilcher took to the skies in a manner that would be used in the future. Unlike Lilienthal, who ran with all his might and threw himself off hills, Pilcher was towed aloft, like a giant kite, by a horse; the system was quite ingenious, with the animal harnessed to a system of pulleys that multiplied its speed several times. Pilcher's visions seem more remarkable the more we study them. He had excellent ideas for the maximum use of available energy and was already laying the groundwork for a gasoline engine of his own design, which he would substitute for his horse-and-pulley system.

He had gone further. He had visited with Lilienthal in the Rhinow Hills and had even flown Lilienthal's glider. Its lifting power surprised and delighted him, and he had rushed back to England to perfect his own craft and give it a propulsion system.

Like Lilienthal, however, Percy Pilcher had failed to solve one of the fundamental and more critical problems of flight — three-dimensional control of equilibrium. Like Lilienthal, he had attempted to gain guidance and control of his craft by shifting his body weight about on a sort of trapeze harness. Then, just four months after Wilbur had written to the Smithsonian, Pilcher tried again. On September 30, 1899, he was towed high into the air by his pulley system, and cut himself loose to begin what promised to be a good glide.

Pilcher's glider had been soaked by a steady rain. Rocked in high winds, it suffered structural failure in the tail assembly. Pilcher plummeted helplessly amid the broken wreckage of his machine. The manner of Pilcher's death weighed heavily with the Wright brothers, who would never forget the lesson.

Wilbur and Orville were impressed with Pilcher's accomplishments and ideas. His launching system was reliable and contained all the energy he needed to get a gliding craft aloft. His plans for a gasoline engine were astonishing. And unlike those who had believed in machines with flapping wings, Pilcher already had been planning to develop a machine using rigid wings, an engine, and propellers. He had been working toward fulfillment of the dual requirements of flight that Sir George Cayley had postulated: wings to sustain him in flight, and concentrated energy through his engine and propellers to drive him forward through the air. And, of course, Pilcher was also using a curved or arched wing, in contrast to such men as Langley, who eventually changed his mind, and others who still insisted on a wing made with a flat surface.

Wilbur and Orville saw at once what the problem was. Neither Lilienthal nor Pilcher had answered the fundamental question of how to achieve stable control. Shifting body weight was at its best a temporary measure, for a simple gentle glide low above the ground, but its intrinsic faults made it useless at great speed or height. The road to death for those flying this way was a certainty.

They must *not* accept the concept of shifting body weight as a control. Somehow, they reasoned, they must change the angle at which the airfoil — the wings — attacked the air through which the aircraft was traveling. Underlying their reasoning were their observations of birds — they had noted how one of these creatures could "pinwheel" about its own body axis — as well as their own ability to envision mechanical systems. Those who preceded them had endured and fought and suffered and died, but they had also "infected us with their own unquenchable enthusiasm and transformed idle curiosity into the active zeal of workers."

Everyone's efforts to date had produced, at most, troubled trembling glides in which the aeronauts were always a split second from loss of control and death. They now knew there was as yet no science of flight. No wonder that the world's most eminent scientists, one by one, had put human flight in the same category as perpetual motion.

Perhaps, some reasoned, success might be achieved by an *association* of searchers in this field of inquiry, for no one man can be simultaneously an inventor to imagine new shapes and new sources of power, a mechanical engineer to design the arrangement of the apparatus, a mathematician to calculate its strengths and stresses, a practical mechanic to construct the parts, and a syndicate of capitalists to furnish the needed funds. On the other hand again, the whole thing perhaps was totally impossible. This, then, was the scene at the time the team of the Wright brothers walked on the stage.

CHAPTER 6

The Secret of the Wrights

FOR THOUSANDS OF YEARS men had envied the birds and sought to emulate their flight. Some of the best minds in history had worked on the problem without tangible results. The failures surely can be attributed to complex technical problems, but they cannot be blamed on a lack of materials necessary to construct a flying machine. Many people believed these were not available until the turn of the last century; this is far from the truth.

Far back in antiquity, there had been a sufficiency of perfectly suitable materials for the building of a glider. For several millennia, man could have built a flying machine without power — only a glider, to be sure, but still a flying machine. The Egyptians, the Greeks, and the Romans could have done it.

In the beginning of the eighteenth century, steam power had become available. A steam engine is not an *ideal* power-plant for an airplane for many reasons, but nevertheless it *is* possible for someone to build a man-carrying airplane powered by a steam engine and fly it. In all the years of the steam engine's development and refinement, no one had done so.

By 1870, the internal combustion engine had been developed; relatively efficient, controllable, lightweight power was now available. By 1890, there had been a century's worth of engineering achievements — railroads, steamships, mechanical reapers, electric lights, telephones, telegraphs, machine tools, calculators — to stimulate and support the inventor, and they were still coming thick and fast; today's technological explosion had barely started.

As we have noted, many of the men responsible for these marvels had turned their attention to the problems of mechanical flight. They had everything available to them that the Wright brothers possessed. Most of them had superior education, better training, better working facilities, and a vast advantage in financial resources — yet they all fell far short of the goal.

Why is it, then, that in this same arena, with the same forces to work with, the Wrights, in four and a half years, succeeded brilliantly where others had failed?

The answer is not simple, but it is there — clear and yet profound.

In the first place, the Wrights identified, defined, and outlined completely the problem they were attacking, which no other inventor — contemporary or earlier — had ever done.

Many of their predecessors, from lack of adequate knowledge, labored under the impression that there were only *one* or *two* problems involved in mechanical flight, and that if they solved these, they would be successful. They hadn't perceived that there were many more snakes in the basket, any one of which could prevent them from succeeding.

The Wrights saw at once that each of the problems was a complex of many parts and approached each one in turn.

The Wrights, with amazing perception, immediately saw and defined the six problems whose solutions were necessary to the attainment of flight.

1. To emulate the birds, one must understand that there are two distinct types of bird flight, and that man for mechanical and gymnastic reasons could hope to copy only one. The darting flight of wing-flapping barn swallows, for instance, required impossible solutions to the problems of mechanical application and human reflexes. The second type, the soaring flight of the albatross or eagle, man could design and emulate, if he could understand its principles.

2. The solution of the secret of lift, with its problems of equilibrium, was related to, but different from, the third problem.

3. There had to be designed a satisfactory three-dimensional control system.

4. An apparatus strong enough to support the weight of a man, yet light enough to fly, must be constructed.

5. The power-to-weight ratio had to be correct.

6. The pilot had to achieve the necessary skill to fly the machine without being destroyed in the process.

But equally significant was the way the Wrights attacked each problem after identifying it. The first problem was to understand and identify the two main forms of bird flight.

The observations of Mouillard while he watched the flight of buzzards in the Egyptian desert confirmed what Wilbur and Orville had already agreed upon. In addition, they were further convinced by observations noted in *Animal Mechanism*, a famous work of E. J. Marey, which they had studied before writing to the Smithsonian.

Watching the barn swallows dart about a barn — whirring themselves in and out of the doors, perching on lofts and rafters, fluttering here and there with an accuracy and an astounding capability despite the potential turbulence of wind drafts, was confusing. It was obvious that the flapping of their wings sustained them. But how? And how did they maintain their extraordinary control?

Wilbur was able to see two vital things about the fluttering flight of a barn swallow. First, the construction of a mechanism that would reproduce the motions of these flapping wings with any degree of success would border on the impossible, and even if it could be constructed, it would weigh too much to raise itself aloft.

Second, and more difficult, was the understanding of the reflexes the swallows needed to maintain equilibrium during these extraordinary darting flights. Wilbur saw that the flight of a barn swallow was a series of gymnastic feats of the first magnitude, and that no man could hope to equal it or to maneuver a machine in this way.

There was another reason that, at this point, he had not completely understood, but that would develop later as the brothers expanded their experiments. This was simply that the required power-to-weight ratio for flapping wings was infinitely greater than would be required in rigid-wing flight. Leonardo da Vinci had made drawings of a proposed apparatus by which a strong man could flap wings and actuate the mechanism by both arms and legs, utilizing the full power of his body.

What Leonardo did not know was that it would take approximately 50 times the strength of a man to sustain himself in the air by the mechanism he had proposed. Few of us have any real conception of the relative strength of a bird and the power used to actuate his wings in comparison to his own weight. A man's pulse is approximately 70 beats per minute; that of a small sparrow will be perhaps 500 to 700. In other words, a sparrow's generation of energy, compared to a man's, is something on the order of 10 to 1.

To produce this enormous energy, the bird must consume approximately his own weight in food every day. If a man were to consume his own weight in food in a day, it would be his last day on earth; he has no way of converting energy at this rate.*

The soaring bird — the eagle, for example — was observed to keep its wings in a rigid position and soar in spirals in the sky, or hover along ridges, balancing adroitly with the winds and currents, but obviously exerting no flapping motion to sustain itself in the air. This was clearly the best approach for man to take, because it was apparent that it would be far better to construct a wing like that of a soaring bird, where no motion of its structure was required.

Theories along this line had been advanced, notably by Lilienthal, though also by others, that involved tangential pressures developed by presenting a flat or even a curved surface toward moving air. That problem involved lift and equilibrium, and the Wrights attacked it later.

They had arrived at the correct conclusion: there was only one mode of bird flight they could hope to emulate. This is what Wilbur meant when he wrote to the Smithsonian that "I believe that simple flight at least is possible to man." Simple flight, of course, was the flight of rigid-winged birds, which sailed in some mysterious way on the currents of the air.

Now they came to the question of lift with equilibrium. It was apparent that if a square, thin surface were presented flat to the

* It is interesting to note that many jet airplanes consume approximately their own weight in fuel every 16 to 18 hours — very much on the order of a bird's consumption.

wind, it would offer maximum resistance, and that if it were turned edgeways to the wind, it would provide very little. Any angle between the vertical and the horizontal would result in some sort of tangential force — a force that would act in some direction other than that of the wind direction. They had reasoned from their kite-flying activities that the direction and strength of this tangential force could be calculated. A center of pressure — the point where the force acted — could be established, but it was quite obvious that the center of pressure would move. This they called the center-of-pressure travel, and assumed that it would move forward on the surface as the angle of the surface to the wind was decreased until the surface finally reached a zero or horizontal angle to the wind, in which case the center of pressure would finally arrive at the leading edge of the surface.

They assumed that the same conditions would apply to curved surfaces, and they were prepared to use the curved surfaces because Lilienthal and others had proven that curved surfaces had more lift than flat surfaces. No one really knew why, but birds' wings were curved and Lilienthal's glider wings were curved, and both provided lift.

This was logical, but would later lead the Wrights into dangerous traps. In any case, it was their conviction that a flat or curved surface could be so presented to the angle of the wind that, if the wind had sufficient velocity and if there was sufficient surface, enough lift could be generated to equal the weight of a man, and flight would be possible.

Also, if the center of pressure moved from the center point of the plane's surface area when the surface was at right angles to the wind, forward to the leading edge of the plane surface when that surface was slanted toward the wind, the problems of lift would have been solved, but the problem of equilibrium would be ever present. To balance the aircraft on that center of pressure would be like balancing on a tight rope in a strong wind. That plane surface would obviously wobble as the skis of a water skier wobble when presented at various angles to the water and at changing speeds. Of their center-of-pressure travel and the difficulty involved in balancing a glider or an airplane caught in its web, Wilbur had this to say: "The balancing of a gliding or flying machine is very simple in theory. It merely consists in causing the center of pressure to coincide with the center of gravity. But in actual practice there seems to be an almost boundless incompatibility of temper which prevents their remaining peaceably together for a single instant, so that the operator, who in this case acts as a peacemaker, often suffers injury to himself in attempting to bring them together." The Wrights saw the problem clearly for the first time.

They could also see that to structure from this flat or curved surface, which they would now call a "wing," they had to find some way of balancing and counteracting the center-of-pressure travel. This balancing arrangement could not be in the form of a movable weight, for many reasons; rather, it had to be some sort of offsetting lifting surface. This is the function served by the horizontal part of the tail of a present-day airplane. The brothers came up with the idea of a small forward plane, to be built in an extended position ahead of their wing. At first they thought it could be secured in a fixed position, but they would later discover that it would have to be movable if it was to maintain the aircraft's balance. The first forward plane, which, at the time, they chose to call the "horizontal rudder" but which we today would call a forward elevator (or canard), became the hallmark of their aircraft design. All Wright planes, in the early days, were distinguished by the forward plane, which extended ahead of the wings.

The fact that the Wrights had incorrectly analyzed the center-of-pressure travel, and its differences on flat surfaces versus curved surfaces, turned out, in the long run, to make no difference. This forward plane would be a happy accident of design, because, as we shall see, it would save their lives many times over.

Many people confuse the problem of lift and equilibrium with that of control. Here again the Wrights saw the difference. It was one thing to maintain balance as the center of pressure moved on the wing; it was quite another to control the motion of the aircraft in three dimensions.

The solution to this problem did not come easily. The brothers labored over it mightily and sought solutions to it no matter where they were or what they did. Their preoccupation was enough to cut them off at times from contact with the outside world. When they discussed the matter, it was in soul-searching or thundering arguments. They kept trying different methods, "talking" with their hands or scribbling out sketches, to see what the other thought about an idea or a suggestion. They were agreed in practice, at least, that if they could change the angle at which the wing attacked the air, and change it rapidly and with reliable response, they would gain an element of control. They devised a system of gears that would change the wing angle of a flying machine, but then, after weeks of work, had to conclude that it would be impossible for them to build a structure strong and rigid enough for the system and still light enough to fly. Their solutions seemed to follow a circle that always returned them to their point of starting — which meant no solution at all.

Then, in the summer of 1899, Wilbur waited impatiently for his brother to return to the house at 7 Hawthorn Street. The usually taciturn Wilbur fairly dragged Orville to a chair to force him to listen; no problem, of course, because each listened eagerly when the other had a new idea.

Orville listened as Wilbur, arms moving like windmill blades, his unusual excitement contagious, explained that he had solved the problems of lateral control. Not in a machine he had built, but in his mind, and with the manner of exchange of these two brothers, it was enough for Orville to grasp clearly what Wilbur proposed.

Years later, Orville would recall:

> A short time afterwards, one evening when I returned home with my sister and Miss Harriet Silliman, who was at that time a guest of my sister's in our home, Wilbur showed me a method of getting the same results as we had contemplated in our first idea without the structural defects of the original. He demonstrated the method by means of a small pasteboard box, which had two of the opposite ends removed. By holding the top forward corner and the rear lower corner of one end of the box between his thumb and forefinger and the rear upper corner and

the lower forward corner of the other end of the box in like manner, and by pressing the corners together the upper and lower surface of the box were given a helicoidal twist, presenting the top and bottom surfaces of the box at different angles on the right and left sides. From this it was apparent that the wings of a machine of the [Octave] Chanute double-deck type, with the fore-and-aft trussing removed, could be warped in like manner, so that in flying the wings on the right and left sides could be warped so as to present their surfaces to the air at different angles of incidence and thus secure unequal lifts on the two sides.

For the next few weeks the bicycle shop saw nothing of Wilbur. He had been making sketches of this new design, trying to blend it with a biplane structure, which he and Orville had agreed was the strongest way to attain adequate surface with light weight. Now he had a plan: sets of wires run through small pulleys between the top and bottom wings would enable him to warp the wings in flight. This is essentially how the wings of today's aircraft are controlled to keep them level or to make them bank; the movable portion of the wing — the aileron — is still located at the tip of the wing and at the trailing edge but is hinged rather than bent.

If he was right, he explained to Orville, then they could achieve with an airplane wing what a bird did by flexing the outer parts, and especially the outer trailing edges, of its wings. He built a model of split bamboo, threads, and connecting trusses for bracing, shaping and reshaping until he had worked out in practice what he had designed. But this wasn't enough. He studied every motion of his delicate model as he moved the warping system back and forth in his hands, jotting down notes, improving here and there, defining and refining. Then it was a feverish rush to build a flyable model that would enable him to test in flight what was, no matter how clever, nothing more than a theory on paper and a bamboo contraption in his workshop.

At this stage the brothers weren't even dreaming of flying a man. Wilbur was desperate to get into the air a model that incorporated wing warping* and could be flown as a kite to test wing warping as an effective flight control; he could at least then see what wing warping would accomplish. By unspoken agreement, since Wilbur had conceived the idea, Orville attended to the mundane and now frustrating daily chores of running the bicycle shop while Wilbur rushed ahead with the kite model. Six days after he had demonstrated his warping idea to Orville, on July 27, 1899, Wilbur was ready to test it. The model was impressive in size, with a wingspan of five feet. Its biplane wings measured a foot in width, or chord (chord is the wing measurement from leading to trailing edge), and the wings themselves were curved along their surface as Lilienthal's had been in his gliders. If this simple device was to work as Wilbur hoped, it would be an important step forward.

Much has been made of the predilection of the Wright brothers toward secrecy. It has been explained as stemming from their fear of having their ideas stolen by other experimenters, but in these early stages it was probably no more than a natural desire for privacy. Wilbur did not want to become a buffoon by flying the kite in the midst of gawking crowds. In their younger days, Orville had been a splendid designer, builder, and flier of kites, and had sent his contraptions soaring to great heights, but he was content to let Wilbur fly the experimental kite because Wilbur had originated the concept he would now test.

In a field to the west of the city Wilbur prepared to try out the system. The only witnesses were several schoolboys who had caught sight of him. This promised to be fun; when a man flew a kite, especially one this size, you could expect something really special.

The youngsters watched Wilbur reel out his control lines. They were puzzled by the new, different shape of the kite and by the way the well-dressed man worked on a series of lines. They saw the lines tugging and pulling at the wingtips of the kite, and the shapes bent to and fro, and they wondered at the way the double-

---

* The Wrights originally used the word *twisting*, or *helical twisting*, to define the changing of a wing's angle of incidence at the tip for lateral control. But the term *warping*, credited to Octave Chanute, was adopted by the Wrights and became generally accepted. Later the French translated it literally as "gauchir" and "gauchissement." In their French patent, however, the Wrights used *tordre* and *torsion* — meaning "to twist."

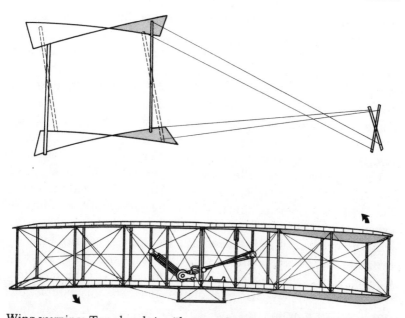

Wing warping: Top sketch is side-view diagram of the Wrights' biplane kite of 1899, indicating general arrangement of strings and effect of wing-warping movements. Operator maneuvered machine by actuating sticks (at right) with fore-and-aft wrist motion. Bottom drawing shows how wing-warping principle tested in the biplane kite worked when incorporated in the *Kitty Hawk Flyer* design. The drawing shows left-wing trailing edge (at right in sketch) warped down, thus producing more lift than the opposite wing and effecting a rolling motion to the right.

winged kite went first this way, and then the other, almost as if the man with the strings were controlling its motion in the air.

Not too successfully, they may have decided, for something suddenly went wrong, and the boys looked up to see the big kite abruptly dip downward and rush wildly at them in a swift dive. No time to run — the boys threw themselves flat on the ground, hands clasped over heads as they readied themselves for the impact, but all they felt was a whistling sound as the kite rushed by above them, despite everything the man did to prevent that downward plunge.

Both Wilbur and his brother were pleased at the way the kite had responded to lateral control but were baffled by the way it had plunged. They had no explanation for this misbehavior, for while it was held aloft, taut at the end of its controlling string, it flew splendidly and answered every command of Wilbur's as he warped the wings. They had no way of knowing at the time that the problem lay not in their design, but in their continuing belief that Otto Lilienthal was the absolute authority on the best curvature for a wing. A wing may be curved in the form of an arc or in the form of a parabola, and there is danger inherent in both designs, but more so in one than the other. At that moment they did not appreciate that there was a killer hiding in the shape of the kite's wings, nor would they — until it threatened their own lives. At the moment, however, the overall results of the kite experiment were absolutely splendid. *They had proved that wing warping worked;* that it indeed provided lateral control by aerodynamic means and could be substituted for the pilot's shifting weight. There were air currents and forces yet to be reckoned with, but no one else had ever achieved satisfactory lateral control in either a model or a full-sized machine, and they had done so on that open field outside Dayton.

They were ready to make the next step, to move up to the ranks of Lilienthal, Pilcher, and all the others who had risked their lives in the air. Using their new design, with wing warping, they would now build a machine large enough, strong enough, and with enough lifting force, to bear the weight of a man.

CHAPTER 7

"... Afflicted with the Belief That Flight Is Possible"

"ONE STEP AT A TIME," Wilbur and Orville had promised their father. In their decision to fly a glider with a man aboard, they planned to move slowly, to record details, and to try to extract from every movement and event a record of those forces that had been encountered. Only after they had accumulated exhaustive tables of notes from their observations, and had analyzed their successes and problems, would they place their own bodies at the mercy of the invisible forces that affected a machine in the air.

They did not forget that Pilcher and Lilienthal had both been killed in experiments. Their first flights with their man-carrying glider must be made under remote control, as it were, with a man's weight simulated by ballast. After these experiments were completed, and after they had learned all they could, they would gamble with their own lives.

The next several months were divided between the summer rush at the bicycle shop and calculations and studies of the full-sized glider they were about to construct. This is a blank period in the history of the Wrights. Their records tell only of the building of the five-foot model, the decision to build the larger man-carrying glider, and the question of where they should test their machine. But that only scratches the surface of these many months that began in August 1899, when they spent long nights in drawing up data and calculations, working out the pressures on airfoils, redesigning the construction details of the glider.

Between the first flight of the five-foot kite glider and the first
test flights of the man-sized machine, more than a full year
would pass.

It was essentially a year of hard, determined study, of tedious
calculations, of effort with no more tangible result than hundreds
of pages of data, of working with wood and sateen and other
materials, of rigging wires, of the thousand and one major items
that had to precede the effort they were planning. This entire
year is gone from our history except for the letters that have
survived.

Angle of incidence, designation of surface, area in square
inches, aspect ratio, surface and curve, rectangular pressure, balance, torsion, tensile strength, square footage, moment of bending: these were the elements of the new world into which they
were moving. How would they actuate the controls of the new
glider when it was occupied only by the ballast? How to launch
it? How to test the wing-warping system? How would they determine actual lift? Would their calculations bear up in practice
or be thrown to the winds with the first awkward tumble of their
untried machine? When would they first feel confident enough
to let the glider carry a man? Discussions continued night after
night; and ever present, as they came closer to their goal of flight
testing their concept, there was the specter of death or severe
injury.

In answer to the concerns of the family, Wilbur spoke for them
both when he said that there would be no escape from risk, that
they must practice what they had already recognized: the only
way to learn to fly is to fly. "If you are looking for perfect safety,"
he said in a kind of gentle admonition, "you will do well to sit
on a fence and watch the birds; but if you really wish to learn,
you must mount a machine and become acquainted with its
tricks by actual trial." And the Wrights were no longer fence-
sitters. Still, the family fears persisted, and finally, in response
to a letter from their father, Wilbur wrote: "I do not intend to
take dangerous chances, both because I have no wish to get hurt
and because a fall would stop my experimenting, which I would
not like at all. The man who wishes to keep at the problem long
enough to really learn anything positively cannot take dangerous
risks. Carelessness and overconfidence are usually more danger-

ous than deliberately accepted risks." The words are quite true today.

By late fall of 1899, they were ready to start looking for a suitable site for testing the large glider, and on November 27, Wilbur initiated correspondence with the U.S. Weather Bureau, describing what they needed. The open fields in the Dayton area had been rejected. To fly a tethered glider like a large kite, no enormous area was needed; but now, as they approached the stage of risking their own bodies on glides from one point to another, they were going to need an open testing ground with steady winds and a smooth surface. Correspondence between the Wrights and government agencies, as well as with private individuals whose names they got from the initial contacts, continued for some months.

In the meantime, they took another important step; they decided to write Octave Chanute. Chanute, an American of French birth, was considered an elder statesman of civil engineering, having built several important steel bridges — including the first to span the Missouri River at Kansas City — and designed some of the country's major railway systems (he even helped develop plans for the New York elevated network). For many years he had collected data on flying machines, had sponsored the work of others, and had actually conducted gliding experiments on the sand dunes of Lake Michigan southeast of Chicago.

Chanute's role in this critical period has been a source of some controversy. Some historians of early flight, perhaps with national bias, have proclaimed him as the man most responsible for modern aviation. Wilbur and Orville Wright themselves felt, and acknowledged in many ways, that Octave Chanute had made a tremendous contribution to their work.

But as quick as they were to praise, the Wrights were later to remind everyone that the control systems in heavier-than-air flight were designed, built, tested, and flown by Orville and Wilbur Wright, and by no one else. Their recognition and handling of this problem was a factor over which Octave Chanute, despite everything else he did, exercised no particular influence.

There were several other notable achievements on the Wrights' long road to flight that they could have mentioned and that Chanute knew nothing about. From the very first, the Wrights recognized Octave Chanute as a most remarkable man who had already made a great contribution to conquering the air, if for no other reason than that he had been a collector of previous information. Also, as time went on and their acquaintance grew, he was to serve as an excellent backboard from which Wilbur could bounce his ideas, particularly in the brothers' struggle to understand aerodynamics in *proper sequence.*

Chanute had come to the United States at an early age, proved himself a dedicated student and brilliant thinker, and risen rapidly in engineering and industrial circles to become one of the most prominent railroad construction engineers in the world. He became interested in aviation as early as 1874, but it would be another 15 years before he felt he could devote full time to research. (He had long admired the work of Francis H. Wenham, the English pioneer whose lecture to the Aeronautical Society of Great Britain in 1866 Chanute later described as a classic.) The concept of sweeping through the skies in a machine under the control of a man, of being able to direct one's own path amid the clouds, flying over natural barriers of terrain . . . it all filled the railroad engineer with a zeal he had not experienced in years. An ardent supporter of any new endeavor in science and engineering, he was soon immersed in the lore of flight, using his own considerable facilities to collect all the information on the work of others who had attempted controlled flight in heavier-than-air machines.

In 1894, with a wealth of material assembled, he published a book that was to become famous in aviation history. *Progress in Flying Machines* was included in the documents sent by the Smithsonian in the fall of 1899 to the Wrights, and this was their introduction to Chanute and his work.

Chanute went beyond theory with several gliders he designed, constructed, and had test flown. Already well past his sixtieth year by the late 1890s, Chanute himself did not fly; accepting the physical demands of glider flight might have been his final adventure. Instead, he employed younger men, who devoted long weeks to studying his machines, practicing carefully on the ground, and finally jumping into the air. Chanute found it vexing that these excursions were brief and awkward and, even by the most generous terms, could hardly be considered true flights.

What galled him most was that his own fertile imagination was unable to bridge the gap between theory and flight.

It was a case of brilliance thwarted. Chanute well understood the value of the curved or arched wing and built machines that reflected his common-sense engineering approach. They were robust and well adapted to gliding needs, but suffered the single fault that they would not fly; the problems seemed to be just beyond his grasp.

One important contribution that Chanute had made in his early experiments was the development of the biplane-type wing for his glider. This design he favored for two interesting reasons. First, he knew that box kites were noted for their stability in flight and that a biplane wing design approximated that of a box kite. Also, being a construction engineer, he was familiar with the Pratt truss, a type of railroad bridge design that used internal bracing to give great strength and rigidity with relatively light weight. Chanute built his biplane wing with this type of internal bracing, and the Wrights adopted it, with substantial construction improvements of their own.

In addition, Chanute had gone beyond Pilcher and Lilienthal, recognizing that flight control by shifting the pilot's body weight could have only limited effectiveness. He proposed for his biplane glider an automatic device intended to function without any effort from the pilot; it would maintain lateral stability by causing the machine's supporting surfaces to adjust themselves to changes in the wind. He was convinced that the human being lacked the sensitivity and the swift instinct to correct, by reaction rather than directed action, the balance of a machine upset by the whims of the air. The birds could do this, he reasoned, because millions of years of evolution had brought them to this stage, but it was far too much to ask of mere man, a creature pinned for the last 500,000 years by gravity to the surface of his planet. Thus, the man must be replaced by an automatic system. It may not be too far-fetched to suggest that Chanute's experience as a railroad design engineer, dealings with vehicles whose course was controlled by banked rails and the inertia of huge masses, influenced his thinking. This line of thinking would eventually become dominant once again in the design of spacecraft controls.

The Wrights disagreed absolutely. They insisted they must

build a control system that could be operated manually, and that this control system must be constructed to maintain longitudinal stability — to keep the nose level — as well.

They believed that the *only* way for a man to attain efficiency — and, in time, instinctive response — was through as much practice with a flying machine as could be had, a belief that undoubtedly stemmed from their experience with bicycles. Wilbur was an excellent rider and Orville a competition racer. Both were unusually adept on their two-wheeled machines. They knew only too well that wobbling, erratic motions and tumbling to the ground almost always preceded instinct and skill, but a man with subtle and automatic reactions could ride with flair and dash, hands clasped behind his neck.

By May 1900, the brothers were in agreement that they should contact Chanute directly; they felt that there must be a wealth of data beyond what they had seen. Wilbur, as chief correspondent, wrote to represent them both, although it was later noted that Orville took exception to Wilbur's frequent use of "I" rather than "we." Wilbur's first letter was to initiate a correspondence of more than 200 letters — a rich legacy in the archives of human flight, for they would record much of the frustrations in the attempts to fly.

On May 13, 1900, Wilbur wrote to Chanute:

> For some years I have been afflicted with the belief that flight is possible to man. My disease has increased in severity and I feel that it will soon cost me an increased amount of money if not my life. I have been trying to arrange my affairs in such a way that I can devote my entire time for a few months to experiment in this field.
>
> My general ideas of the subject are similar to those held by most practical experimenters, to wit: that what is chiefly needed is skill rather than machinery. The flight of the buzzard and similar sailers is a convincing demonstration of the value of skill, and the partial needlessness of motors. It is possible to fly without motors, but not without knowledge & skill. This I conceive to be fortunate, for man, by reason of his greater intellect, can more reasonably hope to equal birds in knowledge, than to equal nature in the perfection of her machinery.

Assuming then that Lilienthal was correct in his ideas of the principles on which man should proceed, I conceive that his failure was due chiefly to the inadequacy of his method, and of his apparatus. As to his method, the fact that in five years' time he spent only about five hours, altogether, in actual flight is sufficient to show that his method was inadequate. Even the simplest intellectual or acrobatic feats could never be learned with so short practice, and even Methuselah could never have become an expert stenographer with one hour per year for practice. I also conceive Lilienthal's apparatus to be inadequate not only from the fact that he failed, but my observations of the flight of birds convince me that birds use more positive and energetic methods of regaining equilibrium than that of shifting the center of gravity . . . My observation of the flight of buzzards leads me to believe that they regain their lateral balance, when partly overturned by a gust of wind, by a torsion of the tips of the wings. If the rear edge of the right wing tip is twisted upward and the left downward the bird becomes an animated windmill and instantly begins to turn, a line from its head to its tail being the axis. It thus regains its level even if thrown on its beam ends, so to speak, as I have frequently seen them. I think the bird also in general retains its lateral equilibrium, partly by presenting its two wings at different angles to the wind, and partly by drawing in one wing, thus reducing its area. I incline to the belief that the first is the more important and usual method . . .

Wilbur was extrapolating his interpretation of the balance of birds, but he had hit on a great truth. He also described "the plan and apparatus it is my intention to test. In explaining these, my object is to learn to what extent similar plans have been tested and found to be failures, and also to obtain such suggestions as your great knowledge and experience might enable you to give me."

Wilbur asked Chanute for his recommendations for an area where he and Orville could test their gliding machines, especially where they "could depend on winds of about fifteen miles per hour without rain or too inclement weather."

His letter included a statement that tells a good deal about the confidence they had come to feel. By now the Wrights were convinced that they had made solid progress in advancing the science of controlling an aircraft, even if their work was still restricted to models, and they were fairly bursting to get into the skies with a machine able to carry a man. Whatever caution or reservation was in Wilbur's mind, he hedged everything that had happened with this significant comment:

"I make no secret of my plans for the reason that I believe no financial profit will accrue to the inventor of the first flying machine, and that only those who are willing to give as well as to receive suggestions can hope to link their names with the honor of its discovery. The problem is too great for one man alone and unaided to solve in secret."

Wilbur would later regret putting those words on paper, for financial profit would indeed become a source of wearying contention between the Wrights and many others.

CHAPTER 8

"You Will Find
a Hospitable People
When You Come Among Us"

THE ROAD TO FLIGHT was mostly a dirt road or a railroad. It was a collection of conveyances and means of locomotion, against which the idea of man's flying through the air must have been indeed laughable. In the years to follow, before the brothers would first command the skies, their efforts included long hikes, rides on bicycles, horse-pulled wagons, boats of a treacherous variety, trains, and even horseless carriages. Footpower, pedal-power, wind-filled sails, locomotives, steam boilers, horsepower, and combinations of all these occupied much of the time of the Wright brothers as they tried, however gingerly, to beat their sateen-covered wings into the air.

The Wrights, after discussions with Octave Chanute and the exchange of correspondence with the U.S. Weather Bureau, selected the area near the village of Kitty Hawk on the North Carolina ocean banks as their first choice for glider tests. They had made the decision in the summer of 1900, but the choice was, as they discovered later, really not the best among all the possibilities open to them. However, at the time Kitty Hawk appeared ideal for experiments in soaring flight, and the information obtained in their search confirmed this choice.*

* Legend has it that the name *Kitty Hawk* originated with the early English settlers. It is an anglicized version of "Killy Honk," the coastal Indians' expression for killing geese, a principal food. (They killed the migrating birds every fall, thus to them "Killy Honk to Killy Honk" represented a white man's year in time.)

Wilbur had searched for an area that would guarantee them winds of 15 miles per hour and fairly open and level ground. On August 3, 1900, Wilbur wrote to the government weather station at Kitty Hawk for more specific information. His letter met with immediate and courteous response from the station observer, Joseph J. Dosher, who, on August 16, replied:

"In reply to yours of the 3rd, I will say the beach here is about one mile wide, clear of trees or high hills and extends for nearly sixty miles same condition. The wind blows mostly from the north and northeast September and October . . . I am sorry to say you could not rent a house here, so you will have to bring tents. You could obtain board."

Dosher, on his own, referred the Wright letter to another resident of Kitty Hawk, William Tate, whom Dosher considered to be the most highly educated man in the local community. Tate knew the area well; he had been postmaster there for some years, and his wife now held the job. On August 18, his curiosity fired by Wilbur's letter, Tate wrote:

> Mr. J. J. Dosher of the Weather Bureau here has asked me to answer your letter to him, relative to the fitness of Kitty Hawk as a place to practice or experiment with a flying machine, etc.
>
> In answering I would say that you would find here nearly any type of ground you could wish; you could, for instance, get a stretch of sandy land one mile by five with a bare hill in center 80 feet high, not a tree or bush anywhere to break the evenness of the wind current. This in my opinion would be a fine place; our winds are always steady, generally from 10 to 20 miles velocity per hour.
>
> You can reach here from Elizabeth City, N.C. (35 miles from here) by boat direct from Manteo 12 miles from here by mail boat every Mon., Wed. & Friday. We have Telegraph communication & daily mails. Climate healthy, you could find good place to pitch tents & get board in

---

The name *Kill Devil Hills,* also legendary, dates back to a shipwreck near there in the early 1800s. A man hired to guard the salvage claimed he had to shoot a pillager. He is reported to have told the ship's owners, "I killed that ol' devil last night." As a result, the general site of the wreck soon became known as "Kill Devil Hills."

private family provided there were not too many in your party; would advise you to come any time from September 15 to October 15. Don't wait until November. The autumn generally gets a little rough by November.

If you decide to try your machine here & come I will take pleasure in doing all I can for your convenience & success & pleasure, & I assure you you will find a hospitable people when you come among us.

Tate's letter, written with such gentlemanly consideration and promise, made the decision easy. The Wrights agreed that the pencil-thin line of beach on the edge of the Atlantic, with its winds so eloquently described by Bill Tate, would be perfect for their needs. Tate had neglected to mention, however, perhaps in his excitement over the project, that this was also Cape Hatteras country, and that the winds that breezed down from the north and northeast also had a tendency to whip into violent storms with little or no warning. There were also other problems unmentioned by Tate and still to be discovered by the Wright brothers, but discover them they would, and remember them all their lives.

The brothers agreed that Orville would attend to the bicycle business, which was going well, while Wilbur set off for the remote sand line of Kitty Hawk, and that, business permitting, Orville would join him later. The brothers rushed through their work to prepare the man-carrying glider while there was still the dependable weather Tate had described, bending ash ribs into the desired lines and shapes, cutting and connecting metal, sewing the sateen cloth, and assembling many parts of the glider without actually putting the machine together. Most of the work was done in the back of the bicycle shop, although Wilbur packed the parts carefully into a large trunk — 50 thin wooden rods, shaped for various components of the glider, as well as tools, spools of wire, metal fittings, and the lustrous, white French sateen that would cover the wings. The spars for the leading and trailing edges of the wings were omitted. Wilbur planned to stop along the coastline of the Carolinas to buy them; he realized that carrying lumber 18 feet long would be too much for a traveler — especially one with the trip he had to make.

They had yet to lift their bodies an inch from the ground in flight, and their trip was intended for learning rather than for great achievement. Indeed, the Wright family was delighted with the thought of Wilbur's going off to the healthy sea climate of the Carolina coastline, for they all believed exposure to sun, breeze, and salt air would help his ailing constitution. It was a quiet adventure, a vacation, as it were, not frivolous, but hardly overburdened with dominant purpose. On September 3, three days before leaving Dayton, Wilbur wrote as much to his father, who was then traveling, explaining he would be "making some experiments with a flying machine. It is my belief that flight is possible and, while I am taking up the investigation for pleasure rather than profit, I think there is a slight possibility of achieving fame and fortune from it . . ."

Those few lines are not only prophetic; they reflect a changing attitude toward the prospect of personal gain. Had there been in the final weeks of preparation, of building the actual glider, a growing conviction on the part of the brothers that they truly *were* close to controlled flight? Not on this trip, perhaps, but certainly in the near future. Think of their attitude at first, hoping to plunge into the mysteries of flight for the sheer joy of the challenge, hoping to achieve only one more small step in the long climb into the sky, *so that their work might help others still to follow.*

Only this hint, then quickly, as if to hedge this speculation about "fame and fortune," Wilbur added, "At any rate, I shall have an outing of several weeks and see a part of the world I have never before visited."

Two days later, Katharine, in a letter of her own to Bishop Wright, reflected the high excitement of the family when she wrote, "We are in an uproar getting Will off. The trip will do him good."

In 1585, Sir Walter Raleigh had sent men to establish a colonial foothold along the Atlantic, and Roanoke Island, within view of Wilbur's destination, was one of the first colonies. It had not been an auspicious beginning, for it became known as the Lost Colony and, beset by grave problems, disintegrated from within and finally disappeared.

Long after the first settlement on Roanoke Island was a memory, more than 130 years later, a richer brand of history was enacted along Cape Hatteras. The skull and crossbones fluttered in these same winds, and of all the brigands and cutthroats who sailed these shores none was more infamous than Edward Teach, better known as Blackbeard. He ended his spell of enthusiastic looting and homicide with an unexpected voyage, his head dangling from the bowsprit of an English sloop sailing up the James River.

Pamlico Sound, which separates Cape Hatteras from this wasteland, is a large body of water extending from the south, at Cedar Island and Cherry Point, all the way up to Bodie Island and Kitty Hawk; here the waterway is constricted sufficiently to lend its widening a new name, Albemarle Sound. Elizabeth City, at the north end of one finger of Albemarle Sound, was Wilbur's destination.

Trunk, baggage, and all, Wilbur embarked from Dayton on Thursday evening, September 6, 1900, on the "Big Four" and Chesapeake and Ohio Railway. No one aboard that train, including Wilbur, imagined that he was beginning a trip that would eventually threaten to put passenger trains out of business. About 6:00 the following evening he arrived at Old Point Comfort, in Virginia, saw to his baggage and crates, and took passage on the ferry steamer *Pennsylvania* for Norfolk. He put up at the Monticello Hotel, and the next morning, September 8, he went to a lumberyard to complete purchases of the boards and materials he planned to use in building the glider at Kitty Hawk. It was the first of many difficulties the brothers would have in the Kitty Hawk area.

He recorded in his notes a few days later that he spent Saturday morning in Norfolk trying to find spruce spars for the glider, but was finally resigned to buying white-pine spars at a nearby mill; these were only 16 feet long, which meant changing the size, area, and some of the design elements of the glider that was still in the trunk. As Wilbur's frustrations mounted, the temperature approached 100 degrees. Wilbur was a man who dressed impeccably, and he would never have thought of appearing in public without his high starched collar and suit jacket. Finally, by late afternoon, he had the white pine, and again he arranged his baggage, trunk, and lumber and departed for Elizabeth City, where he gratefully collapsed in his room at the Arlington Hotel.

Refreshed now, he set about, with renewed purpose, to obtain rental of a boat that would take him across Albemarle Sound, 40 miles of water, to reach the sand dunes of the banks. He was astonished to learn that the names of Sir Walter Raleigh and Edward Teach were far better known to the local citizenry than Kitty Hawk. He later recalled the moment: "I spent several days waiting for a boat to Kitty Hawk. No one seemed to know anything about the place or how to get there."

Four days after reaching Elizabeth City, he made contact with Israel Perry, a sort of riverman who lived aboard his own vessel, a small, flat-bottomed schooner that he used as a fishing boat.

Wilbur checked out of his hotel, only to learn that Perry's boat was three miles downriver and that the only way to reach it was by water. Everything had to be loaded aboard a leaky skiff at the wharf — baggage, trunk, lumber, boat owner, deckhand, and Wilbur Wright; they occasionally shipped water. They rowed the three miles downriver, bailing constantly. An exhausted Wilbur, perhaps sensing he was in the midst of some uncommon madness that common sense would have suggested leaving, saw Perry's schooner with dismay. What he already knew of it was bad enough; what he saw was crushing.

A look at the stern revealed a rudderpost rotten through its entire structure; the wood had decayed, eaten away by weather and insects, and defied the laws of gravity by barely clinging to the stern of the schooner. Wilbur tripped over ropes scattered across the deck; the lines were frayed, split, and in many cases were crudely knotted together. The sails were split and rotting.

The cargo transferred, amid a population of cockroaches, silverfish, rats, and flies, Wilbur had a look at the weather. He felt a light west wind, saw that the surface of the sound was calm enough, and decided that he could stand it for the six hours of expected passage. As he later told his family and friends, a slightly stronger breeze or the first sign of whitecaps would have sent him ashore at once.

It took most of the day for Perry to get ready, and the sun was already below the horizon by the time the schooner slipped into the open waters of the sound, tattered sails flapping. Wilbur watched with alarm as the wind shifted almost as quickly as they pulled well away from land. What had been a pleasant enough breeze became a hard blow that quickly churned the surface into choppy, angry waters. Now that they moved into a crosswind, the poor handling characteristics of the schooner, riding high on the water with a flat bottom, changed discomfort to real danger. In the black of night the wind rose to near gale proportions, and the schooner became almost unmanageable, pitching and rolling wildly, broaching in sickening motion, shipping water, and then, as if to complete the series of tragicomic errors, leaking badly. Each hour became worse than the preceding, and as midnight fell, Wilbur knew that he was in critical danger of drowning. Israel Perry's demeanor became less lackadaisical in proportion to the fury of the now full-blown gale, and he cut straight north in a desperate attempt for shelter.

The night tore apart with a long ripping explosion, and the schooner reeled about violently, its deck askew, wind-driven spray slashing into the three persons aboard — Perry, Wilbur Wright, and the deck boy. Wilbur was soaked through and through, and with the deck boy he fought his way forward, where the foresail, torn loose from its boom, flapped like a demented creature. They secured the sail, gasping for breath, not knowing when the schooner would heel over to its side; and then another blast shook the boat as the mainsail ripped away. Only a jib remained, and in a wild stab at survival, to say nothing of a display of unexpected seamanship, Israel Perry jibed across the wind, skidding the flat bottom in a perfectly timed maneuver to bring the wind onto the stern. Bailing frantically, hanging on for dear life, drenched and frozen, the three men eased into a sheltering cove later in the night. They tied up and collapsed, grateful that their lives had been spared.

It was not until well into the next day, after the fitful repairs that typified everything about this ship, that they moved across calmer waters. As night fell, Wilbur was just able to make out the edges of Kitty Hawk Bay.

He felt jubilant about making shore safely, but this exuberance was swiftly shattered. It was night, and the isolation of Kitty Hawk fell on him as he discovered the wharf to be unlit and deserted, and a small store sealed tightly and abandoned for the night.

Weary to the bone, unfed except for a small jar of jelly Katharine had sent with him (the only food he dared to eat aboard the schooner), he sat stoically through the night, taking catnaps on the deck.

The next morning he unloaded his possessions from the schooner and, with relief, bid Israel Perry and his deckhand farewell. He stood at last on the sandy ground of Kitty Hawk, seven days after leaving Dayton.

CHAPTER 9

"You're Off"

SAFELY ON SHORE, Wilbur made his way to the house of William Tate, with whom he had corresponded the month before. Ten days later, on September 23, he wrote Bishop Wright a wonderfully revealing exposition on his arrival in Kitty Hawk:

> I am staying at present with Mr. W. J. Tate, the postmaster at this place. He is also a notary public and was recently elected a county commissioner of Currituck Co. His occupation is fishing in the fishing season, which begins about Oct. 1st and lasts for about three months. His house is a two-story frame with unplaned siding, not painted, no plaster on the walls, which are ceiled with pine not varnished. He has no carpets at all, very little furniture, no books or pictures. There may be one or two better houses here but his is much above average. You will see that there is little wealth and no luxurious living. A few men have saved up a thousand dollars but this is the savings of a long life. Their yearly income is small. I suppose few of them see two hundred dollars a year. They are friendly and neighborly and I think there is rarely any real suffering among them. The ground here is a very fine sand with no admixture of loam that the eye can detect, yet they attempt to raise beans, corn, turnips, &c., on it. Their success is not great but it is a wonder that they can raise anything at all.
>
> I have my machine nearly finished. It is not to have a

motor and is not expected to fly in any true sense of the word. My idea is merely to experiment and practice with a view to solving the problem of equilibrium. I have plans which I hope to find much in advance of the methods tried by previous experimenters. When once a machine is under proper control under all conditions, the motor problem will be quickly solved. A failure of motor will then mean simply a slow descent & safe landing instead of a disastrous fall.

In my experiments I do not expect to rise many feet from the ground, and in case I am upset there is nothing but soft sand to strike on. I do not intend to take dangerous chances, both because I have no wish to get hurt and because a fall would stop my experimenting, which I would not like at all. The man who wishes to keep at the problem long enough to really learn anything positively must not take dangerous risks. Carelessness and overconfidence are usually more dangerous than deliberately accepted risks. I am constructing my machine to sustain about five times my weight and am testing every piece. I think there is no possible chance of its breaking while in the air. If it is broken it will be by awkward landing. My machine will be trussed like a bridge [based on Chanute's adaptation of the Pratt truss] and will be much stronger than that of Lilienthal, which, by the way, was upset through the failure of a movable tail and not by breakage of the machine. The tail of my machine is fixed, and even if my steering arrangement should fail, it would still leave me with the same control that Lilienthal had at the best. The safe and secure construction & management are my main improvements. My machine is more simple in construction and at the same time capable of greater adjustment and control than previous machines.

I have not taken up the problem with the expectation of financial profit. Neither do I have any strong expectation of achieving the solution at the present time or possibly any time. My trip would be no great disappointment if I accomplish practically nothing. I look upon it as a pleasure trip pure and simple, and I know of no trip from which I could expect greater pleasure at the same cost. I am watching my health very closely and expect to return home heavier and stronger than I left. I am taking every precaution about my drinking water . . .

The bishop was probably more pleased with references to Wilbur's health and his promise to be careful of his drinking water than with the technical details. A man who traveled considerably, Bishop Wright was aware of the varying quality of drinking water in strange locales — a justified concern, after Orville's nearly fatal bout with typhoid fever.

On September 26, Katharine picked up the story to Bishop Wright in a letter from Dayton:

> . . . Orv went south Monday evening, to join Will. They got a tent and will camp after Orv gets there, which will be tomorrow morning. They can't buy even tea or coffee or sugar at Kitty Hawk, so Orv took a supply along. They also took cots and Orv took your trunk. We put your things all in the old trunk. I loaned my trunk to Will. I was glad to get Orv off. He had worked so hard and was so run down. They never have had a trip anywhere, since the World's Fair. They had a hard time getting anyone to look after the shop and do the repairing, but they finally got a young fellow by the name of Dillon, of whose honesty there is no doubt, to stay and watch the store and Cord Ruse comes in to do the repairing. Lorin & I are managers.

On September 28, Orville arrived at Kitty Hawk to join his brother, and the two boarded and lodged with the Tate family until October 4, when they set up their own camp about a half mile from the Tate home. A great deal of work had been accomplished before Orville appeared: Wilbur had worked relentlessly to assemble the glider, despite the added work of reducing the planned wingspan from the original 18 feet without the bow ends; the high-quality sateen had been sewn to the original specifications before they left Dayton, and now had to be cut and resewn. Wilbur cut a two-foot section from the center of each wing covering, and spliced the halves on a sewing machine borrowed from Mrs. Tate. The glider now emerged with a total span, with bows, of nearly 17.5 feet, and was virtually complete about five days before Orville came to Kitty Hawk.

Finally, after a long period with no word from Kitty Hawk, Katharine received a most welcome letter that Orville had written on October 14:

> I wrote you last Sunday, but maybe you have not got it yet. We have been having several big winds, and as the mail is carried out of Kitty Hawk in a small sailboat very likely letters have been slow in transportation this week. I got your letter of Monday last night.
>
> We have been having a fine time, altogether we have had the machine out three different days, from 2 to 4 hours each time. Monday night and all day Tuesday we had a terrific wind blowing 36 miles an hour. Wednesday morning the Kitty Hawkers were out early peering around the edge of the woods and out of their upstairs windows to see whether our camp was still in existence. We were all right, however, and though wind continued up to 30 miles, got the machine out to give it another trial. The wind was too strong and unsteady for us to attempt an ascent in it, so we just flew it like a kite, running down a number of strings to the ground with which to work the steering apparatus. The machine seemed a rather docile thing, and we taught it to behave fairly well. Chains were hung on it to give it work to do, while we took measurements of the "drift" in pounds. [Drift, today, would be called "induced drag."]
>
> In the afternoon we took the machine to the hill just south of our camp . . .

Here the brothers set up a derrick, a kind of triangular wooden tower, about 12 feet in height, which they would use to hold the rope taut when flying the glider as a kite; this was the planned flight practice at the controls before risking actual glides. They could learn to act as instinctively with their glider as they did when riding a bicycle.

This was one of the few times that Octave Chanute was absolutely opposed to Wilbur's plans. Four days after Wilbur wrote Chanute in May of 1900, the older engineer sent off an immediate reply, warning, "As for myself, I have always felt that restraining ropes were a complication which not only vitiated the results but might lead to accidents from rotation of apparatus or collision with supports, and I have preferred preliminary learning on a sand hill and trying ambitious feats over water. I send you a report of my gliding experiments which you may not have."

And as it turned out, Chanute was correct in his warning. The Wrights found that, despite all of Wilbur's plans with the derrick, they must take one step at a time, and they would have to learn the hard way — Lilienthal's way — by getting up in the air and gliding.

However, Chanute's reasoning did not apply to what was going on at Kitty Hawk. In other words, he was right, but not for the reasons offered. The real problem was far greater than "the rotation of apparatus or collision with supports." What baffled the Wrights was a law of aerodynamics that would take them almost two more years to understand. Numbers had tripped them up.

The total wing area of this glider was 165 square feet, even after the enforced shortening of the wings. The wing shape itself was cambered, or curved, to a ratio of 1-in-22. (The word "camber" is standard today in the aviation industry; it is from the French verb *cambrer*, "to curve.")

Lilienthal had urged that wings be built with a camber of 1-in-12, which meant that the highest points of the wing curve would be one-twelfth higher than its width (or chord), the distance, as noted before, from leading edge to trailing edge.

This had proved Lilienthal's point. He had insisted that a glider could never have over 155 square feet of wing area because a wing bigger than this would not respond to his shifting weight.

There were other thorny problems. One was the question of where the designer should place the deepest part of the wing curve. At the leading edge? Eight inches back from the leading edge? Three inches? Nine? Where?

Wilbur and Orville had no idea that the wing they designed was based on inaccurate data. Although they had not yet read Lilienthal's studies of wing camber, they were familiar with his table of "normal and tangential" pressures; these had been collected and printed by Chanute. According to everything Lilienthal had determined through years of experience, the Wrights calculated that their glider, held to the derrick by a rope and supporting the weight of a man figured at 140 pounds, plus its own weight of 52 pounds for a total of 192 pounds, would fly, like a kite, at a very specific angle. This they determined to be a position in which the kite wings attacked the horizontal wind at an angle of about 3 degrees. It is not nearly as fearsome as it sounds. If we hold an imaginary line and rest the glider on this line, facing into the blowing wind, then the wings would be tilted upward about 3 degrees from the absolutely level position.

Having worked out these figures, and assuming that their calculations (which were based on Lilienthal's figures) were correct, the Wrights believed that their glider would not only glide at an angle equal to the best of the soaring birds, but that it would also soar — that is, glide through the air with little or no loss of altitude. Depending on the wind, it would maintain its altitude, standing still over the ground or actually attaining a slight forward motion.

Again, the Wrights stumbled into the quicksand of numbers. Their original wing design (before they shortened the wings) called for an area of some 200 square feet.

Including machine, pilot, and controls, this would provide them with about one pound of weight, from all factors, for one square foot of wing area. The numbers drilled themselves precisely through their calculations.

If the wind blew at 17 to 20 miles an hour, then the glider should support itself. But they had changed dimensions down to 165 square feet, and they figured that they must now have a wind of at least 25 miles an hour to hold the glider steady in the air, pulling against its rope and carrying the weight of a man.

To their distress, nothing of the sort happened; the glider's performance was not even close to what they had counted on. In fact, Wilbur, who was the first to try the apparatus, found that an angle into the wind of almost 20 degrees was required to sustain him and the machine. This was, they discovered to their tremendous disappointment, almost completely self-defeating, for this steep angle of attack not only negated the action of the controls to a great extent, but also guaranteed that the craft they had built would be incapable of decent gliding, let alone soaring.

The performance of their first glider, as far as lifting force was concerned, was only about one half of that calculated from Lilienthal's tables. This means that a wind of 35 to 40 miles an hour would be required to hold the apparatus at the desired angle of attack of 3 degrees. But this was totally out of the question. Winds of this force are considered violent, and usually include erratic gusts. Without any experience in controlling their machine, it would be impossible for the brothers to try to fly in winds like that with any safety.

What these first experiments proved was that the concept of using the tower for satisfactory flight in the wind was totally mistaken. It also indicated that their experiments must press on without the benefit of practice by flying their glider kite-fashion. They had to face the grim truth once again, even as they had long before acknowledged when they first considered the problems of flight: they must follow in the footsteps of Lilienthal and try glides, even if each such adventure lasted for only a few seconds and required a long trudge back up the dunes to reset the apparatus.

Their discouragement was profound, not so much because of their failure as because they didn't understand why it had happened. It was exasperating to find that all of their calculations had turned out to be distressingly wrong.

There was no way out of it. Back to basics. They started flying the empty glider as a kite, from ropes they held by hand. From failure came signs of life. They began to load chains onto the machine to cause it to do some work and to enable them to determine just how much weight it would lift while still maintaining the angle of attack of 3 degrees above the horizontal. Once again they were shocked with the results. In a wind of 18 to 22 miles an hour their glider would support chains weighing only about 75 pounds, or just about half the weight of the loads worked out in their original calculations.

Again, however, there were some positive results. By working the wing-warping control by hand ropes, as Wilbur had done the year before with his glider of a five-foot wingspan, they proved that with 75 pounds of chain and the angle of attack held at 3 degrees, the glider reacted beautifully to their lateral stability control system. The wings warped as they were intended to, and the machine responded with all the agility of a bird riding the wind.

If everything worked out well with a load of 75 pounds and an angle of attack of 3 degrees, what would happen if they doubled the load and increased the angle of the wings from the horizontal to 20 degrees? Again a discovery went into their notes: control effectiveness dropped sharply. Their lateral control suffered, and the longitudinal or pitch control (nose up and down) also deteriorated. They were controlling pitch by use of the movable horizontal elevator, the "horizontal rudder." At a shallow or gentle angle of attack it appeared to work quite well, but at 20 degrees it was virtually worthless.

There was much more to learn, and it weighed heavily on them. They had expected problems in working both control systems as a single movement — controlling the machine from side to side and fore and aft. But simultaneously controlling the glider in both motions, without the practice they had planned, was much more demanding than they had ever anticipated.

In other words, they did not know how to fly and no one could teach them.

As if they lacked for problems, on the afternoon of October 10 they lowered their machine to the ground, left it for a moment to do some other work, and suddenly felt an unexpected gust of wind. They sensed trouble, and as they spun about, helpless, the glider whirled into the air, tumbled for 20 feet or so, and slammed down with sounds that cut them to their bones. What had been a glider was now a twisted and broken pile. In silence, they dragged the wreckage back to their tent, sharing an unspoken desire to walk away from their vexations and go home. They were ready to quit.

Wisely, they held off on any decision until the next morning. When they awoke, they reconsidered. To return to Ohio with so little accomplished went against the grain, so they did what they had always done best: they bent to their work with new spirit, figuring on a few extra days of hard labor. Within five days they were back at flight tests.

Now they had to struggle with the problem posed by an aspect of aerodynamics they did not yet understand. What they observed was that under certain conditions all the lift of the wing was wiped out. They had encountered other invisible, unknown forces. What they did not know at this point was that compli-

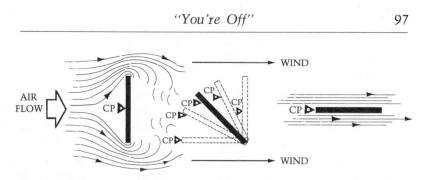

Air flow: When a flat surface is at right angles to the stream of air (left), the center of pressure (CP) is exactly in the middle. As the angle is reduced, the CP (indicated by arrow with white dot) moves forward to the leading edge. It continues moving in that direction as the angle decreases, until the surface is flat, parallel with the air flow when its CP is then directly against the leading edge.

cated forces were moving along their wing as they changed the angle of attack; they did not yet understand the true nature of center of pressure on a curved wing.

To understand what they were up against, we should take a moment to visualize a few simple shapes as they move through the air. If we take a flat surface — say, a square foot of stiff cardboard — and present it at right angles to the wind, then the center of the pressure exerted by that wind will be found in the dead center of the square.

Now let us tilt the top edge of the square forward, shifting its position so that it is now at an angle of 45 degrees to the wind. What happens is that a certain amount of lift is generated by the wind force, and the center of pressure will move forward toward the leading edge.

If we tilt the square further and reduce the angle from 45 to 20 degrees, the center of pressure will continue to move forward on it until, when the angle of the plane is absolutely flat, zero, the center of pressure will have moved forward to the center of the leading edge of the surface.

Now we must leave theory and return to the actuality of the windblown dunes of Kitty Hawk where the Wrights were wrestling with a powerful phantom they couldn't even see, let alone identify. Because, as noted, what happens with center of pressure on a flat surface is entirely different when we introduce camber and thus change the shape of the surface to that of an airfoil with much greater lifting force.

If we take our square foot of cardboard and bend it so that it has a curvature of 1-in-12, and then present it at right angles to the wind, we find that the center of pressure, just as before, is directly in the center.

Now, as before, we decrease its angle of attack to the wind. The center of pressure still moves forward as it did with the flat surface, *but only up to a certain point.* When this critical point is reached, *the center of pressure moves rapidly toward the rear instead of to the front.*

The curvature can be called the Rosetta Stone of lift forces, and its key, the critical point, was what was eluding the Wrights.

What they did not know is that, because the center of gravity of an aircraft and its center of pressure must coincide within certain limits, the sudden aft movement of the center of pressure put so much lift behind the center of gravity that the machine was forced by its own energy to nose-dive into the ground. The greater the lift produced by the wing, the mightier the force that slams it earthward. As a result, the world's entire "flight-training" program, up to this point, had encountered a fatality rate of almost 100 percent.

The center of pressure on a curved surface, as opposed to a flat surface, when at right angles to the air flow, is again at the midpoint of the surface (1). And as the angle of attack is decreased, as shown in 2, 3 and 4, the center of pressure moves forward just as it does on a flat surface. However, when the curved surface is brought to the horizontal position and the angle of attack is zero, the center of pressure moves quickly rearward, contrary to the action on a flat surface, as in 5 and 6. This forces the surface (airfoil), and consequently the aircraft, to dive suddenly and precipitously.

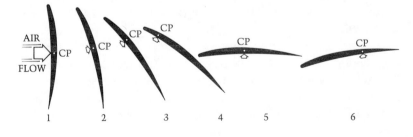

The Wrights had first developed their forward elevator, or canard, to offset the center-of-pressure travel, which they assumed would be in a forward direction, whether on a flat or curved surface. Their contention was that as the center of pressure moved forward, the wing would tend to turn up, as we have said, producing additional instability.

They were still only vaguely aware of a condition known as a "stall," and discerned its potential as a possible source of danger, although they did not understand it in detail.

In any case, the sudden or violent pressure that forced up the leading edge of the wing was an undesirable characteristic, and it impeded the solution to the problem of equilibrium. It had to be offset or balanced by the Wrights' forward elevator.

It was their intention that as this center of pressure moved forward and turned the nose up, the pilot would move the forward elevator to exert a counteracting *nose-down* pressure. Now, although the center of pressure on a curved wing did not travel all the way forward, but only to a certain point, and then swiftly backward, the forward elevator was still effective; it could overcome the rearward center-of-pressure travel just as well as it could overcome a movement forward, simply by being turned in the *opposite* direction. When the glider had a tendency to dive forward, the forward elevator could be turned to force the *nose up*. Although the brothers didn't yet fully understand center-of-pressure travel, their forward elevator could deal with it.

By accident the Wrights had invented a device that solved not only the problem of equilibrium on a flat surface, but that of the reversible center-of-pressure travel on a curved surface, as well. Designed for one purpose, it could serve another.

This was only one unknown feature of their forward elevator. Much more important was that it kept the aircraft from "stalling." Let us understand one additional bit of aerodynamic theory: an aircraft stays in the air only by moving fast enough so that the airstream over its wings provides at least as much lift as the weight of the aircraft. If it drops below that given speed, it approaches a dangerous red line of which all pilots are fully aware and which they are trained from the very beginning to avoid, on pain of death.

As an airplane slows down and approaches the danger point,

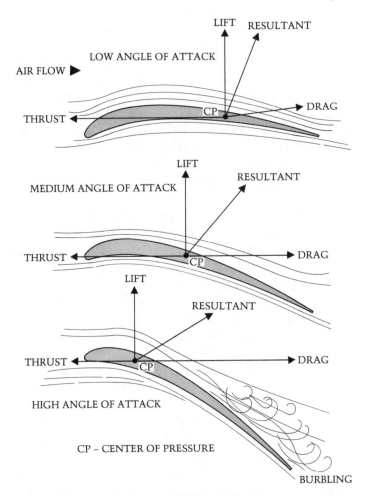

Principle of the stall: When an airplane is in flight, pressure forces act on every part of the wing's surface. The sum total of the magnitude and direction of these forces is called the resultant, and the point where this resultant force intersects the chord of the wing (shortest distance between leading and trailing edges) is termed the center of pressure (CP). At small angles of attack (top) the resultant force is minimal, its direction is upward and to the rear, away from the vertical. As the angle of attack increases, so does the resultant force, and the CP moves forward toward the leading edge. At very high angles of attack, the CP is extremely far forward, and the resultant is much farther back from the vertical. At this point the smooth flow of air around the airfoil is broken, and there is noticeable burbling. Unless the angle of attack is decreased, the airplane will "stall" — the wing will suddenly lose its lifting power.

the angle of attack of its wing increases more and more to compensate for the lack of speed in generating the necessary lift. This process can continue only to a certain point: when the angle at which the wing strikes the air is so great that the airstream passing over the top side of the wing breaks away and turbulence sets in, the wing immediately loses all lift. This is the stall. When it occurs close to the ground, where there is insufficient room for the flier to recover enough speed for the wing to start flying again, the result is almost inevitably a fatal crash.

This is what had killed Lilienthal. The Wrights were well aware of it, were afraid of it, and were determined to avoid it at all costs. In other words, they intended to keep the speed of the glides up to a point where they would not experience the fateful stall. This was their intention, but when they began learning to fly, with no one to teach them, their naïveté and total inexperience became drastically evident. A number of times the Wright brothers did, in fact, stall; each brother in turn experienced more than once the condition where the nose of the machine was allowed to rise so high that the speed died, the angle of the wing became too great to sustain the aircraft, the slipstream of air broke off of the upper surface of the wings, and the machine stalled, sometimes at heights as great as 50 feet.

Under those circumstances, if the machine had fallen, it would have dashed itself to the ground, and the Wright brothers, lying prone, would have had their necks broken.

Now here is the truly fortuitous aspect of their forward rudder design: because the elevator was forward instead of behind, the aircraft, when it stalled, instead of spinning out and killing them the way a conventional aircraft would have done, simply parachuted to the ground in a flat position. Although they hit the sands of their practice area with a hard jolt, the machine was not destroyed nor the occupants injured, beyond being shaken up a little.

Wilbur would be the first one to experience the stall, and the surprising manner in which their aircraft recovered from this dangerous condition would be a relief to both brothers. They would come, in time, to realize that in this "happy accident of design" they had a guardian angel, one that would permit them to continue their practice and learn to become efficient with their machine, yet would spare them from fatal accidents in the process of their training.

There was still another "plus" in the forward elevator config- uration. As the eminent British aviation historian Charles H. Gibbs-Smith has acutely observed, the forward elevator also served as a visual indicator of the airplane's attitude in flight. No matter what other cues are received by a pilot as he flies through the air, he needs a constant reference to the earth's horizon to maintain proper control of his aircraft. This tells him whether his nose is high or low, or is changing pitch, or whether he's banking right or left. He must be able to check the position of his machine in relation to the horizon line in the distance.

The Wrights had precisely that reference, just as if they had planned it that way. The forward elevator gave them a good indication of their angle of attack. Until the advent of the en- closed cockpit, when the pilot could use the engine cowl as a reference, no other would-be flier situated out front in the open had such an advantage.

The first visit to Kitty Hawk was almost over, and nearly all the great hopes with which the brothers had come to the sand dunes, now seemed to be frustrated. They were greatly disap- pointed in the lift capabilities of their machine and in its erratic pitching behavior.

But, in fact, they had accomplished several things far in ad- vance of anything that their predecessors or peers had done. First, their wing-warping system for lateral control had worked per- fectly. Their forward horizontal elevator was a device far more effective for longitudinal control than anything tried before.

Appropriately enough, this safety characteristic was effective only up to a speed of about 60 miles an hour; because it was designed in balance rather than in trail, the forward elevator would become oversensitive at greater speeds — so much so that the machine became unmanageable.

(Only after exceeding this speed, in 1910, did Orville prevail on his brother to take the next step and design a machine with the elevator in the rear. By that time, however, the Wrights had become proficient in flight and had gained the piloting skill

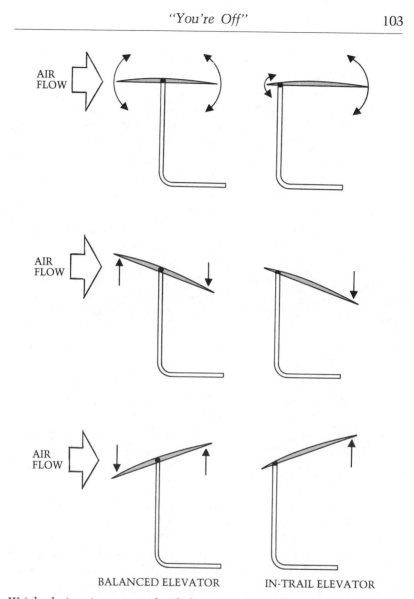

BALANCED ELEVATOR   IN-TRAIL ELEVATOR

Wright designs incorporated a "balanced" forward elevator (left column), the movable surface extending an equal distance on both sides of its hinge or pivot axis, as opposed to an "in-trail" configuration (right column), which would have enhanced controllability in flight. The "balanced" forward elevator was much too sensitive and caused the Wrights great difficulty, especially during their early self-training period. They constantly referred to "blunders" made in the use of the "forward rudder" (elevator).

necessary to avoid a stall. Orville summed up the significance best in a letter he wrote in 1924 to an associate:

"We originally put the elevators in front at a negative angle to provide a system of inherent stability which it would have furnished had the center of pressure on curved surfaces travelled forward, as was supposed, instead of backward with increase of angle of attack. We found that it produced inherent instability. We then tried using our 1900 glider backwards with the rear edge of the surfaces foremost, and found the stability much improved; *but we retained the elevator in front for many years because it absolutely prevented a nose dive such as that in which Lilienthal and many others since have met their deaths.*" [Italics mine: H. C.])

There was yet another critical benefit from the experiments. After their disappointments, the brothers found, to their amazement, that actual wind resistance to their machine — caused by the struts between the wings, the thickness of the wings, the wires, and the supporting members — was much *less* than anything that had been encountered by any other experimenter.

The Wrights had always been acutely aware of the problems of wind resistance and had considered it in every design step. This is what lay behind their decision to operate their glider with the operator in a prone position on the bottom wing. This reduced the resistance of the wind against a man's body to only some 20 percent of what it would have been if the operator had been in a sitting position.

It is an even more notable achievement when we consider that Octave Chanute had issued grave warnings about the prone position, pointing to past events to prove that it would increase the hazard to the pilot. If the machine were to nose-dive suddenly into the ground, then its operator was almost certain to suffer a broken neck. Then, too, if a man could hang from the glider frame, as did Pilcher and Lilienthal, it seemed obvious that his landing would enhance his safety, because he would be touching down in much the same way as a bird, lowering its legs with its wings at a cushioning angle.

Chanute's concern was real. It was based on solid experience, but of course he did not understand the effect of the forward horizontal elevator in the Wright machine.

Orville and Wilbur postponed their return to Dayton until October 23, and this gave them the opportunity both to enjoy sudden good weather and to plan for last-minute gliding with their repaired machine. Taking breaks from their rebuilding efforts by fishing and hunting:

> in which occupation [Orville wrote to Katharine] we have succeeded in killing two large fish hawks each measuring over five feet from tip to tip, in chasing a lot of chicken hawks till we were pretty well winded, and in scaring several large bald eagles . . . This is a great country for fishing and hunting. The fish are so thick you see dozens of them whenever you look down into the water. The woods are filled with wild game, they say; even a few "bars" are prowling about the woods not far away . . .
>
> But the sand! The sand is the greatest thing in Kitty Hawk, and soon will be the only thing. The site of our tent was formerly a fertile valley, cultivated by some ancient Kitty Hawker. Now only a few rotten limbs, the topmost branches of trees that then grew in this valley, protrude from the sand. The sea has washed and the wind blown millions and millions of loads of sand up in heaps along the coast, completely covering houses and forest. Mr. Tate is now tearing down the nearest house to our camp to save it from the sand . . .

They had a good dose of sand when a nor'easter came screaming through the night, and for two days they huddled in their tent as a whipping wind smashed against it. "The wind shaking the roof and sides of the tent sounds like thunder," Orville wrote. With the storm's fury gone as quickly as it rose, he continued, "We spent half the morning yesterday in getting the machine out of the sand. When we finally did get it free, we took it up the hill, and made a number of experiments . . ."

With the help of Bill Tate, they carried the glider almost three miles from their camp to the largest of the dunes, Big Kill Devil Hill, and worked their way up the soft slope along the northeast side of the dune. They looked around to study conditions about them, and agreed that the wind of about 12 miles per hour would do nicely. Caution marked every move and preceded every step,

for by now they were grimly aware of unknown forces that attended their hopes to conquer the air. So, on this late October
afternoon of 1900, Wilbur planned not to glide, but to carry out
a series of very low skimming "semiglides." The 12-mile-an-hour
wind was just right for this purpose, since it would be augmented
by the speed of two men running and holding the glider aloft.

But even the semiglide had to wait. Wilbur lay prone on the
glider, Bill Tate took one wingtip and Orville the other; they
eased the machine forward, no more than a foot over the sand,
and then released their grip. The purpose wasn't at all to have
the glider fly, but to see what happened when the machine, with
a man aboard, contacted the sloping sand surface. This initial
and wisely timid move paid its dividend: the glider eased forward,
dropped onto the sand to skid along easily, in the process spraying
sand into Wilbur's face. He came up spitting out the fine grains
after several such tries and announced that he was ready to have
a go at a real glide.

They climbed higher up the dune and again turned into the
wind to begin their probing stabs at the air. Wilbur remained
very close to the ground, always trying to keep his distance no
more than a foot above the sand. If anything went wrong, his
speed and drop would be at the very minimum. In addition,
Orville and Bill Tate ran alongside, downhill, clutching the wingtips. In this most careful of exploratory attempts Wilbur was thus
able to determine the function of the controls in gliding conditions. He also verified what would be a critical element for the
future: the horizontal front stabilizer and elevator was providing
marvelous fore-and-aft control, once he learned just how far to
move the control in the face of the wind. *This is what it was all
about.* Every time he made even an easy gliding flight he learned
enough to be able to anticipate what would happen on the next
flight, and could then plan his control moves well ahead of time.
Instead of exerting his effort simply in correcting imbalance, he
was able to stay ahead of the machine and catch imbalance when
it happened, thus maintaining his control as the seconds rolled
by. *It was flying,* for however brief a time or short a distance.

On one glide they picked up speed until Orville and Bill Tate
could no longer keep pace in the soft sand, and, by prearranged
signal, they shouted, "You're off!" And off he was, even the

shortened wingspan providing sufficient lift to start the glider hissing along well above the ground. But true to his word, Wilbur immediately depressed the forward horizontal plane to bring the machine back to earth.

What incredible discipline that must have called for! At this instant all his dreams had been snatched from the wind and the sands, and he was *flying!* There was enough wind uphill as well as his own forward motion to impart substantial lift to the glider, and Wilbur had his first experience of the solid feel of a machine with wings that were actually supporting him. The urge to come back on the elevator, to lift higher, to take advantage of wind and downslope and that beautiful lift — I wonder how many at that moment could have held themselves back as Wilbur did. After just a hundred feet, free of any obstructions and still flying well, still balanced and sustaining speed, he eased the glider back onto the sand. It had been flying so well that the men determined that the in-flight portion of the run had been accomplished with a speed of almost 30 miles an hour against the wind, which meant a speed across the ground of 18 miles an hour.

They returned to their camp in quiet jubilation, for these brief moments had dispelled many of their worries and had lightened the despair of the unexpected problems. These short glides had shown that the operator could fly the glider in a prone position, and land on the sand, on wooden skids, without suffering any injury. They knew, however, that the ratio between lifting force and weight was so small that the slightest loss of performance could have kept them on the ground. Their future work depended on confirming the feasibility of the prone position.

On October 23, they left Kitty Hawk, glad to be free of the wretched problems they had endured, but more concerned with putting to use what they had learned, and excited about the mysteries that lay before them.

All of Wilbur's grandiose plans for flying many hours had added up to no more than three minutes in the air, and those minutes were divided into only a few seconds at a time. Indeed, they had done far less in terms of time airborne and distance covered than had Pilcher or Lilienthal, but they knew, without any doubt, that the *principles* with which they were now working were far superior to those of their predecessors.

The wing — their airfoil — promised them still more sleepless nights. They knew they must understand the unsettling characteristic the wing displayed when it approached a negative angle of attack. When that happened — when the chord line went below level, as compared with the flow line of the wind — a disturbing instability set in. That had to be solved before they could return to Kitty Hawk the year following.

And that, too, is an important note for us to remember, for even before they departed from the lonely spit of sand, they agreed that they would again stalk these same winds and loft themselves on their lifting force. Not that all was eagerness. Only five days before their departure, and their expressed determination to return in 1901, Wilbur was in such a state that Orville wrote to their sister, "Will was so mixed up he couldn't even theorize. *It has been with considerable effort that I have succeeded in keeping him in the flying business at all.* He likes to chase buzzards, thinking they are eagles, and chicken hawks, much better." (Italics mine: H.C.)

CHAPTER 10

"Like Learning the Secret of Magic from a Magician"

THROUGHOUT THE STORY of the Wright brothers, from their first serious interest in flight, birds figure prominently. This matter has been a point of controversy among historians, rather than one of agreement. Did their studies of birds have a major effect on their aircraft designs? Did they use the feathered creatures as models or guidelines beyond the most obvious sense?

Wilbur's thoughts on birds are found in detailed notes he kept in 1900, and are produced here just as he wrote them down.

> The buzzard which uses the dihedral angle finds greater difficulty to maintain equilibrium in strong winds than eagles and hawks which hold their wings level.
>
> The hen hawk can rise faster than the buzzard and its motion is steadier. It displays less effort in maintaining its balance.
>
> Hawks are better soarers than buzzards but more often resort to flapping because they wish greater speed.
>
> A damp day is unfavorable for soaring unless there is a high wind.
>
> No bird soars in a calm.
>
> The object of the tail is to increase the spread of surface in the rear when the wings are moved forward in light winds and thus preserve the center of pressure at about the same spot. It seems to be used as a rudder very little. In high winds it is folded up very narrow.
>
> All soarers, but especially the buzzard, seem to keep

DIHEDRAL ANGLE

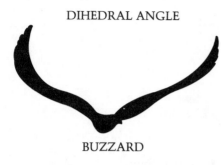

BUZZARD

EAGLE

"The buzzard which uses the dihedral angle finds greater difficulty to maintain equilibrium in strong winds than eagles and hawks which hold their wings level." — Wilbur Wright, 1900

their fore-and-aft balance more by shifting the center of resistance than by shifting the center of lift. Thus a buzzard soaring in the normal position will be turned upward by a sudden gust. It immediately lowers its wings, much below its body. The momentum of its body now acting above the center of resistance turns the bird downward very quickly.

Viewed from directly beneath, the motion of the wings fore and aft seems very small indeed. Neither do birds appear to draw in one wing more than the other. The raising and lowering of the wings is very perceptible whenever the observer is almost on a level with the bird.

A pigeon moving directly from the observer oscillates very rapidly laterally, especially when moving slowly just before lighting. The wings are not drawn in to any perceptible extent first on one side and then on the other as would be the case if the bird were balancing by increasing or decreasing the area of either wing alternately. Moreover, the oscillations of lateral balance are so rapid that gravity alone could not possibly produce them. The bird certainly twists its wing tips so that the wind strikes one wing on top and the other on its lower side, thus by force changing the bird's lateral position.

If a buzzard be soaring to leeward of the observer, at a distance of a thousand feet, and a height of about one hundred feet, the cross section of its wings will be a mere line when the bird is moving from the observer but when it moves toward him the wings will appear broad. This would indicate that its wings are always inclined upward, which seems contrary to reason.

A bird when soaring does not seem to alternately rise and fall as some observers have thought. Any rising or falling is irregular and seems to be due to disturbances of fore-and-aft equilibrium produced by gusts. In light winds the birds seem to rise constantly without any downward turns.

A bird sailing quartering to the wind seems to always present its wings at a positive angle, although propulsion in such position seems unaccountable.

Birds cannot soar to leeward of a descending slope unless high in the air.

Buzzards find it difficult to advance in the face of a wind blowing more than thirty miles per hour. Their soaring speed cannot be far from thirty miles . . .

Now, all this is really quite extraordinary. Learning to fly by watching birds is one of the most difficult feats one can imagine. Even Wilbur's meticulous and perceptive studies of birds, carried out over a period of years, held their own unspoken questions, as evinced in such phrases as "seems contrary to reason," "seems to," and, "seems unaccountable." Although there were many useful direct observations from which certain conclusions could be drawn, and although they provided basic knowledge of the physical actions of an animated body in the air, they did little to solve the problems of manned flight.

Long after their successful flights at Kitty Hawk, the brothers were plagued with others' questions, typified by, "Did you two really learn to fly at Kitty Hawk by watching the flight of birds?"

The Wrights were quick to reply that it simply wasn't so. They explained that their previous observations of birds in flight had led them to certain conclusions with regard to the necessity for aerodynamic control rather than weight-shifting control, and had also provided them with certain insights into aerodynamic design directions, which they considered in order to assure their own progress.

As far as their activities at Kitty Hawk were concerned, they stated that their observations there served only to confirm what they had already decided, rather than leading them to new concepts or methods of construction.

Many years later, with those questions still dogging him, a vexed Orville Wright made it clear that he could not recall anything concerning birds that taught Wilbur and him how to build a flying machine or even to fly. He repeated that watching the feathered creatures had assisted them in confirming theories, and then he finally put the matter to rest: *"Learning the secret of flight from a bird was a good deal like learning the secret of magic from a magician. After you know the trick and what to look for, you can see things you didn't notice when you did not know exactly what to look for."*

CHAPTER 11

"... Permission to Allude to Your Experiments"

UP TO THIS POINT, all the brothers' discussions and writings, especially with Wilbur behind the pen, had made it clear that they were always leaving themselves a way out, to avoid admitting complete failure. The continued references to good health accruing from their visit to Kitty Hawk seemed almost a hedge against the possibility that they might fail altogether, something that would let them retire gracefully from a field in which success had never yet been attained.

All this changed on their return to Ohio, for their subsequent actions made it clear they had been stung by whatever creature it was that infected men with the insatiable urge to fly. They hurled themselves with growing intensity into their project. They could no longer keep from discussing, planning, testing, calculating, and building; and they intended to return at the first opportunity to the windswept sands of the Outer Banks.

On November 16, 1900, Wilbur wrote to Octave Chanute to pick up his correspondence again, and in his first letter he set forth in detail most of their ideas, their successes, and the problems they enountered. Indeed, Wilbur's willingness to confide seemed to have taken on a new impetus since his time in North Carolina, for he gave Chanute the details of the machine, including the dimensions.

"At first the machine was curved laterally to obtain the effect of dihedral angles, but we found the effect very unsatisfactory in gusty winds. Control was much easier after we made it straight . . . We soon found that our arrangements for working the front rudder and twisting the planes were such that it was very difficult to operate them simultaneously."

He also diagrammed the shape and depth of the wing curve and the construction used for the spar and the wing leading edge. In one drawing, which showed how they trussed the double-wing arrangement, he noted that, "We used fifteen-gauge spring steel wire. By tightening the wire *a*, every other wire was tightened."

This, to a man of Chanute's engineering acumen, said a great deal about the Wrights. (He wrote, "Remarkably good construction" on the edge of the Wright diagram.) Clearly, at this stage, Chanute saw that the brothers were not only deep thinkers, but also had the mechanical ability and the design capacity for practical experiments — now that the first field tests were behind them.

Some of the more critical results of the Wright tests were of particular interest, especially the design of the wing curve, where the Wrights committed the same error as others had before them: they disregarded the necessity for smooth aerodynamic surfaces on their airfoils. For instance, Wilbur's words and illustrations showed the rear spar of the wing mounted *above* the rib. He felt this was satisfactory for their needs, for he dismissed the aberration with a single sentence of his letter, "An extra piece of cloth ran up over it to lessen resistance."

Few things will raise a modern aeronautical engineer's hackles faster than remarks of this ilk, for on modern aircraft the slightest disruption of airflow on any wing surface is a major concern indeed. Smooth aerodynamic design is absolutely critical.*

It is understood, of course, that the Wrights were on the threshold of flight, without the benefits of decades of hard scientific accomplishment. The pall of misinformation, or plain lack of knowledge, under which they labored, makes their accomplishments all the more remarkable. Of course, the brothers worked with very slow airspeeds compared with those of modern aircraft, and their aerodynamic obstructions had correspondingly less ef-

---

* I know of no finer example than my experience with changing the wings of one particular jet aircraft. By increasing the rounded dimensions of the wing's leading edge by *one eighth of an inch*, we are able to reduce the aircraft's approach speed to the runway by more than 18 miles an hour.

fect. However, this lack of attention to perfection, so uncharacteristic of the Wrights that it could have stemmed only from their lack of knowledge, proved to have very severe consequences; they might, with proper attention, have saved themselves enormous grief and time.

They made life difficult for themselves in another department, too. During the years in which their experiments progressed, they were constantly changing their wing curves with an attitude that seemed almost careless. They would jump their wing camber from 1-in-23 to 1-in-12 and inevitably run into wildly varying lift and control behavior. They groped in the dark, even about such simple things as the leading edges of their wings, running the gamut from strangely shaped and awkward surfaces to flat areas, all of which contributed to the subsequent control problems that sorely bedeviled them.

Also — and this again has failed to receive its proper notice in the available documents that provide us the legacy of the Wrights — the brothers inadvertently added to their problems, in the course of building their various machines, by developing *nine* completely separate and different means of manipulating the controls of the fore-and-aft, lateral, and directional surfaces. Thus, as soon as they established proficiency with one set of controls, they would plunge into a new jungle of altered aircraft responses by redesigning them.

The key element here is that they had to *relearn to fly* every time they rigged up new controls. This isn't nearly as easy as it may sound. Even professional pilots in today's aircraft exercise extreme caution in moving from one control system to another until they have learned the very different subtleties of operating those systems. In the aircraft built by the Wrights, flying through mists of ignorance about conditions of flight, including the most basic knowledge about the weather, this must be considered one of the most incredible displays of *airmanship* in the history of flying.

Consider this: the aerodynamic surfaces they used were essentially always the same, *but the methods for activating the controls* were at times so different from the preceding ones that they had to create new reflexes and reactions on their own part simply to survive. And all the things we take for granted, including the most basic of instruments, didn't exist in those pioneering days. There were no windsocks, control towers, radios, or weather reports; no dials from which the pilot could learn at a glance airspeed or altitude or anything of the sort.

As if this sort of problem, which would give today's pilots nightmares, weren't enough to confound them, they endured unexpected setbacks, and encountered severe lift, drag, and control problems resulting from their lack of knowledge of aerodynamics (which they still had to extract from nature). At times these setbacks became so severe that the two brothers seriously discussed abandoning their hopes of developing a successful flying machine.

A roughly designed surface was more than aerodynamically awkward; it was positively dangerous. As one example, any aerodynamicist today knows that a ridge along a wing, depending on its position, can set up an instant stall effect if the center of pressure travels back and forth in the vicinity of that ridge.

How did this affect the Wrights? If one studies their gliding and flight tests, there's no question that this ridge-produced stall *did* happen to their test machines, and as lift spilled away from their aircraft, they had only one way to go — down, and out of control.

Even during November of 1900, with the first Kitty Hawk venture behind them, they were assessing the consequences of the quick changes they were making in their designs — changes resulting from their initial tests in the Carolinas.

During this period the brothers were still wrestling with the vagaries of the two-control system. The sensation of flying an aircraft without a rudder is immediately recognizable to the pilot. Indeed, loss of rudder control even in a superbly balanced plane is sometimes considered a full-blown emergency. Yet the Wrights, after their 1900 glider experiments, *didn't have even a vertical rudder on their machine.* They had no guidelines to indicate that *they needed* such a device, and every time they lifted from the ground, that lack of rudder exposed them instantly to a killer situation. This is why I have placed so much emphasis on the fact that it is extraordinarily difficult for an airman to learn to fly the instant he leaves the ground — well, I would have used the term "impossible" instead of "extraordinarily difficult," except that the Wright brothers did accomplish the impossible. When they left the ground it was either fly or crash — nothing in between. It was total commitment and nothing less. The more we think about this situation — the more we place ourselves in their shoes — the more astounding the entire affair becomes. To think that they were doing all this in an environment where hard facts were absent, where their lifting surfaces were subject to sudden changes because of design deficiencies, where they had no idea of forces they would encounter.

All this produces a head-shaking disbelief that it could have happened at all. The brothers were aware to some extent of these problems, and their awareness underscores their own belief, expressed mainly by Wilbur as the spokesman for them both, that sitting on a fence doesn't teach you a thing about learning how to fly. You've got to get in there and have at it.

Another complication they encountered at Kitty Hawk was the scantiness, the primitiveness, of their research and development facilities. Some hand tools and a borrowed sewing machine made up the bulk of their entire testing outfit. They encountered problems with their control system, but they were limited in what they could do to alleviate it because, in Wilbur's words, "As we had neither the material nor the tools to change these so as to correct the trouble we were compelled to test them separately." From every indication we could find, Wilbur referred to the control systems themselves, not to a faulty aerodynamic design. And then there is another point to consider: the controls may well have been adequate, but the pilot experience — or lack of it — could have been the problem faced at any particular moment. It was difficult indeed to separate the wheat from the chaff.

From the beginning of their experiments at Kitty Hawk, the brothers were surprised to find that their glider had two characteristics that they were completely at a loss to explain. The first was that at a 3-degree or even 5-degree angle of attack with winds between 15 and 20 miles an hour (velocities in which they thought they could safely test their controls), the machine failed to deliver anything like the expected lift. In fact, the glider would develop a lift of only about half of what they had originally calculated.

Winds of much greater velocity — 35 to 40 miles an hour —
would be required to fly the glider satisfactorily. This could not
be contemplated seriously; winds of that velocity approached
gale force and would obviously offer dangerous conditions.

The other rather surprising characteristic of their glider was
that it had proved to have a lot less head resistance to the winds
than they had calculated. The brothers did not see, at first, any
connection between these two conditions, attributing the lack of
head resistance to their very fine construction (perhaps, for instance, the extraordinarily well-designed wing covering, the
shape of the struts between the wings, or the way the struts were
fastened to the wings).

Wilbur discussed this reduced resistance in his letter to Octave
Chanute of November 16, suggesting that the inadequate lift
could be due to the low degree of curvature of their wing or,
possibly, an incorrect wing shape. If neither of these was the
case, there must be something wrong in their calculations.

Chanute was at a loss to explain the inadequacy of the lift, but
complimented Wilbur on the reduction of drag or resistance,
which he likewise attributed at first to their fine design. He
continued to write along these lines until he took into consideration the actual glides Wilbur had described.

As we have seen, Chanute was very much concerned, believing
that the Wrights were taking desperate chances by gliding in the
prone position. Even at this point Chanute did not really understand that the forward horizontal elevator would be an enormously effective safety device.

In a letter dated November 29, 1900, Chanute proceeded to
make some calculations measuring the resistance offered by the
body if the man was either sitting up or hanging from the glider
frame, or was prone. Chanute calculated that a man's body in the
hanging or sitting position, upright, would offer to the wind a
surface area of about five square feet; correspondingly, a man in
the prone position would offer resistance of only one square foot.
Clearly, the former condition meant that greater power would be
required to drive the apparatus through the air — at whatever
future time power would be applied.

Chanute, who had congratulated the brothers on what he
termed "a magnificent showing" in reducing the head resistance

by their prone position and other features of their glider, had ended with the rueful qualification "provided that you do not plow the ground with your noses."

Wilbur, in answer to this letter, revealed his own calculations, in which he defended his position.

The Wright brothers had always maintained that it made no difference whether you were flying a powered aircraft or a glider. The power required to move the machine would be the same if the frontal area of the machine was the same.

In the case of the glider, the power would be supplied by gravity, and if the frontal resistance of that glider were so designed, and the operator so positioned, as to produce the minimum resistance, the glide with the power of gravity would be flatter than it would be with the greater resistance of a man in the sitting position. The only difference was that Wilbur maintained that a man in the prone position would have the resistance of *one-half* a square foot of frontal surface versus Chanute's figure of *one* square foot. He indicated this in a letter to Chanute on December 1, 1900, in which he discussed his experiments at Kitty Hawk.

In a response on December 2, 1900, Chanute retorted, "I doubt whether the man endwise can be figured as exposing only $\frac{1}{2}$ sq. foot, even if round-shouldered. I should call him 1 square foot."

Quite surprisingly, on December 3, the very next day, Wilbur Wright answered Octave Chanute's letter, which he must have received that morning. In that answer he devoted a paragraph to analyzing the resistance of a man riding a bicycle; the analysis gives us some idea of the way the brothers had come to apply their intellects to a problem.

> A bicycle rider has ridden 220 yards, without pace, in 12 seconds. This is 3,300 ft. per minute and $37\frac{1}{2}$ miles per hour. The resistance at $37\frac{1}{2}$ miles is 7 lbs. per sq. ft. so that each sq. foot requires $7 \times 3,300 = 23,100$ ft. pounds per minute. At 80 gear the rider makes 520 pedal strokes per mile, or 325 strokes per minute. The length of stroke is $1\frac{1}{8}$ ft. and the weight of rider 150 lbs. The extreme limit of power is $150 \times 1\frac{1}{8} \times 325 = 56,875$ ft. pounds or nearly two horsepower. This is undoubtedly more than the man actually exerts. The friction of tires, bearings and chain

requires a pull of 3 lbs. to overcome, or 3 × 3,300 = 9,900 ft. pounds per minute. Subtracting this from 56,875 leaves 46,875 [46,975] as the extreme power available for overcoming wind resistance. But the bicycle offers a cross section of $2\frac{1}{4}$ sq. ft. whose coefficient is probably $\frac{1}{5}$, so its equivalent area is about $\frac{1}{2}$ sq. ft. and the required ft. pounds 23,100 ÷ 2 = 11,550. But 46,875 − 11,550 = 35,325 is all that is now available for the resistance of the man; and his equivalent area is 35,325 ÷ 23,100 = $1\frac{1}{3}$ [$1\frac{1}{2}$] sq. ft. But the cross section of a man, in racing position is a little over 3 sq. ft. so that his coefficient of resistance is less than one half. If no reduction be made in the area exposed it would require nearly four horsepower to drive him through the air at $37\frac{1}{2}$ miles per hour. If the coefficient for the bicycle racing position be less than $\frac{1}{2}$, I see no reason for estimating the equivalent area of a man in the horizontal position at more than $\frac{1}{2}$ sq. ft., and though I may be mistaken I doubt whether the resistance in the upright position is more than equivalent to $2\frac{1}{2}$ sq. ft.

Clearly, the brothers were not arriving at their conclusions by guesswork.

Wilbur had explained to Chanute in a previous letter (November 16) that within the first two minutes of their trials they had proven fully the efficiency of their "twisting planes" (the wing-warping system). He also said with pride that when they could work the horizontal stabilizer separately and effectively, its response was so immediate that "the ease with which it was accomplished was a matter of great astonishment to us." Wilbur made it clear, too, that their reliance on the accuracy of former experimenters often did them more harm than good, and that even their elevator control was so far from what other men had predicted or "proven" that they had again and again to force themselves to ignore the work of the so-called "greats" in aviation pioneering.

"This may have been partly due," commented Wilbur, "to the steadiness of the wind, partly to the fixed position of the operator, and partly to a *fortunate combination of circumstances of which we were not aware*, but it is our hope that it was due to a new method of grouping our surfaces and to the particularly efficient rudder [the forward elevator] which we used." (Italics mine: H.C.)

Since, until this moment, shifting of body weight by a pilot had been the *only* means of maintaining both lateral and longitudinal stability, it was obvious to Chanute that the Wright brothers had taken an enormous step forward. Chanute, impressed deeply by all he learned from Wilbur's letter, as well as what he could see between the lines, lost no time in answering. This was to establish a pattern of communication between Chanute and the Wrights that in the long run would be considered detrimental by the Wrights, and indeed would affect the development of aircraft design throughout the world.

(Chanute's intentions were good; in a letter written on November 23, he expressed his congratulations on their work and then presented what would become the nucleus of future entanglements and controversy: "I have lately been asked to prepare an article for *Cassier's Magazine,* and I should like your permission to allude to your experiments in such brief and guarded way as you may indicate." Easily enough granted, agreed the Wrights, but in his response, on November 26, Wilbur explained that although he and his brother did not intend to be overly secretive about their machine, there were certain innovations that they wanted to prove by flight demonstration, and they preferred to be guarded about them. At the same time, in his characteristically gentlemanly fashion, Wilbur advised Chanute that he was free to use any or all of certain facts in his article. These included, in their basic form (1) the biplane type of construction, (2) the total overall area of the machine plus the "rudder" or elevator, (3) the prone position of the operator in flight, (4) the fact that "longitudinal balancing and steering were effected by means of a horizontal rudder projecting in front of the planes. Lateral balancing and right and left steering were obtained by increasing the inclination of the wings at one end and decreasing their inclination at the other.")

The Wrights were aware that they walked a thin line in describing their work to others. What would have the greatest effect among other men experimenting with flight was that Chanute's article would make public, though in a general way, the Wrights' system of lateral and longitudinal control. It was back to Orville's comment about watching the magician: you could look forever and be baffled, but the moment he lets you in on his secrets and you know where and how and what to look for, the mystery is gone.

The Wrights did exercise care in what they told Chanute. They provided no details as to just how they effected their helicoidal twist, or wing warping, and by what mechanical means this was rigged, or how their forward elevator was actuated. Yet the cat was at least halfway out of the bag, for by this very basic disclosure, the theory behind two thirds of a three-dimensional aerodynamic control system had been made known.

Innocent enough at first, their statement, coupled with other remarks from Chanute and further comments from the Wrights, would soon set off an explosion in the minds of all those other men around the world who also wanted to fly. Men who had despaired ever of developing their own machines for controlled flight would be inspired by what they read from the eloquent pen of Octave Chanute, and the excitement would sweep across oceans and continents as others revived their attempts to develop machines of less than suicidal capability.

It appears that Chanute was quite innocent in his eagerness to spread the word of the deeds of the Wrights; he wanted to share what they had accomplished and to bring together fledgling airmen throughout the world. The Wright brothers were rather naïve; despite their initial hesitation and the very slight restrictions governing the "withholding" of certain information, they had given virtually free rein to Chanute, who for the next several years, in articles and stories and speeches, would publicize the details of what they were doing. It very nearly cost the Wrights their opportunity to be recognized as the first men to fly heavier-than-air machines under control.

Even now, it is necessary to emphasize again that the credit goes to the Wright brothers, and to no other individual or group, for the development of the flying machine. It was a combination of their unique attributes and qualities that enabled them to focus on the goal, to think out and isolate the difficulties, to resolve the problems, and to implement their solutions in the form of mechanical devices designed and built through their extraordinary mechanical genius. To this combination must be added their incredible good fortune in surviving disease and near-lethal accidents, and in arriving at a type of design that permitted them to fly for a sufficient length of time — and to do so without killing themselves in the process — so that eventually they would possess an instinctive and intuitive coordination of flight controls, which is fundamental to *every* flier.

There were elements that were equally, if not more, critical: they designed and built a proper power-plant when there was none anywhere else in the world at the time they needed their engine. They designed and calculated and created their own propellers with efficiency levels far beyond anything existing then or for many years to come.

As J. G. Crowther stated in *Six Great Inventors,* the Wrights created a gestalt, an "extraordinary collaboration between the two brothers, unparalleled in the history of science . . ." It appears to me, after years of intensive study of the Wrights, as well as my own years in flight and my association for decades with pioneering pilots, that the Wrights were so far ahead of any other designers that they existed in a class by themselves. Had they been diverted from their effort for any reason (and there were moments when the success or the continued attempts of their experiments hung by the most tenuous of threads), or had they split up or one of the two been killed — or gotten married, which might have been worse — the survivor would *not* have continued along the path entered upon by the two as a single mental-physical entity. If through economic or social reasons they had been prevented from pressing on with their tests; if they had not been possessed of the most amazing determination against truly insurmountable odds (as they were presented at the time — physical, mental, spiritual, mechanical, aerodynamic, or whatever one cares to choose); if all these many barriers had not been surmounted and an actual flight achieved *and then five years later* finally demonstrated supremely and overwhelmingly to the world, there would have been no airplanes in the first decade of the twentieth century. And we would have time for endless speculation as to what our present world might be like.

It is entirely possible — and I present this thought as my own judgment — that, without other designers having the benefit of what had been accomplished by the Wrights in aerodynamic design and control, the rest of the world would have remained 20 years behind the standards created by Orville and Wilbur

Wright. (I leave the reader to judge the result on world history if the airplane had been developed *after* World War I instead of *before.* The First World War gave the development of the flying machine such impetus that it became the decisive weapon in World War II. Conversely, let us ask ourselves whether the Allies could have defeated the Axis powers on the ground alone.)

One wonders that Chanute missed the point of how well the horizontal elevator worked for fore-and-aft stability, and how well wing warping worked for lateral stability. When the Wrights described these elements of their machine, including permission to use this information for his magazine articles, the data went in only one direction; Chanute never showed by any comment that he recognized the vital import of these design features. Presumably, he never understood what Wilbur had been describing to him; either it passed right over him or he failed to judge its true importance. Beyond complimenting the Wrights on reducing head resistance and on having the grit to carry out and continue their work, he said nothing. This silence on his part must have puzzled the Wrights, but we shall never know its effect, for neither Wilbur nor Orville ever commented on it.

Chanute also missed the happy accident of the antistall design the Wrights had developed in their forward horizontal elevator, but he can hardly be faulted for that: the Wright brothers themselves had yet to appreciate the significance of what they had done.

Historical accounts of the development of the airplane often include references to Octave Chanute. He has sometimes been called "father of the aeroplane" because of his great research on the work of others, some design work of his own, and his uncanny ability, especially through his engineering genius, to attract reporters and historians.

The references to Chanute have tended to distort certain areas of aviation history, especially those areas that involve the Wrights. The pilgrimage on which I have spent these last years revealed many facts only slowly. With much careful digging (including many interviews with people who had seen or known or flown with the Wright brothers), the monumental work of Wilbur and Orville Wright, as separate from anyone else's, became undeniably evident.

It is during this second series of correspondence between Wilbur and Chanute that one begins to detect that Chanute engaged himself — in fact, he eventually entangled himself — in a mesh of intricate and often irrelevant detail; his great reputation as an engineer undoubtedly prevented his wanderings from becoming immediately apparent to those about him. But it is startlingly clear to us, with the advantage of hindsight, that his great intellectual powers had dropped from their zenith at the time of his first contact with the Wrights or shortly afterward. Hence, on a number of occasions Chanute quite naturally resorted to his practice of recording every detail connected with any sort of engineering project, *often with the result that he missed critical engineering principles or key elements of a project.*

Between the close of 1900 and late March 1901, there is a gap in the correspondence between Chanute and the Wrights. The Wrights were hard at work again in their shop, and Chanute had encountered problems of a personal nature that demanded most of his own time.

In Dayton, Orville and Wilbur discussed between themselves, and with Katharine and Lorin, the results of their efforts so far. Very much at stake was their continued effort in this aeronautical field that so fascinated them and consumed their every spare moment. When they were not working in the shop or discussing with their sister everyday affairs and matters concerning the home, their voices could be heard in animated, often heated, discussions with one another about aeronautics. They were intense, even fierce, about their viewpoints, and loved to shout at one another in sessions that approached bellowing matches. Often, for the sheer joy of examining every aspect of a situation, the brothers would start out severely opposed to one another, and end the argument with each having reversed his position and supporting the point of the other. They considered these sessions to be among the most rewarding parts of their research, and it is that extraordinary dual-minded genius to which Crowther and so many others have alluded.

The discussions between the members of the Wright family came finally to a point of decision, and Orville and Wilbur now decided to spend much of their time and energy in pursuing their goals of developing a man-controlled, powered aircraft. Their original limited goals had been achieved, and they saw that they might soon be able to go much further. Devoting themselves and their resources so fully to their project was not a matter to be decided impetuously; their research would require time, effort, and more and more of their limited funds. They both realized that if they were successful, they *might* gain financially from their efforts; otherwise, all they accomplished would be added to the store of knowledge — that and no more — and they could end up being financially destitute at the end of ambitious but unsuccessful experiments.

By the early summer of 1901 they were agreed on returning to their research and were adjusting their private and business lives to their new schedules. The fever was well upon them, but they could not ignore everyday realities, and their first requirement was to keep their source of income flowing. Three weeks before the brothers decided to return to Kitty Hawk that summer, they hired an old friend, Charles Taylor, for $18.00 a week — $3.00 more than he was then earning — to run the bicycle shop in their absence, although they didn't bother to tell Charlie this would be his job. "They made me a good offer, I lived nearby, and I liked them, so I took the job," was Taylor's response to his new position. Later, he surmised, correctly, that the brothers "hired me to worry about their bicycle business so they could concentrate on their flying studies and experiments." The Wrights also hired a part-time worker to do repair jobs, and left management in the capable hands of Katharine and Lorin. On June 15, 1901, just three weeks before the Wrights were off again to the Outer Banks, Taylor stepped into his new job. He was to play a still more vital role in the success of powered flight, but prophecy was not one of Taylor's talents.

During the first half of 1901, a series of events had been running on parallel tracks, all leading to the brothers' return to the sandy banks of the Carolinas. Wilbur and Orville had been hard at work on an entirely new glider, and quickly saw that they had failed to correct the worst fault of their 1900 design: the wings' deficiency in lifting power. The reason for the deficiency still eluded them, and they examined aspect ratio (span of the chord — the distance between leading and trailing edges), of which they understood very little; camber; modified camber; square footage;

and anything else that happened to come to their attention. They knew they must provide themselves with a wing that would operate in a lesser wind than had the first model, yet support the weight of a man *and* do so with an angle of attack of 3 degrees so that their controls would function as they desired. The glider must be larger, stronger, more efficient, and they must be able to record more accurately the various forces acting on it. They had come to recognize the great value of keeping an accurate record of events. Wilbur had already written to Chanute to ask his assistance in obtaining an anemometer (a device to measure wind velocity) to take with them to Kitty Hawk. In his response of May 15, Chanute indicated he would attend to their request and said that, on a forthcoming trip from Chicago to the East, he would like to stop in Dayton for a visit.

The historic meeting took place on June 26, 1901, and was recorded by Bishop Wright in his diary that day: ". . . O. Chanute spent the evening with our boys." The diary entry for the day following reads, "Mr. O. Chanute spent most of the forenoon and till after 2:00 with us. He is an authority on aerial navigation . . ."

In addition to their professional common ground, they discovered a personal affinity with the white-haired and goateed elder statesman of engineering; he was charming and had a deep intellectual approach to matters of a technical nature, one that had an immediate appeal to the Wrights.

All the Wright family gave Chanute the warmest hospitality. Orville and Wilbur at first observed the rules of Victorian propriety, but they became more informal when they and their guest discussed points of controversy in aeronautics. The visit provided them with a splendid opportunity to throw ideas at one another, and ideas were thrown in abundance.

It would have been surprising for Chanute not to have approached the Wrights without some degree of condescension. He still was not fully aware of the sweeping new principles of flight that had emerged from their research and their tests, yet what he saw and heard impressed him with their character, dedication, and extraordinary alertness. Since he was able to see the parts and assemblies of the new glider they had built and were soon to take with them to Kitty Hawk, as well as their workshops, he also received the strongest impressions of their remarkable native ingenuity and mechanical ability. Design and construction were among the Wrights' strong points, and these were aspects of experimentation that Chanute had never personally enjoyed.

Because of Chanute's age when he first took an interest in developing a flying machine, he himself was unable to translate all of his ideas to reality. Many of his ideas concerning gliders were farmed out to others for implementation. There is an inherent fault in this system, especially when one is dealing with so many unknown quantities, and the machines that he contracted to have built, or that were constructed by associates, were never produced with the degree of perfection or the attention to detail or the ingenuity he so earnestly desired. And now, before him, he saw in the Wright brothers the embodiment of both the intellectual and mechanical capacity to do all that he was unable to do.

Chanute seized on what he saw as a golden opportunity: he would have these two extraordinary young men assist him in furthering some ideas and designs of his own, and he was quick to suggest that the Wrights join him in a mutual effort that summer at Kitty Hawk, including the flight-testing of a glider he was then having built. Orville and Wilbur were aware of the delicacy of their position. They did not wish to refuse Chanute outright, but they feared that the arrangement might interfere with their own work, a notion to which they did not take well at all. In this exchange, Chanute discovered that the Wrights were very definitely their own men. During the careful sparring, conducted in the dignified conversation of the day, he sensed the Wrights' deference to age, experience, and reputation, but he could not shake the stiff-backed determination of Orville and Wilbur not to accept a position as anyone's pupils or minions. They had always shown a great independence, and even a suggestion of interference in their work, which presupposed a need for interference, brought them up very short indeed.

Courtesy restrained their outright rejection of this proposal and several of Chanute's other suggestions while he was their guest. But in the continuing correspondence and later discussions, Wilbur — with Orville's concurrence — rejected, without further question, Chanute's proposals, even when they were offered solely in the form of assistance. Not that all were so offered.

Chanute had had his assistants build a new glider; Edward C. Huffaker had fabricated a rare machine, to the amusement — almost the disbelief — of the Wrights, *of paper tubing.* Chanute hoped that the material would keep the device so light that it would glide more easily than if it were made of wood; it was not a matter of any strength intrinsic in the design. Yet even as Chanute hedged somewhat on his own hopes for the unique craft, he had also sensed an unspoken but nevertheless sharp withdrawal on the part of Wilbur and Orville. He told the brothers that when he left Dayton he would go to Chuckey City, in Tennessee, Huffaker's home town, to judge for himself the machine's progress. Later, through correspondence, he offered the Wrights the assistance of Huffaker at Kitty Hawk; if they would test the Chanute machine, he would pay Huffaker's expenses and have his man assist the Wrights.

Another offer (also tendered during the Dayton visit and repeated by letter) was to send George Spratt, a young man who had abandoned medical practice after several years in response to the siren call of gliding. If Orville and Wilbur would take Spratt with them, offered Chanute, he would work for them at Chanute's expense. Furthermore — and this stiffened the backs of the Wrights to no small degree — Chanute suggested that Spratt's medical services would probably come in handy at Kitty Hawk in the event of a mishap. The Wrights finally did agree to have Spratt join them, but only as an assistant in their glider testing. Reluctant though they were at the start, they came, in time, to value Spratt's friendship.

Despite the cool attitude of Orville and Wilbur to Chanute's offers of men, another gilder, and financial assistance, Chanute was swept up by his own zest for the entire affair and went ahead with his plans to have his men join the Wrights in North Carolina. Wilbur and Orville had already planned a large workshed and hangar, as well as tents, for their second stay on the sand banks, but the likely influx of all this company threatened to reduce their larger quarters to elbow-to-elbow room. And in a moment of weakness, or perhaps because of honest affection for the old gentleman, Wilbur invited Chanute to join them on the windswept sand slopes.

In the matter of financial support, covered in personal visits, conversations, and in correspondence, it should be made clear that Chanute, who made an offer of $10,000, was turned down with finality. The Wrights preferred to handle their own expenses on what they made from their bicycle shop. Bishop Wright had given each of his five children approximately $3000, but Wilbur and Orville were able to carry on their experiments without ever using that money. It was a wise policy, for it assured their unquestioned independence from all others.

Chanute's departure from Dayton set the final stage for intense preparations by Orville and Wilbur, who planned to rush off on July 7 for what they hoped would be perfect flying weather with their new and larger glider. There would be no more waiting until the last moment to dig into the sand for a place to live and sleep. This time they set up every detail in their usual methodical fashion. Their workshop, a framed shed, was 25 feet long and 16 feet wide, with ends hinged at the top near the gable parts to form doors so that the glider could be moved in and out easily. If the weather permitted, the opened ends would also serve as awnings. Wilbur had had enough discouraging experience in trying to obtain materials along the isolated coastline of North Carolina, so they shipped all their heavy materials, tools, and lumber well ahead of time, to be waiting for them at Kitty Hawk. They would have ample supplies, a cooking stove, good lighting, decent bunks, plenty of staples; it would be a comfortable base of operations.

Their final days in Ohio were brightened by the publication of two articles by Wilbur. One, "The Angle of Incidence," which he had written six months earlier, appeared in *The Aeronautical Journal*. It was to be received as an extraordinarily erudite paper, so far ahead of anything else on the topic that it served to establish Wilbur as an authority on aerodynamic experiments. At about the same time, in July 1901, Wilbur's article "The Horizontal Position During Gliding Flight" appeared in *Illustrierte Aeronautische Mitteilungen*, a German magazine.

Finally, with their second large glider disassembled and ready for shipping, they were off by railroad to Elizabeth City. They arrived on July 8 — and were shocked by the unexpected violence that screamed at them from every side.

CHAPTER 12

"It Would Not Be Within Our Lifetime"

THEY HAD TO SHOUT to be heard, even when they were close together. Elizabeth City, on July 8, 1901, was covered with a canopy of black clouds, racing overhead as far as one could see. From across the ocean, whipping past the sand banks as if they never existed, driving low and scudding clouds that bore thick sheets of rain, the wind came howling like a demon. Leaves, branches, and bushes sailed through the air, tumbled and tossed about, then were snatched up by the wind and flung along with a mad urgency.

Everywhere the ground was covered with water in turbulent streams that ran over the sidewalks. The brothers had never seen rain like this; the moment they left the train they were soaked through. They struggled to the hotel lobby, where they stood with water streaming from them, and looked out through the streaked windows at the violence tearing through the city.

The Wrights checked into their rooms, looking upward instinctively as the hotel shuddered in the furious wind blasts. Debris sailing through the air crashed against the walls and roof, and they began to speculate on whether the building would survive the night. They had arrived in the middle of the worst storm in the history of Elizabeth City; on July 9 the winds were recorded at 107 miles an hour, and were believed to have gone much higher when tornadoes spun off from the hurricane.

By July 10, the winds were nearly back to normal, but the rain continued for the next week. On the 11th, riding a boat through an ocean with its surface hissing from the downpour, they reached Kitty Hawk and gratefully accepted the invitation to remain overnight with Bill Tate and his family. The next day the two men hauled their heavy equipment through the rain along four miles of soaked sand to the area of the great Kill Devil Hill dune. They erected their tent and crawled inside to wait. Two days later the storm rode away, and they emerged, with a wild desire to get to work.

One thousand feet to the north of Big Kill Devil Hill, the shed went up quickly. After three days of fitting and hammering, they had it alongside their tent (the same in which they had lived the year before). They put up shelves, spread out their supplies, and, even before the day was out, they were already assembling their new glider. "The building is a grand institution with awnings at both ends," commented Orville in a letter to Katharine.

The shed (which was also the world's first airplane hangar) was completed on July 18. The same day, Edward Huffaker, who had served as an assistant to Langley at the Smithsonian, made his appearance, along with the glider he had built for Chanute. He went willingly to work with the Wrights, providing whatever assistance he could as they assembled their glider. One week later, George Spratt came on the scene. The next day, July 26, the glider was fully assembled.

The brothers had had grave doubts that it would ever see completion; and during the eight days of putting together the various materials, there had been moments of despair, when Orville and Wilbur were just about ready to leave. The great rains, after nearly two months of sunny skies, had caused untold billions of mosquitoes to hatch; they congregated on the visitors so thickly as to blacken their skins. The Wrights were given to understatement, but in writing his sister, Orville said that the mosquitoes "came in a mighty cloud, almost darkening the sun." Work had to stop while the men rigged sheets, swathed themselves in heavy clothes, and made turbans and face masks. They finally piled up driftwood and started a fire that produced dense clouds of smoke. "We attempted to escape by going to bed," Orville wrote, "which we did at a little after five o'clock. We put our cots out under the awnings and wrapped up in our blankets with only our noses protruding from the folds, thus exposing the least possible surface to attack. Alas! Here nature's complicity in the conspiracy against us became evident. The wind, which until now had been blowing over twenty miles an hour, dropped off entirely. Our blankets then became unbearable. The perspiration would roll off of us in torrents. We would partly uncover and the mosquitoes would swoop down upon us in vast multitudes."

On July 26, Wilbur had written to Chanute, warning the elderly gentleman that "You should by all means bring with you from the North eight yards of the finest meshed mosquito bar you can find, as the bar here is too large to keep them off at night. Except for mosquitoes our camp life as been pleasant but exciting at times.

"We expect to have our machine completed today as only a few little details remain to be finished . . ."

Life's mysteries are often unexplained. The next day, the horde of mosquitoes vanished. By the time Chanute arrived at the end of the next week, the camp had developed an almost civilized air, and the late afternoons and evenings began to resemble those of the year before. Orville had brought a mandolin with him, and he would relax by the tent and strum away, with harmony provided by a mockingbird. The orchestration was a pleasant ending to their day's labors.

But the flying did not measure up.

The 1901 glider was considerably bigger than the machine of the previous year, with a wingspan of 22 feet and a chord of 7 feet. As opposed to 165 square feet of the year before, the wing surfaces now measured 290 square feet. The new machine had a larger horizontal elevator, and the entire apparatus weighed in at 98 pounds. No man had ever attempted to fly in a craft of these dimensions. Chanute expressed grave doubts as to whether the glider would get off the ground, which to the Wrights was a clear indication that Chanute failed to understand the true principles of lift. And where he merely had doubts about lifting ability, Chanute professed outright disbelief that, if the machine should ever get airborne, the operator could control it. Again, this was to Orville and Wilbur more proof of Chanute's lack of understanding. Wing warping seemed beyond his comprehension; he still thought in terms of control by the shifting of body weight.

With wing warping, as the Wrights had already confirmed, the size of the machine mattered not at all.

Yet there were those hidden reefs in the sky, against which the Wrights would stumble with heartbreaking results. The gliding experiments that began in late July 1901 are probably the most critical moments in the history of developing the flying machine. It was enough to break the spirit of even Orville and Wilbur . . .

They had modified the wing design of the previous year as the result of tests with the operator aboard. Having failed to obtain the lift in their first glider, they increased the wing camber of the 1901 machine to 1-in-12, from the 1-in-21 of the earlier design. This conformed to the shape prescribed by Lilienthal's tables of air pressure, which were used by Chanute and every other experimenter battering at the doors of flight. It also provides a good example of how the Wrights were misled by the work of others, and, in trying to overcome problems, were forced into making educated guesses that at times represented enormous design changes. This bracketed the problems at hand but failed to solve them. Such drastic alterations in a wing design inevitably must produce vastly different flight characteristics from those they had earlier experienced or expected to encounter.

Again, it is wise to keep in mind that their total flight experience at this point could be measured in seconds for each glide, and that this lack of experience could hardly prepare them for certain violent characteristics they were about to experience and of which they had no knowledge.

As it happened, both Spratt and Huffaker were immensely impressed with the ingenuity and workmanship they saw in the 1901 glider. Both men were experienced in assembling gliders, and Spratt expressed his fear to the brothers that the great increase in camber was dangerous. He had done some experimental calculations on his own, and was one of the few men who disagreed sharply with Lilienthal's tables. His alarm and his open remarks reflected well on his alertness and candor. Spratt knew there would be a problem but was unable to identify the culprit, which, as we have noted, was the swiftly changing center of pressure beneath the wing.

The Wrights in their new design had also committed what to

modern engineers would be an unforgivable sin. Based on a book of data and the dangerous alternative of the educated guess, they made two wing design changes simultaneously and without test: one, an almost clublike blunt leading edge, and, second, an increase of wing camber from 1-in-23 to 1-in-12 when the glider had a man aboard.

They believed that the airstream passing over and under the leading edge of the wing would have some effect on the travel of the center of pressure. Perhaps, they thought, a wing with a very blunt edge would produce a more docile center of pressure travel in the design they were about to test; so, like some of their predecessors, they set up another of those killer situations that had destroyed so many machines before their own.

Early on the morning of Saturday, July 27, they hauled the glider endwise from their workshed. Their aspirations were not matched by the wind on this day; after all the fury they had experienced on their arrival, they now faced such a mild breeze that kite-flying would be impossible.

Wilbur, having had enough delays, for the first time threw caution aside and announced that he would make some glides without first testing the craft minus its operator. The risks were obvious. Wilbur hadn't been in a glider for eight months. His total time in the air under all conditions amounted to approximately three minutes, and now he was about to tackle the hidden reactions of a machine that had never left the ground, even tethered as a kite. The others did their best to dissuade him, but a new and adamant Wilbur faced them down, confident in the new glider and considering the venture to be without undue risk.

The crew carried the glider about halfway up the soft sand of Big Kill Devil Hill. Here, Wilbur climbed onto the bottom wing, settled himself in carefully, grasped the controls, and checked to see that everything was secure. He looked left and right, nodded, and gave the signal for the handlers on each wingtip to run forward as fast as they could and then release the machine for its first flight. They dashed downslope, kicking sand up wildly, until they could run no faster, and cast loose.

Instead of sailing down the slope, the glider immediately settled into the sand. It did not fly — it fell. It was obviously nose-heavy; its center of gravity was much too far forward to permit flight. The crew laboriously carried the glider back uphill for another trip.

Wilbur slid back on the wing to change balance, and again the dash forward was repeated, with the same results.

Wilbur gritted his teeth. An unpleasant silence had descended on the group with this unexpected absence of flight; what they seemed to have on their hands was a machine with the flight characteristics of a barn door. They made five more attempts to launch the glider into a simple airborne slide down the dune, and each time it flopped back into the sand.

And each time Wilbur adjusted his position. Each time he made sure the controls were set properly, that everything was as perfect as it could be. Orville and the others by now were exhausted in the July heat of the Outer Banks, but they bent grimly to the task, carrying the glider back up the dune, always running with all their strength and speed.

Something unexpected happened on the ninth glide. *The machine flew.* Instead of the expected splash of sand and the slither of skids, the glider lifted slightly, no more than two or three feet above the sand, but gliding, on and on, rising and descending slightly, until more than 300 feet lay between Wilbur's launching point and the place where, finally, the skids again slid into the sandy slope.

Behind him Wilbur heard riotous shouting and cries of joy as his "ground crew" ran and hopped and jumped down the slope after him. They knew that whatever had caused the difficulty on the first gliding attempts, that obstacle (or group of problems) was behind them. *They had flown the glider,* and they could hardly wait to share their enthusiasm with its pilot.

They found a grim visage awaiting them. Wilbur climbed slowly from the machine, shaking his head. Something was terribly wrong, he told the others, for he had needed full deflection of the elevator simply to remain those few scant feet above the ground. They argued the matter back and forth. The previous year the front elevator had required only a fraction of the movement Wilbur now needed. Again he repeated that something was radically out of place. The others recommended that they quit for the day and try to figure out what had happened.

But Wilbur shook his head. He insisted that there was only one way to learn if this contraption would fly, and that was to attempt to get it back into the air. In truth, Wilbur Wright was entering an area of the greatest danger. He was fully aware of this enormous risk, but what he did on this day was only one example of the great courage he would display on later occasions.

On the tenth flight, the glider managed a distance of almost 100 feet, moving at about 12 miles an hour into the gentle wind. Then an astonishing thing happened. Aboard the glider Wilbur tensed, as shouted voices echoed his own surprise and sudden apprehension. Wilbur had been applying full down pressure to the elevator to keep the glider from rising too high, but, despite his control movement, the machine suddenly began to rise steadily, higher and higher. This was a complete violation of their plans, which called for keeping the machine never more than a few feet above the ground so that if something did go wrong, the drop back to the sand would not be serious.

But the glider was now 30 feet into the air — as high as the rooftop of a three-story building — and suddenly it began to lose its forward speed. Everyone gasped, for the Wright glider was plunging into the deadliest of all reactions — a complete stall perilously close to the ground. In describing stalls, "close" means too low for the operator to recover from the maneuver, but still high enough for the machine and its occupant to slam into the earth.

Everyone recognized a moment from the past: this was the same situation in which Lilienthal had found himself seconds before he crashed to his death.

In the air, Wilbur heard Spratt shouting to him to correct his flight, to move the controls to bring down the nose of the glider. It was a wasted effort, for Wilbur was already desperately depressing the elevator fully, and the machine continued to rise. Finally, Wilbur seized the last option open to him: he pulled his weight as far forward as he could. The onlookers were braced for the inevitable crash, but, as they watched, stunned, the glider did *not* stall. There was no neck-breaking dive into the ground, but a gentle descent, almost as if the glider were being lowered by parachute, until it settled back to the sand, operator and machine unharmed.

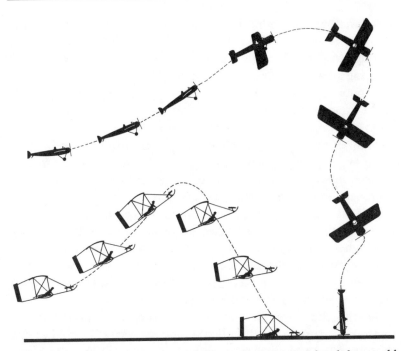

Because of its "happy accident of design," the 1902 Wright glider would "parachute" down after stalling (bottom) instead of falling off on a wing and spinning toward the ground in a descending, helical path, as with conventional aircraft (top and right). Thus the Wrights escaped fatal accidents several times and were able to learn to fly without killing themselves.

Instead of encountering a frightened Wilbur Wright, they faced a jubilant pilot whose smile was radiant. For Wilbur recognized at once that he had passed a towering barrier, that he had encountered the dreaded killer stall, and that he had survived and would survive such moments in the future. He had proved that the forward horizontal elevator could prevent the machine from whipping into the deadly maneuver that had killed Lilienthal. This, then, was the "happy accident of design" that we have mentioned before in the discussion on lift and equilibrium.

Undaunted by his narrow escape, Wilbur insisted on another series of gliding tests that same afternoon. Things went well until Wilbur went into a maneuver he had never met before, beginning with a stall much more severe than the earlier one. The glider nose lifted high and the machine shuddered as it went into a stalled condition, but this time the glider, despite Wilbur's movement of his body and full down elevator, failed to respond in the same manner. He had permitted his forward speed to slow so greatly that the wind was now actually blowing him *backward* over the ground — into what loomed as a lethal tail-slide and tumble to earth. Again, to everyone's amazement, the glider under Wilbur's rapidly improving control recovered from its stall with startling gentleness and eased into a steady, almost floating descent. That happy accident, that forward placement of the elevator was doing its job.

Once the flight tests were again under way — with Wilbur the sacrificial goat if things went wrong — the brothers decided to try to determine how center-of-pressure travel was complicating their attempts to glide. They set up their control lines and flew each wing separately in the form of a kite. They began immediately to get positive results. When the wing was at a high angle of attack, and the airspeed was relatively slow, the wing lifted almost straight up from the men controlling it. When the wind increased to a very high speed, then the wing drew almost level, horizontally away from the kite-flier — downwind, as it were. And if an even greater speed was developed, then the leading edge of the airfoil (wing) would actually dip down suddenly and work its way forward, but *below* the kite-handler.*

Wilbur later wrote down in his characteristic, careful fashion:†

> We noticed that in light winds it flew in the upper position . . . with a strong upward pull on the cord . . . As the wind became stronger, the angle of incidence became less, and the surface flew in [a] position . . . with a slight horizontal pull. But when the wind became still stronger, it took [a] lower position . . . with a strong downward pull. *It at once occurred to me that here was the answer to our problem, for it is evident that in the first case the center of pressure was in front of the center of gravity and thus pushed up the front edge; in the second case, they were in coincidence, and the surface in equilibrium; while in the third case the center of pressure had reached a point even behind the center of gravity, and there was*

---

* See "wind tests" diagram in Appendix C, page 369.
† Wilbur Wright's lecture "Some Aeronautical Experiments," before the Western Society of Engineers, Chicago, Illinois, September 18, 1901.

therefore a downward pull on the cord. This point having
been definitely settled, we proceeded to truss down the
ribs of the whole machine so as to *reduce the depth of
curvature.* (Italics mine: H.C.)

Then, Wilbur added:

On resuming our gliding, we found that the old conditions of the preceding year had returned; and after a few
trials, made a glide of 366 feet and soon after one of 389
feet. The machine with its new curvature never failed to
respond promptly to even small movements of the rudder
[horizontal elevator]. The operator could cause it to almost skim the ground, following the undulations of its
surface, or he could cause it to sail out almost on a level
with the starting point, and passing high above the foot
of the hill, gradually settle down to the ground. The wind
on this day was blowing 11 to 14 miles per hour. The
next day, the conditions being favorable, the machine
was again taken out for trial. This time the velocity of
the wind was 18 to 22 miles per hour. At first we felt
some doubt as to the safety of attempting free flight in
so strong a wind, with a machine of over 300 square feet,
and a practice of less than five minutes spent in actual
flight. But after several preliminary experiments we decided to try a glide. The control of the machine seemed
so good that we then felt no apprehension in sailing
boldly forth. And thereafter we made glide after glide,
sometimes following the ground closely, and sometimes
sailing high in the air.

One can imagine their excitment as they were watched and
helped by the Tates or members of the local life saving station
or by youngsters. Every flight meant more experience and gave
the operator the priceless ingredients of feel and instinctive reaction to his machine, thus reducing the element of surprise he
might encounter on any successive soaring above the ground.
Nothing teaches so well as a few moments at the controls.
No less thrilled than the others, Octave Chanute, who had
arrived on target, made the best possible use of his camera, snap-

ping pictures of various aspects of the glides and creating a marvelous pictorial legacy.

Wilbur continued:

> We made glides on subsequent days, whenever the conditions were favorable. The highest wind thus experimented in was a little over 12 meters per second — nearly 27 miles per hour.
>
> It had been our intention when building the machine to do the larger part of the experimenting in the following manner: When the wind blew 17 miles an hour, or more, we would attach a rope to the machine and let it rise as a kite with the operator upon it. When it should reach a proper height the operator would cast off the rope and glide down to the ground just as from the top of a hill. In this way we would be saved the trouble of carrying the machine uphill after each glide, and could make at least 10 glides in the time required for 1 in the other way. But when we came to try it we found that a wind of 17 miles, as measured by Richard's [a brand name] anemometer, instead of sustaining the machine with its operator, a total weight of 240 lbs., at an angle of incidence of 3 degrees, in reality would not sustain the machine alone — 100 pounds — at this angle. Its lifting capacity seemed scarcely one third of the calculated amount. In order to make sure that this was not due to the porosity of the cloth, we constructed two small experimental surfaces of equal size, one of which was airproofed and the other left in its natural state; but we could detect no difference in their lifting powers. For a time we were led to suspect that the lift of curved surfaces little exceeded that of planes of the same size, but further investigation and experiment led to the opinion that (1) the anemometer used by us overrecorded the true velocity of the wind by nearly 15 percent; (2) the well-known Smeaton coefficient of $.005V^2$ for the wind pressure at 90 degrees is probably too great by at least 20 percent; (3) that Lilienthal's estimate that the pressure on a curved surface having an angle of incidence of 3 degrees equals .545 of the pressure at 90 degrees is too large, being nearly 50 percent greater than very recent experiments of our own with a

special pressure testing machine indicate; (4) that the superposition of the surfaces somewhat reduced the lift per square foot, as compared with a single surface of equal area.

In gliding experiments, however, the amount of lift is of less relative importance than the ratio of lift to drift, as this alone decides the angle of gliding descent. In a plane the pressure is always perpendicular to the surface, and the ratio of lift to drift is therefore the same as that of the cosine to the sine of the angle of incidence.

It was obvious what was happening. Throughout all the theorizing and observing, the brothers were being forced to smash away at the mass of aeronautical information that had been collected and printed and, up to that time, accepted. The great idols of aeronautics were, as the Wrights had found, not infallible.

Wilbur's report then added:

But in curved surfaces a very remarkable situation is found. The pressure instead of being uniformly normal to the chord of the arc, is usually inclined considerably in front of the perpendicular. The result is that the lift is greater and the drift less than if the pressure were normal. Lilienthal was the first to discover this exceedingly important fact, which is fully set forth in his book, *Bird Flight the Basis of the Flying Art*, but owing to some errors in the methods he used in making measurements, question was raised by other investigators not only as to the accuracy of his figures, but even as to the existence of any tangential force at all.

Now Wilbur was showing that the old tenets of aviation were flawed:

Our experiments confirm the existence of this force, though our measurements differ considerably from those of Lilienthal. While at Kitty Hawk we spent much time in measuring the horizontal pressure on our unloaded machine at various angles of incidence. We found that at 13 degrees the horizontal pressure was about 23 lbs. This included not only the drift proper, or horizontal component of the pressure on the side of the surface, but also the head resistance of the framing as well. The weight of the machine at the time of this test was 108 lbs. Now, if the pressure had been normal to the chord of the surface, the drift proper would have been to the lift (108 pounds) as the sine of 13 degrees is to the cosine of 13 degrees, or $(.22 \times 108)/.97 = 24+$ lbs.; but this slightly exceeds the total pull of 23 lbs. on our scales. Therefore, it is evident that the average pressure on the surface instead of being normal to the chord was so far inclined toward the front that all the head resistance of framing and wires used in the construction was more than overcome.

Although, during this second summer at Kitty Hawk, Wilbur had finally made a series of successful gliding flights after changing the camber of their wing, he was still far from satisfied; he was very much aware that the lifting tables worked out by Lilienthal remained inadequate. He and Orville had an improved glider model now, but they were again disappointed in its performance. They were now completely convinced that the whole body of data compiled through a long succession of experiments was in serious error.

The very success the Wrights had gained through their two-dimensional control system was leading them somewhat astray, because they were unaware that controlled flight demands control in *three*, not just two, dimensions. They didn't realize that they had not yet encountered a situation where they would need control in a third dimension, to be coordinated with the other two. Indeed, Wilbur felt ready to prove that there was no need for a tail on a flying machine. It would be, in his opinion, more trouble than it was worth, not serving any obvious purpose.

By now the Wright brothers felt that they had met every requirement of the kind of flight enjoyed by birds. By warping their wings, and being able to control their up-and-down motions, they believed they could roll their machine in much the same way a bird pinwheeled through a turn. If this was good enough for the bird, then certainly it should suffice for the airplane.

That reasoning itself was the trap.

After a series of successful glides with the wings modified to their new camber, Wilbur planned to make his first experiments in turning from a straight course in flight.

The morning of August 9 broke with clear skies and a bright sun and, best of all, an excellent wind out of the northeast. With such ideal gliding conditions, Wilbur was eager to get into the air. Octave Chanute was still camping with the group, along with Huffaker and Spratt. They were joined by Bill Tate, and the assembly of five men carrying the glider, Chanute following more slowly, started up the great sand dune. At the peak Wilbur assumed his comfortable and familiar position on the wing; the handlers grasped the tips and, at the signal, began their rush downslope into the wind. Moments later Wilbur knew by their shouts that he had been released. As soon as he felt the glider to be in reasonable control, with a speed across the ground of some 12 miles an hour, he activated the warping controls. This was the first attempt ever made to initiate a turn deliberately with the wing-warping controls operated by the pilot, although Lilienthal had indeed made turns by weight-shifting.

The turn was to the left and, from the viewpoint of the onlookers, appeared to progress smoothly. But something was going wrong, and Wilbur suffered a sense of uneasiness, which became worse as the turn continued. He had always felt a solid stability to the glider when using the two-control system to maintain straight flight, but now in the deliberate turn the sensation of solidity was yielding to a strange and upsetting instability.

Although he did not know it, he was in grave danger. Wisely, he ended the turn at once and permitted the glider to settle straight ahead.

Perplexed, unable to pin down just what was going wrong, he had the men release him for several more straight-line glides, to make certain that the control system was still working properly.

On the fifth flight of the day, he was released from the dune and started into an intentional turn. Wilbur was anxious, so he paid less attention to his height than was his practice. A desperate move with the front elevator proved too late, and his wingtip struck the ground. Instantly, forward motion on that side ended and the machine spun about wildly and came to a crunching stop in the sand. Despite the softness of the sand, the impact was severe enough to hurl Wilbur off the wing and into the front elevator. The others found him sitting with his hands to his face, with a gloriously battered eye and a bruised nose.

Wilbur was pleased with the flight, nonetheless. He thought he was beginning to understand what was happening with the glider, and that seemed worth a few bruises. What he did not yet understand, and what he was still trying to analyze, was the phenomenon that would one day be recognized as aileron drag.

Again we meet terminology, just as we have encountered camber, horizontal rudder, angle of attack, and other aeronautical terms. Drag is one of the forces of flight, and is most simply defined as resistance to flight; if you don't overcome the resistance created by drag, you don't fly.

What happened when Wilbur activated his controls to turn the machine was that he changed the shape of his wings. Although the right wing came up higher than the left, the increase in its warp created more drag than in level flight. Because the right wing was now being slowed by drag, the left wing began to advance faster through the air. Then, as one thing led inexorably to another, the whole machine started facing the wrong way — to the right — even though it was banked to the left. There was nothing to stop this motion, and the result was that the glider was slipping sideways through the air. This process had already begun when Wilbur allowed the left wingtip to strike the sand; the result of that was his battered face.

Five days later Wilbur again took to the air, but only for short hops. He had returned to greater margins of safety, a move dictated by that vague uneasiness he had felt when first attempting turns. He made several flights on August 14, each only a few feet long, during which he checked his controls and their reactions.

By the 15th he had confirmed that he and Orville were in the thick of a new aerodynamic problem, one that they had just discovered and to which there was no sign of a solution.

Wilbur's notes showed his quiet frustration: "Upturned wing seems to fall behind, but at first rises."

Writing to Chanute on August 22, Wilbur said, "Our machine does not turn (i.e., circle) toward the lowest wing under all circumstances, a very unlooked for result and one which completely upsets our theories as to the causes which produce the turning to right or left."

He and Orville were now faced with two barriers in their attempt to solve the secrets of flight — discouraging enough after their two years of long, tedious, and increasingly dangerous experiments.

These two problems were easily recognizable. First, as we have seen, the Lilienthal tables of lift coefficients could not be relied on with any degree of safety. What the Wrights had proved — and they were not happy about it — was that nobody really knew a thing about what kind of lift could be expected from various types of surfaces. Under those circumstances, *no satisfactory flight program could ever be developed.*

Second, the controls they thought they had been handling so well — the longitudinal control by the front elevator, and the lateral control by wing warping — had turned into a menace. They were not only unsatisfactory, but inherently dangerous. There was a flaw, a missing piece, and it eluded them completely.

As if their spirits were not sufficiently dampened, the skies grew overcast and a heavy rain began to fall. Wilbur was also retreating within himself, back into the gloom that had enshrouded him for so long. In his mind's eye his flying machine, as it entered a turn, became a helpless creature with one wing nearly useless, unable to keep its equilibrium and unfit for flight.

He had good reason to criticize Lilienthal and Langley and the other wise men of science, for many of the calculations and theories then available had proved to be wrong. Thus, no matter how intensive and costly the brothers' attempts to fly, their efforts had been doomed to failure almost from the start.

How far in the future, then, might human flight lie? The distance seemed immeasurable. If the proper lift could not be generated from a cambered wing, and if the proper control could not be exercised, then it would be difficult, if not impossible, to achieve controlled flight with a heavier-than-air machine, and the skies must be left to those men who dangled beneath swollen gas-bags, drifting before whatever wind came their way.

It might be true, after all. The physicists and scientists and mathematicians, the greater body of them all throughout the world, were standing by their proclamation: human flight was not possible.

Chanute, Huffaker, and Spratt had departed.

Morose, patience exhausted, and with still some good flying weather left, Wilbur and Orville closed down the shed, sealed up their quarters, packed selected belongings, and started home. There was the long trek to the wharf, the launch trip to Manteo, then boarding the ferry to Elizabeth City, followed by the train trip to Ohio — much like a funeral ride. In that late summer of 1901, the brothers' spirits were at the lowest ebb since they had begun to think about flight. Wilbur, coming down with a cold, stared straight ahead as the train bore them steadily toward Dayton. At one point he roused himself and offered his opinion that man would probably never fly. And if the day should come when he, Wilbur Wright, was shown to be wrong, and man flew after all, "it would not be within our lifetime . . . not within a thousand years!"

They returned home with grim faces, their mood instantly evident to Katharine. Settled in the house, by unspoken agreement standing behind a curtain of almost complete silence, the two usually voluble brothers were the personification of broken spirit. Later, Wilbur would write of himself and his brother: "When we left Kitty Hawk at the end of 1901, we doubted that we would ever resume our experiments . . . When we looked at the time and money we had expended, and considered the progress made and the distance yet to go, *we considered our experiments a failure."* (Italics mine: H.C.)

By what narrow, tenuous threads hung the fate of airmen . . .

CHAPTER 13

"The Newspapers Are Full of Accounts of Flying Machines"

TIME AND AGAIN, and most often without his having been aware of it, Wilbur Wright had flirted with disaster and death as he swept away from the sloping sand dunes of Kill Devil Hill. He had stumbled into stalls, and only the elevator design had brought the machine gently to earth. He had skidded and slipped through the air, and the result of these motions was to spill the precious lift from his wings, leaving him above the ground in an object with no lifting power. He had dug into the ground and been thrown face first into wooden supports, emerging with a black eye. He had followed the first maneuvers of Lilienthal, as that pioneer was about to die, when the lifting pressures of his wing went berserk and ran madly back and forth and started him into a dive that would have crushed his body and splintered his machine.

There were invisible barriers in the sky, and the Wrights, with Wilbur carrying the load of flight-testing at this point, had managed to trip and even to fall — and emerge virtually unscathed. Bad enough to challenge the elements, but they did so with wings whose shape changed quickly beneath their hands, whose control surfaces and systems were modified again and again, until they knew not what to expect in flight. When they looked for guidance from those proclaimed wiser and more experienced, they found that the information to be had from these sources was worth very little.

It was true that they had managed to become airborne. All

their efforts added up to the discovery of how little they really understood the arena of the sky, and how blind were all those who had preceded them.

It was Katharine, who dearly loved and understood her brothers, who helped their moods slowly to dissipate and filled their lives with the warmth and trust so strong in this family.

It might have ended here. But these two had been bitten by the bug, and they began to lift their heads and look at the situation once again. They considered the things they had learned from others and what they had discovered for themselves, and came to the necessary conclusion:

"The calculations on which all flying machines had been based were unreliable, and . . . every experiment was simply groping in the dark . . . We cast it all aside and decided to rely entirely upon our own investigations."

It was strange, this road they had traveled. They had recognized the major faults of other experimenters and had avoided their pitfalls. They had judged correctly that the shifting of body weight would always be useless in an aircraft of any appreciable size or performance. They had refused to accept the need for major dihedral in wings as the primary source of stability. They had insisted on lateral stability through wing warping and on fore-and-aft stability through an elevator control, and again they were right. They had measured the wind resistance of objects moving through the air and accomplished wonders in reducing drag. They had proven that a prone position for flying was acceptable.

Every time they had made a decision on their own, even though it was contrary to the accepted view, they had been vindicated by their experience. But when they relied on the mathematical tables of others, they were tripped up. They could not accept the wing camber and promised lifting efficiency of wings as expounded by Langley, Lilienthal, Pilcher, and so many others, and they knew that they must derive for themselves the mathematical formulas for the correct wing shape; they had to design and build their own wing.

There was still the other problem, that of control. They had excellent two-dimensional control, but it clearly was not enough for proper flight. If they did not find the missing element, flight would remain impossible. Their work — research, computations, tests, and shouting matches — must continue.

Wilbur again picked up his correspondence with Octave Chanute. The brothers' relations with him at this point were at their warmest, and Wilbur seized on the opportunity to try to analyze difficulties they had experienced at Kill Devil Hill, ones that Chanute had witnessed. Orville Wright would look back on this period, when the gloom was at its greatest, and he would give Octave Chanute a great deal of credit for the continuing growth of the first airplane, principally because of the repeated admonitions of Chanute that they *must* continue their work. They were challenging the unknown, Chanute told them again and again, and they were doing this in the face of adversity and failures on their own part and those of others, and they had accomplished far more than everyone else put together. They must continue.

One of the areas Wilbur discussed at length with Chanute was "Glide Number 3" of the 1901 tests. This proved to be the most perfect of their flights that summer, and Wilbur wondered what they had done right. He also spelled out the problem that so confounded them: the machine did not always turn in the direction in which it was banked.

Chanute wrote to Wilbur that he was "glad to know that you got through your experiments without accident. I think you have performed quite an achievement in sailing with surfaces wider than any which I dared to use, and on which a change of incidence by a wind gust would make so great a difference in the center of pressure . . ." That was, of course, the shop talk familiar to them both.

Six days later, the brothers' work entered a new phase. Chanute again wrote to Wilbur, but about a different subject: "I have been talking with some members of the Western Society of Engineers. The conclusion is that the members would be very glad to have an address, or a lecture from you, on your gliding experiments . . ."

The invitation was extended for September 18 in Chicago, and Wilbur's initial reaction was some superb foot shuffling. He frankly did not wish to test his ideas before so august a body of engineers, and demurred not only to Chanute, but to his own family, as well. Katharine, however, sensed that if Wilbur and Orville could be exposed directly to men with scientific and inquiring minds, who thought well enough of Wilbur to assemble and listen to him, it would bring both of them the rest of the way out of their slump. Katharine was convinced, without fully understanding why, that her brothers had made a great contribution to aviation, and she believed that if either Wilbur or Orville was to address an engineering society, and records were kept of such proceedings, there would be a permanent record of the Wright name in the history of aviation.

Wilbur accepted at last, but only with the proviso that "I am not expected to appear in full dress," and the understanding that he would not be able to prepare what he felt was thorough documentation on his tests. Chanute, who lived in Chicago, agreed to the conditions with delight and invited Wilbur to be his house guest on the trip.

Katharine wrote to Bishop Wright on September 3: "Through Mr. Chanute, Will has an invitation to make a speech before the Western Society of Civil Engineers, which has a meeting in Chicago in a couple of weeks. Will is to perform on the eighteenth. His subject is his gliding experiments. Will was about to refuse but I nagged him into going. He will get acquainted with some scientific men and it may do him a lot of good. We don't hear anything but flying machine and engine from morning till night. I'll be glad when school begins so I can escape."

On September 11 she added: "The boys are still working in the machine shop. A week from today is 'Ullam's'* speech at Chicago. We asked him whether it was to be witty or scientific and he said he thought it would be pathetic before he got through with it!"

And on September 25: "We had a picnic getting Will off to Chicago. Orv offered all his clothes, so off went 'Ullam' arrayed in Orv's shirt, collars, cuffs, cuff links and overcoat. We discovered that to some extent 'clothes do make the man' for you never saw Will look so 'swell.'"

Octave Chanute introduced his guest, and galvanized the au-

---

* Katharine's nickname for Wilbur. She called Orville "Bubo." Both brothers addressed Katharine as "Schwesterchen," "Sterchens," or just "Swes" for short — a German term of endearment for "little sister."

dience by saying that now the control problems of flight were probably behind the two brothers, and that the real problem he saw for the future was to apply the engine with the right power-to-weight ratio to accomplish true flight.

Wilbur's paper was for years afterward regarded as one of the finest documents on the science of aeronautics; perhaps it is all the more remarkable for being Wilbur's first presentation before any group of distinguished men of engineering.

Wilbur opened his talk by contradicting the statements of the man who had introduced him. He stressed that it was not power that was required, but the coordination of systems for controlling the aircraft and the skill of the operator, and that after these requirements were met, it would be a simple matter to bring power to the aircraft.

The engineering paper and the evening proved a huge success, and preparing it together helped the brothers to decide how to attack the problems of aerodynamic lift and flight controls. When Wilbur returned to Dayton, the team began again to work in earnest. They had already agreed that everyone's past efforts had failed to produce accurate information. Everybody had been guessing; no one had any idea of the necessity for technical accuracy. They considered some of the unanswered questions about wings: What should the span-to-chord ratio be? Where will the center of pressure be in level flight? Should the leading edge be blunt or round or *what*? What degree of camber should be used? Should it be 1-in-8, 1-in-24, something in between, and where should it be greatest? What would be the lift-drag ratio in a specific machine, and what kind of horsepower would be required to overcome the resistance of drag?

Wilbur devised a sort of weather vane in the form of a V, on which a flat plane of a certain size was mounted. On the other arm, he would mount the various curved shapes to be tested. By measuring the way the V turned on its pivot when held in a wind, he could test several wing shapes and curves, and compare different curved airfoils with the known performance of the flat plane held in the same wind. His first idea was simply to hold these devices outdoors in the wind, but this proved to be too uncertain and variable for reliable results. To get a steady airflow, Wilbur mounted his test contraption on a bicycle wheel laid flat and attached to the handlebars of a bicycle. The bicycle was then pedaled at specified speeds directly into the wind or in a dead calm.

But even this system, ingenious though it was, did not provide accuracy even remotely close to what they required, because it was too subject to error, humidity, variation in riding speed, and other factors. The next idea to emerge from their search for a testing system was the foundation of all aircraft design — the wind tunnel. This is not to say that the wind tunnel did not exist before their decision to make their own testing facility. Wind tunnels had been used for various purposes by several experimenters, including Wenham and Maxim, on both sides of the Atlantic since the 1870s, but never to test lift-drag ratios or the quality of wing surfaces.*

The Wrights' tunnel was designed to be 6 feet long and 16 inches square, with a pane of glass in the top through which they could observe the action of the airfoils being tested. The wind was supplied by a fan, driven, through a set of gears, by a small internal combustion engine the Wrights had designed and built for themselves in their workshop.

As Wilbur explained to Chanute in a letter of January 19, 1902, "Our greatest trouble was in obtaining a perfectly straight current of wind, but finally, by using a wind straightener, and changing the resistance plane to a position where its ill influence was much reduced, and also by breaking it up into a number of narrow vertical surfaces instead of a single square, we obtained a current very nearly constant in direction. The instrument itself was mounted in a long square tube or trough having a glass cover . . ."

So careful were the Wrights to handle matters with absolute precision in their wind tunnel that, once their experiments began, no large objects anywhere in the room were permitted to be moved, and if Wilbur or Orville was conducting a test, he always stood in the exact place he or the other had occupied in earlier tests. Their assumption was that even such a minuscule change

---

* During the late 1800s, Etienne Jules Marey, who wrote *Animal Mechanism*, had also studied and photographed the flow of air over bodies and surfaces of various shapes; he did this by blowing smoke (to make the currents visible) against objects suspended in a large chamber. He thus introduced a new method of aerodynamic research, which would prove of great value to later experimenters and probably influenced the Wrights.

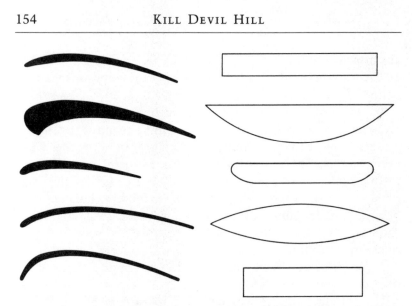

Typical airfoils tested by the Wrights and their planforms: More than 200 airfoils with varying aspect ratios, spans, and camber were evaluated in their wind tunnel. They included flat plates and curved ones; turned-up trailing edges; square and rounded wingtips, bird-wing sections; and square, oblong, and elliptical shapes; plus a range of both monoplane and biplane configurations.

might affect the wind flow and thereby negate the entire test. This is representative of the extreme precision with which they worked; they had determined that only the slightest disturbance could deflect a current a tenth of a degree, which was enough to cause a gross distortion of the results.

In two months of wind tunnel experiments, the brothers, always with the same meticulous care, tested about 200 different wing configurations, combining various aspect ratios, wing curves, cambers, and other factors. No wooden or cloth-covered airfoils, these, but models of airfoils they had laboriously produced from sheet metal, welding leading edges, filling the leading and trailing edges so that their proportions were as close to perfect as it was possible for them to achieve. They tested their airfoils as monoplanes, biplanes, and other multiwing configurations. They built them with dihedral and its opposite, anhedral, with an entire slew of aspect ratio designs — and from all this emerged a vast amount of data on aerodynamics.

For the first time ever, there now existed a scientific body of knowledge that was truly accurate, that was based on tests conducted on rigid engineering and scientific principles, and without which flight would have been impossible. This is not to say it would never have happened, of course; sooner or later other brilliant minds would have taken the steps adopted by Orville and Wilbur. But the Wright brothers performed their tests and accumulated their data years before the idea occurred to anyone else, and their having done so represents another of their truly great contributions to the science of aeronautics. The quality of their research at this point is revealed in a letter Wilbur wrote to Chanute on February 19, 1902.*

Because these data were revealed in great detail to Octave Chanute, and because of the cavalier manner in which the elderly gentleman in turn dispensed so much of this information, the work of the Wrights, which gave them a towering advantage over all other experimenters, was made much less exclusive. Because the experimental results were often printed by Chanute, within five to seven years of Orville and Wilbur's unprecedented laboratory tests other men in the United States and Europe were able to capitalize on their work — to their discomfiture and anger.

Years later, after the Wrights had begun to hold their accomplishments in secret and were negotiating to sell their equipment to foreign governments for military application, Octave Chanute urged them to display openly to the world what they had done. The Wrights' refusal was adamant; they insisted they were so far ahead of the rest of the world that they enjoyed a unique position, and that it would require a decade for others to catch up to them.

In terms of purely scientific achievement, this was true. But what the Wrights did not consider was that their secrets were being leaked to other experimenters, and that these men were enjoying to the fullest the practical results of the backbreaking efforts of the Wrights — without wasting the time to test the hypotheses that led to the results. It was this very situation that would severely cool the relationship between the Wrights and Chanute, but this was still in the future.

By now, at the beginning of 1902, Orville and Wilbur had unquestionably regained their zest for their flying experiments,

* See Appendix B.

and the familiar touch of humor was back again. The St. Louis
Exposition of 1903 was being promoted in the newspapers; in
conjunction with the exposition a prize of $100,000 was being
offered for the best or the first true flying machine. The details
were somewhat hazy, but the staggering sum of the first prize,
and even of the lesser prizes, brought forth a heap of claims of
flying machines that toppled over the edge of idiocy. On February
7, 1902, Wilbur wrote drily to Chanute:

> The newspapers are full of accounts of flying machines
> which have been building in cellars, garrets, stables, and
> other secret places, each one of which will undoubtedly
> carry off the hundred thousand dollars at St. Louis. They
> all have the problem "completely solved," but usually
> there is some insignificant detail yet to be decided, such
> as whether to use steam, electricity, or a water motor to
> drive it. Mule power might give greater *ascensional force
> if properly applied,* but I fear would be too dangerous
> unless the mule wore pneumatic shoes. Some of these
> reports would disgust one, if they were not so irresistibly
> ludicrous . . .

Some six weeks later, in another letter to Chanute: "I think
that the St. Louis Exposition authorities will have to increase the
amount of their prizes, as I have already been offered so many
shares of the prize by various persons who have a cinch on it,
that the sum of my shares would amount to more than the total
prize. Consequently, the St. Louis men must put up more money
or take advantage of the bankrupt law."

But neither Wilbur nor Orville spent any more time considering competitions. All during the winter and spring of 1902, they
worked overtime to prepare the bicycle business for the usual
spring and summer rush and to make sure that Charlie Taylor
and the others who ran and looked after the shop would find
everything in good order. They were also busy redesigning their
glider. Perhaps designing a completely new glider would better
describe their activities, for now they had a solid foundation of
scientific data on which to proceed.

They worked with a passion. Katharine wrote to her father on
August 20, "The flying machine is in process of making now.

Will spins the sewing machine around by the hour while Orv squats around marking the places to sew." Then, almost plaintively, she added, "There is no place in the house to live but I'll be lonesome enough by this time next week and wish that I could have some of their racket around . . ."

On August 25, 1902, they were off again from Dayton, and three days later they were striding along the dry, warm sands of Kitty Hawk, with no hurricanes or choppy seas or sinking boats to bedevil them. They had all their equipment loaded in a wagon, and Wilbur lost no time in getting to their shed. He had brought additional supplies and materials, for now he was planning to stick it out, to remain on the Outer Banks for three or four months if necessary to solve the problems that had brought their efforts to a halt. The brothers were convinced that success would soon be theirs . . . and yet there was still one feature of their glider, not yet known to them, that would try their patience and ingenuity to the utmost, and that would come perilously close to bringing them to defeat. Their rapport — these two young men worked with minds that were not only extraordinarily active, but extraordinarily sympathetic and in tune — would be their salvation.

There were other nagging problems. They had been plagued again by Chanute's insistence in offering (with the best of intentions, they acknowledged) the help of Huffaker and Spratt and still others. But they were veterans at their work now, and experience had taught them that they could accomplish more in one week working by themselves than they could in twice that time with others about, especially Huffaker. They hinted as strongly as courtesy would allow that the camp would be busy and crowded and complicated with work and that they would best be left alone. (Actually, they had hoped Spratt would join them.) Chanute missed the point altogether and reasserted that his associates would meet the Wrights at Kitty Hawk — and that he himself would come, probably with one or more gliders of his own design. The brothers managed to persuade him to delay his visit until October. At least they would have a month to work with the minimum of interference.

Their first week was filled with preparing for the necessities of life on the Outer Banks, for they found their shed in sad disrepair. The howling winds of winter had scooped away sand and buckled the structure in places; boards banged in the wind; tarpaper had been torn away. After they made the repairs, they spent several more days in adding a 10-foot extension to their quarters and workshop. On the basis of their planned lengthy stay, they considered the time well spent. Physical comfort had been considered as carefully as the flying machine.

The glider of 1902 represented subtle but important changes from the machine in which they had met so many frustrations the year before; its design incorporated all their wind tunnel data. The wingspan now reached beyond 32 feet, almost twice as long as the 1900 glider, and 10 feet longer than the machine of the previous year. But the chord was only five feet — two feet less than the wing chord of the 1901 model, resulting in a higher aspect ratio — making the wing slimmer and more graceful. If their wind tunnel tests were right, this wing would have more lifting power and controllability.

The camber represented a drastic change and was 1-in-24; despite this departure from earlier practice (away from the thick wing), the total wing area reached but 305 square feet, only 15 square feet greater than the 290 of the 1900 glider. There was another barely discernible change in the wing. The high point of the wing's curve had been moved backward from the leading edge to about a third of the chord — some 20 inches. This represented an unprecedented departure from all earlier wing forms.

The brothers had also reduced the size of the forward elevator to 15 square feet. It was no longer nearly as rectangular in shape as it had been; it now had the shape of a small wing and did, in fact, assist in the lift generated by the entire machine.

In the 1901 glider, Wilbur had lain flat on the bottom wing, supported by a body-holding system of grips and braces that kept him from rolling too much to one side or another (but had not prevented his flying face first into the elevator when he crashed). For the 1902 glider, the brothers had built a completely different pilot restraint, a hip cradle, which was so tight that when the operator shifted his body position so that his hips moved, that movement in turn operated control wires and warped the wingtips.

It was a psychological control system, in a way. When a wing dips suddenly, especially with the operator lying down, there's an instinctive reaction on the part of the operator to lean or roll toward the high side. In the 1901 machine, to correct wing imbalance, or deliberately to bank, the pilot had had to use foot levers.*

Their ability to work out the hip cradle without ever having tested it in flight is impressive in itself.

There was an entirely new feature to the 1902 glider — a true tail. It was a double, fixed (that is, it had no moving parts) vertical rudder, extending some 4 feet aft of the wings, with a surface area of almost 12 square feet. Each vertical fin was about a foot deep and 6 feet high; and the double-fin arrangement was intended to exert drag when a slip started, tilt the nose down, and keep the machine in a proper bank, allowing the operator to make a turn with constant control. The Wrights hoped to get rid of that pinwheeling motion they had encountered the year before. It was still not enough; it would require much modification and, above all, a new intellectual breakthrough on the part of the brothers before they could consider their machine a real success.

The Wrights had formed a strong friendship in 1901 with George Spratt, and on September 16, 1902, Wilbur wrote a warm letter to their new friend:

> Yours of 9th rec'd. We learned with much regret that there is a possibility that you may not get down here this year, as we had looked forward to your visit with pleasure. Everything is so much more favorable this year than last that it would be a pity to have your ideas of camp life here based on your experience of one year ago. First, we have not seen a dozen mosquitoes in the two weeks and a half we have been here . . . Second, we fitted up our living arrangements much more comfortably than last year. Our kitchen is immensely improved, and then we have made beds on the second floor and now sleep aloft. It is an improvement over cots. We have put battens on the cracks of the whole building including the addition, so it is much tighter and waterproof than before as well as more sandproof. Our new well goes down six or

---

* These were difficult to operate properly, and modern airmen have a rude term for systems of this sort.

eight feet below low water mark on the ocean . . . and we now have good water. We also have a bicycle which runs much better over the sand than we hoped, so that it only takes about an hour to make the round trip to Kitty Hawk instead of three hours as before. There are other improvements too numerous to mention . . . We are having a splendid time . . .

Mr. Chanute is sending down two machines, one built for him by Mr. Herring, and one built by Mr. Lamson (of kite fame). He is expecting to come down himself about Oct. 1st. Mr. Herring will come down to manipulate the Chanute machines.

At present Orville and I are alone in camp. We made arrangements before coming down, to have Dan Tate [Bill Tate's half-brother] with us as soon as we were ready to begin experimenting. This is all the force we absolutely need, as we will do little measuring and photographing till later when we have more men. We do not absolutely need a fourth man, yet he would not be an incumbrance by any means, especially if he was as good a companion as I know you to be.

The Wrights liked Spratt's good humor and his willingness to perform any tasks or chores at hand. But they did not like Huffaker; they regarded him as a moralizer instead of a worker, and that was truly a sore point with them.

After discussing some personal matters in the letter, Wilbur turned to their new glider:

The main thing though is a new machine. We have the two surfaces completed and the uprights in place, but the rudder is not yet quite done. It is 32' × 5' spreading an area of 305 sq. ft. altogether. The curvature is about 1 in 25. We had it out making some tests of its efficiency today and are very much pleased with the results of our measurements. The indications are that it will glide on an angle of about 7° to 7½° instead of 9½° to 10° as last year. The drift is only about ⅛ of the weight. In a test for "soaring" as a kite the cords stood vertical or a little to the front on a hill having a slope of only 7½°. This is an immense improvement over our last year's machine which would soar only when the slope was 15° to 20°, as you will remember.

The long-anticipated flight tests would also determine the validity of the vertical fins, or nonmoving vertical rudders, mounted to the rear of the glider. They were convinced that part of the slippage they had experienced in making turns had to do with the absence of these vertical surfaces, and they were eager to see if they had solved the problem.

Dawn on the morning of September 20 was all that a man could ask for, with a crisp day and a steady wind of 18 miles an hour. Dan Tate joined them as planned, and the three men carried the machine to Big Kill Devil Hill. It was to be an auspicious start in more ways than one. If the glider flew as well as they anticipated, then Wilbur would relinquish the controls to Orville so that both men would be experienced in actual flight.

It was time, they agreed, to share the joys and the perils equally.

CHAPTER 14

Well Digging

THE ATTEMPTS were gentle at first, tentative probes into the air just above the sand; they eased downslope close to the yielding surface "just in case." But with each short glide, with the beautiful response of the new machine to Wilbur's control movements, all doubts of the effectiveness of their wind tunnel tests and new design vanished, as if the sun were burning away ground fog. As the day continued, Wilbur stretched the glides. The machine soared down the dune along a gently descending path of only 7 degrees, and Wilbur was convinced that even better performance was in store for them. He became bolder and increased his height above the sand, and he was delighted with the feel of the craft. Each time he kept climbing higher up on the sand dune to try for greater distances in the glides; for with increasing distance, he had more time in the air to try the control mechanisms. It went better than they had dared to hope, the machine soaring beautifully.

But there was still trouble. Occasionally, mysteriously, the machine trembled for no apparent reason, and those feelings of unease were not entirely removed, as Wilbur explained to the others. Even when he flew straight and level he could feel the winds buffeting him gently, and when they did so the glider transmitted that *sense* of something wrong. It seemed to want to wrest control from its pilot. It would twist, or turn sideways momentarily, yawing from one side to the other, even when its path was a straight line. Crosswinds, Wilbur thought. Winds striking from one side to affect the basic stability of the machine. He was both disturbed and fascinated.

He flew again and again, and then started deliberate, gentle turns. To his astonishment, and accompanied by the cheers of Orville and Dan Tate, the glider maintained its stability and turned amazingly well. Then it was time to try a steeper bank, to make a real turn. Wilbur cast off from the dune and sailed out over the sloping sands; he was already 200 feet from his starting point, when he moved his body to warp the controls and start into a right turn.

All hell broke loose. Something, an unseen force, seemed to slap angrily at the machine. The left wing whipped upward at an angle so steep that if his body had not been restrained by the hip cradle, Wilbur would have fallen out of the craft. But he was held in, struggling to regain control, and he was reacting by instinct. Unfortunately, his instinct betrayed him in this instance; it was not yet in tune with the new control system.

The Wrights would run into the same problem time after time; whenever they changed the actuating methods of their control system, it took time for the pilot to adjust to the new system.

If Wilbur had meant to make the right turn, he would have moved his body to the right in the cradle, and the left wing would

Wright 1902 glider banking to the left. By warping the left-wing trailing edge downward, as shown here, the pilot adds lift on that side, which keeps the tip from striking the ground and enables him to roll the glider back to level flight.

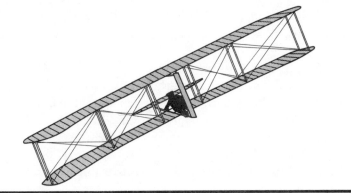

have come up and then he would have recentered his body or forced it to the left to level out again.

This time, however, the left wing came up not because the pilot wished to make a right turn, but because he was struck by a sudden gust; Wilbur, of course, responded instinctively. He responded, however, as if he were still using the old system — he pushed hard with his right foot. Naturally, this had no effect whatever.

It is not surprising that in the process he momentarily stopped paying attention to his pitch control. The result was that as the left wing rose, the nose of the glider rose with it. Alarmed by this situation, he pulled his weight forward, again instinctively.

Each of the Wright brothers always flew the gliders with his right arm tightly around a strut and his left hand actuating the fore-and-aft stick that controlled the forward elevator. In pulling himself forward, Wilbur inadvertently exerted pressure on his left arm as well his right. This merely turned the forward elevator up farther and added to his difficulties, increasing the high angle at which the glider was rearing toward the sky.

Wilbur corrected this by forcing the elevator into the full down position, and the nose of the glider dropped rapidly toward the horizon. Only then did Wilbur recognize the necessity of warping the wings to a level position by shifting his body weight in the cradle to the left; he did this as rapidly as he could, but it was too late. He braced himself as he felt the sickening swoop of the glider slipping sideways, and the next moment there was a thudding impact and a great cloud of sand as the right wing struck the ground.

This was to happen to both Wilbur and Orville on a number of occasions; it had many causes but only one name. They called it "well digging."

Once again that forward elevator had snatched Wilbur from death. When the others ran breathlessly to his side, they discovered that both he and the glider were unscathed. Wilbur lay covered with sand, and explained to Orville and Dan Tate that the fault was that of the pilot, not of the machine. The drastically changed control system, which he had operated in the wrong manner, had turned an easy maneuver into a near-deathtrap. But if ever there was proof of the structural strength of the glider, it was this incident.

After a rest, to catch his breath and his senses, Wilbur was off again from the top of the dune, casting himself back into the very situation that had so confused him. By the time the day was over, he had made 25 glides, the machine was whole, and Wilbur had acquired familiarity with the new control system.

The next time they flew, Orville would make his first flight.

A solo flight. All the way the first time, just as Wilbur had done.

Tuesday, September 23, provided the first opportunity. During the several days between flights, Orville had modified the glider to make the wingtips droop. This change, Orville explained, should assist in mitigating the effects of unexpected winds that struck the glider from the side.

Orville's first flights were training skims, Wilbur and Dan Tate running slowly to provide Orville with the *feel* that only actual movement could provide. He needed this time to gain depth perception, to judge speed across the ground, to feel the sensations of the glider, to acquaint himself with the controls. Wilbur and Dan picked up the speed slightly each time, until the short skimming hops became true glides, and Orville's launching points became higher and higher along the great dune. He was a brilliant student; he had a natural bent for flying the glider; and each success brought a huge grin and a demand for more. But he was pushing the impossible, and several times it became clear that they were trying too much too quickly, for Orville moved the control mechanisms in the wrong direction, and the forward elevator brought the machine down instead of up, with the result that the glider dug in with its skids or struck a wingtip and spun about abruptly in a cascade of sand.

Enough, declared Wilbur. Time for Orville to take a break, and now that he had direct experience, he could learn even more by watching the glider with Wilbur back at the controls. This went on through the day, the brothers exchanging their places on the bottom wing. Orville made a flight of 160 feet. Wilbur sailed out for a distance of 200 feet. Then it was afternoon, and Orville felt enough confidence to try for both height and distance.

It was a heart-squeezing replay of the year before.

Orville crossed over the sands at a height of 30 feet, paying careful attention to the motions and sensations of the glider, trying, as Wilbur had, to determine the cause of the strange sidling effect of their new machine. Wilbur and Tate watched, then fell silent as they saw with horror the nose of the glider climbing ever higher. Speech came; Wilbur shouted his warning as loud as he could, but his words "were drowned by the howling of the wind." He saw a wing rising, and the glider, instead of turning with the bank, began to sidle off in a direction opposite to the bank. Orville, in the meantime, was hard at work, shifting his body within the hip cradle to right the wings and regain full control.

It didn't work. He was back in the trap that had snared and killed so many men before him and that had so nearly killed Wilbur only the year before. The high wing swung higher and the nose jerked up; Orville had flown into a complete stall.

By the time he was fully aware of what was happening, the glider had ceased its forward motion over the ground and was now supported, however briefly, only by the speed of the wind. But it wasn't enough for support. Something had to give and when it did, it was a moment for honest, deep fear, for the glider began to slide backward even as it continued that sickening sidling motion toward the ground. With its speed reduced to less than that needed for controlled flight, the glider was tugged from one side to the other by the slightest buffeting action of the wind, as if it were pitching wildly on a choppy sea. Orville looked behind him barely in time to see the slope of the dune rushing up at him. His speed increasing, the machine completely out of control, he slammed into the steep slope of the dune with a terrific bang.

Orville gripped the controls with all his strength to keep from being torn loose and hurled out of the glider. All about him were the terrible sounds of wood cracking and splintering, fabric tearing, and sand whipping over everything. Because the slope was steep, the wreckage tumbled several feet before it dug into the sand. Wilbur and Dan ran to the wreckage to pull Orville's body free of the entangling wires and broken spars, but to their astonishment and delight they found Orville extricating himself without any difficulty. He had received not a single scratch in the crash. The only damage to his person, in fact, was a piece of torn clothing. No one ever understood how Orville emerged unharmed from the crash that so battered the machine.

Again, it seems necessary to repeat that without the forward placement of the elevator, the Wrights never could have completed their development program to a fully controllable machine without being killed or severely injured. Orville and Wilbur were really no more adept at flying than men like Lilienthal or Pilcher; what they had going for them was a machine that prevented a tragedy from reaching its conclusion. Indeed, the crash from which Orville escaped with such miraculous good fortune appeared to have dealt much more damage to the glider than was the case; they were able to return to the air, after repairs, within only a few days.

Lorin Wright arrived at Kitty Hawk on the morning of September 30 and remained there until October 10. He was an excited spectator as he watched his brothers perform their trials. He also helped as Orville and Wilbur made many more glides.

As long as the brothers flew straight lines, or kept their turns to the most gentle and shallow of banks, the glider behaved. But every time they slowed in flight and were buffeted by winds, or steepened the bank to make a turn, the machine turned wild, went through its disturbing side motions, and whirled toward the ground.

They had flown into what would one day be called the "tailspin": when, as the plane banks, something causes *one wing to stall out while the other is still producing lift,* the airplane is spun about from the lifting force of the outer, faster-moving wing; and the machine rotates as it descends.

What Orville and Wilbur did not know, but were searching frantically to understand, is that the fixed vertical fins at the rear of their glider were actually creating trouble instead of curing their problems. When the glider went into a turn, it first had to bank the wings. In the very process of banking, it eased into a sideslip. This caused the vertical fins, which at this point were immovable, *to function as levers,* and this leverage was forcing the wings to rotate about their vertical axis. Something else happened at the same time. The wings on one side, which were now higher, began increasing their speed, and thus their lift; the wings on the other side, which were lower, slowed down and correspondingly lost lift. The machine was now accelerating around the vertical axis, and the pilot would apply a positive warp to the lower wings to stop this motion. But the pilot's action had just the opposite effect — all it did was to give the lower wings more drag. The spin tightened as the lower wings stalled out completely while the higher wings gained in lift and speed, and around the machine went, the hapless pilot only adding to his woes in his frantic attempts to use his controls to get out of the situation — the action the brothers would later call "well digging."

Wilbur and Orville discussed this problem with raised voices and waving arms, and came to the conclusion that the tail was the cause of the problem. Why this was so still escaped them.

It was Lorin who later told what happened.

After a long evening session of shouting and arguing and scratching out ideas on paper, during which Orville consumed far more than his usual amount of coffee, he lay awake long after the others had gone to sleep. And during this period of restlessness, his mind kept returning to the glider in flight, to what was happening with the controls and how the glider reacted to them.

The next morning, lacking sleep but fired with his images, he presented his thoughts to Wilbur and Lorin when he joined them for breakfast. They knew that when the earlier 1901 glider banked, it would begin to slide sideways through the air, and if the side motion was left uncorrected, or took place too quickly, the glider would go into an uncontrolled pivoting motion. Now, with vertical fins added to correct this, the glider again went into a pivoting motion, but in the opposite direction, with the nose swinging downward. What Orville had discerned in his sleepless tossing was what we have just seen through hindsight: the vertical fins, as they struck the wind on the low side, were adding to the turning movement and were throwing the glider into its spin, its well digging. Indeed, if there had been no vertical fins at all, the machine would have rotated about its axis the other way (as it had done the year before), but with much less severity and consequence.

So, Orville said between mouthfuls, they could change all those

Orville

The source: the eyes of genius

Wilbur

Bishop Milton Wright, 1828–1917.

Susan Koerner Wright, 1831–1889.

Katharine.

Lorin with Leontine, Milton, and Ivonette Wright.

Left: Wright Cycle Company, 1127 West Third Street, Dayton: photographed before the building was moved by Henry Ford to Dearborn, Michigan. *Right:* Wilbur in the shop of the Wright Cycle Company, 1897; the lathe and drill press were powered by a gasoline motor the brothers built.

Otto Lilienthal flying his Type II monoplane hang-glider near Berlin, 1894; he faces the camera, and is swinging his weight to his left to shift the center of gravity and bring down the left wing.

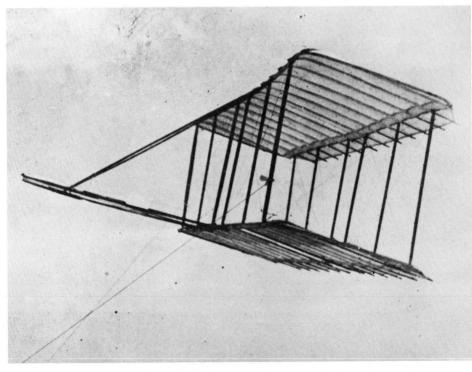

Wilbur's historic letter to the Smithsonian.

The 1900 glider flown as a kite; the brothers were now certain that wing warping was effective.

Left: Mr. and Mrs. William J. Tate of Kitty Hawk, with whom Wilbur first stayed in 1900. *Right:* The Kitty Hawk life saving station and crew.

Left: Fellow campers, August 1901: from left, Octave Chanute, George Spratt, E. C. Huffaker, Wilbur Wright; Chanute's first visit to Kitty Hawk. *Right:* The 1901 glider flown as a kite; note changes in the forward elevator.

Left: Wilbur, the glider, and assorted equipment in the work shed, 1902. *Right:* The kitchen area in 1902; after the discomforts of the first year, the brothers were determined to improve their living conditions.

Left: The 1902 glider, with Chanute, Orville, Wilbur, Herring, Spratt, and Tate. *Right:* The No. 3 glider (second version) being launched, 1902; note single movable rudder.

Wilbur making a turn, still in the second version with single vertical rudder.

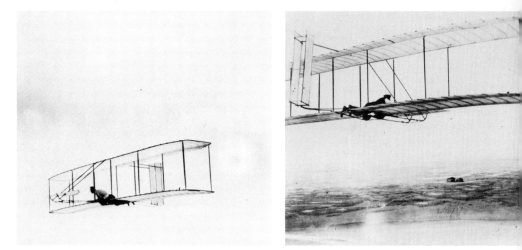

Orville in the first version of the No. 3 glider, October 1902 — note the double vertical fixed rudder.

Left: The bicycle method of testing airfoils; the cycle is a Wright-built St. Clair. *Right:* The wind tunnel, one of various replicas of the lost original, showing the intake with vanes to straighten the air flow.

BALANCE, LIFT, WRIGHT
BROTHERS WIND TUNNEL.
FRONT VIEW. (10-12-30

Left: The balance used in the wind tunnel to compare airfoil performance; the flat horizontal arms were made from hacksaw blades. *Right:* The interior of the 1903 engine, with the crankshaft that Charlie Taylor recalled turning out — "and she balanced up perfectly, too."

The 1903 engine in place, seen from the rear of the aircraft; at left is the cradle, with connecting cables that transmitted the pilot's body movements to the control surfaces.

Kitty Hawk, 1903; Orville in foreground.

The 1903 *Flyer* assembled and ready for a trial.

He might have been first — Wilbur after the aborted flight of December 14, 1903. Downward wing warping can be seen at the wingtips nearest the camera.

December 17, 1903 — man's first step on the "infinite highway of the air."

A discussion at Simms Station, Ohio, May 1904; in a summer of frustration, they would make repeated attempts to get into the air.

Simms Station, November 16, 1904, Orville at the controls. By late autumn, with the combined benefits of a lower density altitude and a catapult, they were making consistent and continually longer flights.

Le Mans, 1908; the Wright *Flyer* is assembled at Hunaudières racetrack.

Left: Preparations for flight; the catapult cable runs forward from the pilot's seat, above the launching rail. The wide vertical structure by the engine is a radiator, also visible on earlier models. *Right:* Raising the catapult weight. The aircraft is off to the right, and its launching dolly lies at the base of the catapult tower.

Left: Wilbur with his good friend Léon Bollée. The automobile manufacturer gave Wilbur the use of his factory and arranged for flight testing at Hunaudières. *Right:* Wilbur with Hart O. Berg, the Wrights' agent in Europe; Berg's wife would be the first woman to go on a fully controlled airplane flight.

Left: Wilbur demonstrates a maneuver as innumerable pilots would do in the years to come. *Right:* Airborne at Le Mans, 1908.

Left: Wilbur's old green cap was copied and sold by the thousands. This promotional piece, although weak on aerodynamic design, represents Wilbur with a fine Gallic air. *Right:* A fanciful application for the new machine; like space travel, another speculation of the time, it would come true.

The Wrights became part of popular culture in France; a 1909 program shows several of the crowned heads they would meet, with Wilbur and a well-depicted *Flyer* overhead.

Fort Myer, Virginia, August 1908: the Army had specified that the flying machine be transportable by wagon; the forward structure was hinged so that each skid and its bracing could be folded back. The observation balloon is some distance to the rear.

Orville's ill-fated flight with Lieutenant Selfridge, September 17, 1908.

Selfridge's death was the first to result from the crash of a powered airplane.

Pau, 1909: Orville, still convalescent from his crash at Fort Myer, watches Wilbur take an anemometer reading.

Left: Pau, February 15: Wilbur prepared to take Katharine for her first airplane ride; like Mrs. Berg's, Katharine's skirts were held in place by a string. This started the "hobble skirt" fashion. *Right:* February 20: Wilbur explains the control mechanism to King Alfonso XIII of Spain (note the changes in the engine since 1903).

Katharine, Alfonso, and Orville — the king had often shown his mettle in the face of Anarchist activity, but had agreed with queen and cabinet to decline any invitations to fly.

March 17: King Edward VII witnessed two flights, one with Katharine as a passenger.

February 15: under the auspices of the Aéro-Club du Béarn, the balloon *Icare* is prepared for an ascent; carrying the balloonist Ernest Zens, the Marquis de Kergariou, Orville, and Katharine, it landed 30 kilometers away at Ossun after a flight of 2 hours, 10 minutes.

Pau, 1909: the Duke of Manchester points out a feature of the *Flyer* to Arthur James Balfour, former Prime Minister of England, and Lord Northcliffe. Northcliffe, a firm friend of Wilbur's and an early enthusiast, established several aviation prizes.

All hands, including dukes, prime ministers, and other onlookers, pitch in to raise the catapult weight.

Northcliffe and Balfour taking the breeze from the *Flyer*'s propellers.

Wilbur at Pau, 1909.

Sheppey I., England, May 1909: the brothers are taken on a tour of the British Aero Club's new flying field. The Short Brothers aviation firm would build the Wright *Flyer* here under license. The driver of the Rolls-Royce is Charles S. Rolls.

June 10, 1909: in a ceremony at the White House, President William Howard Taft presented the Wrights with gold medals of the Aero Club of America (Katharine is at Orville's left).

Dayton Homecoming, June 17-19, 1909. *Opposite:* The flag behind the speakers' platform was made up of schoolchildren from the Dayton area.

Return to Fort Myer, June 1909: Orville on a practice flight before the official test.

The 1909 signal corps machine is recognizable by several features, notably its broad-bladed propellers.

Preparations for Orville's Fort Myer to Alexandria flight, July 1909, and the moment of launch (note oilcan on ground).

In the Fort Myer test flights, the Wrights exceeded Army specifications by staying in the air for over an hour carrying a passenger, and set a record for two-man flight.

Governor's Island, N.Y., September 20–27, 1909: officials of the Hudson-Fulton Celebration with Wilbur and (center) Charles E. Taylor, builder of their first engine.

Aware that he must fly a long distance over water, Wilbur fastened a canoe under the wing of the *Flyer*, but it was not put to any practical test as a flying boat.

Wilbur flew from Governor's Island, at the foot of Manhattan, up the Hudson to Grant's Tomb and back and circled the Statue of Liberty, before the largest audience yet to witness a flight.

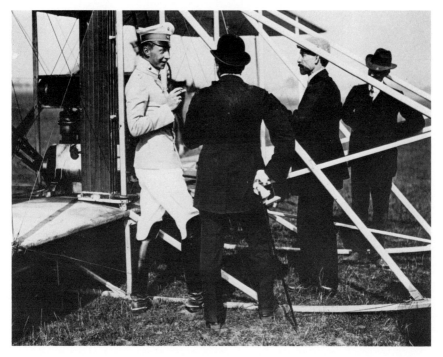

Potsdam, October 2, 1909: Crown Prince Friedrich Wilhelm prepares for flight
with Orville; he was the first member of a royal family to ride in an airplane.

On the back porch at 7 Hawthorn Street.

Le Mans, 1977: Henri Delgove, left, recalls to the author the electrifying flight of August 8, 1908, which he witnessed as a boy of 13 and announced to the town.

Hawthorn Hill.

dangerous side forces on the glider *if they made their vertical fins movable*. This would allow the pilot, as he banked into a turn, to apply pressure that would compensate for this pivoting tendency and keep the machine aligned with the direction in which it was traveling. If the pilot could control the movement of those vertical fins — which would make them vertical rudders — then the pivoting about the vertical axis, and the spinning motion, could not only be stopped, but prevented before it took place.

There was a problem, admitted Orville. There was enough for the pilot to think about with two completely different sets of controls — the wing warp and the elevator — for him to work. To add a third might be too much for any one man to handle.

As Lorin later described the situation, he glanced at Wilbur in a knowing way, expecting Wilbur to say that he had thought of that solution but there was some reason for discarding it.

To Lorin's surprise, Wilbur did nothing of the sort. Instead, he nodded slowly and then declared that it was a great idea, and there was also a way in which they might save the pilot the need to operate three separate controls. Since the pilot would always need to turn the rudders whenever he banked, why not hook them to the same wires that controlled the wing warping? This way, when the operator used the hip cradle as he entered into or emerged from a banked turn, the rudders would also be turning. They went to work on their new design, which called for the removal of the tail's two fixed vertical fins and their replacement with a single vertical rudder 5 feet high by 14 inches from front to back.

There had been other activities and another visitor. From Orville's diary entry of September 26: "I put in a part of the day in constructing a 'death trap' for a poor mouse that has been annoying us by prowling about our kitchen shelves at nights. We are now anxiously awaiting the arrival of the 'victim.'"

On September 27: "At 11 o'clock last night I was awakened by the mouse crawling over my face. Will had advised me that I had better get something to cover my head, or I would have it 'chawed' off."

Orville, his killer instinct held firmly in check, got up and fed the mouse. As he continued in his diary: "I found on getting up

that the little fellow had only come to tell me to put another piece of corn bread in the trap. He had disposed of the first piece."

On October 5, during a heavy Sunday rain, Octave Chanute and his assistant, Augustus Herring, showed up at the camp, along with a multiwing glider designed by Chanute. The very interruptions the brothers had feared were now fully upon them; but Wilbur managed to return to work, and by the evening of October 6 the new vertical rudder was completed. Two days later, with the growing assembly watching carefully, the first tentative tests were flown with the new modifications. They made some 20 glides, both brothers flying, and the longest distance covered was 237 feet. They did not attempt any turns, preferring to feel out the new construction.

On the same day, Herring made his test flights with the Chanute machine, and the Wrights, as well as Spratt, who had arrived on October 1, watched in disbelief. Even on a slope of 13 degrees, on the north side of the dune, Herring was unable to do more than come downhill in short hops and jumps.

The Wrights continued practicing in light winds on the 9th; on the 10th, with the wind blowing at 18 miles an hour, they went full blast at flying their new machine. Wilbur covered more than 300 feet on several glides, but far more significant, so vital it made the distance seem almost unimportant, was the fact that now he was maneuvering the glider through the same motions that had almost killed Orville and him before — and was doing so with complete control and balance throughout.

Where entry into a steep bank condition before meant loss of control and a frightening swerve into the deadly spin, Wilbur was able to glide almost straight out from the dune, drop the nose to pick up speed, and then deliberately pull up at a steep angle until the machine floated like a feather with almost no speed across the ground. Out of this situation, which had killed everyone who had ever entered it, he would nose down and turn and bring the strong winds to bear at a right angle to his course of flight. In other words, he flew intentionally with a maximum crosswind effect and, making perfectly controlled descents, landed the glider safely. He would set up his glide with the wind from the right and land, and then make another flight with the wind from the

left, and all the time the glider flew under precise control, obeying its pilot.

They were overjoyed with their performance. Orville was eager to get into the air, and, after some overenthusiastic working of the controls, he settled down to perform with great skill on his own. They went through more than 30 flights without the slightest difficulty. Their single vertical rudder would snap from center to left or right for a distance of 30 degrees, and all the viciousness that had wrested control from their hands had vanished. They could hardly wait to repeat their glides, and during a period of some 14 days they were able to practice controlling the machine on more than 400 separate launchings from Kill Devil, West, and Little Hills.

Chanute was astounded by what he was witnessing. From his own machine, he had only disappointment. Orville wrote in a diary entry of October 11: "Mr. Herring has decided that it is useless to make further experiments with the multi.-wing. I think that a great deal of the trouble with it came from its structural weakness, as I noticed that in winds which were not even enough for support, the surfaces were badly distorted, twisting so that, while the wind at one end was on the under side, often at the other extreme it was on top. Mr. Chanute seems much disappointed in the way it works."

On October 20, Katharine wrote to her father: "Lorin came home last Wednesday afternoon . . . The boys are having splendid success . . . Mr. Chanute and Mr. Herring were still there when Lorin left. They were all busy setting up Mr. Chanute's machine that was made in California. Herring's machine, made for Mr. Chanute, was a total failure. It would not fly at all."

The Wrights again and again launched themselves into the air. In these last weeks of October at Kitty Hawk, they made more than a thousand gliding flights. They flew more than 600 feet on a number of occasions, and up to 26 seconds for a single flight. They flew in winds of more than 30 miles per hour. Every time they were in the air, turning this way and that, climbing and descending, flying into and against and crossways to the wind, they were gaining the experience and instinctive moves they had sought for so very long. In sum, the final changes in the glider

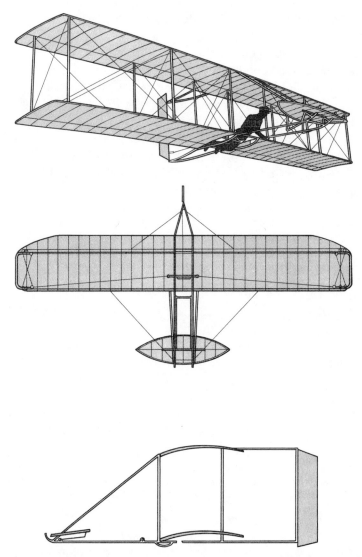

Wright 1902 glider: Three-view drawing of the brothers' first fully controllable and successful machine, which combined rudder and warp controls. During excessive banking, the original 1902 glider had an alarming tendency to fall off in a steep, diving turn — "well digging" as the Wrights termed it — due to drag caused by wing warping combined with fixed rudder leverage. They therefore modified the machine, replacing its fixed double rudder with a movable single rudder connected by cables to the pilot's hip cradle, which controlled wing warping. Complete control was thus at last attained.

were successful beyond all expectations. They had done what they had set out to do: to build a machine that was inherently unstable, but which they could control fully through use of control systems managed by a pilot — and now by two pilots — who became more adept with every flight.

Katharine received a note from Orville that fairly trumpeted their triumphs: "We now hold all the records! The largest machine we handled in any kind of weather, made the longest distance glide (American), the longest time in the air, the smallest angle of descent, and the highest wind!!!"

By now, the word was spreading among the small circle of men who believed that manned flight was, if not immediately possible, certainly worth every effort that could be applied toward its achievement. Leading scientists were keen to learn what events were taking place in the Carolinas. Representatives of foreign governments were making inquiries, and even seeking to purchase Wright gliders.

But there were the final moments at Kitty Hawk, and on the last weekend of October Wilbur and Orville battened down their shed for the coming winter, secured the glider inside, and closed up shop. They had a long walk of four miles to reach the wharf at Kitty Hawk to begin their trip home, and despite the cold day and stinging drizzle, their spirits almost lofted them across the wet sands beneath their feet.

CHAPTER 15

"... And She Balanced Up
Perfectly, Too"

THE BROTHERS were so pleased with their success that they drew
up elaborate drawings* and specifications of their 1902 glider,
and by March of 1903 had applied for a patent for their machine,
its construction, and especially its control mechanisms and their
operation.

The 1902 glider was a fine scientific and engineering accomplishment, but it could not lift from the earth on its own.

There had to be power, contained within an engine that met
the Wrights' restrictions of size and weight and would also deliver
enough of that power to lift and support a machine.

They needed to carry sufficient fuel for that engine to operate
long enough to do the lifting and supporting. Easy enough, but
one more obstacle on the way to transmitting the power of the
engine to a device that would translate engine power into a force
to thrust the machine forward. They had already been thinking
about this operation; back in September 1901, almost 14 months
before, Katharine, writing to her father, had given the clue to
how deeply Orville and Wilbur's hopes ran. She had said that
they heard nothing in the house "but flying machine and engine
from morning till night ..."

The problem of power. This was a delicious thought, for it

---

* The Wrights made their original 3-view drawing of the 1903 *Kitty Hawk Flyer*
on brown wrapping paper. They also did important calculations on the backs of
wallpaper scraps.

meant that the major problems of lift, control, and stability were now behind them.

There is a direct link in everything that relates to flight. The Wrights had developed the necessary airfoil — the properly cambered wing. They built great structural strength and reliability into their machine. Their control systems worked. Now they needed to mate power — or, more properly, power and thrust — to their glider design.*

The chain of necessary events is simple enough in theory. You consume fuel in your internal combustion engine. The heat of the consumed fuel, trapped in the engine, forces pistons to move rapidly and with great force. The force is transmitted through a crankshaft or chains or cables, or a combination of these, to propellers, forcing them to rotate with enough thrust to overcome the weight and drag (friction) of the entire apparatus. It starts moving. It moves because the propellers are linked to the engine. The engine is attached to its mount, and the mount is attached to the wing, so the whole machine is pushed forward. When it moves fast enough, the airflow across the wings is divided to create a pressure differential. When this is great enough, the entire machine has more upward pressure on its wings in pounds than the whole contraption weighs, and, when you add such refinements as controls and the ability to change the angle of attack, you have — presto — flight! . . . maybe . . .

When Wilbur and Orville first started thinking about their powered airplane, it seemed simple.

It seemed so simple, they had started Charlie Taylor on his way to building their engine in December 1902. Devising the engine was in itself a brain-twisting job, because in 1902 the internal combustion engine was still a primitive animal lumbering about on all fours. When it came to the weight-to-horsepower engine they needed to fly, the Wrights found nothing. So, in characteristic fashion, they designed their own. They sought 8 horsepower, which might or might not have been enough to get them into the air. Fortunately, their design was even better than they had hoped, and they were rewarded with a unit of 12 horse-

* For some of their calculations, see Appendix C.

power. The energy of 12 horses contained in a single chunk of metal may not seem like much, but it's 50 percent greater than an engine of only 8 horsepower, and that 50 percent can — *and did* — make the difference.

When they first cranked up their power-plant, it turned at 1200 rpm (revolutions per minute) and delivered 15.76 horsepower. That was in the first 15 seconds. Within several minutes, the rpm dropped to only 1090, and they had available only 11.81 hp. This was still nearly 50 percent more than they had anticipated, so they considered themselves very much in clover. But they were naïve . . .

Of the essentially 12 hp available, about 2.5 hp would be absorbed in the system of drive shaft, sprockets, and chains, leaving but 9.5 hp to raise the machine, its engine, fuel, and operator — a total weight of over 700 pounds. All the power *must* be used, or their machine would simply never get off the ground.

Taylor had been with the brothers from the days of their first full-sized glider. He recalled matter-of-factly, in an interview 46 years after the flight, what had gone into the construction of the power-plant for the first airplane:

If they had any idea in June of 1901 that someday they'd be making a gasoline internal-combustion engine for an airplane and would need some first-rate machine-work for it, they sure didn't say anything about it to me.

But when they returned from the South in 1902, they said they were through with gliders and were going to try a powered machine. They figured they'd need a larger machine to carry the motor and they started work on the new biplane right away. At the same time they tried to locate a motor. They wrote to a dozen companies, some of them in the automobile business, requesting one that would produce 12 horsepower but wouldn't weigh too much. Nothing turned up.

So they decided to build one of their own. They figured on four cylinders and estimated the bore and stroke at four inches. While the boys were handy with tools, they had never done much machine-work and anyway they were busy on the air frame. It was up to me. My only experience with a gasoline engine was an attempt to repair one in an automobile in 1901.

We didn't make any drawings. One of us would sketch out the part we were talking about on a piece of scratch paper and I'd spike the sketch over my bench.

It took me six weeks to make that engine. The only metal-working machines we had were a lathe and a drill press, run by belts from the stationary gas engine.

The crankshaft was made out of a block of machine steel 6 by 31 inches and one and five-eighths inches thick. I traced the outline on the slab, then drilled through with the drill press until I could knock out the surplus pieces with a hammer and chisel. Then I put it in the lathe and turned it down to size and smoothness. It weighed 19 pounds finished and she balanced up perfectly, too.

The completed engine weighed 180 pounds and developed 12 horsepower at 1025 revolutions per minute . . .

The body of the first engine was of cast aluminum, and was bored out on the lathe for independent cylinders. The pistons were cast iron, and these were turned down and grooved for piston rings. The rings were cast iron, too.

While I was doing all this work on the engine, Will and Orv were busy upstairs working on the air frame. They asked me to make the metal parts, such as the small fittings where the wooden struts joined the spars and the truss wires were attached. There weren't any turnbuckles in the truss wires, so the fit had to be just so. It was so tight we had to force the struts into position.

The fuel system was simple. A one-gallon fuel tank was suspended from a wing strut, and the gasoline fed by gravity down a tube to the engine. The fuel valve was an ordinary gaslight petcock. There was no carburetor as we know it today. The fuel was fed into a shallow chamber in the manifold. Raw gas blended with air in this chamber, which was next to the cylinders and heated up rather quickly, thus helping to vaporize the mixture. The engine was started by priming each cylinder with a few drops of raw gas.

The ignition was the make-and-break type. No spark plugs. The spark was made by the opening and closing of two contact points inside the combustion chamber. These were operated by shafts and cams geared to the main camshaft. The ignition switch was an ordinary single-throw knife switch we bought at the hardware store. Dry batteries were used for starting the engine and then we switched onto a magneto bought from the Dayton Electric Company. There was no battery on the plane.

Several lengths of speaking tube, such as you find in apartment houses, were used in the radiator.

The chains to drive the propeller shafts were specially made by the Indianapolis Chain Company, but the sprockets came ready-made. Roebling wire was used for the trusses . . .

We never did assemble the whole machine at Dayton. There wasn't room enough in the shop. When the center section was assembled, it blocked the passage between the front and the back rooms, and the boys had to go out the side door and around to the front to wait on the customers . . .

We blocked-tested the motor before crating it for shipment to Kitty Hawk. We rigged up a resistance fan with blades an inch and a half wide and five feet two inches long. The boys figured out the horsepower by counting the revolutions per minute. Those two sure knew their physics. I guess that's why they always knew what they were doing and hardly ever guessed at anything.

We finally got everything crated and on the train. There was no ceremony about it, even among ourselves. The boys had been making these trips for four years, and this was the third time I had been left to run the shop. If there was any worry about the flying machine not working, they never showed it and I never felt it . . .

Both the boys had tempers, but no matter how angry they ever got, I never heard them use a profane word . . . The boys were working out a lot of theory in those days, and occasionally they would get into terrific arguments. They'd shout at each other something terrible. I don't think they really got mad, but they sure got awfully hot.

One morning following the worst argument I ever heard, Orv came in and said he guessed he'd been wrong and they ought to do it Will's way. A few minutes later

Will came in and said he'd been thinking it over and perhaps Orv was right. First thing I knew they were arguing the thing all over again, only this time they had switched ideas. When they were through though, they knew where they were and could go ahead with the job . . .

I think the hardest job Will and Orv had was with the propellers. I don't believe they ever were given enough credit for that development. They had read up on all that was published about boat propellers, but they couldn't find any formula for what they needed. So they had to develop their own.

There had to be a means of translating the power of the engine into a thrust that would accelerate the machine until it could fly, and then sustain it in flight. This meant propellers.

Propellers. Ah, easy enough. Ships had used propellers for years, and there would be a wealth of data available on propeller efficiency, thrust, and all the other elements they needed; they could transfer marine technology to the science of flight.

However, to their amazement they soon found that there was no collection of data on propellers. The technology was barren, the cupboard containing only dust, and the transfer was an agonizing, frustrating, and blinding task. Once again, they were up against the unknown. They had to start from scratch, for the reality was that no one anywhere in the world had the least idea of how to design an aeronautical propeller.

If the propeller is properly designed, it resembles a section of wing; like a wing, it is an airfoil. It functions in the same way, producing a difference in pressure. There's more pressure on the back of the blade than there is on the front. On the airplane there is less pressure atop the wing than along the bottom, so the airplane wants to ascend — to fly. The propeller, with more pressure behind the blade than in front, tends to move toward the area of less pressure. If you turn that propeller fast enough, the moving tendency gets rather considerable.

As the Wrights pondered their new problem, they realized there was no great difficulty in calculating the angle at which a propeller struck the air. From this starting point they could work out the consequent motion of that body of air in some direction, and the thrust reaction that resulted. But this was, at best, only a start.

Obviously, if a propeller were used to cut through a solid material, like a great chunk of cheese, it would thrust forward the distance of its torque (twist) in one full revolution; this would be easy to calculate. But since air is compressible, there was no known way to calculate the thrust of a propeller when the thrust constantly changed and was affected by compression of the air that the propeller moved and through which it moved. If the aircraft remained stationary, then they could calculate the amount of the propeller's thrust by measuring the pull on a spring scale or other device; but if the airplane remained stationary, there wasn't any purpose to what they were doing.

They had no way of computing how much thrust would develop as the machine moved forward. The faster it accelerated, with a decreasing grip of the propellers on the air, the more thrust would be lost through that movement. And the extent of this loss is what they absolutely had to know. Flight would be impossible unless they could produce enough thrust to maintain the flying speed of the aircraft.

Thrust was one thorn; increased horsepower at maximum rpm had to be determined, too. Also, there would be a limit beyond which their propellers would not be effective. For instance, if they placed the machine in a dive and developed great speed, the propellers could be whirling through the air but not developing any thrust. *

This was an exquisite and complex problem. Years *after* the Wrights had worked out their own solution, when the French first started flying, some of the pioneering greats, such as Henri Farman, Gabriel Voisin, Léon Delagrange, Louis Ferdinand Ferber, and others, as late as 1908, attacked it from an empirical position. They simply plugged ahead on the basis of trial-and-error and groped their way from one guess to another to find the greatest propeller thrust. It must have been an embarrassing sit-

---

* Indeed, in some modern aircraft, propellers sometimes produce drag rather than thrust, and can be — and are — used as air brakes to slow down a machine in flight. This condition occurs when the aircraft motion through the air at this point is greater than the attack angle of the propeller blade.

uation, for despite three and four and even five times as much engine power as was available to the Wrights, the thrust from their propellers gave them less flying power than the *first* Wright *Flyer.*

Obviously, the Wrights had to utilize every ounce of energy from their first engine of only 12 horsepower. In a letter to George Spratt, in June 1903, Orville described how they did it:

> During the time the engine was building we were engaged in some very heated discussions on the principles of screw propellers. We had been unable to find anything of value in any of the works to which we had access, so that we worked out a theory of our own on the subject, and soon discovered, as we usually do, that all the propellers built heretofore are *all wrong,* and then built a pair of propellers 8⅛ ft. in diameter, based on our theory, which are *all right!* (till we have a chance to test them down at Kitty Hawk and find out differently). Isn't it astonishing that all these secrets have been preserved for so many years just so that we could discover them!! Well, our propellers are so different from any that have been used before that they will have to either be a good deal better, or a good deal worse.

Orville had discussed technical points in such a way that we can see clearly his remarkable capacity to grasp details and evaluate them properly. Later, in an article written for the December 1913 issue of *Flying* magazine, Orville stated:

> It is hard to find even a point from which to make a start; for nothing about a propeller, or the medium in which it acts, stands still for a moment. The thrust depends upon the speed and the angle at which the blade strikes the air; the angle at which the blade strikes the air depends upon the speed at which the propeller is turning, the speed the machine is travelling forward, and the speed at which the air is slipping backward; the slip of the air backward depends upon the thrust exerted by the propeller, and the amount of air acted upon. When any of these changes, it changes all the rest, as they are all interde-

pendent upon one another. But these are only a few of the many factors that must be considered and determined in calculating and designing propellers.

One of the many advantages the Wrights had over all their competitors was their hard-earned data from their wind tunnel experiments on airfoils. Because it was clear to them that a propeller was, in effect, an airfoil, they knew that they could apply their data to their propeller blade designs.

They attacked this problem so successfully that they even computed the thrust of their propellers to within *1 percent* of the thrust actually delivered, evidence of the brothers' scientific and practical acumen. No one else in the world had come even remotely close to their progress, and this was but one of the many areas in which the Wrights vastly exceeded every other experimenter. It is a fundamental reason why they attained flight perhaps 10 to 20 years before anyone else could have done so, unless the other inventors had taken their information and experience directly from the tests of Orville and Wilbur Wright.

Another clue to their success was their refusal to attack the problem by empirical means, that is, by the process of trial and error, for there were an almost infinite number of potential propeller designs. To carve these out and test them all, as they had tabulated wing data, would have been impossible in the time available; it would have taken a lifetime.

They realized that they had to devise a formula that would permit them to understand the effects of a propeller in its operation and thus enable them to design and build, at their first try, the best propeller for the transmission of power. In other words, they had to shift from the use of empirical data to theoretical analysis — a huge step even today.

There is no way that one can overdramatize what the Wrights accomplished in their propeller design. The idea of developing a formula to incorporate all the information they needed into an analytical form was something that would challenge a modern computer programmer.

They used all their wind tunnel data for their wings. They selected airfoil number 9 from these tables, because it had provided the best "gliding angle" for different angles of attack of all their test wings — that is, it had the greatest efficiency as it came in contact with the air at varying speeds and changing angles of attack. This airfoil would give them vitally needed stability, and some constancy, in their formula. They reasoned that if this airfoil gave the best glide ratio at different angles of attack for a wing, then it would give the best thrust at different angles of strike in a propeller blade — and a propeller blade on an airplane would have an angle of strike that would change often and swiftly.

But as soon as they crossed over one obstacle they encountered another and much more formidable problem. Orville explained: "It is the width of the blade that determines the angle of attack. The wider the blade, the smaller the angle of attack. If the blade is too narrow, the angle of attack is too great to be efficient; and if too wide, the angle of attack is too small to be efficient." The brothers developed the idea of the maximum blade area for the greatest efficiency, as well as the maximum length and speed of rotation. During this period, their world was filled day and night with mind-numbing calculations. Figures and symbols were scrawled on papers and cloth and walls, but most important, they went into several notebooks that have become keys to our recognition of their genius.

In Wilbur's Notebook H 1902—5, on pages 9 and 10, he illustrated performance estimates of March 6, 1903. His diagrams show what seems to be *wrong*; namely, that the slower the propellers were turning (based on their 12-hp engine), within certain limits, the greater would be the available thrust. Speed of the rotating propeller blade was more important in terms of a specific rpm rather than a maximum rpm, and of course Wilbur was exact in his notes. Therefore, the brothers made the sprocket ratio of the gears of their proposed 1903 flyer at 23-to-8, so that for every 23 revolutions of the engine shaft there were only 8 revolutions of the propellers.

They measured the center of pressure of their propellers from a point five-sixths of the way out from the hub. From this calculation, and based on practical reasons, such as height above the ground, they settled on propellers of 8.5 feet in length. They concluded that they could push a greater mass of air with two propellers of this size, rotating slowly, than they could with one propeller rotating swiftly. They also designed their propellers to counter-rotate; that is, instead of having both blades turn in the same direction, which produces torque, or twist in flight, they had the blades turn toward one another, thus eliminating what would have been an added stability problem.*

After using the most perfect airfoil and arriving at the best angle of attack and blade width, they then had to compute the comparative loss of blade performance. Wilbur worked out such details as the differential between the theoretical tangential angle of pressure exerted by the airfoil in its motion to the normal line of pressure generated by the airfoil in relationship with its chord, for a given amount of torque to be overcome, from which there would develop a certain poundage of thrust. The brothers worked out angles they needed by applying various angle data to a graph computed on the basis of the foot-per-second speed of the rotation of the propeller.

They applied their accumulated data to their graphs and plotted the probable effects of these various forces in miles per hour, or their minimum flying speed. They could then determine that with this differential they would sustain an approximate blade performance loss of 30 percent. Their charts and formulas lent themselves to the calculation of what the Wrights labeled "throwdown," slippage caused by the normal compressibility and out-around effects of flowing air on the propeller blades.

By developing still another formula, they were able to super-impose these data on the graph showing throwdown loss. The only route to establishing this formula for throwdown was by the solution of elaborate quadratic equations. The Wrights, with no formal training, were able to express abstruse and complicated physical concepts and principles in the form of these equations.

The calculations, which we would expect to find in the most modern aerodynamics laboratory staffed by experienced engineers and scientists, and backed by advanced computers and other electronic giants, appeared in the pioneering work of the Wrights in 1903. They are nothing short of miraculous, and they

---

* Counter-rotating propellers would not make news again until 1939, when the first Lockheed Lightning fighter took to the air, its counter-rotating blades considered revolutionary. Today, it is a strong selling point of several twin-engine executive aircraft.

are one more illustration of the superb brainpower the Wright brothers applied to the problems they found.

It is best to repeat it was genius from which all this emerged — of the theoretical quality of Leonardo, Kepler, Copernicus, Einstein, or the practical inventiveness of Steinmetz and Edison. Although they approached their problems in a matter-of-fact way, and although their experiments were conducted with primitive apparatus, perhaps distracting us from the intellectual nature of their efforts, we rob ourselves of a part of our heritage when we fail to elevate Wilbur and Orville Wright to the high reaches of scientific genius. We may have suffered too long the notion that the brothers were some sort of tinkerers who stumbled onto the secret of flight.

Here is an idea of the complexity of what they accomplished. The Wrights began with Newton's second law of motion: acceleration is force divided by mass, or mass is weight divided by gravity. Weight is volume times weight density. The estimates of weight density of air used by the Wrights in March 1903 was .075 foot pounds per cubic foot. And gravity is acceleration at 32 feet per second squared.

The Wrights had determined, as shown by page 12 of the Wright Notebook H, that a pressure of one pound per square foot of propeller disc area would accelerate 10 cubic feet of air at the rate of 42.6 feet per second per second, or a pressure of one pound per square foot of disc area would accelerate one cubic foot of air at the rate of 426 feet per second per second. With this in mind, they concluded that thrust would be equal to a factor of 426 multiplied by the propeller disc area, times foot seconds squared and divided by a term known as gross speed, which was defined as the sum of throwdown and the forward velocity of the machine. They arrived at the value of throwdown by a quadratic equation for which the positive root is the solution; to wit, that throwdown was equal to minus the velocity plus the square root of the velocity squared plus four times the factor of 426 multiplied by the propeller disc area, all divided by two.

Simple calculations by two men with limited formal education!

With their theory of propeller design worked out, the brothers began, early in February 1903, the first attempt to build a prototype propeller. Using a hatchet and draw knife, the brothers designed and carved a piece of wood into an eight-foot propeller with a helicoidal twist based on their wing design number 9. They then tested the propeller on a shed behind the bicycle shop, using a two-horsepower motor to spin the blades.

By the next month they had completed enough calculations to let them take the next step, designing two propellers, each 8.5 feet long. They used three laminations of spruce, and covered the tips with a thin layer of light duck canvas, glued on tightly to keep the wood from splitting. Each propeller was then coated with aluminum paint.

The propellers produced a maximum efficiency of 66 percent (that is, 66 percent of the nine horsepower that reached the propellers was converted to thrust), which was within 1 percent of what they had calculated, and much superior to any driving blade of any other inventors. It was this design that led them to achieve their excellent results with relatively small expenditure of power.

Into the spring of 1903 the Wrights kept working on all other aspects of their machine, trying especially to reduce drag. In his letter of June 7, 1903, to Spratt, Orville discussed drag reduction and said that "We have also made ome experiments on the best shapes for the uprights of our machine, and again found out that everybody but ourselves is very badly mistaken!!! . . . Mr. Chanute seems to very seriously doubt the accuracy of our measurements, as do some others who have made measurements along the same line. We are building our new uprights with simply rounded corners, nevertheless."

Orville closed his letter with a careful "P.S. Please do not mention the fact of our building a power machine to anybody. The newspapers would take great delight in following us in order to record our *troubles.*"

On June 24, 1903, again at the invitation of Octave Chanute, Wilbur gave his second address in Chicago before the Western Society of Engineers. Just as his talk in 1901 had helped clarify the brothers' ideas, so did this later talk. Wilbur fascinated his audience with details of the experiments of 1902; in addition to reporting the actual tests, he stated very fundamental truths regarding flight. He pointed out that, although he and his brother had made over a thousand glides, of which one reached a distance of 622 feet and lasted for 26 seconds, the total amount of their flying time to date did not yet total four hours — less than two hours for each brother.

This was an accumulation exceeded only by Lilienthal, who had required five years to gain five hours of flight.

In his address, Wilbur followed Orville's injunction to Spratt, and avoided any statements about their intention to apply power to their glider. He also avoided any mention of the enormous work and the calculations they had gone through to develop useful propeller thrust. But he did not steer clear of criticisms of work of others, for here Wilbur was on very solid ground indeed. He emphasized the deficiencies of other machines, like those built by Maxim and Langley, in which too much dihedral had been used. He made pointed remarks about the theoretical horsepower needed to sustain a given weight.

Shortly afterward, there was an exchange of correspondence between Wilbur and Octave Chanute, in which Wilbur began to show his irritation with several positions taken by the engineer. Chanute insisted the brothers must reduce all glides to computable data, a notion that struck Wilbur as preposterous. He stressed this to Chanute, explaining it was impossible to do, since the conditions between any two glides could vary so greatly.

The indications from these exchanges, during which Wilbur's irritation became ever more difficult to conceal, were that Chanute's extreme involvement with minutiae simply reflected his advanced age and loss of sharp mental faculties. Wilbur found it necessary to correct the statements Chanute was making about the Wright machine, as well as their flight experiments.

There was another irritation. Chanute was continually asking the Wrights to allow visitors at the Wright encampment on the Outer Banks, something that Orville and Wilbur greatly resented. It was their intention to reach Kitty Hawk early in September, and they used this date as their excuse to avoid having visitors. They needed time, and they needed it alone, they told Chanute, to prepare their facilities and their new machine, and any interference would delay them unduly. They were greatly concerned that Augustus Herring, for whom they had now developed an intense dislike, would show up, as well as that excitable and tremendously impressed military officer from France, Captain Louis Ferdinand Ferber, who was already clamoring to buy Wright gliders.

By this time, Orville and Wilbur were fully aware that they were on the brink of solving a problem that had eluded man for 100,000 years. Despite their coolness about the entire project, at least as perceived by Charlie Taylor, their effort was intense, and the excitement between them was climbing to a high pitch. They did not take kindly at all to the thought of others barging in on them and benefiting from their own long and difficult labors. They struggled to maintain absolute courtesy toward Octave Chanute, but the best they could manage was to convince him that it would be October 25 before their facilities were set up for any work.

On Wednesday, September 23, 1903, the Wrights took the morning train from Dayton for Elizabeth City — and their rendezvous with the beginning of a new age.

CHAPTER 16

"5 Blankets & 2 Quilts"

THE TRIP was familiar but always a little different. Orville and Wilbur were in Elizabeth City late in the afternoon on September 24, and took the first steamer available to Roanoke Island, arriving at Manteo after midnight. In the morning, they boarded a gasoline launch for the trip to Kitty Hawk, and saw their camp by the middle of that day. It was now a matter of rolling up their sleeves and pitching in for some hard, unglamorous work, for in their absence winter gales had slashed away at their camp buildings. Dan Tate shook his head at the torn boards, gaping holes beneath the structures, and sand blown everywhere; he told the brothers the Outer Banks had experienced the worst winter storms he could recall.

The more they studied their structures, the more the Wrights believed Dan, for their building had literally been blown from its foundation. They discovered, to their immense relief, that the 1902 glider had survived its wintry tribulations without damage; the brothers were intent on practicing with it to gain more experience with its controls. Their plan was to practice flying when the winds were acceptable and the weather fit to take to the air. Three days after arriving, they were hovering above the sand dunes, several times managing to move forward slowly in good winds without losing altitude, their linen-covered wings hissing in the ocean breeze. They learned quickly that their reflexes had not suffered at all during the long winter. When the wind was calm or the weather poor, they would concentrate on work to be done in camp. Orville was able to write to Katharine that "the hills are in the best shape for gliding they have ever been, and things are starting off more favorably than in any year before."

On October 1, Wilbur summed up the first few days in a letter to Octave Chanute:

> We reached camp, via Manteo, at noon last Friday, and found everything all right about camp, except that a 90-mile wind last February had lifted our building off its foundation and set it over to the east nearly two feet. We made preparations to begin the erection of the new building on Monday but the conditions for gliding were so fine that we took the machine out and spent the finest day we have ever had in practice. We made about 75 glides, nearly all of more than 20 seconds' duration. The longest was 30⅗ seconds which beats our former records. We did some practicing at soaring and found it easier than we expected. Once we succeeded in remaining almost in one spot for 26⅗ seconds and finally landed fifty feet from the starting point. With a little more practice I think we can soar on the north slope of the Big Hill whenever the wind has a velocity of 9 meters* or more. The wind on Monday was 11 meters at start and gradually increased to a little over 14 meters and then declined to about 9 meters.
>
> Since Monday we have been working on the new building and hope to have it finished in a few days more. Its inside dimensions are 44' × 16' × 9'.

Fifteen days later another letter went off to Chanute from Wilbur: "We were delayed a week by the nonarrival of some of our goods, but now have everything. The upper surface of new machine is completed. It is far ahead of anything we have built before. The lower surface is about half done. It will probably be nearly Nov. 1st before we are ready for trial, especially if we have some nice soaring weather. On Saturday, Oct. 3rd, we had some

---

* That is, meters per second. H.C.

nice gliding, the wind being a little too light for soaring, only 6 to 7 meters; however, we increased our record to 43 seconds and made quite a number about 30 seconds."

The Wrights now held the world's record for glider duration flights. Yet there was a cautious note in Wilbur's letter, for during this period Professor Samuel Langley's highly touted *Aerodrome*, built at enormous expense, had failed utterly in its first flight attempts from a barge on the Potomac River. Langley took a terrible drubbing from the newspapers, which assailed him mercilessly. "Fiasco," "complete failure," and "foolishness" were some of the kinder remarks.

There is a curious circumstance here. The Wrights had worked diligently to produce their small engine of 12 horsepower with a weight of some 180 pounds. But Charles Manly, who attempted the flight in Langley's airplane, had all the advantages of what was probably the most efficient engine in the world; it was a radical design, weighing only 125 pounds and producing an incredible 52 horsepower. Had the Wrights possessed an engine with this kind of performance, they would never have had to calculate down to the *nth* degree every facet of their machine. Compared to what they had, the Langley engine was a marvel of brute power.

In his letter to Chanute, Wilbur commented: "I see that Langley has had his fling, and failed. It seems to be our turn to throw now, and I wonder what our luck will be."

What is not commonly known — although the Wrights were fully aware of the fact and Langley totally unaware — was that there was a growing race between them and Langley to get into the skies with the first truly successful powered and controlled flight. Never having seen it, the brothers had felt they faced serious competition in Langley's machine, but they did not know that Langley's *Aerodrome* was in reality a travesty of aerodynamic design and that, despite its excellent engine, the machine could not possibly fly. Not Orville or Wilbur, not even Octave Chanute, in touch with almost everything else that was happening in flight research, truly understood how far ahead of the rest of the world the Wright brothers stood.

On October 18, Wilbur wrote to his sister to bring her up to date on the events at the camp. As if to keep them from brooding about the awesome task they had set for themselves, nature was keeping them well supplied with distractions:

The second day opened with the gale still continuing with a steady drizzling rain. The wind veered from the northwest to the north during the morning and dropped to about 30 miles, but after dinner it began to back up again. We set to work "tooth and nail" (using a hammer instead of our teeth however) putting braces inside our new building. The climax came about 4 o'clock when the wind reached 75 miles an hour. Suddenly a corner of our tar-paper roof gave way under the pressure and we saw that if the trouble were not stopped the whole roof would probably go. Orville put on my heavy overcoat, and grabbing the ladder sallied forth from the south end of the building. At first it appeared that he was going down to repair some of the rents in the Big Hill which was being badly torn to pieces, for he began by walking backwards about 50 feet. After a while I saw him come back past the side opening in our partially raised awning door . . . I sallied out to help him and after a tussle with the wind found him at the north end ready to set up the ladder. He quickly mounted to the edge of the roof when the wind caught under his coat and folded it back over his head. As the hammer and nails were in his pocket and up over his head he was unable to get his hands on them or to pull his coattails down, so he was compelled to descend again. The next time he put the nails in his mouth and took the hammer in his hand and I followed him up the ladder hanging on to his coattails. He swatted around a good little while trying to get a few nails in, and I became almost impatient for I had only my common coat on and was getting well soaked. He explained afterward that the wind kept blowing the hammer around so that three licks out of four hit the roof or his fingers instead of the nail. Finally the job was done and we rushed for cover. He took off the overcoat and felt his other coat and found it nice and dry, but after half an hour or so, finding that he was feeling wetter and wetter, he began a second investigation and found the inside of his coat sopping wet, while the outside was nice and dry. He had forgotten when he first felt of his coat, that it, as well as the overcoat, were practically inside out while he was working on the roof. The wind and rain continued through the night, but we took the advice of the Oberlin coach, "Cheer up, boys, there is no hope." We went to bed, and both slept soundly. In the morning we found the larger part of our floor under water but the kitchen and dining room were all right, the water being merely even with the under side of the floor boards. The front door step was six inches under water. The storm continued through Saturday and Sunday, but by Monday it had reared up so much that it finally fell over on its back and lay quiet.

According to Dan Tate this storm broke all records for persistence and has been equalled by few in velocity. Five vessels came ashore between here and Cape Henry, the nearest being visible from the top of our Big Hill. My theory is that a cyclone got becalmed off this coast and could not get away again.

The "whopper flying machine" is coming on all right and will probably be done about Nov. 1st.

That date was noteworthy, however, for an entirely different reason. A letter arrived from Chanute (written on October 24) announcing he would be arriving before long, and in the envelope was a news clipping describing Langley's preparations for a second attempt at flying his machine. Langley was insisting — to the press, which loved a good story, and to the army, which was paying for Langley's expensive tests — that his problems lay with the launching mechanism, not with the machine itself.

Wilbur fretted over the news, because if the army continued to sponsor Langley's tests, he could be ready long before the Wrights and could have his second shot at flight before the Wrights could attempt even their first. Neither of the brothers knew, of course, that the Langley machine was a monstrosity and they need have no fear of its ever flying, but they did know that their machine could not be ready for weeks; there seemed to be every danger of Langley's being the first.

They had had close calls before 1903, and this trip had not

been without its share of problems in flying their year-old glider. Indeed, on October 3 Orville escaped only by a hair's-breadth what could easily have been a fatal accident. A sudden gust of wind literally threw him from his hip cradle and rolled him onto the lowered wing, from which position he was forced to scramble back frantically to reach the controls — barely in time to avoid a crash. In the days following, Wilbur *did* crash, slamming a wingtip into the ground hard enough to jostle him severely and rake a trough in the ground. And there was still another incident: a down-draft jerked the glider toward the sands despite Orville's hard maneuvering, and a wingtip struck the side of Wilbur's head sharply enough to give him a fine headache.

Nevertheless, the fear of being second prompted the Wrights, after intense discussion, to decide on a gross violation of their self-imposed safety code. They would fly this new machine as an airplane without first testing out its lift or systems as a glider. George Spratt was appalled and tried to dissuade them; the slightest miscalculation in design, not discovered before they tried powered flight, might wreck the machine on its first attempt to get into the air, and they would lose more than they might ever gain.

Wilbur would have none of it. He had absolute confidence in his ability to fly, and in Orville's, as well.

They went to work, day and night, trying to be ready before the end of the first week in November. By November 4, Orville noted in his diary that they were "within half day of completion" of the flying machine. The next day they tested the engine. It balked and missed explosions, not surprisingly since it had breaker points instead of spark plugs and a sort of fuel pan instead of a carburetor. Also, because of a rather sketchy lubricating system, it tended to overheat — and bind up, lowering the number of rpm's — after a short time. After final tuning it was brought down to a steady and reliable running. The irregularities of the engine explosions put them in an agony of frustration, for by the time they had gotten the balky creature to run well, certain damage had been done — the hubs to which the propellers were fastened jerked loose from both drive shafts. Then they found problems with the magneto. By now it was very evident to Spratt that, no matter how intently the Wrights worked, it would be a long time before they could make any attempt at their first flight. He decided to leave immediately.

Spratt's departure was no doubt hastened by a decline in creature comforts. Many of the food supplies were starting to run low; getting new supplies was difficult; and the brothers preferred to live on short rations rather than waste any time going for food. The weather had also become an implacable foe. On November 1, five days before Spratt left, Orville had written to his sister:

> About a week ago the weather turned very cold (about zero according to my backbone) and another rain set in which continued for several days without intermittence. We found that a fire was absolutely necessary, especially on account of Spratt, who suffers much from cold. We took one of the carbide cans and, after punching some holes in the bottom for air, built a fire in it inside the building. Of course the smoke was so intense that there was no standing up in the room, so we sat down on the floor about the can with tears streaming down our cheeks enjoying its kindly rays of heat. Everything about the building was sooted up so thoroughly that for several days we couldn't sit down to eat without a whole lot of black soot dropping down in our plates. We decided a change was necessary, so we got a little stove pipe and built a stove out of the can, adding strap iron legs to it, and a number of patent dampers, so that now we have about as good control in our stove as we have on our machine . . .

George Spratt left Kitty Hawk late in the afternoon on November 5 in a launch, and took with him the two drive shafts, to be sent to Dayton by express from Norfolk, as well as a letter he would mail to Charlie Taylor that contained instructions for repairing the shafts. As Spratt reached Manteo on his way to Norfolk, Octave Chanute arrived at Manteo on his way to the camp. Chanute was present from November 7 to 12, and it was not the most pleasant of visits, mainly because of the weather, the short rations, and the fact that there was no flying machine ready to take to the air. As to the food, by now, Orville wrote to Katharine, "we had to come down to condensed milk and crack-

ers for supper, with prospects of coffee and rice cakes for breakfast."

It was not long after his arrival that Chanute announced he
must leave soon because of pressing business matters elsewhere.
The cold had become so severe that Wilbur was prompted to note
that the nights called for "5 blankets & 2 quilts. Next come 5
blankets, 2 quilts & fire; then, 5, 2, fire & hot-water jug. This is
as far as we have got so far. Next comes the addition of sleeping
without undressing, then shoes & hats, and finally overcoats."

On his way from the Outer Banks, Chanute stopped at Manteo
to send back several pairs of gloves, which were received most
gratefully.

On November 15, Orville wrote to both his sister and father:

> We are now alone again, the first time for about a month.
> Mr. Chanute came just as Dr. Spratt left. Spratt, by the
> way, left about two hours after the breaking of our pro-
> peller shafts, taking them along with him to express at
> Norfolk. We got Pop's letter yesterday saying that they
> had been received and were nearly ready to be sent back.
> We will not get them for three or four days yet. At the
> time they broke we were trying to get the engine in order.
> The strains on the shafts were enormous as a result of
> the sprockets being a little loose. The weight of our ma-
> chine complete with man will be a little over 700 lbs.
> and we are now quite in doubt as to whether the engine
> will be able to pull it at all with the present gears, as we
> will not be able to use more than $\frac{3}{4}$ of our power in
> getting started. The screws came loose before we had
> time to either measure the speed of the engine or the
> thrust of the screws. Mr. Chanute says that no one before
> has ever tried to build a machine on such close margins
> as we have done to our calculations. He said that he
> nevertheless had more hope of our machine going than
> any of the others. He seems to think we are pursued by
> a blind fate from which we are unable to escape.

Orville related that they had taken out their 1902 glider and
placed it on the 60-foot launching rail system they had built,
placing the rails on the slope with a wheeled launching dolly;

they then made experiments in coasting down the hill and taking off into the winds to soar. They had excellent success in these tests and managed some good glides, but they were exercising great caution. Now that they had the stove in their shed going continuously, the heat had so dried out the linen-and-wood framework, they dared not attempt any flight in high winds.

Nor were the Wrights at all pleased with the visitor's attitude toward their work. Orville explained further that Chanute "has been trying to purchase the Ader machine built by the French government at an expense of $100,000.00 which he was intending to have us fix and *run* for him. He thinks we could do it! He doesn't seem to think our machines are so much superior as the manner in which we handle them. We are of just the reverse opinion . . ."

If Katharine and Bishop Wright had been concerned that these delays and discomforts might possibly be making the brothers depressed, Orville dispelled all such thoughts by adding, "I am now taking up my German and French again, and am making some progress. The lack of a German dictionary prevents me, however, from reading much, the vocabulary in the grammar being quite limited . . ."

There were certain indicators of wry head-shaking on the part of the brothers. They were amazed at the power of the Langley machine — four times greater than their own — but they were able also to see that Langley had headed down blind alleys and was too much concerned with details that had no effect on the aerodynamic performance of his aircraft. "Our track for starting the machine (total cost about $4.00) amused Mr. Chanute considerably," wrote Wilbur to his father, "as Langley is said to have spent nearly $50,000.00 on his starting device which failed in the end to give a proper start, he claims . . ."

By November 19, water was freezing on the ponds by the camp, but the next day the propeller shafts arrived and the brothers threw themselves into their work. As quickly as they could, they prepared for another engine test. When the shafts were in place, they were plagued again by the irregular firing of the engine and the violent jerking of the chains. By the next day they seemed to have solved the engine problem; Wilbur recorded in his notes

that the trouble lay in the system that fed fuel to the engine.
Orville wrote to Charlie Taylor:

> The shafts arrived day before yesterday noon
> (Friday) . . . You did a most excellent job of brazing, and
> we are highly pleased that the bearings were not injured
> at all. I suppose you remember how the chains and pro-
> pellers jerked when we were testing them at home, but
> you ought to have seen them here. We thought that when
> we could get both propellers on the shock would be di-
> vided between the two, but on the contrary we found the
> shock greatly increased on each. The jerking of the pro-
> pellers back and forth would loosen up the sprockets in
> spite of all the tightening we could do. This play was
> probably the cause of breaking the brazing loose, although
> they had been already brazed so many different times
> that the fit was very poor. While the shafts were away
> we had lots of time for thinking, and the more we
> thought, the harder our machine got to running and the
> less the power of the engine became, until stock got down
> to a very low figure. We had designed our propellers to
> give 90 lbs. thrust at a speed of 330 rev. per minute (about
> 950 of engine), which we had figured would be the re-
> quired amount for the machine weighing 630 lbs. When
> the weight of the machine went up to over 700 lbs. the
> thrust required might be 100 lbs., and we got to doubting
> whether the engine would have the power, using the
> gears we have, to give the necessary thrust. As soon as
> the shafts arrived we set them up and got ready for a test.
> The engine, of course, had been run only a few minutes
> since we had been here, so that two of the cylinders were
> full of oil and only exploded now and then. As a result,
> after about ten seconds' run, both sprockets were loose.
> We used a chain and six-foot 2 × 4 to tighten them and
> the nuts, but ten seconds' more run and they were loose
> again. We kept that up all Friday afternoon, and by eve-
> ning stock had gone still lower, in fact just about as low
> as it could get, about 100 percent below par. But the
> darkest hour comes just before dawn. The next morning,
> thanks to Arnstein's hard cement, which will fix any-
> thing from a stop watch to a thrashing machine, we stuck
> those sprockets so tight I doubt whether they will ever

come loose again. After a few minutes' run to get the adjustments, and to burn out the surplus oil, the engine speeded the propellers up to 351 rev. per min. with a thrust of 132 pounds. Stock went up like a sky rocket, and is now at the highest figure in its history. We had made some allowance at nearly every point in our calculations, so that with the increase of weight we expect the thrust necessary to be only a little over 90 pounds, but of course that is coming down to our closest figures. When Mr. Chanute was here he said that from 25 to 30 percent should be allowed for loss from transmission. As we had allowed but 10 to 15 percent, we saw that the gears we have would not allow us to speed the engine up enough to get the thrust. However, the loss of transmission is not as much as we had calculated, or the power of the engine is more, for the propellers speeded up more than we had ever hoped for (standing still) but gave exactly the thrust we had calculated that it should give at this speed. We will not be ready for trial for several days yet on account of having decided on some changes in the machine. Unless something breaks in the meantime we feel confident of success.

We have had the old machine out only a few times of late on account of its dilapidated condition, which renders it quite unsafe. Our record of 1 min. 11$\frac{4}{5}$ sec. will probably stand for some time, anyway . . .

I suppose you find things a little chilly of mornings. We had ponds of ice all about our camp the other morning and the wash basin was frozen to the bottom. But the carbide can has kept us very comfortable indoors . . .

Several days of poor weather turned into several days of terrible weather. Light rains worsened until Kill Devil Hills was the scene of howling winds and biting cold, and to add to their misery it began to snow. Unexpectedly the weather changed; on November 28 the wind changed to an easterly heading and the thermometer rose. Immediately, they were hard at work to ready the machine for its first test flight, and they ran the engine with a new apparatus that would judge engine and wind speed simultaneously. Engine speeds averaged 1000 rpm, and in one test the geared-down propellers wound up to 350 rpm, a much better performance than they had anticipated. They were jubilant with the results, and the lingering doubts about the machine being able to support itself in the air vanished. They conducted a half-dozen runs of two to three minutes each, and then, examining the machine, they saw something that made it clear that these tests were an excellent idea.

Along one of the propeller shafts, barely visible, was a hairline crack. Under the stresses of flight, the shaft might well have flown apart, destroying the machine in the air or sending it, tumbling out of control, to the ground.

Most people at this point would have seen good reason to quit. The Wrights knew that Langley might try again — if he had not done so already — and they felt their chances of being first into the air were becoming slighter every day. They were also aware that they could look forward to worsening weather, to screaming winds, sleet, and snow; they knew about winter at Kitty Hawk. Yet they vowed that, no matter what, they would stay at Kitty Hawk long enough to make at least one attempt at flight.

They also agreed that to waste more time on the old propeller shafts would be a dead end. Accordingly, on November 30, Orville left for Dayton to make new shafts of spring steel.

Their expectations of the weather were borne out; on December 3 there was a great storm, but at least this time Orville was not present to share the miseries suffered by his brother. He was in Dayton, hard at work, and on December 9, as Bishop Wright noted in his diary, "Orville started at nine o'clock, with his new propeller shaft, for Kitty Hawk . . ."

He also brought news of Langley. On December 8, Charles Manly had again tried to fly Langley's *Aerodrome* on the Potomac. The great craft had been boosted from its launch rail, where, poised in midair, the engine howling, it had promptly broken in two and tumbled into the river. Manly had nearly drowned in the snarled wreckage; only the courage of an assistant, who dove at once into the frigid river, had saved his life. The newspaper reactions to this second expensive disaster were razor-sharp, and Langley was slashed to ribbons in the national press. Manned flight was, in the general consensus of editors as well as congressmen, stupidity that had about as much chance of success as perpetual motion.

But on December 12, 200 miles to the south of the Potomac, new propeller shafts were in place, and the Wright brothers moved their own machine outside its hangar to prepare for their first trials. They were chagrined to find the sands of Kill Devil Hills lying quiet under a lazy breeze. There simply wasn't enough wind for them to take off from level ground, and they had to settle for testing their aircraft along its launching rails. Again, fate, as we shall see, intervened on their behalf. The frames supporting the tail snagged on the end of the launch track, breaking the point of the rudder. Back in the hangar, repairs and modifications became the immediate business.

December 13 was perfection. The skies and the winds were made to order. A warm breeze of 15 miles an hour sighed across the desolate sands. The moment for flight could not have been better.

But Orville and Wilbur spent the day relaxing. They caught up on some personal chores, read books, walked along the beach. December 13 was a Sunday, and the brothers had given their word to their father they would not break the Sabbath by working.

CHAPTER 17

"Success Assured Keep Quiet"

AT HALF PAST ONE on the afternoon of Monday, December 14, the brothers extended a flag from the side of the workshed, which could be seen from the Kill Devil Hill Life Saving Station just over a mile distant. This was the prearranged signal that a powered flight would be attempted, for the brothers wanted every opportunity to have witnesses present if they were successful in sustaining their aircraft for any distance.

Soon after the flag went up, John T. Daniels, Robert Wescott, Thomas Beacham, W. S. Dough, and "Uncle Benny" O'Neal came to the shed and the waiting airplane. They pitched in to move it a quarter mile to the intended launch site. To make it easier to move the 600-pound airplane that distance, the brothers had the men roll it on its 60-foot track (which Wilbur had named the "Junction Railroad") to the end; then they would pick up the rear sections of track and move them forward to become the front section. It took about 40 minutes to get the machine into position.

The airplane's skids rested on the launching dolly — a six-foot plank that itself rested on a smaller wooden section attached to two small wheels in tandem. The wheels were modified from bicycle hubs, with ball bearings to reduce friction, and ran along the metal top of a two-by-four-inch monorail.

By now, two small boys and a dog had come along to watch the strange behavior of these stranger adults. They stayed only long enough for the engine to start, with its popping clatter, whereupon they took off in full flight for the nearest hill, scurrying beyond the crest to safety.

The rail rested along the gentle slope of the hill, and the machine was secured on its launching dolly by wire to keep it from moving until the operator signaled for the craft to be released. The brothers moved the coil box into position, connected the wires to start the engine, and moments later heard staccato thunder and saw their propellers whirling. They removed the wires and the coil box, inspected everything carefully. Just after three o'clock, Wilbur tossed the coin. He waited as Orville called out his choice — Wilbur won. The older brother slid onto the wing, snugged himself into the hip cradle, looked to his right to see Orville nod. Another man was at the left wingtip. Wilbur judged everything about him. The machine rested on a downslope because the wind was but five miles an hour. He might fly, and he might not. The wind made it all marginal. Wilbur readied himself.

It was a long moment for the witnesses. They had seen the gliders, but now the powered machine, propellers whirling and engine rumbling like hard, irregular thunder, fascinated them. They could see only the gross details, of course, but had they known what to look for and study, they would have determined the first powered aircraft to have a wingspan of 40 feet and 4 inches, a camber of 1-in-20, a wing area of 510 square feet, and a length of 21 feet and 1 inch. Without the pilot, it weighed 605 pounds. The practiced eye would have seen that from side to side this was *not* a symmetrical craft: the engine was placed to the right of center on the bottom wing to reduce the danger, in a crash, of the engine falling upon the hapless pilot. And the pilot, as he had done with the gliders, lay prone, but now to the left of center in order to sustain proper balance. Also, the right wing was some four inches longer than the left wing, to compensate for the engine, which weighed between 30 and 40 pounds more than the pilot — depending on whether he was Wilbur or Orville.

A hand lever operated the elevators, which extended well ahead of the wings, moving it up or down as the pilot intended. The new machine had twin movable rudders rather than the single vertical rudder of the 1902 glider, and the rudders were linked by wires to the wing-warping system. To coordinate controls, the

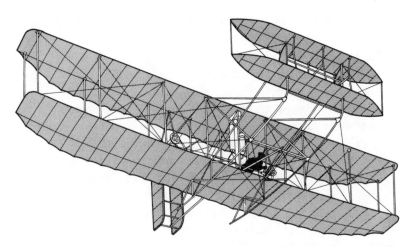

To control the Wright *Flyer* in full three-axis flight, the pilot lay prone, with head forward, his left hand operating the elevator lever, his right hand gripping a strut, his hips in a "cradle." By shifting his hips sideways, he pulled wires attached to the cradle. This caused the wingtips to warp and the rudder to turn (a double action from one movement). He thus controlled roll and directional steering.

pilot in the hip cradle worked the rudders and wing warp by wires attached to his hip cradle. If he wanted to turn to the left, he moved his body in that direction, and the cradle moved to the left. This warped the right rear wingtips to the down position, and the left rear wingtips to the up position, and at the same time, automatically, the rudders moved to compensate for yawing effects in the turn. By now the Wrights understood their system well enough to know the heavier machine needed two rudders. These counteracted fully the added resistance of the wing with the greater angle and the resulting tendency of the craft to swing in a direction opposite to a desired turn; they also assisted the turn by their effect on the airstream.

The engine rumbled, the propellers whirled, and Wilbur shouted that he was ready to fly. He reached down before him and grasped the restraining wire to release its grip.

Nothing happened. The wire was pulled so tight, his hands could not overcome its restraining force. Orville's yells brought the men to pull back on the *Flyer* to slacken the wire, and Wilbur at once jerked it free.

> ... Before I myself was ready [Orville related], Will started machine. I grabbed the upright the best I could and off we went. By the time we had reached the last quarter of the third rail (about 35 to 40 feet) the speed was so great I could stay with it no longer. I snapped watch as machine passed end of track. (It had raised from track six or eight feet from end.) The machine turned up in front and rose to a height of about 15 feet from ground at a point somewhere in neighborhood of 60 feet from end of track. After thus losing most of its headway it gradually sank to ground turned up at angle of probably 20° incidence. The left wing was lower than the right so that in landing it struck first. The machine swung around and scraped the front skids (bows running out to front rudder) so deep in sand that one was broken, and twisted around until the main strut and brace were also broken, besides the rear spar to lower surface of front rudder. Will forgot to shut off engine for some time, so the record of screw turns was mostly taken while the machine was on the ground. The engine made 602 rev. in 35½ s. Time of flight from end of track was 3½ sec. for a distance of 105 ft. Angle of descent for the 105 feet was 4° 55'. Speed of wind was between 4 and 8 miles.

That evening, in a letter to their family, Wilbur provided this account:

> We gave machine first trial today with only partial success. The wind was only about 5 miles an hour so we anticipated difficulty in getting speed enough on our short track (60 ft.) to lift. We took to the hill and after tossing for first whack, which I won, got ready for the start. The wind was a little to one side and the track was not exactly straight downhill which caused the start to be more difficult than it would otherwise have been. However the real trouble was an error in judgment, in turning up too suddenly after leaving the track, and as

A

PITCH
AXIS

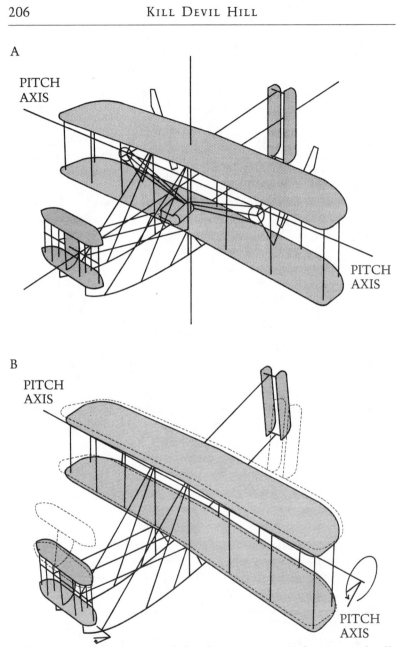

PITCH
AXIS

B

PITCH
AXIS

PITCH
AXIS

Flight control: Motion around the three axes — pitch, yaw, and roll,
indicated by the center lines in A above — was controlled by means of
movable surfaces. In B there is a nose-down motion around the pitch
axis; when the elevator is moved to a nose-up position, the aircraft will
be restored to level flight position.

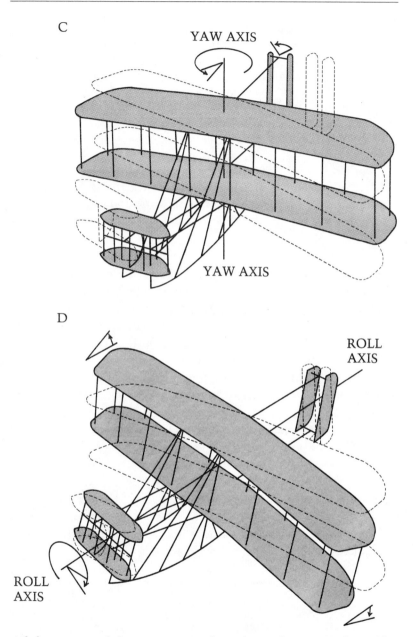

C

YAW AXIS

YAW AXIS

D

ROLL
AXIS

ROLL
AXIS

A left turn around the yaw axis is indicated in C; by moving the rudders to a right-turn position, the pilot will regain directional position. Motion around the roll axis in D shows the left wings as they are lowering; by raising the left wing, the pilot will return the aircraft to level flight.

the machine had barely speed enough for support already, this slowed it down so much that before I could correct the error, the machine began to come down, though turned up at a big angle. Toward the end it began to speed up again but it was too late, and it struck the ground while moving a little to one side, due to wind and a rather bad start. A few sticks in the front rudder were broken, which will take a day or two to repair probably. It was a nice easy landing for the operator. The machinery all worked in entirely satisfactory manner, and seems reliable. The power is ample, and but for a trifling error due to lack of experience with this machine and this method of starting the machine would undoubtedly have flown beautifully . . .

The details notwithstanding, neither of the brothers thought Wilbur had achieved a successful flight — only its promise. The machine had left the ground higher than its landing and in an unsustained flight, and obviously had touched down out of control. Thus, it failed to meet the hard definitions of sustained and controlled flight.

As the observations of both brothers showed clearly, Wilbur understood his fault in trying an angle of climb so steep that the *Flyer* almost at once lost its airspeed and began settling to the ground. With the high angle of attack, slow speed, and limited power, this was inevitable. If Wilbur had not overcontrolled immediately on lifting from the track, December 14 would have been the date of the first successful powered flight. Wilbur recognized that the forward elevator, much larger than in their 1902 machine, was now *too* sensitive. They now knew what to expect, and, as they started their repairs, Wilbur wrote out a telegram he dispatched the next day to Bishop Wright:

MISJUDGMENT AT START REDUCED FLIGHT ONE HUNDRED TWELVE POWER AND CONTROL AMPLE RUDDER ONLY INJURED SUCCESS ASSURED KEEP QUIET.

They could hardly wait to make another flight the next day. The *Flyer* was repaired, and they chafed to get into the air. But the winds hardly stirred. When they awoke Thursday, they couldn't believe their ears. A subdued roar came to them, a rumble that rose and fell in the distance. They looked toward the ocean and saw the surf boiling before a bitter, howling wind of nearly 30 miles an hour.

They went outside and stared. Finally, there was nothing to do but return to their shed to be out of the numbing wind. They sat about, depressed, listening to the wind shrieking through loose boards, blowing jets of sand around them.

They shared the same thoughts. They were already two months behind schedule, and this wind could easily become a screaming gale or hurricane.

They might not have another chance until next spring.

CHAPTER 18

"Two Folks Parting Who Weren't Sure They'd Ever See Each Other Again"

IT IS IMPORTANT to understand what exactly is meant by the term "flight."

> In the history of flying one is often faced with claims for this, that, or the other "first" [states Charles Gibbs-Smith], regardless of whether the achievement in question has any true historical significance. Whatever tributes can be paid to certain experimenters on the score of ingenuity, persistence, or personal courage, it is essential to decide whether their contribution was important historically, and to what degree . . .
>
> In order to qualify for having made a simple powered and sustained flight, a conventional aeroplane should have sustained itself freely in a horizontal or rising flight-path — without loss of airspeed — beyond a point where it could be influenced by any momentum built up before it left the ground: otherwise its performance can only be rated as a powered leap; i.e. it will not have made a fully self-propelled flight, but will only have followed a ballistic trajectory modified by the thrust of its propeller and by the aerodynamic forces acting upon its aerofoils. Fur-

thermore, it must be shown that the machine can be kept in satisfactory equilibrium. Simple sustained flight obviously need not include full controllability, but the maintenance of adequate equilibrium in flight is part and parcel of sustentation . . . [Sir George Gardner, the then Director of the Royal Aircraft Establishment at Farnborough stated in 1958:] "Clearly it is necessary to distinguish between an undoubted sustained, powered, and controlled flight, and a 'powered leap' . . . Nothing much less than a quarter of a mile would seem to remove all reasonable doubt that a flight was indeed sustained."

Gibbs-Smith then makes a critical point:

As it is the ability of the machine to be sustained successfully in the air which is the criterion, it is important to note that it is distance through the air which matters, not over the ground. . . .

Even totally unflyable aeroplanes, as well as many objects which are not flying machines at all, can be made to leap through the air for considerable distances . . .

He quotes the man he regarded as the most eminent authority on the subject — Wilbur Wright:

"From our knowledge of the subject we estimate that it is possible to jump about 250 feet, with a machine which has not made the first steps towards controllability and which is quite unable to maintain the motive force necessary for flight. By getting up good speed a machine can be made to rise with very little power, and can proceed several hundred feet before its momentum is exhausted . . . There is all the difference in the world between jumping and flying."

So the flight of December 14 was never considered successful by the Wright brothers. It failed to meet their own criteria, but it did show them that they were doing things the right way, that their equipment functioned, and that their hopes for future success were well-founded. As they waited out the gusty winds on the morning of December 17, while sand whistled along the floor, they knew that getting into the air would be flirting with death itself. But there came a time when you simply threw the dice and had it; you took your whack at what you wanted so desperately to do, and that was it.

As I imagine the discussion they must have had that morning, I get cold chills, because I know what was about to take place. And I know that *their machine had never been flown before.* The forward elevator had been changed and enlarged from the previous year and, if anything, was drastically oversensitive, but the only way they could determine such a reaction was to fly the airplane under the safest of all conditions.

Although the brothers had been practicing with gliders, their total experience with a power machine was the three and a half *seconds* of Wilbur's attempt three days before. Their tank contained enough fuel to fly the machine about eight miles in calm air; although the brothers did not seriously set their aim on such a distance, they had discussed the possibility of remaining low over the sands and flying off the four miles to the village of Kitty Hawk. Ideal conditions could make it possible, they mused . . . But conditions were far from ideal; the winds blew at 24 to 30 miles an hour.

At ten in the morning they marched into the teeth of the wind and raised their signal flag for their witnesses and helpers to join them. In the meantime they began laying their launching track, less than 200 feet west of their large work hangar and pointing straight north. It was so cold that the brothers often had to return to their shed so that they could cup their hands over their stove to get feeling back into their fingers. However, they were perfectly dressed, as was their custom, for the occasion, in full suits, right on down to starched white collar and tie.

Finally, four men from the life saving station appeared, hands in pockets, jacket collars pulled up high, to watch the proceedings and, if needed, to help. Daniels and Dough had been there on the 14th, and with them were infrequent visitors from former times, W. C. Brinkley and A. D. Etheridge. A fifth spectator was a teenager from Nags Head, Johnny Moore, who happened to be at the station on a visit and had joined the others on the trek to the Wright camp.

Orville set his tripod and camera in place, aiming carefully so that when the release was pressed the airplane would be shown just as it left the track; he assigned this task to John Daniels. Thirty minutes after the flag was raised, the 600-pound glider had become an airplane, with its engine running to warm up. The two brothers stood aside from the others, talking quietly. It was to be Orville's turn first today, and he doffed his usual bowler and put on a cap, taking the extra precaution of fastening it securely with a safety pin. "After a while they shook hands," Daniels later explained," and we couldn't help notice how they held on to each other's hand, sort o' like they hated to let go; like two folks parting who weren't sure they'd ever see each other again."

Orville slipped aboard the bottom wing, grasped the controls, and secured himself within the hip cradle. He studied the instruments around him. First was a Richard hand anemometer mounted on the front center strut adjacent to his body; this one instrument actually held two units. The upper part had an eight-blade fan within a cylindrical case that rotated as air blew against it; the rotation was transmitted along a shaft to a recording device two and a half inches below. This presented a watch-type face with two hands. The rotating fan drove a long needle to indicate distance covered in meters, and the shorter hand measured that distance in units of 10 meters each. As the craft traveled through the air, the hands kept track of the actual distance flown through the air; when the plane stopped, the hands also stopped, thus providing an on-board record of distance traveled. The second instrument — a stopwatch — was as vital then as it is today; by combining the reading of the two gauges the pilot knew the distance traveled within a specified time and could later calculate his speed from the flight log. A Veedor engine revolution recorder, the third instrument, kept a record of propeller turns; it, too, provided an accounting of distance traveled through the air.

Resting on the wing, waiting, with the wind rocking the craft from side to side and swinging and howling through the struts and wires, Orville counted the final moments. He knew he was taking a staggering risk. He and Wilbur had broken their own promise to test-fly the machine as a glider before powered flight, for it was larger, heavier, more demanding than any other craft of theirs, and even their control system was not truly familiar to them. Wilbur took his position at the right wingtip and then motioned to the five onlookers, urging them, as Daniels related, "not to look sad, but to laugh and hollo and clap our hands and try to cheer Orville up when he started." Wilbur turned back to his position as the five whooped and shouted and clapped hands. Above all this noise, the sputtering engine and its staccato barking, the whirl of the propellers and muted thunder of wind and shouting of onlookers, there came Orville's cry that he was ready; and his hand moved; and an instant later the restraining wire released the machine.

> On slipping the rope [he recorded in his diary], the machine started off increasing in speed to probably 7 or 8 miles [an hour]. The machine lifted from the truck just as it was entering on the fourth rail. Mr. Daniels took a picture just as it left the tracks. I found the control of the front rudder quite difficult on account of its being balanced too near the center and thus had a tendency to turn itself when started so that the rudder was turned too far on one side and then too far on the other. As a result the machine would rise suddenly to about 10 ft. and then as suddenly, on turning the rudder, dart for the ground.

The *Flyer* dashed out about 100 feet from the end of the tracks and in a final lunge for the ground that covered an additional 20 feet, it whacked solidly against the sand, skidding along and cracking one skid as it slid straight ahead and came to a halt. Orville's hand reached out at once to shut off the fuel supply petcock. The props whispered as they wound down, blurred, showed their blades instead of a blur, and clacked to a halt.

In light of the conditions and circumstances, the results were greatly impressive. Orville had flown into the teeth of a gale of

27 miles an hour and had managed to cover a distance of some 120 feet. He had been in the air for 12 seconds, and he had struggled against the double-planed elevator, which, put as kindly as we may, was simply too big, oversensitive, and a thundering pain to the operators who tried to gain consistency of control. The single greatest obstacle in these flights was a matter of overcontrol.

The Wrights were not yet aware of the great strain they placed upon themselves in controlling their machine. Not even an expert and skilled pilot could have flown this first Wright machine without practice and plenty of room for maneuvering. Too often, the airplane handled like a berserk dragonfly because of the extreme oversensitivity of the forward elevator, which should have been designed in trail instead of in balance. Of course, its placement on the glider had served to good purpose before, as we know.

Few people are aware that flying is less a matter of doing things right than it is of being able to correct swiftly and accurately, and as smoothly as possible, those situations that go wrong. *Flying is constant correction.* Newcomers to flight training almost always hear words that have been repeated countless times: "The toughest part of flying is to fly straight and level." That is, to fly a steady course without changes in direction or height. It's impossible to do so without these constant minor corrections to the controls, and here were the Wrights, seeking maximum distance under control, in an almost-angry flying machine, *and* doing so in weather conditions that would have been challenging even for a modern aircraft of equal size!

After Orville's first trial, which produced a ground distance of 120 feet (an air distance of 600 feet because of airspeed and wind factors), and while they were repairing their craft, the brothers discussed the excessive sensitivity of the front elevator. If they had made glider tests, as was their original plan, they would have taken a few days to reduce the size of the elevator or in some way modify the system to reduce the sensitivity. But time had become so bitter an enemy, as strong as the cold itself, that structural changes were out of the question. Now that they understood the problem, they would attempt further flights using extreme care in controlling the amount of elevator travel.

Orville recorded that

> at 20 min. after 11 o'clock Will made the second trial. The course was about like mine, up and down but a little longer over the ground though about the same in time. Dist. not measured but about 175 ft. Wind speed not quite so strong [which, of course, accounted for the flight of a little longer distance in the same length of time]. With the aid of the station men present, we picked the machine up and carried it back to the starting ways. At about 20 minutes till 12 o'clock I made the third trial. When out about the same distance as Will's, I met with a strong gust from the left which raised the left wing and sidled the machine off to the right in a lively manner. I immediately turned the rudder to bring the machine down and then worked the end control. Much to our surprise, on reaching the ground the left wing struck first, showing the lateral control of this machine much more effective than on any of our former ones. At the time of its sidling it had raised to a height of probably 12 to 14 feet . . .

The problem was not so much the sudden gust from the left as it was that *Orville still didn't know how to fly.* When the gust hit him, the nose also started up; Orville immediately threw in full down elevator so that he could hold his altitude. At the same time, he operated the warp control to raise the lowered right wing. The wing came up so swiftly, as Orville recalled, that "on reaching the ground the left wing struck first . . ." What had happened was simple enough. Orville had worked the controls in reaction to the wind gust, and had overcompensated.

Ten years later, Orville wrote: "With all the knowledge and skill acquired in thousands of flights in the last ten years, I would hardly think today of making my first flight on a strange machine in a twenty-seven-mile wind, even if I knew that the machine had already been flown and was safe. After these years of experience I look with amazement upon our audacity in attempting flights with a new and untried machine under such circumstances!" *

It was approaching midday, and Wilbur prepared for the fourth flight. It began at exactly twelve o'clock.

---

* There is an extremely interesting point here. Orville Wright's diary, as it was printed (and I imagine it was intended to be verbatim) in Fred C. Kelly's *Miracle At Kitty Hawk*, states clearly that "on reaching the ground the left wing struck first . . ." Kelly's other book on this matter, *The Wright Brothers*, an authorized biography, quotes Orville as stating "the right wing was lower than the left and struck first." However, the source for the latter may have been Orville's account written 10 years later, "How We Made the First Flights," which appeared in the December 1913 issue of the American publication *Flying*. In preparing the *Flying* article, Orville may have made the description conform to a photograph taken by Wilbur at what appears to be the moment of impact. On the other hand, the picture could have been snapped just before Orville raised the lower right wing in an attempt to recover lateral control. (At the time Orville wrote his diary entry he had not seen the photo.)

Because of these and other historical contradictions, I decided the only solution lay in obtaining a look at the actual diary of December 17, 1903, where, in his own handwriting, Orville states, ". . . on reaching the ground the left wing struck first . . ."

CHAPTER 19

Flight

THE PEOPLE of Kitty Hawk had always been generous and kind to Wilbur and Orville — friendly and warm, sharing their food and worldly goods, sparing no effort to assist in any way they could to provide physical comfort, and open in their respect for the brothers. Most of them, however, felt less than convinced about the Wrights' being able to fly; Kitty Hawk was an area where the reaction to flight was often expressed in such familiar bits of folk wisdom as "If God had wanted man to fly, He would have given him wings."

Bill Tate, who from the beginning had been a close friend to the Wrights, was not present at the camp on December 17, 1903. This was not a sign of lack of faith; he had assumed that "no one but a crazy man would attempt to fly in such a wind."

The brothers had different ideas. Shortly before twelve o'clock, for the fourth attempt of the day, Wilbur took his position on the flying machine, the engine sputtering and clattering in its strange thunder. His peaked cap was pulled snug across his head, and the wind blowing across the flats reached him with a sandpapery touch. As he had felt it do before, the machine trembled in the gusts, rocking from side to side on the 60-foot launching track. He settled himself in the hip cradle, feet snug behind him, hands on the controls, studying the three instrument gauges. He looked to each side to be certain no one was near the wings. There were no assistants to hold the wings as they had done with the gliders, for Wilbur believed that unless a man was skilled in what he was doing he ought not to touch anything, and he had insisted on a free launch, for he knew the craft would require only 40 feet in the stiff wind to lift itself into the air.

Wilbur shifted his head to study the beach area. Today was different. The wintry gale had greatly reduced the bird population, as far as he could see. It had been that way since they awoke. Very few of the familiar seagulls were about beneath the leaden skies.

Wilbur turned to each side again, looked at his brother, and nodded. Everything was set, and Wilbur reached to the restraining control and pulled the wire free. Instantly, the machine rushed forward and, as he expected, was 40 feet down the track when he eased into the air. He had prepared himself for almost every act of the wind, but the gusts were too strong, and he was constantly correcting and overcorrecting. The 100-foot mark fell behind as the aircraft lunged up and down like a winged bull. Then he was 200 feet from the start of his run, and the pitch motions were even more violent. The aircraft seemed to stagger as it struck a sudden down-draft and darted toward the sands. Only a foot above the ground Wilbur regained control, and eased it back up.

Three hundred feet — and the bucking motions were easing off.

And then the five witnesses and Orville were shouting and gesturing wildly, for it was clear that Wilbur had passed some invisible wall in the sky and had regained control. Four hundred feet out, he was still holding the safety altitude of about 15 feet above the ground, and the airplane was flying smoother now, no longer darting and lunging about, just easing with the gusts between an estimated 8 and 15 feet.

The seconds ticked away and it was a quarter of a minute since Wilbur had started, and there was no question, now: the machine was under control and was sustaining itself by its own power.

It was flying.

The moment had come. It was here, now.

Five hundred feet.

Six hundred.

Seven hundred!

My God, he's trying to reach Kitty Hawk itself, nearly four miles away!

And, indeed, this is just what Wilbur was trying to do, for he kept heading toward the houses and trees still well before him.
Eight hundred feet . . .

Still going; still flying. Ahead of him, a rise in the ground, a sprawling hump, a hummock of sand. Wilbur brought the elevator into position to raise the nose, to gain altitude to clear the hummock; for beyond this point lay clear sailing, good flying, and he was lifting, the machine rising slowly. But hummocks do strange things to winds blowing at such high speeds. The wind soared up from the sands, rolling and tumbling, and reached out invisibly to push the flying machine downward. The nose dropped too sharply; Wilbur brought it up; and instantly the oscillations began again, a rapid jerking up and down of the nose. The winds were simply too much, the ground-induced roll too severe, and the *Flyer* "suddenly darted into the ground," as Orville later described it.

They knew as they ran that the impact was greater than that of an intentional landing. The skids dug in, and all the weight of the aircraft struck hard, and above the wind they heard the wood splinter and crack. The aircraft bounced once, borne as much by the wind as by its own momentum, and settled back to the sands, the forward elevator braces askew, broken so that the surfaces hung at an angle. Unhurt, aware that he had been flying a marvelously long time, mildly disappointed at not having continued his flight, stuck in the sand with the wind blowing into his face and the engine grinding out its now familiar clattering, banging roar, Wilbur reached out to shut off power. The propellers whistled and whirred as they slowed, the sounds of the chains came to him more clearly, and then only the wind could be heard. The wind, the sand hissing against fabric and his own clothes and across the ground, and perhaps a gull or two, and certainly the beating of his own heart.

It had happened.

He had flown for 59 seconds.

The distance across the surface from his start to his finish was 852 feet.

The air distance, computing airspeed and wind and all the other factors — more than half a mile.

He — they — had done it.

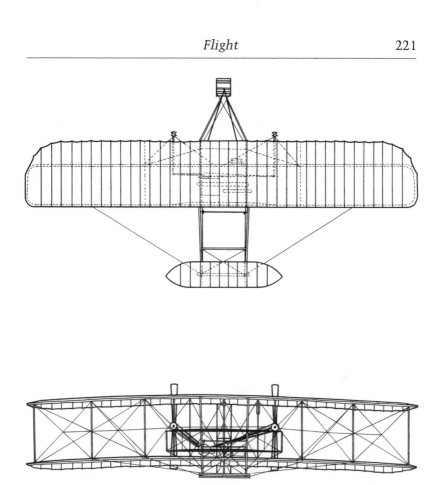

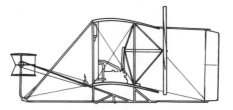

Wright 1903 machine: Span — 40 feet, 4 inches; chord — 6 feet, 6 inches; gap — about 6 feet, 2 inches; camber — about 1-in-20; wing area — 510 square feet; horizontal rudder (elevator) area — 48 square feet; vertical rudder area — 21 square feet; length — 21 feet, 1 inch; weight — 605 pounds. In 1903 this airplane, called the *Kitty Hawk Flyer*, made one attempt on December 14 and four flights on December 17, and never flew again.

The air age was *now*.

Just 56 days before, Simon Newcomb, the only American scientist since Benjamin Franklin to be an associate of the Institute of France, in an article in *The Independent* had shown by "unassailable logic" that human flight was impossible.*

---

* Following Orville's first successful flights at Fort Myer in 1908, Professor Newcomb was reported to have been asked if he thought passenger planes would be the next step. "No," the professor allegedly said, "because no plane could ever carry the weight of anyone besides the pilot."

CHAPTER 20

"Longest 57 Seconds"

THEY RAN UP to the machine, where Wilbur stood waiting for them. No one ever recorded what Wilbur's words were at that moment, and no amount of research has been able to unearth them. It is unfortunate, but they are lost forever.

We do know what *happened*. The broken elevator structure was but a minor accident: "The main part of the machine was not injured at all," remarked Orville later. "We estimated that the machine could be put in condition for flight again in a day or two." In fact, it had been their plan that after this fourth flight, they would break for lunch, and then it would be Orville's turn to gain additional altitude and, with luck, fly all the way to Kitty Hawk. The weather station was about four miles distant, and their gasoline tank, fabricated by a tinsmith back home in Dayton, held two quarts of gasoline in a cylinder 12 inches long by 3 inches in diameter. This would have given them an endurance of 18 minutes and a range of 9 to 10 miles, depending on the wind. That plan, obviously, was to go by the wayside, because of the repairs now needed. They separated the elevator from the main body of the *Flyer* and began carrying the machine back to camp. They were greatly pleased, because it was still eight days before Christmas, when they planned to be home, and now they knew they had a reliable machine they could fly for far more impressive distances than they had before.

Fate stepped in as they reached camp.

> We set the machine down a few feet west of the building
> [Orville reported], and while standing about discussing
> the last flight, a sudden gust of wind struck the machine
> and started to turn it over. All rushed to stop it. Will who
> was near one end ran to the front, but too late to do any
> good. Mr. Daniels and myself seized spars at the rear, but
> to no purpose. The machine gradually turned over on us.
> Mr. Daniels, having had no experience in handling a ma-
> chine of this kind, hung on to it from the inside, and as
> a result was knocked down and turned over and over
> with it as it went. His escape was miraculous, as he was
> in with the engine and chains.

Daniels himself, with a touch of grim hilarity, referred to the
moment as his "first — and God help me — my last flight. I
found myself caught in them wires and the machine blowing
across the beach and heading for the ocean, landing first on one
end and then on the other, rolling over and over, and me getting
more tangled up in it all the time. I tell you, I was plumb scared.
When the thing did stop for half a second I nearly broke up every
wire and upright getting out of it."

Further flights that year were now out of the question. As
Orville described the machine, "The engine legs were all broken
off, the chain guides badly bent, a number of uprights, and nearly
all the rear ends of the ribs were broken. One spar only was
broken."

The men examined Daniels carefully; he was a mass of
scratches and cuts, his clothes were torn, and he was still rather
dizzy. They shook hands all around, and the visitors took Daniels
with them to attend to his injuries.

Orville and Wilbur, stiff with cold, went to their living quarters, where they prepared and ate lunch. They rested for several
minutes, washed their dishes, and, ready at last to send word of
their achievement, at about two o'clock in the afternoon began
the walk to the weather station four miles distant in Kitty Hawk.
From the station, still run by Joseph J. Dosher, they could dispatch a wire via government facilities to Norfolk, where the

message would be continued by telephone to a commercial telegraph office near Dayton. The message, as it was received in Dayton, read:

176 C KA CS 33 PAID.   VIA NORFOLK VA
KITTY   HAWK N C DEC 17
BISHOP M WRIGHT
                    7 HAWTHORNE ST
SUCCESS FOUR FLIGHTS THURSDAY MORNING ALL AGAINST TWENTY ONE MILE WIND STARTED FROM LEVEL WITH ENGINE POWER ALONE AVERAGE SPEED THROUGH AIR THIRTY ONE MILES LONGEST 57 SECONDS INFORM PRESS HOME ##### CHRISTMAS.
                    OREVELLE WRIGHT   525P

While this slightly garbled message was being transmitted, including the error of flight time of 57 seconds rather than 59, the brothers went to the life saving station nearby, to talk with the crew on duty. Captain S. J. Payne, who skippered the facility, told the Wrights he had watched through binoculars as they soared over the ground.

Orville and Wilbur went on to the post office, where they visited Captain and Mrs. Hobbs, who had hauled materials and done other work for them, spent some time with a Dr. Cogswell, and then started their trek back to their camp. It would take them several days to dismantle and pack their *Flyer* into a barrel and two boxes, along with personal gear, and they went to work with their usual thoroughness. It was a strange and a quiet aftermath, and several times they went back outside to stand and look at the ground over which they had flown.

CHAPTER 21

"Most Unmitigated Impudence"

THE ERRORS began with the telegraphed message and continued with an unfortunate series of misadventures with the press. The latter account in the greatest measure for the Wrights' uncommunicative attitude toward reporters, an attitude that was not to change. The more they dealt with the press, the more they were exposed to its machinations, fabrications, thefts, and deliberate misinformation, and the more contemptuous they became.

On December 18, one Dayton newspaper, the *Daily News*, reported that the Wright Brothers had emulated the aerial work of Alberto Santos-Dumont. The editors, unable at this stage of history to tell a gas-bag from an airplane, derogated the Wrights as cheap imitators of something they knew nothing about.

A few lines from the Associated Press dispatch, a condensed version of the first story that appeared in the Norfolk *Virginian-Pilot*, December 18, will give an idea of what the brothers faced:

> The machine flew for three miles . . . Preparatory to its flight the machine was placed upon a platform . . . on a high sandhill and when all was in readiness the fastenings to the machine were released . . . The navigator, Wilbur Wright, then started a small gasoline engine which worked the propellers. When the end of the incline was reached the machine gradually arose until it obtained [*sic*] an altitude of 60 feet . . . Protruding from the center

of the car is a huge fan-shaped rudder of canvas, stretched upon a frame of wood . . .

The *Pilot* carried headlines across the front page that read: FLYING MACHINE SOARS 3 MILES IN TEETH OF HIGH WIND OVER SAND HILLS AND WAVES AT KITTY HAWK ON CAROLINA COAST, NO BALLOON ATTACHED TO AID IT. The paper's Ed Dean wrote the grossly inaccurate story that Orville later said was "ninety-nine percent wrong." Dean had been told about the flight by H. P. Moore, a member of the *Pilot*'s circulation department and friend of the Norfolk telegraph operator, from whom he got the news. Moore, who aspired to become a reporter, offered the story to 21 newspapers. Only five bought it, and only three of the five printed it: the New York *American,* the Washington *Post,* and the Cincinnati *Enquirer.*

On the afternoon of December 18, the Dayton *Evening Herald* ran a large, page-one story of the flight based on a 350-word Associated Press dispatch sent that morning to AP members. The AP report, a condensation of the *Virginian-Pilot* story, repeated many of the same errors, among them that the flight "lasted three miles" and references to "six-bladed propellers at the rear to shove it forward." Headlined the *Herald*: DAYTON BOYS FLY AIRSHIP, MACHINE MAKES HIGH SPEED FLIGHT IN THE TEETH OF A GALE AND LANDS AT THE POINT SELECTED. PROBLEM OF AERIAL NAVIGATION SOLVED, ASCENT MADE AT ISOLATED SPOT ON CAROLINA COAST, WHERE WRIGHTS EXPERIMENTED FOR THREE YEARS.

The Dayton *Daily News* item on December 19, datelined Norfolk, followed up its balloon story of the day before: "Orville and Wilbur Wright, Inventors of the 'Wright Flyer,' which made several successful flights near here Thursday, left today for their home in Dayton, O., to spend Christmas with their parents." End of story.

Although locally the Dayton *Journal* could have been the first with the news on December 18, telegraph editor Frank Tunison chose to ignore it. The next day the *Journal* ran the original account, followed on December 20 by an attempt to correct the misinformation, but the follow-up story still fell woefully short of the mark. It began: "Bishop Milton Wright of this city has received a telegram from his sons, Wilbur and Orville Wright, who are at Kitty Hawk, North Carolina, the fourth autumn, experimenting in gliding through the air on an airplane of their own make, and regulated by devices of their own invention." The news article went on to quote Orville's telegram in full and described the plane in some detail.

On the train, coming home from North Carolina, Orville and Wilbur prophetically concluded that they now possessed the machine that, even in this infant stage, held great potential as a weapon of war. They were also aware of staggering commercial possibilities — which had not existed on the morning of December 17, 1903, but were obvious that afternoon — and the Wrights had already made their decision that it would be absolutely necessary to patent every feature of their aircraft before releasing its vital details for others to use for their own gain. Anyone could copy their airfoil, for instance, if he knew its shape; he wouldn't have to make all the calculations the Wrights had had to make in designing it.

Bishop Wright could not conceal a certain pique as he wrote in his diary on December 18: "The [Cincinnati] *Enquirer* contained flaming headlines on the Wright's flying. Dayton *Journal* and Cin. *Tribune* contain nothing! though I furnished press reporter the news . . ."

Katharine had wired Octave Chanute the report from Kitty Hawk. On December 19, Chanute wired back: PLEASED AT YOUR SUCCESS. WHEN READY TO MAKE PUBLIC PLEASE ADVISE ME. This was two days after the successful flight, but Chanute apparently had not yet read or heard the news from other sources. Stranger still, reporters knew of the flights, and magazines and newspapers were sending telegrams and otherwise trying to get exclusive rights to the story. Above all, they wanted photographs of the men and their machine. Even on December 22, the day before the brothers arrived in Dayton, Bishop Wright's diary tells it well: "I was at home all day. Reporters were calling . . ."

On December 22, Bishop Wright wrote to Carl Dienstbach, American correspondent of *Illustrierte Aeronautische Mitteilungen*: "The Norfolk dispatch was evidently a friendly, though incorrect report. My sons say their four successful flights the 17th instant were 'from the level.'" The father added a postscript:

"Wilbur is 36, Orville 32, and they are as inseparable as twins. For several years they have read up on aeronautics as a physician would read his books, and they have studied, discussed, and experimented together. Natural workmen, they have invented, constructed, and operated their gliders, and finally their 'Wright Flyer,' jointly, all at their own personal expense. About equal credit is due each."

Referring to a particularly distorted account, the brothers had wired their sister, rather wryly: HAVE SURVIVED PERILOUS TRIP REPORTED IN PAPERS. As Bishop Wright recorded in his diary on December 23, "They came [home] at 8:00. They had some interviewers in the way but suppressed them."

This was a natural reaction to the unexpected events that followed their flights at Kitty Hawk. They were inventors, wholly self-reliant men who lived and worked in a world of scientific accuracy. Theirs were scientific minds concentrating more on work than conversation, and people connected with the press were a strange breed. To the brothers, telling a story or relating an event was simply a matter of presenting the facts in an honest fashion.*

The year 1903 ended with this notation in Bishop Wright's diary: "The past year was full of stirring events. I was serene and happy through it all, though grieved at the folly of many, and the wickedness of not a few. I believed that God would at last vindicate the right."

At this point in the development of the airplane the Wrights had made only a beginning, and they were well aware of it. They knew they had stripped from nature the secrets of flight; that they had developed the proper power-to-weight ratio; that they had transferred that power by their propeller design into proper thrust; that they had devised a three-dimensional control method for their machine; that they had the right wing curve; that they had the right lift to carry the proposed weight. They had proved

---

* A public relations executive once remarked to an aviation group that what the Wright brothers needed after their first flight was a good PR man — somebody who could handle the press, who could talk in terms understandable to the reporters, who understood the newspapers' special needs, and knew how to guide and deliver accurate and comprehensible information. (On the other hand, if the Wrights had employed this kind of expert, they would have received a deluge of demands on their time that would have greatly hindered their further research.)

all this, but their airplane was still just barely marginal in its design, and it was hardly able to sustain itself in any kind of adverse conditions.

As important, they themselves still had had very little experience in powered flight and were much too shaky and uneven in their flight procedures. From the standpoint of modern training and modern machinery, *they were at all times on the critical edge of disaster.* Their forward elevator had saved their lives, and they had also managed to acquire a minimum number of skills, which, coupled with their share of good fortune, had kept them from being killed. At the end of 1903, their flight time of less than two hours each in the air was the total of bits and snatches, spread over four years! They were still very much in the class of the shaky novice, where piloting was concerned, and the air itself was filled with invisible forces, that could cause them to lose control and be dashed to the ground.

Beginning in 1904, the Wrights concentrated on improving their aircraft and its controllability. They realized that annual return trips to Kitty Hawk for every flight test would cost too much in time, effort, and money, and that they must find a local place for their experiments. Orville, especially, believed that their aircraft could easily handle flying in Ohio. In a letter of January 7, 1904, to George Spratt, Orville wrote, in connection with the flights at Kitty Hawk: ". . . That we had quite a surplus of power was shown by the fact that on leaving the rail we could rise 8 or 10 feet in going forward about 50 feet. Of course this really amounted to about 150 feet through the air . . ."

Orville also revealed something of their attitude toward capitalizing on their efforts: ". . . Since our return we have been receiving daily offers of stocking our company for us from some of these professional promoters, who would like to get the chance to swindle some of the people who think there is an immense fortune in the flying machine. Even our friend Herring has made us a very generous offer, a copy of which I am making for your amusement . . ."

Augustus Herring, confirming the Wrights' earlier opinion of him, had suddenly discovered that it was truly he, and no one else, who had perfected the first airplane, and, in a gesture of overwhelming largesse, had offered to set up a company in which he, Orville, and Wilbur would have equal shares. Wilbur wrote the next day to Chanute: "A copy is . . . enclosed of a letter received a few days ago from Mr. Herring. This time he surprised us. Before he left camp in 1902 we foresaw and predicted the object of his visit to Washington; we also felt certain that he was making a frenzied attempt to mount a motor on a copy of our 1902 glider and thus anticipate us, even before you told us of it last fall. But that he would have the effrontery to write us such a letter, after his other schemes of rascality had failed, was really a little more than we expected . . ."

Before writing these letters to Spratt and Chanute, Orville and Wilbur had come to a decision regarding the press. They knew that their machine had potent military implications, even if, at this point, their grasp of its military application was hazy. Indeed, their discussions of the subject were limited to the enormous value such a machine would have in allowing one side to detect the movement and location of enemy forces, thereby bringing about a situation where continued wars would be folly. They did realize that an enormous financial return might be possible, and they were fully determined to control the information dispensed about their machine and their work.

They had therefore issued the following statement to the Associated Press on January 5:

It had not been our intention to make any detailed public statement concerning the private trials of our power "Flyer" on the 17th of December last; but since the contents of a private telegram, announcing to our folks at home the success of our trials, was dishonestly communicated to the newspapermen at the Norfolk office, and led to the imposition upon the public, by persons who never saw the "Flyer" or its flights, of a fictitious story incorrect in almost every detail; and since this story together with several pretended interviews or statements, which were fakes pure and simple, have been very widely disseminated, we feel impelled to make some correction. The real facts were as follows:

. . . On the morning of December 17th, between the hours of 10:30 o'clock and noon, four flights were made, two by Orville Wright and two by Wilbur Wright. The

starts were all made from a point on the level sand about
two hundred feet west of our camp, which is located a
quarter of a mile north of the Kill Devil sand hill, in Dare
County, North Carolina. The wind at the time of the
flights had a velocity of 27 miles an hour at ten o'clock,
and 24 miles an hour at noon, as recorded by the anemometer at the Kitty Hawk Weather Bureau Station . . ."

The Wrights went on to report how they felt about the nature
of their flights, what they meant, how they were carried out, the
actual distances flown, and the difficulties in conducting these
flights against the kind of wind encountered; in essence, they
made it clear how far the development of the flying machine had
progressed. Then came their final paragraph:

From the beginning we have employed entirely new principles of control; and as all the experiments have been
conducted at our own expense without assistance from
any individual or institution, we do not feel ready at
present to give out any pictures or detailed descriptions
of the machine.

The Associated Press, which only shortly before had trumpeted
its sensational story of "two six-bladed propellers" and a "navi-
gator's car" and the rest of its incorrect trappings, sent out the
Wrights' statement — but without the first paragraph, the one
that told of the fictitious stories and fake interviews carried by
the newspapers.

To Orville and Wilbur this was one more example of deceit. It
was clear that the press would continue to protect its own; and
their statement was to a large extent ignored. So much misinformation by this time had been published, there had been so
much ridicule and distortion, that the real truth, as the Wrights
knew it, received little attention.

On February 5, 1904, Wilbur was moved to write as follows to
the editor of the *Independent*:

My attention has this day been called to a case of most
unmitigated impudence in the *Independent* of February
4. On page 242 an article was published under my name

which I did not write and which I had never seen. The bulk of the article consisted of carelessly arranged or garbled extracts from two addresses, which I delivered before the Western Society of Engineers, and which were published in the *Journal* of that Society in the issues of December, 1901, and August, 1903. Following this came extracts from two press dispatches which appeared in the daily papers of December 19, 1903, and January 7, 1904. A few sentences from a strange source were interpolated, in which an attempt was made to describe the methods by which the power machine was sustained and propelled. This part was entirely fanciful and untrue. The pictures which accompanied the article were not obtained from us, nor were they from any of our photographs.

I have never given to any person permission or encouragement to palm off as an original article extracts from these copyrighted addresses and newspaper dispatches. Neither have I given to the *Independent,* nor to any one, the least permission or excuse for using my name in the furtherance of such attempted fraud. Nor have I given the faintest permission to attach my name to any article of any kind in any paper, excepting the statement which my brother and I gave to the papers on January 6, 1904. Our attention had previously been called to cases in which conscienceless but enterprising reporters had utilized these addresses as mines from which to draw material for pretended interviews, but it remained for the *Independent* to serve them in the form of a forged signed article . . .

All the time the Wrights were wrestling with the press, they were finding other problems elsewhere. The brothers knew that they were in legal country, that there were patents to establish, and that they needed protection for the findings of their research. Applying for patents on their machine and its control system on their own met with little success. At last they faced the facts of life, and secured the services of a recommended patent attorney to protect their inventions.

Now, free to continue their work, they began a new program of hard research and development. They had flown — proof lay behind them. They knew, however, that their machine needed much work. It was not equipped to handle certain problems in the air; it was oversensitive in control; it needed more power. It needed a complete redesign to enhance its overall performance and render it more reliable. The Wrights also hoped to explore some of the possible avenues of application. One of their first steps was to abandon their first powered airplane. The *Kitty Hawk Flyer*, which had made five flights (one on December 14 and four on December 17), was never rebuilt for test purposes. In January 1904, within a month of their first flights on the Carolina banks, they began construction of a new machine, which would be larger, heavier, more powerful, and capable of improved performance. At the same time they set about finding a new location for the continuation of their flying activities. Torrence Huffman, president of the Fourth National Bank of Dayton, offered them the use of a pasture on his farmland, known as Huffman Prairie, located eight miles outside of the city. They set up a shed on this property near Simms Station, a stop on the interurban trolley that ran hourly between Dayton and Springfield, Ohio.

Bordered by trees, poles, and power lines, and with livestock wandering about, the field, approximately 100 acres, turned over to the Wrights was less than perfect, but Huffman gave it to them without charge, and they did not complain of gifts. Wilbur later wrote to Chanute that

> . . . we must learn to accommodate ourselves to circumstances. At Kitty Hawk we had unlimited space and wind enough to make starting easy with a short track. If the wind was very light we could utilize the hills if necessary in getting the initial velocity. Here we must depend on a long track, and light winds or even dead calms. We are in a large meadow . . . skirted on the west and north by trees. This not only shuts off the wind somewhat but also probably gives a slight downtrend . . . The greater troubles are . . . that in addition to cattle there have been a dozen or more horses in the pasture and as it is surrounded by barbwire fencing we have been at much trouble to get them safely away before making trials. Also the ground is an old swamp and is filled with grassy hummocks some six inches high so that it resembles a

prairie-dog town. This makes the tracklaying slow work. While we are getting ready the favorable opportunities slip away, and we are usually up against a rainstorm, a dead calm, or a wind blowing at right angles to the track.

By the middle of April, the Wrights had completed their workshed, and the new airplane was nearly ready for testing.

CHAPTER 22

"We Certainly Have Been 'Jonahed' This Year"

THE MACHINE the Wrights built for their flight tests in 1904 at Huffman Prairie was to be stronger, heavier, more powerful, and faster than the *Kitty Hawk Flyer*, and its potential for greater performance excited Orville and Wilbur. "We are hard at work getting ready for spring," Wilbur wrote to Chanute on March 14, 1904. "The new machines will be of the same size as the old one but will weigh a little more, 800 lbs. probably. By gearing the engine to run a little faster we will not only carry the additional weight but will have enough surplus to increase the speed to about 40 miles an hour."

The *Wright Flyer II*, as it was called, had a modified wing for greater speed; it was now cambered to 1-in-25 instead of 1-in-20, and the engine delivered 15 to 16 horsepower, the exact output depending on many small modifications that could be made. The pilot of the *Flyer II* still lay prone, and the wing warp and rudder controls were still linked. Because the wind conditions at Simms Station were different from those at Kitty Hawk, the brothers reckoned that they might increase the length of their launching track, the "Junction Railroad," from 60 to 160 feet.

There was only one thing wrong with the flight tests that began in May of 1904: *Flyer II* wouldn't fly.

In the words of Orville:

> When it [the machine] was ready for its first trial, every newspaper in Dayton was notified, and about a dozen

representatives of the press were present. Our only request was that no pictures be taken, and that the reports be unsensational, so as not to attract crowds to our experiment-grounds. There were probably fifty persons altogether on the ground. When preparations had been completed, a wind of only three or four miles [an hour] was blowing — insufficient for starting on so short a track — but since many had come a long way to see the machine in action, an attempt was made. To add to the other difficulty, the engine refused to work properly. The machine, after running the length of the track, slid off the end without rising into the air at all. Several of the newspaper men returned the next day [actually, on May 26], but were again disappointed. The engine performed badly, and after a glide of only sixty feet, the machine came to the ground. Further trial was postponed till the motor could be put in better running condition. The reporters had now, no doubt, lost confidence in the machine, though their reports, in kindness, concealed it. Later, when they heard we were making flights of several minutes' duration, knowing that longer flights had been made with air-ships, and not knowing any essential difference between air-ships and flying-machines, they were but little interested . . .

In their first dozen takeoffs in 1904 they managed only once — out of all their attempts — to achieve a distance of 300 feet. They had calculated that they needed a wind of at least 12 miles an hour to become airborne with the 160-foot track, but that meant rearranging the track whenever the wind shifted, so that they could make their takeoff into the wind. They made so many wild launches from their rail system, the airplane sliding or skidding out of control immediately after takeoff, that they began to amass an alarming number of accidents and broken parts. They would set up the *Flyer II* on its rails, everything ready to go, and wait, looking at distant trees, high grass, and smoke to tell them when a wind was coming. Then one of the brothers, by prearrangement, would climb quickly to the controls, the other would start the engine, and they would wait for the wind to reach them and would launch hastily, almost frantically, into it.

One such launch almost killed Orville. A sudden blow they had been waiting for approached, and they fired up the engine and started the *Flyer II* down its track. Orville rose swiftly, and almost at once the wind was gone; the becalmed airplane, propellers thrashing, fell to the ground. The impact hurled Orville off the wing, a main spar cracked, and the wing collapsed atop the helpless pilot. Had not the upper spar broken precisely where it did, it is likely that Orville would have suffered a serious injury.

To understand what was happening, we must return to December 17, 1903, when the brothers made their first successful powered flights, and consider the weather conditions: water had frozen during the night of the 16th and they had awoken to ice all around them.

According to the Kitty Hawk weather report, signed by J. J. Dosher, the temperature at the time of their flight was approximately 34 degrees. They were at sea level, there was a 27-mile-an-hour wind, and the air was clear and dry; in effect, the air was thick, and gave all the airfoils that bit into it — the propellers as well as the wings — much more efficiency. These were prime flying conditions.

At Huffman Prairie, on May 23, 1904 — the day they made their first attempt to fly in front of the press — the temperatures reached 81 degrees in the early afternoon. Huffman Prairie is 815 feet above sea level, and there was high humidity (66 percent). All these factors combined to produce the opposite effect — air that did a poor job of supporting their *Flyer*, and in which even the engine worked with less efficiency and put out less power.

The support qualities of the air for sustaining flight — the combined effect of these ingredients — have come to be known as "density altitude."

A high density altitude drastically robs an airplane of its ability to perform, and the Wrights had an aircraft of marginal performance at best; to get into the air, it needed everything it had. Between the two sets of conditions present at Kitty Hawk on December 17, 1903, and at Simms Station in late May 1904, there was a density altitude differential of about 4700 feet!

The brothers had also consistently reported trouble in getting

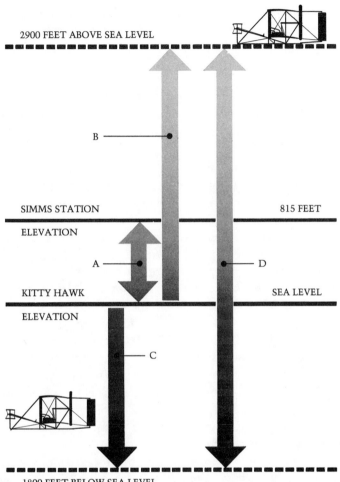

2900 FEET ABOVE SEA LEVEL

B

SIMMS STATION   815 FEET

ELEVATION

A   D

KITTY HAWK   SEA LEVEL

ELEVATION

C

1800 FEET BELOW SEA LEVEL

Why at first the 1904 *Flyer* failed to fly: The diagram above shows the relative elevation of Kitty Hawk (sea level) and Simms Station (815 feet), where the normal density altitude difference on a standard day is 815 feet (A). On May 23, 1904, the temperature at Simms Station was 81° F., resulting in a density altitude of 2900 feet above sea level (B). This compares with Kitty Hawk's temperature of 34° F. at first flight time on December 17, 1903, which produced a density altitude of 1800 feet *below* sea level (C). Because of these temperature extremes, the density altitude differential between the two takeoff points was approximately 4700 feet (D). This is a principal reason the Wrights failed to fly successfully in Ohio until they constructed a starting or launching mechanism, consisting of a catapult, which they first used in September 1904.

the engine to fire on all cylinders, so it was obviously not developing its full horsepower. In addition to that, they had changed the wing camber from 1-in-20 to 1-in-25, reducing the curvature and thus reducing the lift. This combination had a deadly effect on performance.

Still another important condition existed at Simms Station on that unpleasant day, May 23, 1904. It was the problem of acceleration, whose solution in one form or another was absolutely essential for flight.

Any airplane with a given amount of power converted to thrust will accelerate at a given rate until the drag of the air on the airframe is equal to the thrust. The greater the power an airplane has, the greater the acceleration.

If there had been no wind blowing at Kitty Hawk, the Wrights' 12-horsepower engine would have required a track 755 feet long in order to get the aircraft to accelerate to its flying speed of about 30 miles an hour. On their 60-foot track, with no wind, the craft would have needed an engine of 120 horsepower — 10 times the power they had — to get sufficient acceleration to take off. Fortunately, on December 17, 1903, the wind blew at 27 miles per hour. Although the brothers were apprehensive about controlling the aircraft in this much wind, it was the wind that had saved the day. Against that 27-mile-per-hour wind, the airplane needed an acceleration of only 3 miles an hour to gain a flying speed of 30 miles an hour, and consequently, only 40 feet of the 60-foot track was needed for takeoff.

These were the real reasons (which the Wrights only partially understood) that the *Flyer* did not fly satisfactorily in those early attempts during the late spring and summer of 1904 — and not, as some have held, because of some scheme of the Wrights to fabricate a series of failures in order to deceive the press.

The abortive attempt to fly before the press on that afternoon of May 23, the many other unsuccessful attempts in June and July, and their ignorance of what was causing their difficulty, must have made the summer of 1904 a nightmare to the Wrights. Time after time, to the brothers' great irritation and puzzlement, the *Flyer* either failed to rise from the track or settled quickly to the ground, unable to maintain flying speed.

On June 14, Wilbur wrote to Chanute, "We certainly have been 'Jonahed' this year." Then, on June 21, he wrote that "Kitty Hawk grounds possess advantages not found at our present location." He complained of lack of wind and of the engine not delivering full power, but he unwittingly gave a clue to the problems, which neither he nor Orville completely understood. Speaking of one of their trial flights, he continued, "On this one Orville almost got away, but after about 200 ft. he allowed the machine to turn up a little too much and it stalled." *

Finally, toward the end of the summer, the brothers realized that they needed some assistance in accelerating the machine for takeoff. In typically imaginative fashion, they devised a catapult, which they would continue to use for some years. They built a tower, rather like a small derrick, that would stand behind the *Flyer*, with a system of pulleys that raised a weight, first 800 pounds and later increased by stages to 1600. A line of people pulling on a long rope would raise the weight to the top of the tower, cocking the catapult. The rope, passing under the track to the far end and through a pulley, ran back to the *Flyer*, where it was hooked to an automatic release mechanism.

When they were ready to start, they would pull a cord that released the weight, which fell and snapped the *Flyer* forward.

The device was first tried on September 7, 1904, and gave the airplane enough acceleration to get it airborne. After that, flights in the cooling autumn air became longer and more satisfactory. By October, the temperature of the air had become low enough so that density altitude was no longer an important factor. The catapult overcame the other deficiency of acceleration, and the brothers again began breaking records.

Now they were able to fly with some degree of success. There were 105 flights made in 1904, almost all short flights, but the longest, on December 1, lasted for five minutes and eight seconds and covered a distance of 4515 meters, or about three miles. During this flight Orville circled Huffman Prairie two and a quarter times. Earlier in the year — September 20, in fact — they

---

* This is the first time the brothers used the term *stall*, now so familiar to airmen.

were able to fly in a complete circle from takeoff to landing. The
brothers were making true progress.*

For the year 1904 their total flight time came to 45 minutes,
and the experience they had gained brought them to believe the
time had come for them to reap whatever reward they could
obtain from their invention. Deciding first to offer their airplane
to the United States Government, they wrote to Robert Nevin,
their congressman, on January 18, 1905, summarizing their accomplishments of the previous year:

> The series of aeronautical experiments upon which we
> have been engaged for the past five years has ended in the
> production of a flying-machine of the type fitted for prac-
> tical use. It not only flies through the air at high speed,
> but it also lands without being wrecked. During the year
> 1904 one hundred and five flights were made at our ex-
> perimenting station, on the Huffman prairie, east of the
> city; and though our experience in handling the machine
> has been too short to give any high degree of skill, we
> nevertheless succeeded, toward the end of the season, in
> making two flights of five minutes each, in which we
> sailed round and round the field until a distance of about
> three miles had been covered, at a speed of thirty-five
> miles an hour. The first of these record flights was made
> on November 9th, in celebration of the phenomenal po-
> litical victory of the preceding day, and the second, on
> December 1st, in honor of the one hundredth flight of
> the season.
> The numerous flights in straight lines, in circles, and
> over "S"-shaped courses, in calms and in winds, have
> made it quite certain that flying has been brought to a
> point where it can be made of great practical use in var-
> ious ways, one of which is that of scouting and carrying
> messages in time of war. If the latter features are of
> interest to our own government, we shall be pleased to

* The first eyewitness account of a powered airplane flight in history was written
by Amos I. Root and published in *Gleanings in Bee Culture,* January 1, 1905.
Root reported on the flights of September 20, 1904, when an airplane made a
complete circle for the first time. Two weeks later, in the magazine's January 15
issue, Root wrote a detailed description of the Wright plane, closing his story
with some sage advice: "No drinking man should ever be allowed to undertake
to run a flying machine."

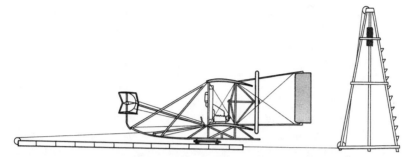

Takeoff assistance: This sketch shows arrangement of the unique weight-and-derrick launching device first used in September 1904. Subsequent tower sizes, drop weights, and rail lengths varied somewhat. When the weight dropped, the machine was pulled rapidly along its rail, and, as it neared the end, the pilot raised the nose. At that instant the rope released itself and the airplane took off.

take up the matter either on a basis of providing machines of agreed specification, at a contract price, or of furnishing all the scientific and practical information we have accumulated in these years of experimenting, together with a license to use our patents; thus putting the government in a position to operate on its own account.

If you can find it convenient to ascertain whether this is a subject of interest to our own government, it would oblige us greatly, as early information on this point will aid us in making our plans for the future . . .

Congressman Nevin brought the matter to the War Department's Board of Ordnance and Fortification and received a letter signed by Major General G. S. Gillespie:

I have the honor to inform you that, as many requests have been made for financial assistance in the development of designs for flying-machines, the Board has found it necessary to decline to make allotments for the experimental development of devices for mechanical flight, and has determined that, before suggestions with that object in view will be considered, the device must have been brought to the stage of practical operation without expense to the United States.

It appears from the letter of Messrs. Wilbur and Orville Wright that their machine has not yet been brought to the stage of practical operation, but as soon as it shall have been perfected, this Board would be pleased to receive further representations from them in regard to it.

The men on this board simply did not understand the stage to which the Wrights had brought their machine. The Wrights were unable to explain this, and felt that they had definitely been turned down, so they began looking elsewhere. France, England, and Germany looked like possible markets. In fact, they had already applied for French and German patents on their airplane — in March of 1904! (France granted them a patent on July 1, 1904.)

It should be noted here that the Wrights in 1904 and 1905 were actively promoting their invention as well as developing it. Despite the lack of widespread publicity about their success at Kitty Hawk, they had sparked more than a passing interest within official circles abroad, if not at home. In October 1904, Lieutenant Colonel John E. Capper visited the brothers in Dayton on behalf of the British government. (In 1905 the British War Office indicated a definite interest in seeing the Wright machine fly.) And in December of 1905 the Wrights signed an optional contract with Arnold Fordyce, representing a French syndicate that included Captain Louis Ferdinand Ferber, the artillery officer who had been experimenting with gliders of both the Lilienthal and Wright types, and Henri Letellier, owner and publisher of the French newspaper Le Journal. The contract called for the delivery of one flying machine at a cost of one million francs ($200,000) for use by the French army. Interestingly, only a few weeks earlier, Frank S. Lahm, an American businessman residing in Paris, received details of the Wright flights from his brother-in-law, Henry M. Weaver of Mansfield, Ohio. Lahm, a balloonist and member of the Aéro-Club de France, was also the father of Lieutenant Frank P. Lahm, who in 1906 won the first International Balloon Race in France and two years later — with Orville as pilot — became the first U.S. Army officer to fly in a heavier-than-air machine.

The following spring, 1906, a French commission composed of Fordyce, Commander Henri Bonel, Captain Henry J. Régnier,

Captain Jules H. F. Fournier, and the American attorney Walter V. R. Berry met with the Wrights in Dayton for the purpose of negotiating certain changes in the contract signed by Fordyce. But the parties failed to reach agreement, and the option lapsed.

Meanwhile, when Octave Chanute learned that the U.S. Army had rejected the Wright proposal, he strongly urged the brothers not to sell airplanes to foreign powers until every possible avenue for some sort of agreement with their own government had been thoroughly explored and exhausted.

All during the spring, summer, and early fall of 1905, the brothers continued their construction changes and experiments. They had improved upon their engine, propellers, controls, and response in the air to such an extent that British historians, who certainly occupied an unbiased position, later referred to the 1905 Wright machine as the "first practical airplane in the world." They considered this machine, with its improvements, as important an achievement as the first *Kitty Hawk Flyer* of 1903.

Many of these changes showed little to the eye, for structural strength had become increasingly dominant in planning by the brothers. The 1905 machine was stronger than its predecessors in almost all ways — it had greater operating load capacity, could withstand the shock of air turbulence, endure "G" loads imposed by flight, and survive harsh contact with the ground. It demonstrated field service capability, withstood the wear and tear of daily operation and like an obedient charger, accepted gracefully, almost thankfully, the constant improvements the brothers molded into it with loving, capable hands.

The tail was longer in its reach from the main structure to increase directional stability and control; the wing possessed a more effective leading edge, and a new engine of larger cylinder bore delivered up to 25 horsepower (thereby more than doubling the power available at Kitty Hawk). The brothers were after longer flight times: if they were to follow their program of safety, remaining basically within their planned flight area, this meant performing wide turns instead of flying straight and level across the countryside. It is much easier to do the latter, for flying in circles means steeper and more demanding maneuvers that impose greater loads on machine and pilot. Under these conditions basic problems and deficiencies emerge from the cocoon of gentle flight, and become very obvious indeed.

One example will suffice; it also shows how surely and swiftly the Wrights solved each new difficulty. Previously they had modified their propeller blades to be wider and thinner than those of the 1903 *Flyer*. Efficiency went up, but the brothers also noticed a failure of the new propeller blades to perform in accordance with their calculations.

The Wrights placed great store in their theoretical work; failure to realize performance in flight as forecast in their laboratory was most disturbing to them. They guessed quickly that a new element affected the propellers — perhaps under the pressures of actual flight, the blades twisted away from their shape at rest. To test this theory, they attached to each blade a small surface (they called them "Little Jokers"), much like a miniature elevator, that extended at an angle and distance that should cure the suspected tendency of the blades to twist in flight.

Experiments in the air confirmed their new theory and their ingenious "fix." With the mystery removed, they again changed the propeller design, eliminating the "Little Jokers" and adding a backward sweep to the blades, calculated precisely to avoid the pressures of flight and to keep the blades free from distortion. The entire program was in fact extremely complicated; it was beyond the understanding or capacity of any other aspiring pilots or scientists anywhere in the world, who had yet even to match the efficiency of the *first* propellers produced by the brothers. Yet the only reference to this problem found in historical texts, is often limited to a description of the 1905 machine as having "bent end" propellers installed.

The pilot-operator of the 1905 *Flyer* still used the hip cradle control system. He still lay prone on the lower wing, and it was the very success of the 1905 flights that was soon to bring on the demise of this never really acceptable pilot position. It had been created by the need to reduce frontal air resistance to its absolute minimum in the gliders and the earlier low-powered *Flyers*, and for this reason was retained in the 1905 model.

Simms Station in the early months of 1905 was no place for a fledgling aircraft, with its storms, howling winds, ice, snow, and fields sodden from spring rains and the melt of accumulated slush. Not until June 23, 1905, did the Wrights take to the air again from their Ohio field, and this was for a flight of just under ten seconds, a starkly inauspicious beginning for what would follow.

In fact, none of the first ten flights of 1905 exceeded the fourth flight at Kitty Hawk in 1903. The maximum distance achieved was 750 feet, and during these tests the brothers again and again smacked into the ground with severe force. "We have made several changes in the operating handles," Wilbur wrote Chanute in July, "and have had some trouble instantly acquiring familiarity with them. We are sure they will be a good thing when we have learned the combination properly, but they have cost us several rather unlucky breakages, aggregating several weeks of delay."

Heavy rains also delayed them. Flying from a marshy bog was simply not the way to go. Then it was August and the subtle changes became blazing advances. On the first flight of August 24, Orville covered a distance over the ground of 1556 feet in just under 32 seconds. Later that day Wilbur flew a ground distance of nearly 2300 feet. Four days later he increased the distance to 2775 feet, and in a later flight, also on the 28th, he managed a distance over the ground of 4257 feet in 79 seconds. He was getting closer and closer to the coveted one mile of flight.

It came to the brothers on September 6th. Orville made a "first flight of the day" test and remained airborne for just over 40 seconds, to cover a distance of just over 2000 feet. On his second flight he remained aloft for an astounding time — just six seconds short of *five minutes* — and circled the airfield four times, landing at the starting point, after flying a distance over the ground of 15,609 feet!

Three miles in the air!

The next day Orville flew several times and virtually completed his record-breaking flight of the 6th — and in the process, as Wilbur related with dry humor: "Four complete circles. Twice passed over fence into Beard's cornfield. Chased flocks of birds on two rounds and killed one which fell on top of upper surface and after a time fell off when swinging a sharp curve."

September 26: Wilbur flew for more than 18 minutes and, during his circling the field 16 times, covered a distance of more than 11 miles. The flight ended only when the *Flyer* ran out of fuel.

September 29: Orville flew for four seconds short of 20 minutes and covered a distance of 12 miles — again ending what could have been a much longer flight if he had not run out of fuel.

October 3: Orville covered more than 15 miles in just over 26 minutes, 11 seconds.

October 4: Orville extended the duration to 33 minutes, 17 seconds, and flew a distance of 20.7 miles.

October 5: Wilbur carried off the best flight of the year. He was aloft for 39 minutes and 23 seconds for a distance of 24.2 miles, during which he averaged 38 miles an hour and circled the field for 29 complete rounds! *This one flight alone covered more distance and time than the total of all the flights made throughout 1903 and 1904.*

This was spectacular, but of far greater import to those who understood flight (precious few at the time) was that the Wrights had separated their joint control system. They now had separate pitch, roll, and yaw controls — and the first fully controllable airplane ever built. And that would have more impact on flight than simply collecting time in the air and distance over the ground.

The next day Wilbur would make one more flight, and when it ended, the brothers entered into a period that today we must regard as bordering on the tragic. For it was then that the Wrights made a definite decision to embark on a course that many consider to have been detrimental to the continuing development of aviation, not only at that time, but for several years to come. Wilbur wrote to Chanute: "Some friends whom we unwisely permitted to witness some of the flights could not keep silent, and on the evening of the 5th the *Daily News* had an article reporting that we were making sensational flights everyday. It was copied in the Cincinnati *Post* of the next day. Consequently we are doing nothing at present, but before the season closes we wish to go out someday and make an effort to put the record above one hour. If you wish we will try to give you notice in time for you to be present . . ." But at the beginning of November 1905, a great storm moved into the area. High winds and thun-

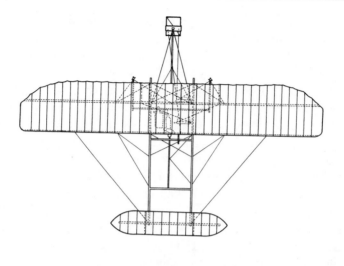

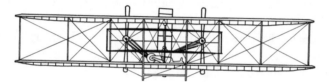

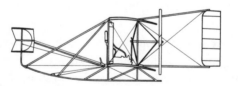

Wright 1905 machine: Span — 40 feet, 6 inches; chord — 6 feet, 6 inches; gap — 5 feet, 11¼ inches; camber — 1-in-20; wing area — 503 square feet; horizontal rudder (elevator) area — 83 square feet; vertical rudder area — 34.8 square feet; length — 28 feet; height — 9 feet, 5⅛ inches; weight — 710 pounds. The motor, propellers, and other parts of the Wrights' second engine-driven machine, built in 1904, were used in constructing *Flyer III* in 1905, a model generally referred to as the first practical powered airplane in history. Its final flight in this configuration was on October 5 — 24 and ⅕ miles in 39 minutes, 23 seconds, including about 30 circles of the Simms Station field.

dering rain for days on end prevented the record-breaking flight from being attempted.

By the end of 1905 the Wrights had decided to end their flying. Stung by the press, angered by their own government's rejection, convinced that almost everyone with whom they came in contact was out to exploit their work and to cheat them, the brothers, in effect, went underground. Flight was their secret, and they were going to guard it to the utmost. If they continued to fly, they would only expose the details of their machines, and the newspapers would be ever more watchful. No matter that the great bulk of the press remained skeptical and scornful; they could make every attempt to take pictures and thus expose the *details* of their machine. The Wrights did not believe that what they had already accomplished, even though it could be patented, was enough protection for their interests.

The overwhelming later disbelief in Europe about the Wright airplanes stemmed largely from the fact that their flights in 1904 and 1905 in their own community went, for the most part, unreported; certainly reports of these flights were not widely disseminated beyond the Dayton area.

There were some who would later insist that the Wright brothers rigged these tests so that the machines could not fly! They insisted that the engine problems were faked and that the takeoff run was deliberately shortened. Some suggested that the elevator was being used to cause an immediate stall.

Dan Kumler, city editor of the *Daily News* in Dayton at the time of the flights, recalled in a 1940 interview (as told in Kelly's biography) that many people who had been on interurban cars passing the Huffman field, and had seen the Wrights in the air, used to come to the *Daily News* office to inquire why there was nothing in the paper about the flights.

That is hardly in agreement with the statements made by some writers that, until two days before the flights were ended in October 1905, they were never seen by anyone in the area! Indeed, there were so *many* eyewitnesses calling the newspaper that, according to Kumler, they got to be a nuisance. Asked why nothing had been printed in his paper after so many people demanded to know about the flights, Kumler responded: "We just didn't believe it. Of course you remember that the Wrights at that time were terribly secretive."

The interviewer, in open disbelief, asked Kumler the inevitable question: "You mean they were secretive about the fact that they were flying over an open field?"

Kumler pondered the question, a grin came slowly to his face, and then he said, "I guess, the truth is that we were just plain dumb."

Was Kumler the only editor with knowledge of the flights? Even the owner of the paper, James M. Cox, admitted that "none of us believed the reports" of the Wrights' flying.

The managing editor of the Dayton *Journal*, Luther Beard, knew Orville Wright, and one day asked him outright if he and his brother were actually flying. In fact, the question was asked on the trolley returning from Simms Station, because, although Beard did not believe the story of the flights, he had been told by a number of children that *they* personally had seen the flights. He asked Orville if it was true, and Orville allowed as to how it was so. Still later, on another occasion, Beard asked Orville, "Done anything of special interest lately?"

The reply: "Oh, nothing much. Today one of us flew for nearly five minutes."

Beard wanted to know where they went on such a journey.

"Around the field."

And it was Beard's decision that this didn't rate even a mention in his paper. After all, Santos-Dumont had already flown over Paris and circled the Eiffel Tower, and *that* was *news*. Obviously, Beard and other editors had no conception of the difference between a heavier-than-air machine and a primitive gas-bag with rudimentary directional control.

In any case, from November 1905 until May 1908 the Wright brothers were so adamant in their distrust of individuals, groups, and governments, that they stopped all flying and never left the ground for the entire period — as we shall see, nearly a catastrophic decision.

An incident at Simms Station in the fall of 1905 had been the crowning blow. They observed two men stalking the pasture adjacent to their workshed. Thinking first that they were hunters, they paid no attention. Then they realized there was very little to hunt. The men's actions were even a little strange when they came up to the shed: they did not introduce themselves, but asked if it was all right to look around. Since there was no more sneaking about, the Wrights agreed, and the men were told, "Go right ahead, but please don't take any pictures."

One man, carrying a camera, laid it down and ran to the shed. He was amazingly knowledgeable about their aircraft and called every part of the machine by its correct name. Obviously, this was no newsman. It was not until later that the Wrights learned his identity — he was chief engineer for Langley of the Smithsonian Institution! To the Wrights, the man's deviousness in not identifying himself was the worst kind of deceit, and the episode confirmed their decision to institute tight security around everything they did.

On October 19, 1905, at the continued urging of Octave Chanute, the Wrights wrote a third letter to the War Department, in an attempt to wake the sleeping giant. "We have no thought of asking financial assistance from the government," they began. "We propose to sell the results of experiments finished at our own expense." (On the same day, the brothers wrote to the British War Office, renewing their proposition to furnish a flying machine for scouting purposes; they also sent word to Captain Ferber, reporting that they were now prepared to supply a powered airplane capable of flying at least 40 kilometers.)

At its meeting of October 24, 1905, the Board of Ordnance and Fortification acknowledged receipt of the letter from the Wrights, who had also requested the government to define the requirements that a flying machine must meet before its acceptance. The board still held the Wrights and their claims in open disdain, and said they had no intention of formulating any specifications for the performance of the flying machine. They would not take any further action on the subject "until a machine is produced which by actual operation is shown to be able to produce horizontal flight and to carry an operator."

Two weeks before, the Wrights had flown over 24 miles in a single flight. Alas! The military mind!

Now, by remaining behind their wall of silence and secrecy, known only by a trickle of information from such men as Chanute, or others who had seen them fly, the Wrights condemned themselves to steady criticism. People who were interested in what they had accomplished and tried to unearth details, only to be rebuffed by the brothers, concluded that the Wrights were unable to perform what they claimed. And if the Wrights were telling the truth, then their having erected a wall around themselves would work only to the benefit of other individuals and governments, for their refusal to fly gave the others the time they needed to work on flying machines.

During this bleak interval, other inventors of lesser capability, who copied and plagiarized all they could learn about what the Wrights had done, were moving into the limelight with much shouting and fanfare.

The next two and a half years were grueling for the Wright brothers. It is a dreary picture that we have of these two proud and sensitive men, of great integrity and innovative capacity, but with stubborn minds and undemonstrative characters, rejected by their own government, wandering part of the time around Europe and being exposed to political intrigue, graft, doubts, misrepresentations — all that the international financial world offers up. The Wrights, of course, were not without their true friends and powerful supporters; through connections with some American financiers they retained Hart O. Berg, an associate of Charles Flint and Company, as their agent in France. This was the opening move in two years of negotiations with France and other foreign governments, as well as with private interests.

It must be emphasized that during this time, although they still refused to show any of their machinery or equipment, and still refused to fly, the Wrights were far from idle in their research and development. They considered their 1905 *Flyer* to be not only an excellent machine in terms of performance, but also one that was eminently practical and that would be able to fulfill the requirements of any contract they might sign.

Orville later (in 1908) summed it up when he stated, "A practical flyer having been finally realized, we spent the years 1906 and 1907 in constructing new machines and in business negotiations. It was not till May of this year that experiments were resumed at Kill Devil Hill, North Carolina . . ."

But that was only skimming the surface of the turbulent waters boiling beneath.

CHAPTER 23

"As You Rise, the Objects Become Clearer"

THE 1905 MACHINE went through a complete restructuring. The new vertical engine of 35 horsepower promised greater reliability and speed, and after flying 38 minutes in one flight and 35 in another, the brothers knew that long flights could not be made with the pilot remaining in the prone position. By the end of the 38-minute flight Wilbur's neck was so stiff, he could scarcely move his head.

They would have to arrange for upright seating and for double the space so that the craft could carry both pilot and passenger. If the aircraft was to be used for training, then the passenger would be a student, and the plane would require two sets of controls, which would add to the complications of construction. If the passenger was a military observer, he would need room for equipment as well as the flexibility to record information. These were some of the paramount considerations for the new machine, and the Wrights were in a somewhat difficult position. They sought contracts, promising they could deliver according to specification, but they absolutely refused to show any of their plans, or to demonstrate their aircraft, until they had in their hands a signed contract for purchase of the airplane they insisted they could deliver. In late 1905, Samuel Cabot of Boston, through Chanute, had offered to form a stock company through Lee, Higginson & Co., but was turned down by the Wrights.

On several occasions they were close to making business deals that would have been very profitable, but that required a slight break in their security wall. They would not budge from their position, and whenever the terms of a major business contract were at issue, the Wrights simply turned their backs on the deal. Quickly, those who dealt with the brothers learned that money itself was not the primary consideration.

In the spring of 1907, notwithstanding their inflexibility, it seemed that a contract would soon be coming, through a syndicate they were forming abroad. Wilbur sailed for Europe in May for a series of talks in London, Paris, and Berlin. Orville arrived in Paris in late July, and Charlie Taylor joined them in August. Also in July, the brothers had an airplane shipped to France, where it remained for more than a year — its crate sealed — on the docks of Le Havre. If they had flown that machine in 1907 in France, it would have been a sensation and would have earned the brothers the instant acclaim of all the world. For even as late as the spring of 1907, there had been only two flights made in Europe, both by Santos-Dumont — one in October and the second in November of 1906, the latter a spectacular giant hop of about 720 feet in a lumbering, unmaneuverable thing called the *14-bis*. This feat had commanded enormous attention all through Europe.

The potential contracts were battered and bruised by obstinacy on both sides — the Wrights, and the men and groups with whom they were dealing. The brothers seemed unable to come to an agreement with anyone, and even as they stumbled from one collapsing deal to another in Europe, back in the United States, through the continuing interest and efforts of Samuel Cabot and his brother Godfrey, the capabilities of the Wright's flying machine were brought directly to the attention of President Theodore Roosevelt, whom the Wright family especially admired.

Roosevelt studied the papers brought to him and in that same year (1907) passed them on to William Howard Taft, the Secretary of War. Once again the governmental wheels ground with agonizing slowness; not even the weight of the President could speed up the process. It would take the War Department's Board of Ordnance and Fortification two years to understand what the Wrights were proposing to the U.S. Government.

The Wrights' stubbornness might have lessened had they recognized the real dangers at hand. As they prowled the halls of business and finance, so others were prowling through their own secrets of flight and were stealing the brothers blind. These men were building new flying machines that, because of what the Wrights had done, had far greater chances of success than ever before. Chanute was aware of these machinations, and he implored the brothers to lower their demands, to make *some* kind of deal, even if it meant disclosing some of their secrets during contract negotiations.

Still, the Wrights remained unperturbed. That is, until the fall of 1907 and the spring of 1908, when other people began to make short flights and called the attention of the world to their deeds. Their flights were nothing like those of Orville and Wilbur. They weren't fully controlled nor were the craft as maneuverable as the Wrights', *but they were flights.* Not hops, not jumps, but flights. Crude flying — but it was enough. Voisin, Farman, and Delagrange in France, and Glenn Curtiss in the United States. Not only had the Wrights endangered the contracts they wanted so badly, but they were in jeopardy of losing the recognition they deserved as the first to fly. By this time most people scorned the claims of the Wrights. Then, in the early part of 1908, when it seemed history might just shrug off the brothers, their luck turned around. Both the French *and* the U.S. Army Signal Corps offered contracts — on the Wrights' terms.

On February 8, 1908, the brothers received the Signal Corps contract. Six weeks later, on March 23, they had in hand the contract with Lazare Weiller, a wealthy Frenchman, to form a syndicate that would control the rights to build, sell, or license the use of the Wright airplane in France. The French company would be known as La Compagnie Générale de Navigation Aérienne. A member of the syndicate was Henri Deutsch de la Meurthe, who had made an effort to organize a French company sometime previously. The new company included Hart O. Berg, Charles R. Flint, and other financiers and businessmen. Both contracts were drawn up as the Wrights had demanded originally: their machine would remain hidden until the Wrights released it.

But it was a Pyrrhic victory. They did not receive anything even remotely close to the million francs they had originally intended to secure for their flying machine, and they had lost two and a half years of flight-testing by not flying — during which time they steadily yielded their great lead over the rest of the world competitors in flying.

The news that F. W. Baldwin had flown the *Red Wing* in March of 1908, and Curtiss the *June Bug* in June, at Hammondsport, New York, arrived four and a half years after the Wrights first flew at Kitty Hawk. They themselves had not flown since October 1905, and the intervening time had been disastrous to their strength and confidence in managing their own affairs and in controlling their future. No matter that Wilbur wrote to Chanute, "We don't feel that anyone will come up with anything like the capability of our Flyer for at least five more years." Wilbur simply could not recognize that once men knew that other men had flown — that it could damned well be done again because there wasn't any doubt about its being possible — then people would throw themselves into an extra effort to join them. Neither was Wilbur aware of the extent to which these new aeronauts were taking advantage of what he and Orville had done.

Besides giving the Wrights a great deal of encouragement and valuable counsel, Chanute had also made a significant contribution to the *Flyer*'s basic design. His experience in bridge construction produced the original truss arrangement for the biplane configuration, which the brothers had adapted for their machine. But Chanute, as we know, had leaked great amounts of vital information to aeronautical groups all through the United States and Europe. In fact, Chanute's generous dispensing of information had revitalized moribund hopes in Europe for heavier-than-air flight. And historians can trace easily to Chanute himself, addressing the Aéro-Club de France in Paris in the summer of 1903, the reams of information on the details and capacity of the Wright gliders that served as the catalyst to get Europeans turning once more to the skies.

The news of the flights at Kitty Hawk provided, as suggested, an additional spark to European interest. No matter that the flights in December of 1903 were wasted on an unimpressed American press; the news hit Paris like an explosion and galvanized hundreds of bright and hard-working inventors to new activity. There was yet another factor: by 1906 the drawings in the Wright patents were available to anyone who wanted badly enough to get them. And they gave proof — in vivid, technical detail — of how to get into the air.

If we look back to those moments, we recognize a problem that has bedeviled the aircraft business from the beginning. There is, first, the genius of the inventor, his ability to devise and put into tangible form a new design — both revolutionary and practical at the same time. And then there is always that problem of *selling* the product. There is engineering and there is marketing, as distant from one another as the two poles of this planet. Today, we know this, but the Wrights, from 1903 to 1908, had no such knowledge of the marketplace.

Nonetheless, they had once again confounded all the rules by actually receiving two vital contracts. Now they had to deliver. For both contracts, they had to meet certain flight-test requirements.

The Signal Corps demanded a machine "capable of carrying two men and sufficient fuel supplies for a flight of 125 miles, with a speed of at least 40 miles an hour." At this point, they had flown, in powered craft, only about 70 minutes each. There was that new requirement of upright seating in the new machine, not only for the pilot, but also for the second occupant, and all the drag that it would create. They felt they could overcome the increased drag through the application of more power. Despite Orville's having said that he worked during 1906 and 1907 on a new machine, they had actually done very little to the basic design and construction of the 1905 *Flyer*. Operating the machine from a sitting position also meant they would have to design, build, and test a new control system.

Thus the Wrights forged ahead into the knotty problems of working out another actuating system for the flight controls — one of the nine different systems they eventually developed for their various flying machines. Only this time they decided to try an entirely new concept rather than modifying the controls that already existed. And to prepare themselves for the upcoming demonstrations of flight in America and Europe, they would need to regain unused skills in flying. For the proper winds and a great deal of room and privacy in which to practice, they returned to Kitty Hawk in May 1908. They packed their 1905 *Flyer* with the more powerful engine and upright seats they must now adapt to their machine, and left for the Atlantic coastline, where they had not been since the epochal December of 1903.

The few years had devastated their old camp. The buildings were a sagging wreckage. Their old materials were gone. Wind, rain, and sand had battered their once-snug facility. The work needed to get the camp in shape added to the pressure. Then, too, the Signal Corps contract was no secret, nor was the one with the French syndicate, so the Wrights were news. Where no one before cared about the location of Kill Devil Hill, where they had lived and worked, now newspapermen lurked behind the dunes and in distant woods or walked along the seashore, watching everything the brothers did.

Although the Wrights were not seeking publicity, they were not trying to avoid reporters, either. But facts still became distorted. They didn't fly until May 6, yet the Norfolk *Virginian-Pilot*, which had inaccurately told its readers of the first flight in 1903, carried a wild story to the effect that on May 1, 1908, one of the brothers had flown 10 miles out over the ocean! This erroneous report was picked up by other news services and disseminated worldwide.

By now, several major papers expressed an interest in confirming whether the Wrights were flying. The first newsman to reach Kitty Hawk was D. Bruce Salley, a free-lance correspondent from Norfolk. He arrived on May 4 and promptly queried the New York *Herald* in hopes of selling a story. As a result of Salley's inquiry, however, the *Herald*'s editors sent Byron R. Newton, their top reporter, down to get a first-person, eyewitness account of what, if anything, was happening. (Newton, a crack investigative journalist, would later become Assistant Secretary of the U.S. Treasury and, afterward, collector of customs in New York.)

Other correspondents soon arrived at Tranquil House, the little boarding place at Manteo, where they stayed during the practice flights. Besides Salley and Newton, the news contingent now included William Hoster of the New York *American*, P. H. McGowan of the *London Daily Mail*, and writer Arthur Ruhl and photographer James H. Hare of *Collier's Weekly*.

One morning Charles W. Furnas, an excellent mechanic who lived in Dayton, walked into their camp and, to their astonishment, offered his services in any way the Wrights could use him.

He was put to work immediately and soon showed himself to be so capable that Wilbur and Orville considered him an "insider" rather than a visitor.

The Wrights had modified their 1905 machine, converting it for use by two occupants in a sitting position and installing a slightly different arrangement of levers for the operation of the control system. It also featured a 35-horsepower engine with vertical instead of horizontal cylinders. Although Wilbur flew on May 6, and both brothers flew on May 8, the first flight any of the newspapermen witnessed occurred early in the morning of May 11. Not wanting to upset the Wrights, they watched from a distance.

As news copy, however, the brothers were subjected to all sorts of annoying speculation. Other men were flying every day and were making headlines; the Wrights up to this time had been on the ground. It was great fun for some of the reporters to tease the Wrights, to speculate on whether they *could* fly. Newsmen write stories that sell papers, and one of the ways to sell papers is to create controversy. Could the Wrights really fly? Maybe not! The reporters dug up anyone who would declare the Wrights to be bluffers and printed whatever nonsense they could find. And while they wrote these stories, they were of course doing everything they could to get new information on the Wrights, above all to get photos of them and their equipment, using their crude telephoto lenses to get pictures of the Wright plane in the air. Yet the newsmen kept their distance from the Wrights' camp.

The reporters, however, were the least of their problems. The brothers were running constantly into snags. They had difficulty getting their engine to make the necessary revolutions and to do so reliably. Designing and building the new control systems couldn't be rushed; they demanded slow and careful work. There were also problems of construction and of constant repairs to the aircraft, as well as all the mundane tasks of everyday living.

On the morning of May 14, 1908, Wilbur, to express their gratitude to Charley Furnas, took him on a flight about Little Hill of the Kill Devil Hills; Furnas was the first person ever to fly as a passenger in an airplane.

Then Orville flew with Furnas for over three minutes, clearly demonstrating that the Wright airplane would be capable of meeting the U.S. Army's specifications. And the press was there to see it; as Newton wrote, "Some day Congress will erect a monument here to these Wrights."

What it was like for the pilot and passenger to fly in the aircraft was vividly described by Orville and Wilbur in an article they wrote for the September 1908 issue of *The Century Magazine*.

In order to show the general reader the way in which the machine operates, let us fancy ourselves ready for the start. The machine is placed upon a single rail track facing the wind, and is securely fastened with a cable. The engine is put in motion, and the propellers in the rear whir. You take your seat at the center of the machine beside the operator. He slips the cable, and you shoot forward. An assistant who has been holding the machine in balance on the rail, starts forward with you, but before you have gone fifty feet the speed is too great for him, and he lets go. Before reaching the end of the track the operator moves the front rudder, and the machine lifts from the rail like a kite supported by the pressure of the air underneath it. The ground under you is at first a perfect blur, but as you rise the objects become clearer. At a height of one hundred feet you feel hardly any motion at all, except for the wind which strikes your face. If you did not take the precaution to fasten your hat before starting, you have probably lost it by this time. The operator moves a lever: the right wing rises, and the machine swings about to the left. You make a very short turn, yet you do not feel the sensation of being thrown from your seat, so often experienced in automobile and railway travel. You find yourself facing toward the point from which you started. The objects on the ground now seem to be moving at much higher speed, though you perceive no change in the pressure of the wind on your face. You know then that you are traveling with the wind. When you near the starting-point, the operator stops the motor while still high in the air. The machine coasts down at an oblique angle to the ground, and after sliding fifty or a hundred feet comes to rest. Although the ma-

chine often lands when traveling at a speed of a mile a
minute, you feel no shock whatever, and cannot, in fact,
tell the exact moment at which it first touched the
ground. The motor close beside you kept up an almost
deafening roar during the whole flight, yet in your excitement, you did not notice it till it stopped!

The brothers went hard at their flying, for despite their retreating into their sheds when newsmen nosed about, they were fully
aware of the press of time. During one period of flying every day
for nine days, for a total of perhaps 15 minutes in the air, Wilbur
let the controls get away from him and overcontrolled with the
front elevator. Later, he confessed to a possible mistake with the
pitch control, but added that it might have been an unusually
strong gust that had overcome the machine. In any case, the
result was the same: the airplane was flying downwind at about
50 miles an hour when, without warning, it shot earthward and
crashed into the sand, to be reduced at once to a tumbled and
tangled heap of wreckage.

This was another case of miraculous escape from severe injury,
for which the brothers were becoming famous among their close
circle. Wilbur emerged from the grinding crash with a bruised
cheek, some hurt ribs, and a solid blow across his nose.

There is a point here to be stressed. After a crash — or a
crackup, to use the older vernacular — a pilot understandably
suffers a certain amount of apprehension, of fear. The sky — and
the plane — have become enemies. The cure for this situation is
immediately to get the man back into another machine and into
the air again, so that when he completes his postaccident jaunt
he will emerge from the second aircraft with a grin instead of a
deepening frown.

The Wrights could not afford such a luxury; they had only one
machine. Every time they crashed, they had to wait days, sometimes weeks, thinking over and chewing on what had dashed
them into the ground — all the while they were repairing the
very winged steed that had thrown them. Anyone who has ever
done test-pilot work, or has had to climb into another aircraft
following an accident, or who has had even a narrow escape

from a crash, will never forget the symptoms of terror that accompany one's re-entry into the cockpit, the hollow feeling in the pit of the stomach, the uncomfortable dryness in the mouth — and, above all, that strange magnification of every sudden sound and movement. To those who have experienced these joyless occasions, there is never a lapse of memory as to their details!

So those of us who have been there are brought to wonder how the Wrights, who never admitted to such emotions or reactions, but beyond all question certainly experienced them, ever managed to maintain their stalwart courage, given their extraordinarily poor circumstances. Searching through every word they ever committed to paper, talking with those who knew them, studying each line and scrap of information, we find not the slightest hint that they ever lost confidence in what they were doing or let fear interfere with their work. This lack of fear was not shared by the rest of the family or their friends. During the flights at Huffman Prairie, Charlie Taylor often told his friends that every time the brothers took off, it was the last time he expected to see them alive. And a neighbor who lived across the field would, whenever the *Flyer* darted earthward, run frantically from her home with muscle lotion to administer to either Orville or Wilbur, who she was certain must be in a terrible state.

I believe there is no better way of describing this trait of the brothers than to say that they had, in the old American phrase, plenty of guts.

Wilbur's crash in the 1905 *Flyer* during the tests in 1908 at Kitty Hawk forced the brothers to make major decisions. The crash had been so severe that there was no hope of resuming practice flights at Kitty Hawk that year. Time was running swiftly away from them. They had planned, because of their contract, to set up another airplane, a new 1908 *Flyer*, which would be demonstrated to the Signal Corps at trials at Fort Myer in September. If they were not ready, their entire contract would be jeopardized.

Now, just as the pressure for the army tests was steadily mounting, the French syndicate notified the brothers that patience was running out in France; no further delays would be tolerated by those financially and politically involved. The Wrights must perform — almost immediately — in France. They had two obligations that had to be met simultaneously, and they made a decision that tore at them.

For the first time, Wilbur and Orville were to be separated in the flying endeavors that had shaped their lives.

CHAPTER 24

"If It Is Your Desire to Enter the Exhibition Business . . ."

ORVILLE RETURNED TO OHIO, where he plunged at once into the construction of the new 1908 *Flyer* to be used in the tests for the U.S. Army Signal Corps. Pressed by the French syndicate not to waste a moment before conducting the European trials, Wilbur took a train to New York and embarked on May 21 on the steamer *La Touraine*, arriving eight days later in Le Havre and continuing his journey without delay, so that he was in Paris the night of May 29.

His plans were to assemble the *Flyer* that he and Orville had sent to France in 1907, and that had remained since then on the Le Havre docks. When assembly and checkout were completed, he would make the promised flights before French officials. During this period, tension within rival camps of experimenters mounted steadily, for comparisons were inevitable. The claims of the Wrights, compared with actual performance delivered by other experimenters, were so superior that they were disbelieved by honest men. The newsmen reported the almost daily flights of Voisin and Farman, among others, and the arrival of Wilbur Wright in France, although of interest, was also a source of much skepticism. The brothers were referred to unkindly as posturers who talked loudly but delivered little or nothing, and the magazine *Les Sports* identified them as *les bluffeurs*; it later declared, "*le bluff continue.*"

Wilbur became the calm eye in a developing hurricane of attention. No pressure seemed to affect him. He calmly did what he had to do, taking his time, deliberating most carefully as he studied different locations in France to find what he described as a satisfactory "flying ground."

He viewed the château grounds of Pont Piétin; the race course at Gavres, north of Blain in Brittany; the estate of M. Robert Esnault-Pelterie, near Versailles; and other locations near Sartrouville, Fontainebleau, Vincennes, Châlons, Sermaize-les-Bains, and Vitry. None of these met his satisfaction, however, and he reached a decision only after M. Léon Bollée, president of the Aéro-Club de la Sarthe, offered him space in his automobile factory and suggested a "flying field" at the racetrack in Le Mans. Wilbur examined the factory space and the racetrack and found they would be quite suitable.

In June he received a disturbing letter from his brother. "On my way back from Kitty Hawk," wrote Orville, "I stopped at Washington. On account of the bad weather I could not get around much, tho' I took a pretty good look over the grounds at Fort Myer, and the country for some distance around. That is about as tough ground to fly over as one could well expect." Orville did not overestimate his problems; the army contract required that the aircraft depart from Fort Myer, Virginia, and fly around a balloon tethered five miles away at Alexandria before returning to its takeoff point. No other aircraft of any type had ever flown cross-country. With only skids beneath his wings, a forced landing would be grim. The brothers, in their practical way, had always sought out flying areas where there were plenty of good landing sites.

Wilbur, for his part, had to disregard the negative stories ground out by the backers of Farman and Voisin, who did all they could to discredit him in their passionate defense of the pride of France. He preferred to accept the warmth and friendship offered by many other Frenchmen.

He lost no time, once the racetrack had been decided on as his flying field, in building his hangar and workshed and bringing the crated 1907 aircraft from Le Havre to the Bollée factory. But when, on June 17, he opened the crates, he found the airplane battered, in many places broken, and generally in terrible shape. He was going to have to rebuild completely some portions of the craft, and in his distress at what he faced he fired off an angry letter to his brother, castigating Orville for the terrible packing job.

Orville replied in a letter dated June 30, 1908, explaining: ". . . The materials in the boxes, especially the large box, were all fastened, excepting a few light strips for rib repairs. The trouble comes at the customhouse. After taking out the engine last year they didn't take the trouble to put back all the nails. That was the reason the rocker-arm post was broken . . ."

No matter; all the explanation in the world could not lessen the extent of the reconstruction task facing Wilbur. He checked into a hotel at Le Mans until his hangar was completed and then, following his practice at Kitty Hawk, left the hotel and moved in with his machine. He hired a French mechanic, of whom he subsequently wrote, "His knowledge of English and mechanics is rather more limited than I had hoped to find it."

And he found he was to need that mechanic, although his services would remain less than what Wilbur required. In 1907 the Wrights, through their French syndicate, had contracted with Bariquand et Marre, a French company, for the construction under license of several of its aircraft engines. On June 4, 1908, Wilbur went to the plant to study the engines personally; he couldn't believe what he found. The engines were mechanical horrors, and the modifications made by the firm had all but ruined the power-plants on which he would depend so greatly. Even the original engine, sent as a model, had been gouged and bent and rendered almost worthless. With each succeeding trip to the factory, Wilbur's patience grew shorter, and, in one of the rare occasions in his career that people can remember, he became absolutely furious at what he considered obstinacy and stupidity, and dragged everything away from the plant. In a manner so typical of Wilbur Wright, he rebuilt his own engine.

By June 25, 1908, he had repaired the old engine. On July 4, he was running it in a full power test when a sudden shriek pierced the air. The scream came from a split hose that led from the engine block to the radiator, and as it broke loose it sprayed a vicious stream of scalding water that burned the skin over Wilbur's chest and along one arm.

How any man could have continued at this point — suffering from third-degree burns and in severe pain, working with men who barely understood him, repairing a nearly demolished airplane, and rebuilding an engine from the block up — is almost beyond my comprehension. Yet this was Wilbur Wright, who not only carried on what he considered to be his responsibilities and his duties, but disguised from his family, in his letters, the extent of his injuries.

There were other pressures. Every week was a time for aviation meets. The usual group of Voisin, Delagrange, and Farman in France, and Curtiss in America with the *June Bug*, commanded the growing attention of a delighted press — and drew enormous crowds to their exhibitions. In the world of aviation there was now a very serious doubt as to whether the Wrights really talked more than they *might* be able to fly.

Wilbur was galled by few things, and even then his response remained low key. Orville, who was working on the article for the September issue of *Century*, sent some of his remarks to his brother. On June 28, from Le Mans, Wilbur responded:

> . . . You should also call attention to the fact that the European revival of interest in aviation dates from 1903, in which year Mr. Chanute, who had been our guest at Kitty Hawk in 1901 and 1902, gave an address before the aeronautical societies of Paris in which he gave a full account of the results of our work, with photographs of many of our flights with motorless gliding machines. Moved by this address, M. Archdeacon employed a couple of young mechanics, the Voisin brothers, to build a gliding machine (*Revue d' Artillerie*, [Mar.] 190[4], article by Capt. Ferber) of the Wright type. Mr. Chanute published drawings to scale of the 1902 Wright glider in the Aérophile of [August] 1903. This journal is the official organ of the Aéro-Club of France. The machines furnished by the Voisin brothers in more recent years to M. Farman and M. Delagrange trace their ancestry and general design to this Wright-pattern French glider of 1903.
>
> Capt. Ferber, of the French artillery, also built several gliding machines of a pattern he called the "Wright type," but the resemblance was merely in outward form, the essential features of control not having been made known at that time.

When the news of our first motor flight of 1903 reached Europe, it was not credited because it seemed too extraordinary to be true. We on our part were satisfied with having made announcement of the result accomplished publicly and promptly, and were not sorry to permit matters to rest quietly till we should have had time to perfect the machine. But when the news of our 1905 flights reached France there was an extraordinary turmoil of excitement among French aeronautical enthusiasts. Night after night the rooms of the Aéro-Club were the scene of the most heated discussions, some maintaining that a flight of 24 miles was quite impossible, and the claim of having made it a mere "bluff." From the days of the Montgolfiers the French had proudly claimed the leadership in all things connected with the navigation of the air, and they were not ready at once to admit that any but a Frenchman could have accomplished such a thing as had been done in America almost without warning. But many believed and at once formed a section of aviation in the Aéro-Club. A number began the erection of machines, of whom Santos-Dumont, with a machine embodying the French idea of the Wright type, but with double-deck supporting planes with rudder at the front instead of the rear, was the first to obtain notoriety by actually leaving the ground. More recent efforts by various European experimenters are well known to newspaper readers.

Orville, at home in Dayton, was working day and night to complete the new machine he would demonstrate later in 1908 to the Signal Corps. When he read in *Scientific American* about Curtiss's *June Bug*, he responded to the information immediately and sent off a copy to his brother in Le Mans. Orville wrote to Glenn Curtiss:

I learn from the *Scientific American* that your *June Bug* has movable surfaces at the tips of the wings, adjustable to different angles on the right and left sides for maintaining the lateral balance. In our letter to Lieutenant Selfridge of January 18th, replying to his of the 15th, in which he asked for information on the construction of flyers [Wright *Flyers*] we referred him to several publications containing descriptions of the structural features of our machines, and to our U.S. Patent No. 821,393. We did not intend, of course, to give permission to use the patented features of our machine for exhibitions or in a commercial way.

This patent broadly covers the combination of sustaining surfaces to the right and left of the center of a flying machine adjustable to different angles, with vertical surfaces adjustable to correct inequalities in the horizontal resistances of the differently adjusted wings. Claim 14 of our Patent No. 821,393, specifically covers the combination which we are informed you are using. We believe it will be very difficult to develop a successful machine without the use of some of the features covered in this patent.

The commercial part of our business is taking so much of our time that we have not been able to undertake public exhibitions. If it is your desire to enter the exhibition business, we would be glad to take up the matter of a license to operate under our patents for that purpose.

There was another matter of deep and growing concern to Orville that affected the work of the Wrights, and Orville sent off further correspondence to Wilbur on the subject. It was the problem of their relationship with Octave Chanute, whose overzealous and sometimes misinformed advice was becoming more and more difficult to bear. Indeed, the Wrights had been forbearing for a long time out of respect for Chanute, but as Wilbur said gingerly, he suspected that some of Chanute's faculties were declining to such an extent as to render him a bit indiscreet in matters involving the Wrights.

Chanute published papers frequently, and two were of special interest to the Wrights; both appeared in print in July 1908, one in the United States and one in Germany. They were quite similar, and they were prompted by the publication of the U.S. Army Signal Corps flying machine specifications and the call for bids to meet them. It was clear to Chanute that the Signal Corps, having little or no knowledge of its own about what specifications should be used, had "borrowed liberally" from the capabilities of the Wright machines, so there was little need for him, Chanute, to retain great secrecy in his writing.

On July 19, 1908, Orville wrote to Wilbur:

> I notice that Chanute has written an article for the *Mitteilungen,* in which he again criticizes our business methods, says we have spent two years in fruitless negotiations because we have asked a ridiculously high price, but that now we have gone to the other extreme in making a price to our own government. He predicts that Herring will fail, but that we will succeed, unless we meet with an accident. I think I will write him. He has also become a convert to airships, and thinks they are going to have great value in war. He says the use of the flyer [Wright *Flyer*] is greatly overestimated, generally, and that its uses will be very restricted. He seems to be endeavoring to make our business more difficult . . .

This was the first really clear indication that the Wrights were falling out with Chanute. Such occasions would now come with increasing frequency. Yet all through the month of July, Wilbur was able to push to the back of his mind the pain from his burns, the frustration at having to rebuild almost an entire airplane, his anger at what had happened to his engine, his pique at such people as Chanute, his contempt for others like Herring, and his amusement with those who stated that the Wrights could not really fly — and he continued to work in his imperturbable, serious, and dedicated manner.

Meanwhile, the Hunaudières racetrack at Le Mans was visited by the famous aviator Blériot, who had already made a number of successful flights and was known all through his native France. (He would later gain greater fame by being the first to fly across the English Channel.) The summer of 1908 would mark the beginning of a new phase in the growth of aviation in Europe and, of course, the world. Another visitor was an Englishman — Charles S. Rolls, an active balloonist and founder of the Rolls-Royce motor car company. They came to Le Mans strictly for the purpose of meeting Wilbur and observing what he was doing. These visits had enormous impact on their own immediate and future work.

CHAPTER 25

"If You Don't Hurry"

WE MUST UNDERSTAND the true extent of the activities taking place at this time. One of the strange elements in the history of the airplane's development was that in each country where there had existed any serious interest in the flight of heavier-than-air machines, there were only a very few people who were sufficiently motivated to pursue the subject with diligence and some personal sacrifice.

In Germany, after the death of Lilienthal, all aviation matters had sputtered to a virtual standstill. Only sporadic attempts by relatively unknown individuals were to be found in unsuccessful trials at flight. The same pattern was followed in England after Pilcher plunged to his death, and experiments had ground to a halt. Here were two great countries, England and Germany, technical leaders of the world, and in both lands lively interest in aviation had given way to a cessation of activity. Not only were the ranks of new experimenters nearly empty, but the leading scientists and engineers of each nation loudly voiced their conclusions that it would *never* be man's lot to fly. The tests of Pilcher and Lilienthal seemed not to matter; interest was simply not there, and those who professed belief in man's control of the air were regarded as imbeciles shouting into the wind.

Much the same was true in France, where ballooning was a widespread art. And in our own land, except for the attempts of a very few, the situation was the same. You could count the serious experimenters of the world on the fingers of one hand.

In the fall of 1907, with news of the flights of the Wright brothers trickling through part of the scientific and engineering community, a small group of serious men began to gather about Alexander Graham Bell, already renowned for his invention of the telephone. They called themselves the Aerial Experiment Association and included among their number men like Lieutenant Thomas E. Selfridge and Glenn Curtiss, but despite their high caliber and their activities, they made almost no progress in the design of flying machines.

The reason the Wrights had forged ahead with such success was well stated by Fred Kelly in *Miracle at Kitty Hawk*. The Wrights, said Kelly, had the imagination to grasp the fundamental problems of flight and, as well, the technical skills and the dedication to pursue building the devices necessary to solve those problems.

When aviation enthusiasts in France learned of the 1903 powered flights at Kitty Hawk, they divided into two groups. The first believed the stories were true, that it was criminal for France to have allowed this to happen, and that every effort should now be made to match and then exceed the Wrights in technical ability; France, through the Montgolfiers, was the home of aviation and should not throw away its heritage.

Their opponents, who had split off from them, felt that the stories of the 1903 flights were lies so gross, they could be ignored, and that there was no need for haste. They could continue as they were, pursuing the subject in leisure and with great care, and, as always, France would still be the first into the skies with true aircraft. When the news of the long flights at Simms Station reached France, the confidence began to erode. The news also filtered through to select groups in Germany, England, Italy, and Spain.

Then more and more Frenchmen came to understand that the only nonsense about the Wrights' flying was in their own minds — and the French were galvanized to new action. They went to work at flying. Wealthy enthusiasts sparked new attempts by putting up great cash prizes for aviation accomplishments. One prize was simply for the first flight to be made (as a "flight" has been defined earlier). Others were for the first flight of one kil-

ometer, for the first flight to be able to circle and return to the
point of departure, and so on.

The Wrights had already met every one of these goals years
before.

In a vague way, most French designers emulated the designs of
the Wrights. However, this was a "surface configuration," rather
like copying the shape of a car but forgetting to put an engine in
it. They never really took the trouble to study the fundamentals
of the Wright design, which is hardly surprising since the Wrights
thought in specifically technical and scientific terms and their
copiers were simply imitating general shape.

We have seen that the Wrights designed their machine to be
inherently unstable; that very instability made the aircraft re-
sponsive to three-dimensional control.

This the French did not understand. To them, Orville and
Wilbur when gliding were in complete control of their machines
and this made them akin to the birds. In fact, the French called
them *"les hommes-oiseaux"* — the birdmen. But, as Gibbs-Smith
defines it, the Wrights took the "airman's approach" to flying, in
which the pilot identifies with his machine. Thus they were
dubbed.

But stability, especially the built-in stability sought urgently
by the French so that they might steer an airplane as one did a
car or a boat, was their undoing. The "chauffeur's approach"
(another description by Gibbs-Smith) simply didn't work in the
sky, with its turbulence and motion; there, stability had to be
regained constantly when outside forces snatched it from the
hands of a pilot — and that called for instant control response.
Without it, the French machines could only stumble and stagger
above the ground.

One of the problems resulted from the French designers' insistence on great dihedral in their gliders and airplanes. Let the
essential lifting force of the wing provide stability, they declared.
There is no need for control in roll. Thus, they were still in
difficulty even *after* they had added longitudinal control by the
use of fore-and-aft elevators, and a rudder for directional control.
How important is roll control? If a pilot is flying a modern, stable,
balanced, aircraft today, and he loses his ailerons, he considers
it a full-blown emergency, *which it is.*

It was not until they saw how maneuverable the Wright *Flyers* were that the French fairly rushed to add roll control to their own machines. Yet they were still in trouble, because with so much dihedral in their design, the sharply upward-inclined wings worked against the effect of the warping and aileron systems they had introduced.

Again, to indicate how wide was the gulf separating the Wrights from the rest of the world: it was not until late 1906 that Santos-Dumont made his first powered hops for distances less *than the ground measurement* of Wilbur's flight of 852 feet in 1903 (which is estimated to be more than a half mile through the air). And then in 1907, on November 9, Henri Farman, a French pilot of British extraction, finally managed to fly his Voisin-built airplane at Issy-les-Moulineaux for 1 minute and 34 seconds and to cover a distance of 1030 meters — almost 3400 feet.

Two years before this the Wrights had flown 38 minutes and 24 miles on one flight.

The Farman-Voisin, an attempt to improve on the Wright *Flyer*, carried a forward elevator for longitudinal control and rudders in back for direction, but managed its turns only by dangerous skidding motions, since there was no way for the pilot to control the angle of his wings. Any severe weather or wind gusts would have hurled the aircraft out of control to the ground.

In January 1908, the indomitable Farman finally managed to make a circle with his shaky aircraft during a flight that lasted for 88 seconds. This was the first circling maneuver ever accomplished by an aircraft in France, and the enthusiastic citizenry, who either did not know or disbelieved what the Wrights had achieved years earlier, shouted to the world that this was the "first circle" ever flown by anyone, anywhere. The brothers shook their heads and smiled, for they knew the Farman-Voisin machine had skidded like an elephant on ice to make its turn and that it was years behind the Wright *Flyer*. Those who knew about the Wright brothers, however, were not amused. False information once believed — as with Farman — is just about as good as the real thing, and though the Wrights' supporters *knew* that the Wrights had flown a perfectly controlled circle at Huffman Prairie on September 20, 1904, the French and all Europe did not. Then, in April 1908, Léon Delagrange, with another machine built by the Voisin brothers, managed a flight of 6 minutes and 30 seconds, during which he covered approximately two and a half miles in the air. France went mad with joy and greeted Delagrange as if he had just accomplished an event far beyond the ability of all mortal men.

In a sense, the reaction of the French had a good effect on Orville and Wilbur; they now saw the folly of continued, self-enforced secrecy. This is what Chanute as a businessman had seen and why he was so critical of the Wrights: while they tried to work through all their problems, others *were* catching up, and, more important, most people now disbelieved the Wrights and celebrated their new heroes.

Another sour note sounded from the United States. People were hearing news about Glenn Curtiss and his associates. At Hammondsport, the *Red Wing*, which Curtiss had helped design, staggered into the air with Baldwin at the controls and flew for only 19 seconds, but it covered a distance of 319 feet — *and in photographs people saw an airplane flying, and that was all that mattered to them.* Had not these machines flown under control? Obviously, or they would have crashed. Had they not flown considerable distances and for minutes at a time?

While Wilbur was still searching for a flying field, Delagrange went to Milan and managed to remain airborne in his Voisin for 18 minutes and 30 seconds, while he covered a distance of nearly nine miles. Delagrange *was flying.* And to the public, he was flying with spectacular success.

News reached the Wrights that Farman was taking his Voisin to New York, and there was a deluge of newspaper publicity. He planned to arrive on July 29, 1908. The pressure was building, and on July 29 Orville wrote to his brother: "Farman was expected to arrive at New York today. If you don't hurry he will do his flying here before you get started in France."

Wilbur studied the letter with grave misgivings, for he was still recovering from his scalding burns, working without a competent mechanic, rebuilding his engine, and constructing his airplane, all on his own.

If there could have been a moment more discouraging than this, it is difficult to know what it might have been. Yet the

Wrights shone through it all. Calmness under pressure had always been their hallmark, and their displays of temper were reserved for the arguments between themselves, but almost never revealed to outsiders.

Dr. Albert F. Zahm, of the Smithsonian, who had befriended Orville in the United States, came up with a marvelous idea. Wilbur was in France? He, Zahm, had many contacts in Europe, and he felt the opportunity was perfect for Wilbur to meet a beautiful, wealthy woman, who wanted to meet *him* — object, matrimony. Zahm wrote all this in a letter to Orville, explaining the details, and one can only imagine the wry grin that crossed Orville's face as he penned his own note to Wilbur, which he forwarded with Zahm's letter. On July 5, 1908, Orville wrote: "I inclose a letter from Prof. Zahm . . . I had half a notion to accept the proposition for you. My power of attorney seems of little use for anything else!"

But Wilbur was too busy for beautiful women or fortunes at this moment. Wilbur was going to attempt to fly.

CHAPTER 26

Il Vole! Il Vole!

THEY CAME from all across France, this very select group of men who built their own wings, or financed their countrymen, or worked to design new craft that would be at home in the skies. A small group, really; by actual count of one eyewitness, no more than 26 people in all at the Hunaudières racetrack at Le Mans. Blériot, Archdeacon, François Peyrey, René and Pierre Gasnier, Ernest and Paul Zens, Robert Guérin, Captain Alexandre Sazerac de Forge, Count Henri de Moy, two Russian army officers, and, of course, Léon Bollée and Wilbur's own representative in his syndicate, Hart O. Berg.

Saturday morning, August 8, 1908, was bright and crisp. Even the attitude of the men was genial; they were laughing — enjoying the spirit of the moment and the warmth of the heavens. Only Berg paced impatiently, for on his shoulders had rested an enormous burden. He had taken a good deal of abuse for his inability to bring these two men to produce actual proof of their claims. The pressure on him had become intensified by the flights of Frenchmen in recent months. Now he was maintaining an outward calm, trying to radiate confidence — and sweating out what was going to happen.

Studying the spare, almost gaunt figure of Wilbur, Berg was, in fact, less than confident. He did have great faith in this cool, almost chilly American, but he knew better than anyone else in France just what tremendous pressures Wilbur Wright had endured. And he knew.

For more than the reasons that Berg had already enumerated to himself, this airplane, this strange machine of the Wrights, *had never flown*. Even the set of controls had never been tested in flight. Berg shook his head in private dismay and watched Wilbur, seemingly as untroubled as a man who had never known a frustrating moment in all his life, working on the flying apparatus.

Now Wilbur was studying those controls again. He had done so more times than he could remember. He knew he must have everything straight in his mind before committing the plane to flight. Handles on the elevator lever now controlled the wing-warping system. This system had never been in his hands off the ground, and what seemed to press most heavily on his soul was that stark realization that his total flying time in any powered machine — absolutely the total — was *hardly more than one hour*. Of this total, nearly all had taken place almost three years before.

And when he had last flown, only twenty minutes at Kitty Hawk, that adventure had ended in a splintering crash. The crash had been his most recent flying experience.

Any failure of this first flight attempt at Le Mans would be disastrous. It would play perfectly into the hands of all his detractors and scoffers; and, almost certainly, the success of others and the long spell on the ground for the Wrights would doom their experiments in France. No one would believe, at least those who wrote the official records, that Orville and Wilbur truly had led the world into the air. They would go down in history as *les bluffeurs*. Bitter medicine indeed to contemplate, and he had enough on his mind without this nerve-jangling nonsense.

"We'd heard that something was going on at the track, that an American inventor was building a plane," Henri Delgove, then a boy of thirteen, told the author in June 1977. "Most people were saying it's a joke — he's no flier, he's a liar."

Henri Delgove and a young friend decided to see for themselves on that fateful August 8. They left their parents' Saturday picnic, took their bikes, and rode out to the track late that afternoon, just as the crew was moving the plane from the shed and placing it on a rail behind the tower, or catapult. They watched from a distance as the strange thing with wings was placed on the launching rail. The American climbed aboard and settled himself in. Henri's powers of recall were remarkable:

> There was a small number of official people, twenty or twenty-five, members of the Aéro-Club in Paris and other authorities. But brats like us were not permitted on the course, so my friend and I climbed a fence just behind the grandstand and waited to see what would happen. They were trying to start the engine. It went bang and stopped. Finally at about six in the evening it started. Then a weight dropped from the tower and off it went. At the end of the first two hundred yards or so he [Wilbur] bent his plane to the left and made a complete circle.

The eyewitnesses watched, incredulous, as the Wright *Flyer* rose steadily into the skies and then, soon after takeoff, the wings dipped, the aircraft rolled into a left bank, turning under complete control, and Wilbur came around 90 degrees, leveled off, flew straight, and then, again, swept into a steep bank as the *Flyer* raced into another circle, responding perfectly. On the ground there was amazement and cheering as the *Flyer* sped away.

Young Henri Delgove watched in fascination as he saw the machine race through the air and turn like a gigantic swift bird and disappear from view behind the grandstand. In his recollection, Henri said it appeared to be "side-gliding." (He probably meant "side-slipping.") "It's going to crash!" Henri shouted to his friend. They gripped one another in their excitement, waiting to hear that strange engine clattering and popping and, as Wilbur came into view again, "There he is! He's still flying!"

The *Flyer* swooped down, cutting another circle as Wilbur brought the machine into the wind; the engine sound changed and then the plane was just above the ground and the skids touched smoothly and with feathery lightness as it came to a ' alt. Wilbur saw the small mob running madly toward the *Flyer*, and he shut down the engine to stop the propellers. As he alighted, Henri Delgove and his friend laughed at the sight — the American going crazy trying to push away the hysterical Frenchmen who rushed to him to embrace him and hug him and kiss him on the cheeks, and everyone was shouting and laughing all at the same time in a fine and wonderful madness.

The boys rushed up to join the group but remained on the fringe, listening intently. The Frenchmen were talking up a storm, but, said Henri, "Mr. Wright, he was a wonderful man — so calm and soft-spoken." Asked if he spoke to Wilbur, Henri Delgove replied, "Oh no, I was but a boy — and too shy."

The two youngsters could contain themselves no more, and in a flash they were on their bicycles, pedaling furiously down the road until they raced into the old medieval town of Le Mans, with its great castle and cathedral, screaming at the top of their lungs, "Il vole! Il vole! He flies — he flies — he's no liar, he's a flier."

At the racetrack, the wild Frenchmen were pleading with Wilbur to fly again immediately. But he refused. Enough for the first test. Berg was jubilant. His early faith in Wilbur Wright was vindicated; he would no longer have to be on the defensive. He finally got Wilbur to one side. He *must* fly again, just as soon as possible. If not today, then, of course, certainly tomorrow.

Wilbur told him no. Tomorrow was a Sunday and he would not break the Sabbath.

On Monday, August 10, Wilbur prepared for his second day of flying at Le Mans. The past Saturday, there had been 26 adult witnesses on the racetrack.

On Monday morning there were 4000.

Wilbur wrote to his brother on August 15, 1908:

> Last Saturday I took the machine out for the first time and made a couple of circles. On Monday I made two short flights. In the first I wound up with a complete ¾ of a circle with a diameter of only 31 yards, by measurement, *and landed with the wings level.* I had to turn suddenly as I was running into trees and was too high to land and too low to go over them. In the second flight I made an "eight" and landed at the starting point. The newspapers and the French aviators nearly went wild with excitement. Blériot & Delagrange were so excited they could scarcely speak, and Kapferer could only gasp and could not talk at all. You would have almost died of laughter if you could have seen them. The French newspapers, *Matin, Journal, Figarc L'Auto, Petit Journal, Petit*

Parisien, &c., &c., give reports fully as favorable as the
Herald. You never saw anything like the complete rever-
sal of position that took place after two or three little
flights of less than two minutes each . . .

As soon as the news spread to other parts of the world, there
came an immediate reaction from Henri Deutsch de la Meurthe,
who had been the mainstay of the whole French syndicate that
had contracted to support the Wrights in Europe. On this matter,
Wilbur added the news that

> Deutsch telegraphed to inquire whether he could have
> the 100,000 frs. stock and definitely took it. The English
> Mercedes-Daimler Co. have written to know whether
> they can have England on same terms as the published
> Weiller contract. They also would like to arrange the
> German business, I presume through the German Daim-
> ler Co. I have asked them to send a man to talk over
> matters.
> We certainly cannot kick on the treatment the news-
> papers have given us; even *Les Sports* has acknowledged
> itself mistaken . . .

(Years later Mme. Léon Bollée, whose late husband had been
so helpful and kind to Wilbur in 1908, visited Orville in Dayton,
accompanied by her daughter Elizabeth, then the Countess Jean
de Vautibault. Mme. Bollée recalled that Wilbur had told her he
would make his first flight in France on the day her baby was
born, which he did, on August 8. The daughter's most prized
possession was a brief message signed by Wilbur Wright, stating:
"To Elizabeth, the little girl whose bright eyes opened upon this
grand world when my flights in France had their beginning."
Wilbur counted Léon Bollée a true friend and credited much of
the success at Le Mans to him.)
Immediately after his flight on Saturday, Wilbur had been invited into the town of Le Mans, which wished to celebrate the
great moment brought to them by this spare American. Wilbur's
refusal was polite but firm: he wished only to prepare the machine for the forthcoming flights on the following Monday. While
everyone else still gaped or chattered with excitement, Wilbur

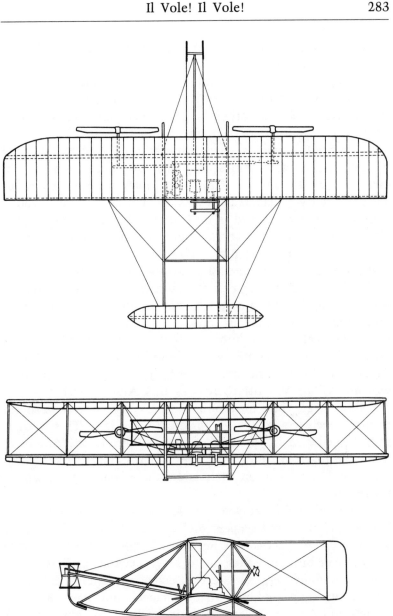

Wright 1907-1909 machines: Span — 41 feet; chord — 6 feet, 6 inches;
gap — 6 feet; wing area — about 510 square feet; horizontal rudder
(elevator) area — 70 square feet; vertical rudder area — 23 square feet;
approximate length — 31 feet; approximate weight — 800 pounds. Note:
At least seven airplanes were built by the Wrights between 1907 and
1909, and the dimensions vary; the drawing is of the "1907 model."

retired to his hangar and without fuss of any kind remained there all through Sunday.

More than one person was taking new stock in this man from some place in America known as Ohio. He seemed to have one characteristic above all others — and the French often remarked on the calm simplicity of the man. Most of the people were aware that a powerful syndicate was backing him. And that he had traveled thousands of miles and, therefore, must be a man of means, of wealth and political power. They were not ready for an American who labored the same hours as the local French workmen and who carried an ordinary lunch bucket, just as they did. It did not take long at the Bollée factory for word to spread that here was a man so simple in his work and his daily conduct that he must be considered a great man, one with a scientific outlook on life. A genius, perhaps, but a man who, above all else, was not ostentatious; a man who put on no airs and thought of himself as no more than an equal.

There was also a great humor in their relationship with Wilbur Wright, for the Frenchmen with whom he worked in the Bollée factory could not pronounce his name correctly. To them there was no Wilbur Wright; there was this American they called "Veelbure Reet." But this pronunciation was very close in sound to the French words *"vieille burette,"* old oilcan. This is what they named him in their affection. Old Oilcan, the American from that place in Ohio. From the men who labored daily with their hands for bread on their table, there could have been no higher praise.

Wilbur's thoughts strayed from Le Mans. The reaction of the French and their newspapers told him all he needed to know about his own success. But he worried about Orville, knowing his younger brother was soon to leave Dayton for Fort Myer, where he would demonstrate the second airplane to the army. Wilbur quickly passed over his own success on August 8 and in his letter of August 15 cautioned his brother: "In your flights at Washington I think you should be careful to begin practice in calms and keep well above the ground. You will probably be unable to cut as short curves as I do here, but you will have it easier on your speed test in a straight line . . . Be awfully careful in beginning practice and go slowly."

It was good advice. Wilbur's caution held no deprecation, because Orville's machine had been built with a lesser wingspan and was heavier and faster, in order to meet Signal Corps contract requirements; yet with the limited power available it would not be as maneuverable as the older craft Wilbur was flying. Eleven days after Wilbur's first flight at Le Mans, Orville was on his way to the army site, his machine packed in crates, and his father noting with some deep concern in his diary of August 19: "Orville started to Washington City, this evening at 10:12, via Harrisburg, Pa. Both he and Wilbur peril their lives; perhaps Orville most by the unsuitableness of the grounds at Ft. Myer."

The brothers appreciated, but weren't overly fond of, the growing family concern for their well-being. Even Wilbur finally reacted to the warnings, and just before his first flight in Le Mans, wrote to Katharine that "I am afraid that you are doing too much worrying. You will soon have us worrying about you. You may depend upon it that if anything very serious happens I will let you know of it, so you need not pay too much attention to newspaper talk . . ."

In his letter of August 15 to Orville, Wilbur also stated:

> On Thursday I made a blunder in landing and broke three spars and all but one or two ribs in the left wings and three spar ends of the central section and one skid runner. It was a pretty bad smashup, but Kapferer who was present pronounced it as fine a demonstration of the practicability of flying as the flights themselves. It did not shake me up a particle.
>
> I have not yet learned to operate the handles without blunders, but I can easily make turns of three hundred feet diameter. On the other hand I find the winds here tremendously gusty. I have not dared to tackle anything above 5 or 6 miles an hour yet . . . We have obtained the use of the Camp d'Auvours a few miles east of Le Mans . . . and will move as soon as the machine is repaired . . .

(At Hunaudières racetrack he had made a total of nine flights in six days, the longest just over eight minutes.)

Now at the Camp d'Auvours military parade ground Wilbur

erected a new and larger shed than that in which he lived and worked at the racetrack. His letter continued: "The grounds there are a half kilometer wide and extend with no obstruction by large trees for five or six kilometers. It ought to be much better than here and the home flight will be much easier as I will have less turns to make . . . My [scalded] arm is still sore . . . The repairs on the machine will probably take five or six days in all."

Wilbur's thoughts on cross-country flying were somber. No one could predict what would lie beneath a pilot if his engine quit, and we must remember that most of the flights made by the brothers *were all at very low altitudes.* (A forced landing from a few thousand feet in a small airplane flying 40 miles an hour is not particularly frightening to contemplate, but from less than 50 feet or so, it is terrifying even today.) What disturbed Wilbur was that Orville, in flying his army tests, had no choice but to make cross-country flights over inhospitable terrain, and that was the basis for his muted alarm and words of caution.

Two weeks before Orville's first flight, he received another letter from Wilbur, dated August 25:

> The excitement aroused by the short flights I have made is almost beyond comprehension. The French have simply become wild. Instead of doubting that we could do anything they are ready to believe that we can do everything. So the present situation is almost as troublesome as the former one. People have flocked here from all over Europe, and as I wish to practice rather than give exhibitions it is a little embarrassing. But I tell them plainly that I intend for the present to experiment only under the most favorable conditions. If the wind is more than five miles an hour I stay in. In a calm you can detect a mismovement instantly, but in winds you do not know at first whether the trouble is due to mistakes or to wind gusts. I advise you most earnestly to stick to calms till after you are sure of yourself. Don't go out even for all the officers of the government unless you would go equally if they were absent. *Do not let yourself be forced into doing anything before you are ready.* Be very cautious and proceed slowly in attempting flights in the

middle of the day when wind gusts are frequent. Let it be understood that you wish to practice rather than give demonstrations and that you intend to do it in your own way. Do not let people talk to you all day and all night. It will wear you out, before you are ready for real business. Courtesy has limits. If necessary appoint some hour in the day time and refuse absolutely to receive visitors even for a minute at other times. Do not receive *any one* after 8 o'clock at night . . .

A few days ago I was presented with a medal of the International Peace Society of which Baron d'Estournelles de Constant is president. Another for you was also given into my charge.

That English crowd, Daimler Mercedes, is ready to make a contract similar to the Weiller contract but at a higher price. However I fear that they are more interested in selling stock than doing regular business and I am waiting to make further investigations, and consider other offers.

It is not probable that I will be able to go to Washington unless absolutely needed. I can only say be extraordinarily cautious. Choose your own times. Good Luck . . .

Orville, advice and all, was moving ahead steadily with his own program. At Fort Myer he moved his equipment and dismantled aircraft into the huge balloon and dirigible hangar; in addition to an excellent workspace, which Wilbur had had to do without, he had other assets. On his arrival on August 20, he was accompanied by Charlie Taylor, who had worked so long and well for the brothers. And also present was Charley Furnas, the young mechanic who had appeared so unexpectedly at Kitty Hawk.

The presence of these two capable and willing workers proved invaluable to Orville, for whom the preparations were difficult and the actual flight tests as close to impossible as he could have imagined.

Yesterday I went over the grounds for five miles in several directions from the Fort [Orville wrote on August 23 to Wilbur in Le Mans]. I have about decided on a course

directly towards Alexandria. There would be quite a number of good landing places on this course, though there is
one large forest of over a mile wide in which there are no
breaks whatever. The starting point at Ft. Myer is 240 ft.
above sea level. The ravines are sea level, and the turning
point 160 ft. Three of these deep ravines must be crossed.
The lowlands are more cultivated and therefore more
open and suitable for landings . . .

I am not looking for much trouble, if I can get the
practice which I expect. The parade grounds are rather
small, but I think quite as large as the part of the grounds
which you could use at Le Mans. The committee which
will pass upon the trials are Major Squier, Major Wallace,
Lieuts. Lahm, Selfridge, and Foulois. Everyone seems very
friendly and the newspapermen are kindly disposed.

I am now at the St. James but I expect to change to the
Cosmos Club within a day or two. Mr. Zahm is taking
me there.

I expect to begin the first flights about the first of
September; I may be ready a day or two before that. I can
choose my man that goes with me in the trials. If Lieut.
Lahm wants to go I think I will ask him, or maybe Lieut.
Foulois whom I like very much. He is a little fellow, only
weighing 130 lbs.

The goods [the airplane] came through in perfect shape.
They were packed exactly as were the goods sent to Europe. Our trouble there is with the customhouse tearing
everything loose and not fastening them again.

At this time there were growing complications with Augustus
Herring, whose association with the Wrights went back to their
powered flight in 1903 at Kitty Hawk and for whom their distaste
had not diminished. Herring had tried to pass on to Professor
Samuel Langley the secrets of the Wrights and had been immediately rebuffed by that gentleman of high honor. Undaunted,
Herring went off to Glenn Curtiss with much of the information
only he knew, including invaluable data that had been gathered
with such tremendous difficulty by the brothers. Concluding his
letter to Wilbur, Orville wrote: "Herring announces that he is
not going to ship his machine by express but is going to fly it
here from New York. The Signal Corps does not hesitate to

express its scepticism. Herring was granted an additional 30 days."

Obviously, no one was going to fly an airplane from New York to Washington in 1908.

Four days later he wrote to Katharine and complained that "I haven't done a lick of work since I have been here. I have to give my time to answering the ten thousand fool questions people ask about the machine. There are a number of people standing about the whole day long . . ."

The last days of August were spent in testing and retesting the engine Orville would fly. On September 1, he moved the airplane from the balloon hangar to the balloon tent, and on the day following, with everything in readiness, he prepared for his first flight. One can only wonder at Orville's remarkable self-control when a minor ground accident cancelled his plans. The machine was being moved by a hand-pushed dolly to its launching rail and dropped heavily to the ground. Orville did not know what damage might have been caused, and he refused to fly until, of course, he could inspect the entire machine carefully and slowly. It was not as bad as he had feared, but he refused to hurry the preparations.

The day came — September 3, 1908. Across the ocean, Wilbur Wright had shattered the aplomb of France, and his name was sweeping the entire continent. In the United States, his younger brother, now sporting a mustache and a derby, formal and anonymous in his starched collar and tie, boarded a streetcar at the Cosmos Club and rode to Fort Myer.

Yet Orville was not planning a test, as defined by the Signal Corps. This was to be *his* first experiment with his new machine, and he wasn't about to rush into a situation where he would be judged for his contract on the basis *of his first flight*. Orville was understandably apprehensive. Army officers and a small throng of observers had collected, convinced that Orville was intending to start and complete his entire test along with this first experimental hop. Orville couldn't believe they were all so uninformed about his flight problems.

A single glance at a scene he had studied many times by now was enough to fly every alarm flag in his mind. The area from which he must fly, and return to land, was barely 700 by 1000 feet. Neither Orville nor Wilbur had ever made a flight within such a confined space.

Which meant that, on his first flight in an untested machine, and without having flown for a long time, he must circle *immediately* after he took off.

Not many of the people who came to watch believed he could perform this maneuver. Some even expected to see him crash.

CHAPTER 27

"Undreamed of, Even by Yourselves"

IN FRANCE the song whirled through the country like a flame. *"Il vole! Il vole!"*

He flies! He flies! — a popular refrain taken up in the cabarets and theaters.

It was different in the United States. "Show me" would have better expressed the general feeling.

Orville launched from the short track, lifted into the calm air as the falling weight slung him forward and upward, propellers whirling, and immediately swung into a banked turn and raced around the wickedly restricted flight space in 1 minute and 11 seconds. But in those 71 seconds he swung about the field one and a half times, and when he landed and shut down his engine, he heard a strange and growing roar that became louder and ever more intense.

It was the sound of people going wild, giving vent to unprecedented emotions, a crowd of beholders that rushed forward, screaming as loudly as they could, overwhelmed by the miracle that had taken place before their eyes.

Orville had had enough problems with the press to have turned from it forever; however, we have seen that he remained always courteous, that he spoke with newsmen whenever they requested conversation with him, and that he did not hold any journalist responsible for bad reporting until he could judge him personally. But he did consider reporters to be especially hard as human beings, often bereft of personal considerations, and he generally kept them in a special classification. He was, therefore, all the more astonished by what he saw when he landed. He might have expected a crowd of Frenchmen to unleash their emotions, as Wilbur had described, but he was quite unprepared for the sight of some of the toughest newsmen he knew running to meet him in tears.

The fact that Wilbur had been flying successfully in Europe for more than a month before Orville's brief circling dash around the army post had never really sunk into the American consciousness. It was something the people had ignored. It had happened thousands of miles away, so it "wasn't real." Again we are faced with the old saw that until you've seen it, you can't understand it or even believe in its reality.*

What with Wilbur's first flight on August 8 at Le Mans and the many flights to follow, 1908 goes down in history as the Year of the Wrights. They had become world famous. Reports raced back and forth between Europe and the United States, and the press, with frenzied public backing, tried every day to outdo itself in hysterical acclaim.

Not even the flight of Charles Lindbergh, not even the sight of astronauts walking on the moon, were to stir the public fervor in Europe more than the deeds of the Wright brothers. It is difficult to establish this fact in our own time, but to the people of 1908, press and public alike, man had truly been given wings for the first time. Wings to move through the atmosphere and, as some of the greatest scientists were quick to point out as they climbed onto the Wrights' bandwagon, even to go beyond the atmosphere — to move through that dimly conceived blankness beyond the planet. This is what men of science tendered to the public as they gave their impressions of what the flights of the brothers would *mean* in terms of the future. It was a barely recognizable, yet nonetheless inescapable, beginning of not just an air age but — far beyond that — a space age to come.

---

* Nothing seems to have changed from the Wright *Flyer* to the most advanced machines built today, and anyone who seeks success in the aviation industry, right now, must never forget this basic rule of marketing new aircraft: Observers and prospects who are not part of the industry itself must be *shown*. They must be flown, and the performance of the new product must be demonstrated.

It is worth our while to recount here some of the actual statements made, because they belong to the heritage we all share. After piling scorn, even condemnation, on the Wrights, France and all Europe admitted their error and turned their voices to praise of Wilbur Wright. To their great credit is the reaction of the people abroad; they recognized the Wrights handsomely:

Léon Delagrange: *"Well, we are beaten! We just don't exist!"*

An unidentified reporter in France: *"No one can estimate the consequences which will result from this new method of locomotion, the dazzling beginnings of which we salute today."*

Louis Blériot: *"For us in France and everywhere, a new era in mechanical flight has commenced . . . It is marvellous."*

René Gasnier: *"It is a revelation in aeroplane work, who can now doubt that the Wrights have done all they claimed? . . . We are as children compared with the Wrights."*

Paul Zens: *"Mr. Wright has us all in his hands."*

The newspaper *Le Figaro*: *"It was not a success, it was a triumph!"*

François Peyrey: *"I shall try to give an idea of the incomparable mastery of the American aviators in the marvellous art of imitating the birds. For a long time — for too long a time — the Wright brothers have been accused in Europe of bluffing; perhaps even in their own land. Today they are hallowed by France, and I feel an intense pleasure in counting myself among the first to make amends for such flagrant injustice . . . It would also be just as puerile to challenge the first flight of December 17th, 1903 in North Carolina as it would be to deny 'les expériences' in La Sarthe [Le Mans] . . . From the stands . . . an immense acclamation goes up from the witnesses of this prowess . . ."*

The *London Times*: *"All accounts . . . published in this morning's papers from the correspondents on the spot, attest the complete triumph of the American inventor . . . The enthusiasm was indescribable . . . All accounts agree that the most admirable characteristic of yesterday's flight was the steady mastery displayed by Mr. Wright over his machine."*

Major B. F. S. Baden-Powell, past president of the (later Royal) Aeronautical Society of Great Britain: *". . . That Wilbur Wright is in possession of a power which controls the fate of nations, is beyond dispute."*

And then Gibbs-Smith noted, in words I personally find so eminently pleasing: *"Nor was praise wanting for Wilbur himself, whose quiet charm and modesty became a legend."*

And Orville was hard at work. In a cryptic entry in a Signal Corps log that now needs no amplification: "Friday, September 4, 1908. Wind: Direction S.S.W. Velocity 3 miles. Distance covered: 3 miles. Maximum height: 40 feet. Condition of engine after flight: good. Left the shed at 5:15 P.M. Returned to the shed at 6:10 P.M. Time in flight 4′ 15″, engine was running 6 minutes."

Then there were problems . . .

"Saturday, September 5, 1908. Wind: Direction S. Velocity unknown. Left the shed at 4:20 P.M. Returned to the shed at 5:05. Did not fly on account of high winds and rain."

The day following, Orville wrote to Wilbur: ". . . Curtiss was here Thursday and Friday. They have not been able to make the motor [built by Curtiss] on the [Baldwin] dirigible run more than a minute or two without missing about half its explosions. Ours runs without a miss. Selfridge has been trying to find out how we do it! . . ."

The presence of Curtiss and the purpose in Selfridge's seeking engine information appear to have been a catalyst for Orville. In one of his rare shows of quiet and personal anger, for it was more than pique, he set about with a hidden vengeance to show once and for all that he and his brother had long before left the rest of the world in the wake of their wings. He was going to fly, faster and longer and better than *anyone* — save for his own brother, and if he should exceed any performance by Wilbur, it would be only a matter of good fortune. But everyone else? Ah, it was time for the lesson —

He had new things going for him — greater fuel capacity, the sitting position instead of the prone, more power in the engine, and, above all greater skill and absolute confidence in himself and his machine.

We need judge only by the dates in 1908 —

September 4: Four minutes and 15 seconds in the air.

September 7: Flight time 55 seconds.

September 8: Eleven minutes and 10 seconds airborne.

September 9, first flight: Fifty-seven minutes and 31 seconds — circling the field 57 times!

September 9, second flight: One hour, 2 minutes, and 15 seconds in the air.

September 11: Airborne for the first flight for 10 minutes and 50 seconds. And again, the same day, a flight of 1 hour, 10 minutes, and 24 seconds.

September 12: Onlookers gaped in disbelief — flight time up to 1 hour, 14 minutes, and 20 seconds.

There were other reasons for headlines. On September 9, Orville, for the first time in public, took up a passenger — Lieutenant Frank P. Lahm, who flew with Orville for 6 minutes and 24 seconds. Three days later he took up Major George O. Squier for 9 minutes and 6 seconds. The plane's ability to carry a passenger seemed to the onlookers nearly as remarkable as the fact it could fly at all.

Every time either of the Wrights set a new mark in the air, the press went beyond reporting the specific event; it published editorial comment. Echoing the sentiments of the *London Times*, a reporter who watched Orville's flights wrote that "it would have been childish to have said that the reports of their flights in 1903–4–5 were anything but the truth. No one could be able to handle aircraft in the air the way these men did and set the records if not only their technology but their skill had not stemmed from a long period of experimentation and effort."

At the height of their fame, now reaching around the world, the Wrights became the subject of conversation and speculation. People in Europe wondered if Orville shared the charm, modesty, and humility Wilbur made so evident in France. When reporters in the United States praised Orville, for the same virtues, people wondered if jealousy had ever entered the brothers' extraordinary engineering minds. But that question was quickly dismissed, for through all else there emerged the sense of integrity; their deep confidence in one another; the rapport, as they worked on technical matters, that was so close, they seemed of a single mind; and their total trust not only in each other, but in all the members of their family. That each brother could and did contest the ideas of the other was already well known — accounts of their shouted arguments were a source of much delight — but there was never doubt that their disputes were only a means for them to arrive at a common solution.

At the time when Orville was wreaking havoc with the aeronautical records and astonishing observers in Virginia, Wilbur,
for many reasons, had yet to exceed a flight of more than 21
minutes in France. Although he suffered frustration with his own
flights, his admiration for his younger brother was unbounded.
On September 13, 1908, Wilbur wrote to Katharine:

> "You ought to have seen it! You ought to have seen it!
> Great big sing!" I refer to the excitement roused by Or-
> ville's dandy flights. However, I suppose you have seen
> some of it in America too. When I made my first flight
> over here the sudden change from unbelief to belief
> roused a furor of excitement I had not expected to see
> renewed, but the news from America seems to have been
> sufficient to repeat the stir. I have had almost as many
> congratulations on Orville's success as I had a month
> ago. I suppose Orville must be overwhelmed with them.
> Well, it was fine news all right and lifted a load off of my
> mind.

Wilbur's problems included bad weather and the overheating
of his engine. After each flight he worked on the power-plant,
which was an earlier model than the one Orville was using, in
an attempt to increase its cooling efficiency. On September 5, he
was airborne for 19 minutes, 48 seconds, an excellent flight but
still far below what he had accomplished at Huffman Prairie. On
the 10th, he was up for 21 minutes, 43 seconds. Finally, on the
16th, he managed to stay aloft for a new record of 39 minutes, 18
seconds — commendable but still well behind what his younger
brother was doing with repeated flights of well over an hour each.
Nonetheless, every flight was a sensation. People came by the
thousands to look up in wonder, and even to pray on their knees
before this unquestioned miracle of man's having been given the
gift of flight. Wilbur's quiet and unassuming ways made him a
French national hero (his strict punctuality for appointment was
particularly impressive). And when it came to doing things his
own way, Wilbur was stubbornness personified. No one could
make him fly unless *he* was satisfied that conditions were proper.
Almost everything he did or said became national news, and
finally, after much coaxing, he agreed to receive an honor during

a formal dinner of the Aéro-Club de la Sarthe on September 24, 1908, in Paris. But he did so on the condition that he would not be asked to speak before the group. Promises notwithstanding, the excited audience begged him to talk. He rose slowly to his feet, his eyes moving across the waiting throng.

"I know of only one bird, the parrot, that talks," he said at last, "and it can't fly very high." Whereupon he resumed his seat.

The press tried in every way possible to find new things to say about Wilbur Wright. Praise was extravagant, and newsmen endowed the Wrights with qualities they themselves had never imagined they possessed. As Wilbur related, "Instead of doubting that we could do anything they were ready to believe that we could do everything."

An enormous amount of news space was devoted to his personal life, to his unassuming decency, his integrity, his refusal to be swayed by the tremendous acclaim showered upon him. Much was written about the keen intelligence he had concealed behind his working like any other laborer. He was described, and by the scientists of France as well as the press, as a man of exceptional knowledge, deeply learned and capable not only in aviation but other fields of science, as well; and overnight, as is still true of celebrities, he became known as a leading expert on art, literature, medicine, and all the affairs of the world.

He especially relished his new relationship with the newspapers. Their representatives were welcome at Le Mans, he assured them, and as quickly as reporters and correspondents arrived on the scene to stare and poke and ask questions, he would grin and put them to work, Tom Sawyer–fashion, fetching tools, helping to drag the airplane in and out of its hangar, dragging and pulling on the rope that lifted his catapult weight. They loved it. Wilbur had intended it as a joke and found that the joke was on him — anyone who had even the slightest chance to help fought for the privilege.

A visit within his quarters and working area was greatly prized; every detail went into news stories that were read everywhere in France and throughout Europe. Reporters wrote glowing descriptions of Wilbur's workshed, praised his neatness, marveled at his precision even in storing tools and working materials, and wrote long copy on how Wilbur's canvas cot was hauled up by rope each day to the ceiling of his workshop so that it would not interfere with his operations. For he was still living and sleeping in his workshed, although requests poured in, asking him to accept hotel suites and other extravagant forms of hospitality.

Scores of dignitaries, curious and skeptical, came from hundreds of miles around to see for themselves whether the American, Wilbur Wright, could really fly. Among the more eminent of the qualified investigators were Griffith Brewer, of the Aeronautical Society of Great Britain, and Charles S. Rolls, of Rolls-Royce, who, with Louis Blériot, had first met Wilbur in June. At Le Mans, Brewer had the distinction of being the first Englishman to fly, when he accepted Wilbur's invitation to go up as a passenger. He was followed in flight almost immediately by Rolls, a fellow balloonist, and other members of the society. (Rolls subsequently became the world's first private buyer of an airplane.) Later, Brewer would devote much of his life to exposing the fraud perpetrated by the Smithsonian Institution and Glenn Curtiss and his associates at Hammondsport, New York. It was a deceitful scheme aimed at discrediting the Wrights and establishing the original Langley *Aerodrome* as the world's first successful heavier-than-air flying machine.

Most startling to Wilbur was the avalanche of fan mail that descended upon him. If the letters carried scientific questions and were obviously serious, Wilbur did his best to respond, doing so in laborious detail. Many writers merely expressed their good wishes and congratulations. But there were also hundreds of letters from women who sought eagerly to make his acquaintance, to meet him and to dine with him. Many letters contained proposals of marriage — complete with physical and intellectual credentials and proof of social position. Wilbur consigned such correspondence to the stove.

Even as *"Il Vole, Il Vole"* sent its tune through France, it became the fashion for people from Paris and nearby communities — and some not quite so near — to visit the parade grounds at Camp d'Auvours. One woman of high social status traveled all the way from Paris just to watch the American whirl through the skies like a great linen bird; and here was this fellow they called Old Oilcan sound asleep in his shed, refusing to fly just because he did not like the weather at the moment. The idea that the safety of the flight, not her expectation, was what counted seemed to her inexplicable. *

No man in the world at that time could have known more pride than Bishop Milton Wright, and his pride was less for the flights of his sons than for their steadiness of character in the teeth of the gale of publicity and acclaim. On September 9, 1908, the bishop wrote from Dayton to Wilbur (and sent a similar letter to Orville):

> Indeed they treat you in France as if you were a resurrected Columbus; and the people gaze as if you had fallen down from Jupiter. Enjoy fame ere its decadence, for I have realized the emptiness of its trumpet blasts. "And false the light on glory's plume, As fading hues of even."
>
> You and Orville are, however, secure of a place with Fulton and Morse and Franklin in the temple of fame. "Conquerors of the Air." Its extensive results are, as yet, uncomprehended and undreamed of, even by yourselves. Did Fulton have any vision of an ocean greyhound, or Franklin of wireless telegraphy? . . . I wish it were so you could be in the home circle.

Yet there were the moments little known by the admiring public. In a letter written to Katharine on September 10, Wilbur disclosed the tremendous stress he had borne, separated in a foreign country from a life heretofore supported by his family's love and strength:

> I received word last evening of Orville's flight of 57 minutes, and today learn of his having passed the hour in a second flight later in the day. It is a record for sure! I have not done much for several weeks, partly because of windy weather, partly because of accidents which have necessitated repairs, and partly because I have been so nervous and worried that I have not felt like doing much

* There is no point in being too critical, for in this respect the world has hardly changed since 1908. I have spent too much time at Cape Canaveral and the Kennedy Space Center, when some electronic or mechanical flaw held the countdown on a manned mission, listening to the groans and complaints of visiting observers who could not fathom why a spacecraft would not depart for the moon on *their* schedule.

hustling. You can scarcely imagine what a strain it is on one to have no one you can depend on to understand what you say, and want done, and what is more, no one capable of doing the grade of work we have always insisted upon in our machines. It compels me to do almost everything myself and keeps me worried . . .

On September 13 Wilbur wrote to his father:

Orville's fine flights are making more of a sensation than my first flight over here and I thought then people would go crazy they were so excited. Well it will be a relief to me to have some of the responsibility removed from my mind. While I was operating alone there was the constant fear that if I attempted too much and met with a serious accident we would be almost utterly discredited before I could get the machine repaired, with no materials and no workmen. The excitement and the worry, and above all the fatigue of an endless crowd of visitors from daylight till dark had brought me to such a point of nervous exhaustion that I did not feel myself really fit to get on the machine. But I am much better now and our position is so secure that I can work with less strain than when I felt that I was surrounded by a pack of jealous & chauvinistic Frenchmen who would be glad of the least excuse for stopping their cheers & beginning to hoot.

However I must say that here in the district of La Sarthe every one from the prefect or governor down to the humblest citizen has seemed a genuine friend from the beginning almost. They look on me almost as an adopted citizen and show their friendliness in a dozen different ways. For instance, the old green cap which Orville brought home last fall and which I have been wearing over here when at work has set a new style and the stores have their show windows full of "Wright" caps. Some of the other manifestations are not so pleasant. From daylight till dark a crowd hangs about the building peering in at every crack. Almost every evening a crowd of two or three thousand people comes out to see if I will make a flight, and goes home disappointed if I do not. Some of them have come twenty, forty or even sixty miles on bicycles and a few from foreign countries. One old man of 70 living about 30 miles away made the round trip on a bicycle every day for nearly a week. I sometimes get so angry at the continual annoyance of having the crowd about that I feel like quitting the whole thing and going home, but when I think of the sacrifices some of them have made in the hope of seeing a flight I cannot help feeling sorry for them when I do not go out. If I can get through this season in such a way as to make a reasonable competence secure I am done with exhibitions & demonstrations forever. I can't stand it to have people continually watching me. It gets on my nerves.

Mr. Lahm is immensely proud of the fact that his son [Lieutenant Lahm] made the first trip with Orville . . .

Frank S. Lahm, a member of the Aéro-Club of France residing in Paris, was already a minor celebrity because of the flight his son had made in Virginia.

If one recalls what had happened to Wilbur Wright when he was eighteen, that terrible moment when a hockey stick came smashing into his mouth, and his long seclusion afterward, this feeling of his becomes easier to understand.

The interest of the people was no longer morbid or derisive; the curiosity had become adoration. Nevertheless the crowds were there, but Wilbur felt loneliness in the midst of these thousands. He was homesick for his family, but this remained a secret he told no one in France.

On September 13 he wrote to his brother, who now seemed to have been separated from him for years, "The newspapers for several days have been full of the stories of your dandy flights, and whereas a week ago I was a marvel of skill now they do not hesitate to tell me that I am nothing but a 'dub' and that you are the only genuine champion skyscraper. Such is fame! Your flights have naturally created an immense sensation in Europe and I suppose that America is nearly wild . . ."

A letter from Orville to Wilbur, written on the same day, contained a chilling prophecy:

I suppose you have had full reports of the flights I have been making this week . . .

The Navy department seems much interested. Lieut.

Sweet, who was detailed by the Navy department to witness and report on our flights, is very enthusiastic. He says he believes that every war vessel will soon be equipped with machines. They will want machines to carry two men, fly for four hours, and carry floats so that they will not sink in case the engine stops . . . Every one here is very enthusiastic, and they all think the machine is going to be of great importance in warfare . . .

The exchanges of the brothers moved swiftly from technical and business matters to their human concerns. On September 15, Wilbur added personal details in a letter to his sister: "Commander Bonel is our warmest friend in France and seems to have a personal affection for us. You will notice his picture in one or two of the photographs I sent home. The boy about 14 or 15 years old in the same pictures is his son, an awfully nice boy. I have several youthful friends over here. The Baron d'Estournelles has a little boy about 10 and a little girl of 6 who are great partners of mine. They both speak English very well, and are sweet, well trained little folks . . ."

September 18, 1908, dawned a rare day indeed — perfect, beautiful, splashing softly across the French countryside. It was cool and serene despite the strong sun, and there was scarcely a breath of wind. A perfect day for flying. And it could not have come at a more propitious time, for Wilbur had just completed his preparations for an official trial. Not an exhibition this time, but a demonstration for the record, and an attempt for the Michelin and Commission d'Aviation prizes. Wilbur felt a great strain lifted from him. He had triumphed in his first flights in France, and Orville had taken all America by storm. Their friendly rivalry on both sides of the Atlantic had spread their names and fame around the world. Fame, and the realization that for the entire race of man a new era had dawned. The new age had come like no other. Not slowly, not making its effect known gradually, but just as swiftly as the explosive rush of their own wings.

And *they* had done it. It was a beautiful moment, a savoring of life, a marvelous time to be alive and triumphant within themselves. At eight o'clock in the morning, the dew still fresh in the fields about him, Wilbur prepared the machine for what he intended to be a record-smashing flight.

Someone came up to him, and he glanced up as a telegram was held out.

In horror he read the news. Orville Wright had crashed! His passenger, a military officer, was dead, and Orville was in a hospital with serious injuries.

CHAPTER 28

"As a Result of His Trust in Our Machines"

NOT EVEN when Orville lay in delirium from typhoid fever and he had sat so long at his side had Wilbur felt so helpless.

The telegram said that the accident had happened about five in the afternoon of the day before, Thursday, September 17. Orville had been circling the field at Fort Myer. Everything was going well, and the observers had had no hint of trouble. Then, on his fourth circuit of the field, voices rose in fright. Screams lanced out as the aircraft pitched over and dove straight for the ground, to crash with terrible impact. Lieutenant Thomas E. Selfridge had been flying with Orville as the army's official passenger.

Wilbur wished desperately for more details, but the telegram was brief. Orville was alive, with a fractured left leg, four broken ribs, a fractured and dislocated hip, and a back injury. Selfridge, whose skull had been fractured, had lived to reach the hospital with his pilot, but had died an hour later. He was the first man to die in the crash of a powered aircraft.

For two days Wilbur was nearly paralyzed from the shock. He and Orville had never done anything without sharing the moment; their intervals of being apart had all been brief and had been spent on working toward a common goal; this tore at his soul. At last, on September 20, he was able to write to Katharine:

> I received the news of the awful accident at Washington only on Friday morning about eight o'clock, just as I was

finishing preparations for an official trial for the Michelin
& Comm[ission] d'Aviation prizes. The death of poor
Selfridge was a greater shock to me than Orville's injuries, severe as the latter were. I felt sure "Bubbo" would
pull through all right, but the other was irremediable.
The weather was ideal, a day of a thousand, but in view
of the positive news of Selfridge's death, I did not feel
that it would be decent to proceed as though I were
indifferent to the fate which had befallen him as a result
of his trust in our machines. So the trials were postponed
till next week.

I cannot help thinking over and over again "If I had
been there, it would not have happened." The worry over
leaving Orville alone to undertake those trials was one
of the chief things in almost breaking me down a few
weeks ago and as soon as I heard reassuring news from
America I was well again. A half dozen times I was on
the point of telling Berg that I was going to America in
spite of everything. It was not right to leave Orville to
undertake such a task alone. I do not mean that Orville
was incompetent to do the work itself, but I realized that
he would be surrounded by thousands of people who with
the most friendly intentions in the world would consume
his time, exhaust his strength, and keep him from having
proper rest. When a man is in this condition he tends to
trust more to the carefulness of others instead of doing
everything and examining everything himself. A man
cannot take sufficient care when he is subject to continual interruptions and his time is consumed in talking to
visitors. I cannot help suspecting that Orville told the
Charleys [Charles Furnas and Charles Taylor] to put on
the big screws instead of doing it himself, and that if he
had done it himself he would have noticed the thing that
made the trouble, whatever it may have been. If I had
been there I could have held off the visitors while he
worked or let him hold them off while I worked. But he
had no one to perform this service. Here Berg helps to act
as a buffer and gives me some chance to be alone when
I work. People think I am foolish because I do not like
the men to do the least important work on the machine.
They say I crawl under the machine and over the machine
when the men could do the thing well enough. I do it

partly because it gives me opportunity to glance around to see if anything in the neighborhood is out of order. Hired men pay no attention to anything but the particular thing they are told to do, and are blind to everything else. When we take up the American demonstrations again we will both be there. It is much easier to do things when you have someone at hand in whom you have absolute confidence.

Tell "Bubbo" that his flights have revolutionized the world's beliefs regarding the practicability of flight. Even such conservative papers as the London *Times* devote leading editorials to his work and accept human flight as a thing to be regarded as a normal feature of the world's future life . . .

No matter what he heard from others or read in the news accounts, or heard even from his own family, Wilbur was wise enough and had sufficient experience to withhold final judgment about the cause of the crash until he heard directly from his brother.

One lesson that was to be learned from the very outset of flight — and the Wrights had learned it instantly when they read details of their "six-bladed propeller" that pushed, pulled, levitated, and propelled, of their "navigation car," of their flights "10 miles out to sea," and so forth — was that eyewitnesses to a flight were very rarely competent to report on the events that had taken place. They might be honest, but generally they lacked the background knowledge for judging a moment or a detail, and often drew conclusions that might appear correct but were based on weak premises.

Jerome Fanciulli, a former reporter for the Washington *Post* and the Associated Press who had covered aviation from its infancy, was at Fort Myer when Orville crashed and had met several times with Orville at the National Press Club in Washington before the 1908 flight demonstrations began. I have discussed the crash with Fanciulli, whose presence at the scene makes his words all the more valuable. It is interesting to compare Fanciulli's eyewitness account with Orville's.

"When he crashed I was one of the first to reach the plane. There never was a correct story of what happened. The newspapermen wrote that a propeller broke, but there was no truth to that. There wasn't anything to it except that Lieutenant Tom Selfridge was very heavy. He was the heaviest passenger Orville had taken up. When Orville made his turn, never having had that experience with so heavy a passenger before, the airplane started sliding down. And of course Orville didn't know, but if he had put his plane into a nose dive he would have come out of it all right."

Orville had not stalled, Fanciulli said. "No, he slid sideways. He sideslipped and struck the ground with his wing — and cartwheeled. It happened because he had extra weight and was making a sharp turn with very little power. And he might not have had enough height even to dive out of it. I'd say he was about a hundred and fifty feet, perhaps."

Fanciulli spoke of his warm friendship with the Wrights, even though he was a young *newspaperman* at the time. "Katharine was very devoted to Orville when he was in the hospital. She would read Wilbur's letters out loud in front of me. They just took me in as if I were one of the family. They certainly showed a great deal of confidence in me, which I not only respected but valued very highly. I first met Katharine when she came to Fort Myer. She was delightful. Where Orville was concerned, her devotion was absolute. She looked after him and read those letters from Wilbur; that sort of thing. She was a rather vivacious person, but calm, intelligent, charming. She was very dignified . . . You got the impression she had a very strong character."

"In the hospital," Fanciulli recalled, "there was some conversation between Orville and Katharine about Wilbur being a little too bossy. There was no question that Katharine and Orville were closer than Katharine and Wilbur. Most of all she remains in my memory as a fine, strong character."

As to the strength of the brothers, and whether they may have developed a fear of flying, especially after surviving a number of crashes, Fanciulli said, "I never saw any indication of that. They felt that once they got things going, they wouldn't do a lot of flying themselves anymore. They wouldn't have to. They could get others to do the flying for them."

This seemed strange; the brothers — particularly Orville — loved to fly. Fanciulli shook his head. "I think it was more a case

of not having anything to gain by flying, anything that would
advance their knowledge. I think that was their attitude. Although, of course, this may have been the influence of the people
who were financing their company. Maybe they felt the Wrights
ought not to fly. And very few people are aware of it, but Orville
never did get over his injuries completely."

And Augustus Herring?

"He was a very clever fellow, a faker," was Fanciulli's response.
"He had it written all over him. I went to New York when he
was trying to get a Signal Corps contract. I went with some
members of the Aero Club of America and several others. We
visited his shop. He had a beautiful shop, beautiful propellers,
and all that sort of thing. But as young as I was then, I immediately sized him up as a faker. I reported my opinion to General
Allen of the Signal Corps."

(Later, Jerome Fanciulli would be involved in major negotiations and as a go-between for the Wrights, Glenn Curtiss, and
the other leading aviation figures of that day. Although Fanciulli
managed the Curtiss Exhibition Company between 1909 and
1912, he remained a good friend of the Wrights.)

From Dayton, a convalescing Orville wrote this accident report
on November 14, 1908, to Wilbur in France:

> It is two weeks today since I left the hospital at Fort
> Myer, yet I am just beginning to get about the house on
> crutches. I sit up several hours at a time, though I suffer
> some from the pressure of the blood in my feet and legs,
> after so long a period of disuse. This is the first I have
> written since the accident.
>
> I have tried to get reliable information concerning the
> accident, but I find most witnesses observed very little
> of the details of what happened.
>
> We had made three rounds of the ground, keeping well
> inside of buildings, trees, etc., so that the turns were of
> necessity pretty short. On the fourth round, everything
> seemingly working much better and smoother than in
> any former flight, I started on a larger circuit with less
> abrupt turns. It was on the very first slow turn that the
> trouble began. Just after passing over the top of our build-
> ing at a height which I estimate at 100 or 110 ft., but

which Lieut. Lahm, Chas. Taylor, Furnas, and many others thought to be 150 ft., and while traveling directly towards Arlington Cemetery, I heard (or felt) a light tapping in the rear of the machine. A hurried glance behind revealed nothing wrong, but I decided to shut off the power and descend as soon as the machine could be faced in a direction where a landing could be made. This decision was hardly reached, in fact I suppose it was not over two or three seconds from the time the first taps were heard, till two big thumps, which gave the machine a terrible shaking, showed that something had broken. At the time I only thought of the transmission. The machine suddenly turned to the right and I immediately shut off the power. I then discovered that the machine would not respond to the steering and lateral balancing levers, which produced a most peculiar feeling of helplessness. Yet I continued to push the levers, when the machine sudden[ly] turn[ed] to the left (the right wing rising high in the air) till it faced directly up the field. I reversed the levers to stop the turning and to bring the wings on a level. Quick as a flash, the machine turned down in front and started straight for the ground. Our course for fifty feet was within a very few degrees of the perpendicular. Lieutenant Selfridge up to this time had not uttered a word, though he took a hasty glance behind when the propeller broke, and turned once or twice to look into my face, evidently to see what I thought of the situation. But when the machine turned headfirst for the ground, he exclaimed, "Oh! Oh!" in an almost inaudible voice.

I pulled the front rudder lever to its limit, but there was no response in the course of the machine. Thinking that, maybe, something was caught and that the rudder was not completely turned, I released the lever a little and gave another pull, but there was no change. I then looked at the rudder and saw that it was bent to its limit downward, and that the pressure of the air on the under side was bulging the cloth up between the ribs. The first 50 ft. of that plunge seemed like a half minute, though I can hardly believe that it was over one second at most. The front rudder in that distance had not changed the course more than five or ten degrees. Suddenly just before reaching the ground, probably 25 feet, something changed — the machine began to right itself rapidly. A few feet more, and we would have landed safely. As it was, the skids hit out at the front end. All the front framing was broken and the machine turned up on edge just as it did in the last flight in the South.

The only explanation I have been able to work out of the cause of the plunge for the ground is that the rear rudder, after the stay wire was torn loose by the propeller, fell over on its side and in some mysterious manner was caught and held in this position, with a pressure on its under side . . .

Almost a year later, June 6, 1909, Wilbur had thought long and hard about the details of the accident, and had gathered more detailed information. The account of the accident and its cause that he wrote to Octave Chanute is the best summation:

. . . After looking over the Ft. Myer machine we have decided that the trouble came in the following manner. One blade of the right propeller developed a longitudinal crack which permitted that blade to flatten out and lose its pushing power. The opposite blade not being balanced by an equal pressure on the injured blade put strains on its axle and its supports which permitted it to swing forward and sidewise a little farther than the normal position and at the same time set up a strong vibration. This brought the uninjured blade in contact with the upper stay wire to the tail and tore it loose, the end of the wire wrapping around the end of the blade and breaking it off. The blade which broke off was not the one which originated the trouble. The machine was pointing almost toward Arlington Cemetery at this moment, but swerved to the right where small trees made a bad landing place. Orville in the meanwhile had stopped the engine and attempted to turn to the left so as to land in the regular grounds, but found the tail inoperative. He therefore twisted the wings so as to present the left wing at the greater angle in order that the increased resistance might hold that end of the machine back and face the machine up the field. The maneuver succeeded very well and the machine had faced back toward the derrick and descended a third or more of the distance to the ground without any indication of serious trouble. He next moved the lever to straighten the wing tips so as to go straight ahead, but the machine instantly turned down in front and made almost straight for the ground. He thinks the tail had fallen over on its side with possibly a slight negative angle and that, when he moved the handle which operates the wings and tail, the latter was twisted to a positive angle and received a pressure on the under side, which caused the plunge. He pulled the front rudder to the limit, but for a time the response was very slow. Toward the end something seemed to change and the machine began to right, but it was too late. The ground was struck at a very steep angle and with terrific speed. The splitting of the propeller was the occasion of the accident; the uncontrollability of the tail was the cause . . .

Now, in September of 1908, Wilbur moved slowly through the shock of Orville's crash and serious injuries, the death of Selfridge, and his own bitter self-criticism that he had left undone something that could have prevented the crash. What also troubled Wilbur, more than anyone even suspected at that time, was that the public might instantly reverse its opinion and turn against him because of what had happened at Fort Myer. When this reaction did not take place, he accepted the continued support — which in many ways was even more enthusiastic than before — with enormous gratitude.

His feelings are clear in the closing passages of the letter he wrote to his sister on Sunday, September 20 — a day of rest before he would make new attempts to stretch his performance in France:

". . . The comments of the newspapers on the disaster are almost all very sympathetic and hopeful for the future. I have had dozens of telegrams expressing sympathy and confidence in us and our machines. Offers to accompany me are more numerous than ever. Mr. Nernst, the inventor of the Nernst lamp, was here Thursday evening and saw me fly in a golden sunset, thirty-two minutes at about 80 ft. height. He had seen Delagrange make a flight of about twenty-five minutes in the morning, before leaving Paris. He nearly went crazy with enthusiasm over my flight. "It was so different," he said. The next morning when he heard of Orville's accident he sent me a long telegram and said he would like to go with me, whenever I was ready to fly. Everyone takes almost as much interest in Orville's recovery as I do myself. He has certainly won the sympathy and admiration of the world, all right.

I am awfully sorry that you have had to pass through so much trouble of a nerve-wracking character this summer . . .

Now, Wilbur was pressed to make up for his brother's enforced absence from the air. No longer could he enjoy that friendly, almost daily, transatlantic dueling that their leapfrogging, record-breaking flights had engendered before the accident. He now felt he alone must uphold the Wright name in a way the world had not yet seen; he was determined as never before to prove the Wrights' proper claim to leading the world into the air and to prove that, no matter what anyone else was doing now, Orville and Wilbur Wright were still years ahead of the others.

September 21 was a Monday. The Sabbath behind him, Wilbur returned to flying — and thrilled France and all the world with a flight, for the official record, of 1 hour, 31 minutes, 25 seconds, during which he set a new world's distance record of 41 miles.

He was just beginning.

CHAPTER 29

"Princes & Millionaires Are as Thick as Fleas"

WILBUR TOOK TO THE AIR like a man possessed. Three days after setting his world record, he was in the air for a flight of more than 54 minutes, covering over 34 miles. On September 25, he flew for over 36 minutes. Three days later his flight endured for more than 1 hour, 7 minutes, along a distance of nearly 30 miles. And on October 3, he made two flights, one of which represented another niche in the skies: he flew nearly 35 miles, for more than 55 minutes, carrying a passenger and instantly gaining recognition for his machine's ability to perform with more than a single occupant.

Through the entire fall at Camp d'Auvours Wilbur kept at his flight demonstrations. The news from home was getting better as Orville continued to improve. He felt spiritually enriched by the way people in France expressed sympathy and understanding about Orville's accident and by their unflagging support of him. And he knew that others, those very dear to him, understood what he had felt. On September 24 his father had written:

> You may rest assured that I have deeply felt for your situation in France. The loneliness of [being] so far from home and friends, your difficulty in getting suitable workmen, your defective supply of parts of your machine, your burned arm, your overwork and unaided cares, the annoying attentions of the multitude, the inconsiderate

attention and requirements of notables, the immense responsibilities on your lone shoulders — all joined to make it hard on you. And the thunders of the world's applause could but ill comfort you under the handicaps and mishaps and depressions you had to encounter. It took good metal to stand the strain. Most of men under it, would have been like your broken propeller-shaft, at Kitty Hawk, in 1903. But you will come through all, safely and gloriously. We shall yet see you here in triumph . . .

The friendship of the officials and people of Sarthe is a beautiful thing — toward a stranger. I hope you will ever maintain and cherish it . . .

The distance overcome and perseverance, to see the flights is pathetic. What compassion Jesus showed toward the multitude drawn out by curiosity!

No doubt, not a few would have welcomed a chance (by your mishap) to hoot, though they cheered your success along with the multitude. Men are savage . . .

We look forward to the time when you can be again in the home you have always so loved. All Dayton awaits your coming . . .

On September 28, Wilbur felt the urge to write cheering words to his brother. "Today I made a flight of an hour and seven minutes," he wrote, "making 24 circuits of the two poles a kilometer apart, 48 kilometers in all . . .

"If I swipe the 5000 franc prize of the Commission of Aviation I will try to send some home . . ."

He won the prize!

Then, on October 7, Wilbur received a letter from Octave Chanute, one of many, but this one more personally detailed than was usual for the elderly gentleman. Chanute had just returned to Chicago after making a trip to Washington for the purpose of visiting Orville in the hospital.

When I left Orville . . . he was pronounced quite out of danger . . .

He had so endeared himself to all the Army officers and men with whom he had come into contact, as well as to the hospital attendants, that they were eager to do all they could for him, but, of course, a military hospital is not as comfortable as one's own home. At the Cosmos Club, where he had been staying, he had become very much liked and the members kept continually asking about him, only regretting that the surgeon's orders prevented calling upon him.

Your sister has been devotion itself. Fearing that he might lack something she stayed up at the hospital every night and deprived herself so much of sleep that I ventured to remonstrate with her about it . . .

I congratulate you heartily upon the magnificent success which you have achieved in France, upon the recognition which is now accorded you and upon the prospect that you will reap a fortune from your labors . . .

One of the more delightful touches of Wilbur's dry humor was in his letter of October 9 to Orville. "Every day," he remarked, "there is a crowd of people here not only from the neighborhood, but also from almost every country of Europe. Queen Margherita of Italy was in the crowd yesterday. Princes & millionaires are as thick as fleas . . ."

Through it all, Wilbur flew with almost passionate intent. During more than 100 flights at Camp d'Auvours, he carried passengers on no less than 60 of them. The most impressive of these flights took place when he carried aloft M. Léon Bollée, the man who had befriended him by offering the space at his auto factory in Le Mans. Bollée weighed 240 pounds, and Wilbur carried him merrily about the field with two complete swooping circles of the area. Just as Orville's passenger flights in America drew the most attention, so did this one with the heavyweight, especially for this machine and its limited power.

Wilbur grasped the attention of Europe with another sensational feat: he took aloft the first woman ever to fly in an airplane. Hart O. Berg approached him with the question: Would Wilbur take up his wife for a flight? Wilbur consented, but with a proviso that was to have ramifications beyond that day. The Wright *Flyer* had two seats atop the bottom wing, exposed fully to the airblast, and women's fashions of the day featured great flaring skirts. For both aerodynamics and modesty — Wilbur considered them of equal importance — he suggested that a rope be tied about Mrs. Berg's ankles to gather in her skirt and hold it in place. The flight received great attention: everything Wilbur did was news, and the first woman in an airplane was sensational news. And just as the Wright cap had been sold everywhere in Europe as a new fashion, so with this one flight the "hobbled skirt" became an overnight hit. Every girl, of course, had to be prepared to go flying with her beau, and the new style sold out wherever it appeared.

By now Camp d'Auvours was a world center for celebrities, millionaires, politicians, and the royalty of Europe, who flocked to where Wilbur Wright whirled and soared through the air as no man or machine had ever done before. The chance for a flight in this remarkable aircraft was so attractive a possibility that the great figures of Europe came from hundreds of miles in the hope they might be passengers, which would raise them to a level of esteem not to be obtained through any other activity. And the flights were less and less often brief hops, for in 1908 Wilbur made seven flights lasting more than an hour, and three of more than an hour and a half.

Then it was year's end, December 31, and Wilbur Wright was determined not to let this year go by without a last mighty journey through the air — and an attempt to win the Coupe Michelin. The weather did not cooperate; it was winter and menacing clouds began to gather. Ignoring weather in which he would not ordinarily have brought the machine from its shed, Wilbur climbed aboard with the engine turning over and released the holding wire. The machine flew perfectly in the cold, heavy air, but after he had been up for a while it began to rain, and the icy water stung deeply into Wilbur's face and body. He pressed on, and then sleet began to knife into his skin. Undaunted, he continued his flying, and when he landed, he had closed out the year *with a flight of 2 hours, 20 minutes, and 23.2 seconds, during which he covered a distance of 77 miles!*

He had just broken every flight record in the world — and in the process he won the coveted Michelin trophy, which also brought him 20,000 francs.

CHAPTER 30

"Quite Short, Well-Proportioned Men of Infinite Patience"

THE YEAR 1909 began a new phase in the lives of the Wrights. The contract with the French syndicate called for the brothers to train fully at least three pilots, who would then train others for France. Selected as students were the Count Charles de Lambert, Paul Tissandier, and Captain P.-N. Lucas-Girardville. Wilbur had already started some training flights at Auvours, but these took place with frequent interruptions and no real consistency because of the worsening weather conditions of the French winter. At the suggestion of Tissandier, Wilbur selected the area of Pau, an ancient fortress town at the gateway to the Pyrenees, and birthplace of Henry IV of France. It was here that Wilbur Wright would establish the world's first flying school.

By now, in the opening days of 1909, Orville was well on the way to recovery from his crash, and Wilbur's suggestion, received a few weeks before, that Orville come to France, bringing Katharine with him, began to look like an excellent idea. Katharine would take a year's leave of absence from her teaching, and it would be a splendid opportunity for Orville to continue his mending. It would be more than just a trip; they could all be together again, sharing the triumph they had earned after so many years. And Pau would be a marvelous place to stay, one of the great winter resorts of France. The townspeople of Pau were eager to have the Wrights. Wilbur's flying had put Le Mans on the world aviation map and the same would happen if he started his flight school at Pau. The community had built a house to furnish living quarters and a workroom on the grounds about eight miles from town, and arrangements had been made for Orville and Katharine to have free guest accommodations at the best hotel in Pau for as long as they wished to remain.

Orville, often in pain, was still walking with difficulty, but he and Katharine sailed for France on January 5, 1909, and joined Wilbur in Paris on January 12. Some black cloud seemed to be following Orville, for on the trip from Paris to Pau, on January 16, the train in which he and Katharine were riding smashed into another train, and Orville was severely shaken up and subjected to even more pain. The violent jolt tumbled him badly; from that day on he would never enjoy a ride in a train. The jarring motion hour after hour had a peculiar and painful effect on the permanent injuries he had suffered in his crash.

Notwithstanding an ocean voyage and train wreck, Orville and Katharine held a joyous reunion with Wilbur, who had returned from Paris to Pau two days earlier. The climate, the surroundings, and the awe in which the Wrights were held were a tonic for Orville, and he continued to recuperate steadily.

Life became a series of small and happy adventures, including the delights of mixing with the nobility and with political leaders of Europe. They never knew who or what group would appear suddenly in their midst, as on March 17, 1909, when King Edward VII of England, then wintering at Biarritz, arrived with his entire entourage to meet the Wrights and to watch Wilbur fly. They had more than they bargained for, since this was the day on which Wilbur first took up his sister for her view of the world at — for those days — high speed and high altitude.

Wilbur was still exhibiting his dry humor. Each flight required the derrick catapult to be cocked with the 1600-pound weight, and this called for many bodies pulling on the rope to carry the weight to the top of the pylon derrick. On more than one occasion Wilbur had a most unusual work crew setting up his launch catapult, for royalty and other famous men clamored to do their share. One of those assisting Wilbur was Lord Balfour, the former prime minister of England, who quickly threw off his coat and grasped the catapult rope. When people looked at him in surprise, he stood straight and informed the audience that any event as important as the flight of a man overshadowed the importance of any man on the ground and that he was going to do everything he could to contribute to this miracle.

Wilbur had made great friends with Lord Northcliffe, owner of the *London Daily Mail,* and the Englishman made it known among his own friends that he never ceased to wonder at Wilbur's gentleness of spirit and his quiet manner. These characteristics, combined with what he knew to be Wilbur's great knowledge of aviation and mechanics and many other subjects, endeared Wilbur to Northcliffe.* He was never less than amazed, he told his friends, that this American lacked a high school diploma, had done very little traveling, and yet worked modestly, in the midst of the world's most powerful men, with an aplomb that, as far as anyone could recall, never left him. Yet, like Wilbur, Northcliffe was not beyond his own little jokes, and would often direct others about him to certain tasks that made affairs easier for Wilbur when he was preparing for flight. One day Northcliffe pointed to a fine-looking young man heaving desperately on the catapult rope.

"Ah, you see that chap over there?"

Wilbur nodded.

"Well, he is the Duke of Northumberland. A very high station, indeed."

Wilbur nodded again.

"And this particular endeavor in which he is now engaged," continued Northcliffe, "namely, pulling on that catapult rope, is probably the only worthwhile thing that he has ever done in his life."

There was no escaping the names of Wilbur and Orville Wright all through Europe. Their names were on the lips of tens of millions, and they had swiftly become household words in a dozen languages. Songs were written for them and about them.

---

* Speaking of the Wrights early in the First World War, Lord Northcliffe had this to say: "I never knew a more simple, unaffected trio than Wilbur, Orville, and Katharine . . . Their heads were not in the least turned by the various attentions bestowed on them, nor by the many great financial offers given them to make demonstrations. They were Americans of English descent, and had a great affection for this country . . . [Katharine], in writing to me the other day, said: 'We here make no pretense at being neutral, we are heart and soul for England and her Allies in this great struggle' — and I think that family proved it by taking a beggarly sum for one of the greatest inventions of the world."

Whatever they wore set new clothing styles. They kept their audiences delighted with their simplicity and modesty, which the Europeans found a charming contrast to the brashness they often encountered in Americans. Yet the Wrights, enjoying as they did these marvelous moments, were eager to complete their work in Europe and return home. They wanted to build another aircraft, an improved machine, and complete the Signal Corps contract tests so disastrously interrupted the past September.

While they were in Pau, the Aeronautical Society of Rome offered them $10,000 for a machine and the training of an operator. The Italian government was also interested in the airplane.

On March 1, 1909, Wilbur wrote to Bishop Wright:

> I am expecting to finish my work here in a couple of weeks and then go to Rome for a month before coming back to America. It will be a full year in Europe. On the whole I have had an interesting time over here, but I will be very glad to get back home again . . .
>
> For several weeks we have been having visits from a number of distinguished visitors. Mr. Balfour, the former prime minister of England, was here a couple of weeks ago. Then the king of Spain made a special trip to see us,* and a few days later M. Barthou, one of the French cabinet ministers, came down and took a ride with me. He told me that the government would soon confer the Legion of Honor on both Orville and me. Although the camp is eight miles from Pau crowds of people come out every day and visitors flock there from all parts of Europe. The crowds are better handled than at Le Mans and give little trouble . . .
>
> It will not be necessary to put a mortgage on your Grant County property. We can scrape together a few dollars for you if you need it.

How pleasant it must have been to refer to this matter with tongue in cheek! For years the Wrights had been strict with their

---

* King Alfonso XIII of Spain declined an invitation to fly; he had promised the queen not to.

money. Their total out-of-pocket expenditures, right up to the point where they made their flights on December 17, 1903, had not quite reached *one* thousand dollars. They were frugal, careful of every dollar spent. They had never accepted any money from anyone until they established man's first flight, and after that they joined the French syndicate, with various backers, as a business arrangement, not a revenue source to carry out their research. And now the money, through prizes and competitions and especially new contracts, was starting to come in, steadily, ever growing. Without question, the Wright family would never again be concerned about finances.

H. Massac Buist was an ebullient Frenchman with a zest for life, a startling intelligence, and a penchant for seeking out moments that promised the greatest excitement. He was a natural to travel in style to Pau so that he could personally witness the great events taking place there and record them. His impressions — entertaining as well as informative — originally appeared in the March 6 and 13, 1909, issues of the British publication *Flight*. Buist saw things as did few other people and described them with perception and flair:

There must be a human side to flying, despite the colourless, abstract, and appallingly erudite tomes that teem from the Press and turn and turn about with fancy-free, hair-raising treatises on the precise manner in which we are going to wake up one morning to find the sky darkened with an enemy's aerial fleet, that seemingly never has to come to earth for petrol-tank or other replenishments.

These things being so [Buist informed the world], I resolved to go in quest of the present Mecca of the movement — Pau. Are you minded to go too? For me the excursion was rendered delightful every mile of the way, because I journeyed along the true pilgrim's course, the high road, albeit in rare luxury because on a 6-cyl. Rolls-Royce car, the route followed enabling us to halt many times on the way to visit other workers at the science of flight, as at Châlons, Issy-les-Moulineaux, Juvisy, Buc, and elsewhere, so that our interest grew and grew with the miles of roadway left behind, reaching the culminat-

ing point at Pont Long . . . It seems impossible to take a
ply in the human phases of flight without being interested in the personalities of the brothers Orville and Wilbur Wright.

To follow the daily flights conveniently one needs a
motor car, for the journey from Pau to Pont Long occupies
an hour and a half by horse-drawn conveyance, and that
is a tedious waste of time where minutes are precious.
The town is quitted by the Bordeaux road. A series of
large sign-boards, bearing each the legend "Champ
d'Aviation" saves all trouble at the parting of the ways.
By car one comes in twenty minutes' driving on some
flat, open land on the left, with a large, solid-looking,
reddish-brown building set back a couple of hundred
yards or so from the roadway. This substantial and neatly-
designed structure houses, perhaps, the most wonderful,
as it is the simplest, machine yet devised by the mind of
man — the four-year-old Wright biplane that the greatest
men from all parts of the world have journeyed hundreds
of miles to see, and that a king has been proud to sit on,
though he might not make a flight . . .

We have set out at eight o'clock in the morning, with
Miss Katharine Wright and the mail on board, and as the
only other members of the party besides myself are Mr.
Griffith Brewer, who represents Messrs. Wrights' patent
rights in this country, and the Hon. C. S. Rolls, who, as
a sometime friend, has been granted the honour of being
the first Englishman who has been allowed to order a
Wright aeroplane for use in Britain, we are *personae gra-
tae* at the Wright establishment . . .

The second mechanic has rolled back the huge sliding
doors that furnish an opening of more than 40 ft. to
enable the aeroplane to be taken in and out of its house.
One's eyes kindle at a moment like this, on seeing for
the first time the machine that folk have read about in
all parts of the civilised world, and when on the tip-toe
of expectation to catch a first glimpse of the brothers who
will go down in history as the first of mankind to ride
the wind at will.

One had just time to note with surprise that the four-
year-old machine was spick and span, with aluminium

paint over every part except the canvas, when a pale little man with a thin refined face, small regular features, very blue eyes, closely set and with somewhat of a poet's expression in them, a cap slightly too small for him, a stick, and a limp, came into view round one corner of the machine and, after a cheery "Good morning, sister," greeted the other members of the party with a quiet cordiality that gives genuine pleasure to a welcome. He need not have said "sister" for any stranger to have guessed the relationship; you could not mistake it. "How little he is" was the thought that came in mind to me when I first set eyes on . . . Mr. Orville Wright.

Before one had time to observe him more at the moment, however, a clean-shaven man, scarcely any taller, fair, tremendously active of movement, clad in an old cap, a black leather motor cyclist's type of coat, and trousers that were plainly strangers to the press, came forward in the characteristic act of rolling up a ball of string and thrusting it into one of his pockets. He hailed "sister" also; but one would need to be told of the relationship, so utterly unlike his sister or his brother is Mr. Wilbur Wright . . . The greatest trial of their lives — their separation on account of their simultaneous demonstrations of human flight in France and America — is happily overpast, for they are working together again, consequently they are as happy as schoolboys . . . I have never seen them taciturn, or curt, or secretive, or any of the other things which I had been led to believe were their outstanding characteristics . . .

The brothers present a case of absolute contrasts working in such perfect harmony as to gain every advantage to be derived from two distinct types of intellect being brought to bear on a single proposition. Both are quite short, well-proportioned men of infinite patience. They smile readily, give you a very firm grasp when shaking hands, and express themselves with more than common clearness; but for the rest, you believe they are brothers merely because folk whose word you cannot doubt tell you so. Making due allowance for the fact that Mr. Orville is only beginning to recover from the effects of his accident, nevertheless one realises in many minor ways that he does not normally possess the lightning-like rapidity of movement characteristic of Mr. Wilbur, whose walk is a series of rapid strides, in which his legs seem to have an inclination to get slightly in advance of his body. The quick turns of the head, the sudden darting glances that he will cast at sky, horizon, machine, or man, taking in all he wants in an instant, and the energy and decisiveness of his utterances are all in keeping. He is plainly a man accustomed to arrive at his decisions while things are yet happening. His deep-set eyes are well-spaced, and he rarely opens the lids fully. When he does it is for a moment only, as to glance into the air, usually with a sideward swing of the head and a wrinkling of the brows, one gathering the impression that he possesses the power of actually viewing the wind, so penetrating is the gaze. His features are large, strong, well-cut, and in handsome proportion, the top of the head being quite bald and the face clean-shaven, with thin straight lips, the corners of which sometimes play when his features break into a smile, on which occasions the eyes also laugh at you. When smiling, too, the mouth broadens and you become aware for the first time of a line that leads from either side of the cheek to about the corners of the mouth — those two lines which the eye of the camera seems to dwell on as the sole feature of the "flying-man," but which the human eye does not discover under any other circumstances. Truth to tell, the camera is no friend either to the brothers or to their sister. I have never seen a photograph . . . that portrays any one of the trio truthfully . . .

By comparison, Mr. Orville Wright does not possess any pronouncedly distinctive personality. That is to say, your eye would not be drawn to him among a crowd of men in the fashion in which it would instinctively dwell on Mr. Wilbur. Perhaps this is because Mr. Orville's features, including the jaw, are all small, while his eyes are not deep-set like his brother's and have somewhat of a dreamy expression, so that if you were asked to define the mental temperaments of the two brothers in a phrase you would say that Mr. Wilbur learned things through his eyes, while Mr. Orville got his knowledge by intuition, with which he is undoubtedly dowered to a rare

degree . . . He is seldom still for more than a few minutes
. . . He continues to follow every detail of the flights and
preparations for them, shouting instruction or advice
from time to time, and being immensely proud that already he is able to climb over the tension wires to get at
the motor. Despite the tremendous shock caused to his
nervous system by his accident, he has flown in France
with his brother, went up in a balloon only a week ago,
and often it is plainly as much as he can do to restrain
himself from taking control of the aeroplane and making
a flight.

There never were men who took the work more enjoy-
ably . . . merely because for them the joy of living lies in
the pursuit of their fascinating ambition. "Oh, they have
just had no end of fun learning to fly," says Miss Katharine Wright. "To hear them argue around and knock the
bottom out of each other's ideas, then at the end of three
hours to find Orv where Will started off, and Will where
Orv began, is just the killingest thing imaginable, and
makes them both burst out laughing — but it saved them
no end of useless experiment . . ."

They are extremely satisfied with their ground at Pont
Long. "The conditions for flying here are any amount
better than they were in America," said Mr. Orville. "See
there, where those trees make the nearest boundary?
That's a thousand feet away, the greatest length I ever
had to fly in; so I had to keep on the turn all the time.
But here you can make a circle of seven or eight kilo-
metres without getting out of the bounds of the grounds.
That's grand for teaching."

"Say," quoth Mr. Wilbur, coming up at that moment,
"I never knew such a place for shifting winds as this is.
In America we used to be able to set the starting-rail and
leave it for six days at a time; and in the North of France
it rarely shifted more than a quarter during the day. But
here the cold wind comes down off the mountains in the
morning, follows the sun right round, so," — describing
a half-circle with the wave of the arm — "then goes back
to the hills at night, so it's most everywhere in the course
of the day. I guess I didn't start just now because it had
shifted round to behind us."

"Don't matter, she ought to rise all right whether the

wind's in front or behind," observed Mr. Orville. "I used
to start regularly with the wind anything up to ten and
even fifteen miles an hour behind me at Washington. I'll
just get the anemometer and signal you with my stick
when to let go. The breeze is dropping or rising from six
to three miles an hour every few seconds this morning."

"Yah!" says Mr. Wilbur, with a jerk of his head and a
humorous pursing of his lips, as he strides off in his
tremendously energetic manner to superintend the adjustment of the starting tackle. And a few moments after,
Mr. Orville, holding the anemometer high in his left
hand, gave a shout as he let his stick drop to signal that
the breeze had subsided to three miles an hour. Instantly
Mr. Wilbur released the starting-catch, the big machine
scudded forward as the weight dropped, and a moment
later it was successfully launched in flight for the first
time in Europe with the wind behind it at the actual
moment of starting . . .

A common enthusiasm makes teaching a delight alike
to instructor and pupils. And it is a pleasure to observe
that none of the "fledglings" ever dreams of taking any
credit to himself. When anybody comments on their
flights the invariable reply is to the effect that "I did
nothing. It's such a wonderful machine, everything
comes so easily with it. The only tax is on the attention,
not on the muscles, which tire rather by our eagerness
than from any strain to which we put them." . . .

Now that the brothers are world-famous and the cy-
nosure of all eyes, it must be a happy reflection for their
hale and aged father that he was immensely helpful to
them in completing the final stages of their great discovery. His faith in the ability of his boys to achieve their
purpose never wavered, and they tell you with pride that
whenever their father went to see them during the experimental days he always brought good luck, which incidentally invariably extended to their having a good
flight. "Father — he's just splendid," they will say with
affectionate pride; and one sees as by reflection the renewed hope that must have come to them time and time
again during the troublous days from the cheery presence
and practical assistance of the grand old clergyman, who,
for all that the presence of Miss Wright in Europe leaves

him lonely at home, would not curtail her visit by a day. To the contrary, he is anxious for her to visit as many places of interest as possible. The link that ties the brothers is by no means the only one that is uncommonly strong in the Wright family. Indeed, as a family they are united to a rare degree. And that unity of purpose is manifest in their characters as it is in their activities.

CHAPTER 31

"Jas. Whitcomb Riley Came After Noon, & Others"

EVENTS QUICKENED in pace, in almost every aspect of their lives. Training pilots, selling airplanes, making business deals, traveling through Europe, and entangling themselves in fiercely contested legal battles over their patents kept them too busy to do what they wanted most of all — to keep improving their machines, to better their skill, to advance their performance.

On March 20, 1909, Orville sent a message to his brother Lorin: "I am sending inclosed a draft on New York [bank] for $5797. For pity's sake don't lose it as I spent seven francs and over an hour's time getting it . . ."

Messages went back and forth across the Atlantic. Bishop Wright wrote Wilbur and Orville: "I am glad to notice that they credit Wilbur for Sunday observance and freedom from tobacco. It will do more good than all the worth of the money you will ever get out of your invention . . ."

And the money was starting to pour in like rising breakers tumbling on the shore. April 2, Orville from Paris to Lorin: "I am sending inclosed a draft on New York for $21,297.19. Please deposit it in building associations at 4 pc. I think it best to distribute it somewhat . . ."

By April they were in Rome, and on the 14th, Katharine wrote her father: "We had J. Pierpont Morgan, his sister, daughter and a friend out to visit the camp yesterday afternoon. They were very pleasant people."

The training regime in France had accelerated through March, and now they faced more of the same in Italy. When that was done, they planned even more work. "It will probably be May before we are ready to start home," Orville wrote Lorin. "We have made a contract for some demonstrations at Berlin before the end of September, which will bring us back here again as soon as we are through in America . . ."

Orville was in Paris early in April when he received a detailed note from Wilbur, who had arrived in Rome:

> I reached Rome on Thursday morning after a rather tiresome trip. The cars were very crowded from Paris to Genoa.
>
> The goods arrived on Wednesday and were taken out to the shop on Thursday. There is a beautiful big shop here, two or three times as big as Bollée's, built at the time of the automobile boom but almost unused now. It makes a splendid place to set up the machine. It is located outside the north gate of the city, on the old Flaminian Way along which Caesar passed on his way to the conquest of Gaul, &c., &c., &c.
>
> The grounds for flight had not been fixed when I arrived but finally the place near the fort at Centocelle ("Chentochelly"), to the southeast of Rome, has been settled upon. It is a very good place, flat but not quite level, there being a gradual slope toward the southeast. The wind will be up the slope in the morning and down the slope in the evening. A train line runs about a half mile from the shed, with cars about an hour apart. The view over the *campagna* toward Frascati is very beautiful. The town is situated on the slope of the Alban Mountains, about twelve or fifteen miles away, I should judge.
>
> The shed is being constructed on the "knock-down" plan and its erection has not yet been commenced. Berg offered to bet forty francs to ten centimes that it would be ready before we were, but I am no robber. I hope we will not be delayed too long.
>
> The weather was rather good on Thursday and Friday but rainy yesterday and today. I am not looking for ideal weather, but I hope the worst season will be over by the time we are ready to fly.

On Friday we were granted an audience by "His Gracious Majesty" [King Victor Emmanuel]. Berg has employed a stenographer but I have not seen his postage bill yet. Berg pretended that the officers of the Aéro-Club had requested the meeting in order to boom their club. They only have fourteen members so far. "His Gracious" &c. is about the size of the little twin, and his feet failed to reach the floor by at least a foot when he sat down, but he gave us a very cordial reception and promised to come out to the grounds whenever we should be ready for him.

I have not had any time to look about the city yet, and probably will not unless we have plenty of windy days.

[P.S.] Tell Chas. Taylor that sticks with ferrules on the ends must be smaller than the hinge they fit into. It is scandalous to send out such stuff as he sends.

The flights by Wilbur Wright at Centocelle began on April 15 for a total of 42 flights. Twenty-three were training flights with Lieutenant Mario Calderara, of the Italian navy, one with Lieutenant Umberto Savoia, and one with Captain Castagneris Guido. The remaining flights were made with various passengers who desired to be taken up. Several flights were made without the use of the drop-weight derrick and five without the derrick or starting rail.

On the day the king of Italy visited Centocelle, Wilbur took up a Universal cameraman and a bioscope camera to capture the surrounding countryside on film, thus producing the first motion pictures ever taken from an airplane. It was a remarkable record of pioneering aerial photography. Bishop Wright made a laconic entry in his diary of Monday, April 19, 1909: "Moving pictures of Wilbur's flights were shown at theater."

Three weeks later he made another entry that well concealed his personal elation: "The children sailed for New York on the *Kronprinzessin Cecilie*, due at New York next Tuesday."

Then, on the day they arrived in Dayton, May 13, 1909, the bishop wrote: "Flags, Chinese lanterns, and electric lights are being arranged. Eleven carriages met the Wright brothers and Katharine at the depot . . . and a four-horse carriage pulls them home, where thousands meet them around our house. Over 10,000 came at night."

It is enough to say that Dayton went quite mad with joy when the brothers returned from their stunning successes in Europe.

And then it was quickly back to business. Wilbur, four days after arriving home, wrote to Octave Chanute:

> We reached home last Thursday after a good trip of 15 days from Rome. We are all improved in health since leaving home. I have gained about a dozen pounds in weight. Orville is in splendid general health and is getting to use his leg quite well again. He had no trouble in walking about the deck of the steamship without a cane. My sister is also much better than when she finished her 1908 season of nursing. We had a very nice time abroad, but it is a pleasure to be back home again.
>
> We are very busy at work on the machine we will use at Ft. Myer. The old one was so badly broken up that we will make all but the motor and transmission new. It is probable that we will reduce the area a trifle.
>
> On our way home we stopped a couple of days in London, and met a great number of your friends who wished to be remembered to you. The English are fitting up a very nice flying ground at Sheppey Island near the mouth of the Thames, and we have taken orders for about a half dozen machines which are being constructed for us by Short Brothers. We have had opportunities to close out our English business but have preferred to hold on to it for the present. We sold in France and Germany, and will probably close a contract for Italy very soon. After sailing we learned that Lt. Calderara at Rome had met with an accident but we have no reliable information regarding it as yet. I left him with greater misgivings than my other pupils, because he was a cigarette fiend, and was being very badly spoiled by the attention and flattery he was receiving. De Lambert and Tissandier were splendid fellows in every respect and very trustworthy. I hope you are in good health and that we shall see each other soon.

Chanute immediately responded on May 19:

> It is with great pleasure that I receive your friendly letter of 17th and the good news about all of you which it contains.

I have, of course, rejoiced over your triumphs in Europe and was particularly gratified with the sensible and modest way in which you accepted your honors, both abroad and since your return to this country. It encourages the hope that you will still speak to me when you become millionaires.

Please tell Miss Katharine and Orville that I congratulate them upon having seen the sights of the "Eternal City" under such happy auspices.

As for myself, my health is good, but I begin to feel advancing age and my capacity for work is being diminished. I have lately bought a house and given it to my daughters, and I shall hope to receive you in it, if your engagements bring you this way.

I do not yet feel certain that I will be able to go to Washington to see you fly, but I shall hope to do so.

There were certain interruptions in the work of the brothers as they prepared for the Signal Corps flight tests. On June 10, 1909, they were received at the White House by William Howard Taft. Before a standing audience of a thousand men and women, the President presented the two guests of honor with Aero Club of America gold medals. In a brief but deeply moving ceremony, the President praised the genius, hard work, persistence, and modesty of Orville and Wilbur Wright: "You made this discovery by a course that we of America like to feel is distinctly American — by keeping your nose right at the job until you had accomplished what you had determined to do." He then expressed the hope that the flying machine would be used for "peaceful benefits for all nations," and not just for the purposes of war.

The President, six feet two inches tall and a hefty 300 pounds, stood between Orville and Wilbur, and then, for the benefit of the photographers, bestowed special attention on Katharine, assuring her she should have every right to be extremely proud of her brothers. "Miss Wright blushed as she shook the President's hand," reported *The New York Times*, "but her eyes were alight with pleasure."

One week later the brothers again were interrupted in their now frantic preparations for Fort Myer. Orville, Wilbur, and Katharine were the center of a massive two-day celebration (June

17 and 18) in their hometown of Dayton. There were three parades, two enormous banquets, and a public reception attended by all the city schoolchildren, an event at which Bishop Wright with beaming pride delivered the invocation.

More gold medals were bestowed on the brothers. There were medals voted by the Congress, by the State of Ohio, and by the City of Dayton. The climax of the celebration, which brought the city to a standstill, came on the second night, with sensational fireworks in the form of portraits of Wilbur and Orville, eight feet in height, intertwined with the American flag.

In those two days all business was suspended — except by the Wright brothers. In every spare moment they rushed back to their workshop to work on the new airplane, which had been scheduled for the next army trials in July.

A few comments by Bishop Wright: "Thursday, June 17th, 1909. Reception at 10:30. We came home and stayed till night. Jas. Whitcomb Riley came after noon, & others . . . Went over at night to fireworks.

"Friday, June 18th, 1909. It was a lovely day. Went at 10:30 to fair ground. Children sing 'Star Spangled Banner.' I made the invocation . . . [General] Allen spoke and presented the Congressional medal, Gov. Harmon the Ohio medal; Mayor Burkhart presented the City medal. Return home. Attended the parade in afternoon. Also automobile parade at night. Grandstand, 1st & Monument Ave."

Concise, casual, matter-of-fact. Not *quite* ho-hum. Warmly received, accepted, enjoyed. The pleasure running deep, quiet.

But Wilbur and Orville were chafing at the bit. They enjoyed the huzzahs showered upon them, but, knowing the Signal Corps demonstration was unfinished business, they were impatient to get back to work. They still felt they had to prove themselves. On Friday, June 18, while Dayton rocked to the festivities honoring the brothers, an entry in the Signal Corps' "Log of Wright's Aeroplane" for the tests to be resumed stated succinctly, "Aeroplane arrived from Dayton, Ohio."

The next day, Bishop Wright neatly penned another short note in his diary: "Wilbur and Orville pack clothes and start to Washington City on 10:00 train at night — via Harrisburg . . ."

CHAPTER 32

"The Senate Adjourned . . ."

EVERYTHING IN LIFE has its own meaning. To Orville and Wilbur Wright, whatever conquests they had made, whatever they had achieved, there were still matters left unfinished. The brothers were the idols of the civilized world. They had received awards and honors beyond their dreams. Financial rewards were pouring in on them. Millions of people cheered and praised them as men and as great inventors. They were enshrined, in whatever halls of fame existed, as the two men who had turned the world on a course never before known to man, and from which we could never again turn away.

But there was unfinished business at hand. The successes and the honors and the new affluence were not enough. Orville and Wilbur had not finished their tests for the Signal Corps, and they would not rest until they had completed their flight demonstrations and proved the superiority of their machine against any others in the world. This was now a case in which winning was a matter to be settled once and for all.

On Thursday, June 24, 1909, they completed assembly of the new machine to be used in the U.S. Army Signal Corps demonstration flights and competition. There were no laurels on which they could or would rest — not yet. Proof in flight was everything.

On June 25 and 26 they tested their new engine. The magneto and battery worked as designed. They snugged down the machine, cabled it tightly, wound up to 1640 revolutions per minute.

The machine appeared to want to fly as much as did the brothers. The pylon tower for launching the *Flyer* was assembled.

Bishop Wright and Reuchlin, the oldest Wright brother, arrived in Washington on June 28. Again those marvelous notations in the father's diary: "Orville met us and took us to the Raleigh House, where we took rooms in the 8th story.

"The Senate adjourned & Congressmen came to witness a flight. A rain went south. Wind strong."

A simple notation. "The Senate adjourned & Congressmen came to witness a flight . . ."

Orville and Wilbur discussed the tests, and Orville put his foot down. He, Orville, had started these tests, and no one else was going to finish them. They would both make test flights, but in the official demonstrations it would be Orville at the controls. They agreed.

Now, with over three weeks of testing and preparation behind them, including 20 practice flights to be certain of control response, propeller thrust, and structural integrity, they called in the officials. The requirements were established. The conditions were set.

Late on the afternoon of July 27, Lieutenant Frank P. Lahm took his seat aboard the *Flyer*. On hand were President Taft, the cabinet, other high public officials, and an estimated crowd of 10,000 enthusiastic spectators.

The engine turned over smoothly. The log for the "aeroplane" says it brusquely: "Left shed at 6:10 P.M. Start 6:35 P.M. Time in flight 1 hr. 12 min. 37⅘ sec. Circles around field 79½ times. Returned to shed 7:30 P.M. Maximum height 150 ft. . . ." The flight had fulfilled the army requirement of remaining in the air for one hour carrying two persons, and broke a world record held by Wilbur Wright, who in 1908 at Le Mans had flown with a passenger for 1 hour, 9 minutes, and 41 seconds.

The next flight was to be an official speed trial from the proving ground at Fort Myer to Shuter's Hill, in Alexandria, five miles distant, where the airplane would circle and return to its takeoff point. In between there was no suitable ground to land if the engine failed. But Orville ignored the danger. He would be flying *above* it; the surface didn't matter to him.

Ten years later, Orville set down his terse description of that tremendously significant flight, which not only met but exceeded the terms of the Signal Corps contract:

"Lieutenant Benjamin D. Foulois (now General Foulois) was the observer on this test flight.

"The motor made 1,310 R.P.M. in flight, developing 32 horsepower. The ten-mile course from Fort Myer to Alexandria and return was covered in 14 minutes 40 seconds — an average speed of 42.58 miles. The timing of this flight varied a good deal. Foulois' time, taken on the machine with a stop watch, gave a speed of a little over 42.9 miles . . ."

The last barrier was down. The last questions were answered. The last promises were fulfilled. *And more . . .*

The army disbursed $25,000 for the aircraft, and then added $2500 for each mile per hour over the requirement of at least 40 miles per hour.

There were more flights. The speed was increased. Refinements to the aircraft improved its handling qualities. But to the brothers, all this was inevitable. More power, more efficiency, more experience meant there was only one way to move — toward improved performance. And there was another matter of unfinished business, but this time they needed to prove nothing; they had only to meet the specifications of others.

Orville and Katharine sailed for Europe, bound for Germany, where Orville would fly demonstrations for the German Wright Company and then train two men to the point where they would be competent enough to instruct other pilots. On August 19, 1909, Orville wrote Wilbur: "We reached Berlin this morning. Berg had secured the best rooms in this hotel [Esplanade] for us for nothing. We have a large sitting room about 25 × 30 feet, two large bedrooms and two bath rooms."

Wilbur could not resist a quip and on August 30 wrote back: "I see by the papers that you and Bill [Kaiser Wilhelm II of Germany] had quite a confab. I advise that you move into a hotel about like the Brittania [*sic*] at Rome. If you stay where you are too long Swes [Katharine] will never be able to live on the salary she gets when she goes to teaching school after Christmas . . ."

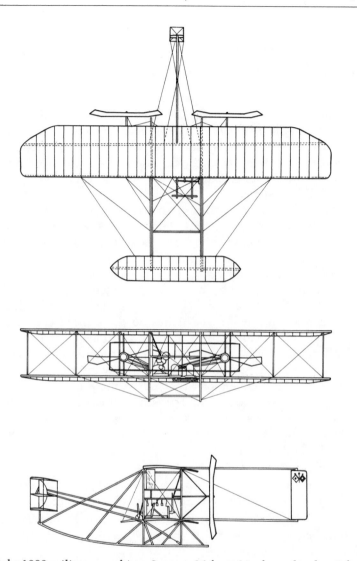

Wright 1909 military machine: Span — 36 feet, 6 inches; chord — 5 feet, 10 inches; gap — 5 feet; approximate wing area — 415 square feet; approximate horizontal rudder (forward elevator) area — 80 square feet; approximate vertical rudder area — 16 square feet; length — 28 feet, 11 inches; weight — 735 pounds. This airplane, purchased by the U.S. Government for $30,000, is the machine flown in army tests at Fort Myer in 1909 and is sometimes referred to as Signal Corps No. 1. It was the only unit of its type constructed and was specially designed to meet speed requirements.

The next response from Orville made its own point: "I am sending a draft for $40,000 . . ."

Flying details followed in a letter from Orville on September 23:

> I finished on Templehofer [Tempelhof] field last Saturday with a flight for the one-man duration record. I was compelled to stop after an hour and 46 minutes on account of the water supply being exhausted. The little drive arm on the water pump had broken, and as a result the water had all boiled away . . . I made a flight on every appointed day excepting one, and on that day a pouring rain set in just as I was ready to start. The machine was out in the rain for nearly an hour and was thoroughly soaked through. One of the glued joints in the propeller was loosened as a result . . .
>
> In the early flights in winds the machine was jerked from under me a number of times, and I would find myself sitting five or six inches up the back of the seat. I have now learned, by watching the tape, when these rolling gusts are coming and prepare for them, so that I can keep the seat much better. Saturday afternoon, however, I got caught by one that raised me 8 or ten inches off the seat. As I try to hold myself in the seat by pushing myself tight against the back I rode for quite a distance before I slipped down to the seat. I am going to tie myself to the seat with string . . .

All this time they had flown without any support or safety system that secured them to their aircraft. The idea of flying in a bare seat on an open wing without a restraint harness is, to us, beyond belief. No pilot with any experience today would even think of such madness . . .

The rolling gusts to which Orville referred are, of course, downdrafts. The machine, on being caught in this invisible downward thrusting of an air current, is slammed downward, and the pilot, if he is not secured to his seat, is lofted up and out of that seat — and can quite easily be thrown from the aircraft. From this episode the safety belt was born.

Orville found flight conditions in Germany none to his liking.

When the brothers began to encounter rough air conditions earlier that year, they fastened a tape, or ribbon, to a vertical spar, and by watching it swing from one side to the other they could judge, roughly, the direction and strength of the sudden winds.

Orville continued: "I have never passed through so many and such severe whirlwinds as in the flights here. But they were usually in certain parts of the field and I could keep out of the worst of them if I chose. I would be flying along very nicely when of a sudden the machine would begin to quiver, and in looking at the tape I would see it swerve to one side at an angle of over 45 degrees, and then in a few seconds, without my making any change with the rudder, it would swing an equal amount to the opposite side . . ."

The brothers were opening new frontiers — not just through their own flying, but by making flight possible for other pilots. Bishop Wright noted in his diary on October 2, 1909: "Orville, at Potsdam, is reported to have flown over 1,600 feet high — 1,637 ft. He took up the Crown Prince of Germany, 60 ft. high; gets a present of a diamond and a ruby [stickpin] composing the letter 'W' and a crown."

In the United States, Wilbur was busy with public demonstrations of the Wright *Flyers*. New training schools were getting under way. There were competitions to be entered and great prizes and honors to be won, and all they required of the Wrights was *flying*. On October 4, 1909, Wilbur made a flight in the New York area before more than a million cheering people gathered for the Hudson-Fulton Celebration. Ever safety-conscious and innovative, and aware that he would be flying over a very wide river, he strapped a canoe with a covered deck under the framework of the *Flyer*, between the skids. Should he be forced to land in the water, he would be able to settle smoothly on the river's surface, and both machine and pilot would remain afloat until rescued; the flying boat was born.

He took off from Governor's Island in New York Harbor, swung north to fly up the Hudson River to Grant's Tomb, turned about and flew south, back to Governor's Island. It was a flight that amazed New York and made international headlines, for it was a demonstration of confidence in a machine and mastery by the pilot before the single greatest audience ever assembled to see a man fly.

The flight also had some far-reaching implications. As Wilbur flew over the many naval vessels and ocean liners lying at anchor in New York Harbor, he sounded the first warning, however softly, that those enormous battlewagons would not always be the mainstay of the world's naval fleets.

Wilbur was perhaps more involved in flying and business activities in the United States than was his younger brother in Europe. He had moved training operations from Fort Myer to College Park, Maryland, where previously Orville had flown after the conclusion of the army flight tests. It was much more suitable for training than Virginia, and while Orville was flying at Tempelhof in Berlin, Wilbur completed their contract with the Signal Corps by training Lieutenants Frank P. Lahm and Frederic E. Humphreys. He also gave lessons to Lieutenant Benjamin D. Foulois, officially designated as the army's first aviation pilot, who later became chief of the Air Corps in 1931.

On October 31 Wilbur wrote his father:

> After a two days' trip to New York I am back in Washington again for a few days. I have practically finished my work here and will go back to New York on Wednesday and meet Orville and Kate who will probably land on Thursday morning. Lieutenants Lahm & Humphreys are managing the machine very well, and Lt. Foulois is also learning rapidly.
>
> My trip to New York was in connection with a deal to dispose of our American rights. It is proposed that we transfer our business for U.S. and Canada to a company of which J. P. Morgan, Cornelius Vanderbilt, Judge Gary, George Gould and others will be the chief stockholders.* We are to receive $100,000 in cash and one third of the stock of the company, and also a 10 per cent royalty on the selling price of each machine made by the company. I think the deal will be consummated but the papers are not yet signed . . .

---

* The Wright Company was organized in November 1909 for the manufacture of Wright airplanes, with Wilbur as president. Orville succeeded his brother on the latter's death, and he remained president until the firm was sold, in 1915.

When in New York last week I received another
$10,000 from the Hudson-Fulton people, thus making a
total of $12,500 out of the $15,000 agreed upon. It is
doubtful whether I ever get any more, as the treasury is
about empty.

Wilbur wrote Chanute on December 6, 1909:

We are all home again after a rather strenuous summer
and autumn. Orville and my sister had a splendid time
in Germany, and Orville returned much stronger in every
way than when he went away . . .

We have closed out our American business to the
Wright Company* of which the stockholders are Messrs.
C. Vanderbilt, Collier [Robert J. Collier, of *Collier's
Weekly,* donor of the Collier Trophy† and America's first
private citizen to buy a Wright plane], Belmont, Alger,
Berwind, Ryan, Gould, Shonts, Freedman, Nicoll & Plant.
We received a very satisfactory cash payment, forty percent of the stock, and are to receive a royalty on every
machine built, in addition. The general supervision of the
business will be in our hands though a general manager
will be secured to directly have charge. We will devote
most of our time to experimental work.

All of us are in very good health. Father, though in his
eighty-second year, is still quite active. My own health,
owing to the outdoor life of the past year, is better than
in former years. I trust that you retain well your strength
and enjoyment of life.

You could almost hear the clock running down.

The great decade of the Wrights — stretching from 1899 to
1909 — had reached its culmination. It was ten years since Wilbur had written to the Smithsonian Institution and asked what
they could tell him about man's attempts at that mysterious and
elusive art, flying. Ten years of study and deep discussions about

* Construction of the new firm's factory in Dayton began in January 1910.
† In 1912 Robert J. Collier established this most prestigious annual award for the
greatest achievement in aeronautics (now including astronautics) in the United
States with respect to improving the performance, efficiency, or safety of air (or
space) vehicles, "the value of which has been thoroughly demonstrated."

the movement and curvature of the wings of birds, the intricacies of wind tunnels, gliders and snapped spars and bruised muscles and soaring away from the dunes of the Outer Banks of the Carolinas.

There were to be more flights; there would be new designs. And Orville would set world gliding records on his old proving grounds at Kill Devil Hill. But for the moment they had enough of the strain, the struggle, the traveling, the sickness and accidents, pain and wonder. It was time to unwind the mainspring of frenetic activity. It was time to savor life without rushing, and without proving anything to anybody.

Orville and Wilbur Wright, with the support of their family, especially Katharine, had achieved goals far beyond their expectations when first they turned, with curious eye and questing mind, to the skies. They had, in the pursuit of flight, achieved wealth and fame on a scale they had never conceived from their place in the small bicycle shop in Dayton. They were revered and honored throughout the world, for, like Prometheus bringing back fire from the secrets of nature, they brought to all men, everywhere, the magic of flight, which, until they dedicated their lives to it, had been only a dream.

They were the finest example of a growing, searching, healthy society spread across the United States, but it was to the world that they left their legacy.

Man was finally able to move in three dimensions.

Flight was only the name of the new and powerful servant. For from this moment on, the face of the planet would change, and we would enter a new era and a new way of living. Wings gave us speed, and we were free of the terrible weight of time as we traveled between continents and nations. Wings mingled men and their cultures and altered forever our consciousness.

Life is more than victories and goals achieved. There are the mundane and the prosaic, and the things we do not like; they all make up the canvas of our lives. Not all men are of the best will, and the Wrights discovered, sadly, that if they were to protect their creation from the grasping reach of others, they would have to wage battle in the courts of law. Orville and Wilbur emerged victorious from every court fight over infringements on their patents, both here and abroad. But they may as well have tried to stop the incoming tide with the wave of a baton; court decisions and practical enforcement are not one and the same. The Wrights came to despise these legal wranglings, which sapped their strength even more than the physical punishment of crashing to earth from the sky.

They still had much to say and great things to accomplish. They had inventions to perfect, including automatic flight-stabilizing systems that were the miracle of their time. There were awards to be won and praises to be received, but from now on they would stay away from the piercing searchlights of public acclaim. They wished it to be this way.

The Wrights were home.

Epilogue

WILBUR HAD LONG WANTED to leave, for future historians, a special statement with which he hoped the history of flight would be set on its proper course. And though he criticized some of Otto Lilienthal's theories and conclusions, Wilbur neverthe-less still respected the German experimenter for his relentless efforts to fly. With these points in mind, in early May 1912 he prepared a text for the bulletin of the Aero Club of America:

> When the general excellence of the work of Lilienthal is considered, the question arises as to whether or not he would have solved the problem of human flight if his untimely death in 1896 had not interrupted his efforts . . . One of the greatest difficulties of the problem has been little understood by the world at large. This was the fact that those who aspired to solve the problem were constantly pursued by expense, danger, and time. In order to succeed it was not only necessary to make progress, but it was necessary to make progress at a sufficient rate to reach the goal before money gave out, or before acci-dent intervened, or before the portion of life allowable for such work was past. The problem was so vast and many-sided that no one could hope to win unless he possessed unusual ability to grasp the essential points, and to ignore the nonessentials . . . When the detailed story is written of the means by which success in human flight was fi-

nally attained, it will be seen that this success was not won by spending more time than others had spent, nor by taking greater risks than others had taken.

Those who failed for lack of time had already used more time than was necessary; those who failed for lack of money had already spent more money than was necessary; and those who were cut off by accident had previously enjoyed as many lucky escapes as reasonably could be expected.

Lilienthal progressed, but not very rapidly. His tables of pressures and resistances of arched aeroplane surfaces were the results of years of experiment and were the best in existence, yet they were not sufficiently accurate to enable anyone to construct a machine with full assurance that it would give exactly the expected results. Under such conditions progress could not but be slow. His methods of controlling balance both laterally and longitudinally were exceedingly crude and quite insufficient. Although he experimented for six successive years 1891–1896 with gliding machines, he was using at the end the same inadequate method of control with which he started. His rate of progress during these years makes it doubtful whether he would have achieved full success in the near future if his life had been spared . . .

I've searched everywhere for answers, pored over countless documents and interviewed many authorities. But nowhere have I read a more articulate analysis of the basic problems of aeronautical experimentation. The genius of the Wrights went beyond science and invention. They were masters at expressing themselves in the clearest, most succinct terms. Their writings will always remain the best source for the truth.

Tragically, just 15 days after Wilbur wrote those words, he was dead — a victim of typhoid. When the fever claimed Wilbur on May 30, 1912, the Wright family was at his bedside. That same day Bishop Wright wrote in his diary:

"This morning at 3:15, Wilbur passed away, aged 45 years, 1 month and 14 days. A short life, full of consequences. An unfailing intellect, imperturbable temper, great self-reliance and as great modesty, seeing the right clearly, pursuing it steadily, he lived and died . . ."

Later that year, the Wrights moved into a mansion they had built at Hawthorn Hill, in Dayton.

There, Bishop Wright died in 1917, at the age of eighty-eight.

Katharine and Orville lived in this house until 1926, the year Katharine married Henry J. Haskell, and then Orville lived there alone.

One would have thought that after the brothers' great triumph, the world, content with this historic achievement, would allow the family to live out their lives.

This was not to be the case. It is true that the Wrights had patents, but a patent only gives an inventor the right to sue against infringement or to defend himself against litigation. As a result, the Wright family was embroiled in a number of acrimonious lawsuits. Everyone trying to fly, it seemed, began using the Wright system of control, or a variation of it, as well as the wing-curve and propeller data so painstakingly gathered by the brothers. The mental anguish Wilbur suffered as a result of this series of legal battles over the Wright designs merely compounded the problems of his failing health in those final days.

Also at this time, other early pioneers of flight, notably Glenn Curtiss, with the help of the Smithsonian Institution, became involved in a shameful plan to discredit the Wrights. They engaged in the deception by revamping the structure and control system of the crash-prone Langley *Aerodrome*. Finally, in 1914, the *Aerodrome* flew successfully for a short hop, prompting claims that its failure to fly in 1902 was the fault of the launching mechanism, not the airplane. "Therefore, Professor Samuel P. Langley had actually designed and built the first man-carrying flying machine capable of sustained flight." This statement, endorsed by the Smithsonian, was a shocker, and the cause of a prolonged dispute.

The whole ugly episode cast a shadow over the real accomplishments of the Wright brothers, a burden Orville was forced to carry alone for many years. This was the main reason Orville had refused to place the *Kitty Hawk Flyer* in the Smithsonian. Instead, he kept it in storage; then, in 1928, he sent it to the Science Museum in South Kensington, London, on loan.

The Wrights' old English friend, Griffith Brewer, was loyal to the end. With that strong sense of British fair play, he devoted a great part of his later life to correcting the record — championing the Wrights' sole and rightful claim to having been the first to design a successful flying machine and to fly it. Brewer died in 1948, at Walton-on-Thames, England.

Eventually, as the result of the efforts of many individuals, as well as the actions of a concerned Congress, Orville accepted the Smithsonian's official apology, and the *Flyer* came home to rest, one of the great heritages of the American people.

Orville lived to see the world change because of what he and his brother had created, but, unfortunately, he did not see man change with it. He lived through two costly world wars in which the technology born at Big Kill Devil Hill played a devastating role.

But on the happier side, we may imagine his feelings when he was invited to take over the controls of a four-engine Lockheed Constellation airliner, or when he walked aboard airplanes whose wingspans were greater than the length of his first flight on December 17, 1903.

He saw the propeller yield to the jet engine, and he saw the stovepipe gimmickry of another American visionary, Robert H. Goddard, develop into huge rockets with brilliant exhausts that marked their ascent beyond the atmosphere of his world.

In 1947, Orville Wright had not long to live. But that year he saw man fly at supersonic speed, tread the edge of space and cradle the atom for future propulsion. He also saw the birth of the first of the great electronic computers — and he knew that what he and Wilbur had begun at Kitty Hawk was almost ready to take man to heights undreamed of by the greatest minds of earlier centuries.

Orville Wright passed from us on January 30, 1948. Even as his loss was mourned, what he and his brother had begun continued to hurl into the future with ever mightier bounds.

Nine years after his death, only 54 years from his first flight, man orbited the first satellite of his planet. Four years later — in 1961 — the first man raced around the world with a speed of 300 miles *a minute.*

Sixty-six years after he slipped his restraining cable at the foot of a sand dune in North Carolina, three men departed from the Earth with a speed of seven miles *a second.*

In the same time it took Wilbur Wright to cover 852 feet in the first full flight of a powered airplane, the first manned expedition to the moon *flew a distance of four hundred and thirteen miles.*

When Neil Armstrong stepped on the lunar surface in July 1969, he looked up to see a glowing blue and white jewel in the heavens. A heaven as black as the blackest velvet, blacker by a thousandfold as it embraced this marvel of life we call Earth. And as that distant orb turned, nearly a quarter of a million miles away, Neil could see the line that marked where the Atlantic Ocean met the sands of the Carolina coast. Not clearly, but enough to be certain of what he was seeing.

That was where it had all begun 66 years before, where two courageous men, with the dreams of birds in the sky, with wood and cloth and metal, with their grasp of complicated physical principles, and their delight of soaring in cool breezes, opened the heavens so that Neil and men like him could scuff the dust of other worlds from their boots.

The lives of Wilbur and Orville Wright were indeed "full of consequences"; no other technology in the history of the world has advanced so rapidly over such a short period of time. And never again has that giant leap for human progress been symbolized more dramatically than when Apollo 11 soared through space and reached our lunar satellite. For astronaut Neil Armstrong carried with him to the moon a piece of the original linen wing fabric that had flown on the Wright machine of 1903.

The *Kitty Hawk Flyer* had landed.

Appendices
Bibliography
Index

Appendix A

To fully grasp the true significance and magnitude of the Wrights' discovery, the notable accomplishments and progress of others on both sides of the Atlantic must be placed in proper historical perspective. And in assessing these relationships and their relative importance, certain other events and activities in the lives and work of the brothers that followed those early formative years of aeronautical experimentation should also be examined more closely.

That the Wrights were first to achieve "powered, sustained and controlled" flight cannot be disputed, yet in some quarters it still is. But so far every claim of predating the Wrights at Kitty Hawk in 1903 has been disproved.

Granted, in 1890 Clément Ader of France did accomplish an unassisted takeoff with his steam-powered *Eole*, but the machine could not sustain itself nor could it be controlled. And the story that he flew his government-subsidized *Avion III* for more than 980 feet in 1897 turned out to be patently false. In 1894, Sir Hiram Maxim's giant biplane test-rig succeeded in lifting itself off its launching rail for a second or two before crashing, but no one pretends that it could ever fly.

The German-born American Gustave Whitehead (Weisskopf) claimed to have flown monoplanes successfully in 1901 and 1902, one flight allegedly covering a distance of seven miles over Long Island Sound. However, all the accumulated evidence to date shows that these "flights" were nothing more than flights of fancy.*

* Gustave Whitehead is alleged to have made his first "recorded flights or hops" on August 14, 1901, near Bridgeport, Connecticut, but there is no solid proof supporting such reports. Also, some 35 years later, affidavits attesting the Wrights had visited Whitehead in Bridgeport between 1900 and 1903, and while there had gained valuable "inside information" from him, were labeled "utterly false" by Orville. In a letter to Fred L. Black of the Edison Institute at Dearborn, Michigan, dated October 19, 1937, Orville denied that the brothers had ever been to Bridgeport until 1909, "and then only in passing through on the train." About the Whitehead plane, Orville added that the design "is in itself enough to refute statements that the machine flew."

Preston A. Watson, a Scotsman; Karl Jatho, of Germany; and Richard Pearse, of New Zealand; were also reported to have flown successfully in 1903 — before the Wrights. But not one of them did. In fact, Watson has since stated that he had flown only a glider; Jatho made some powered hops in a semibiplane, all unsustained and uncontrolled; and Pearse later admitted his efforts to fly actually took place in 1904, but were totally unsuccessful.

In February 1906, a little more than two years after the Wrights triumphed at Kitty Hawk, Dr. Samuel Pierpont Langley, who with the financial help of the U.S. Government — *and* the Smithsonian — had struggled so hard to be first in the air, died of a stroke, at the age of seventy-two. Writing to Octave Chanute on Langley's death, Wilbur, whose quarrels were not with the professor but with the Smithsonian hierarchy, paid this tribute:

"No doubt disappointment shortened his life. It is really pathetic that he should have missed the honor he cared for above all others, merely because he could not launch his machine successfully. If he could only have started it, the chances are that it would have flown sufficiently to have secured to him the name he coveted, even though a complete wreck attended the landing. I cannot help feeling sorry for him. The fact that the great scientist, Prof. Langley, believed in flying machines was one thing that encouraged us to begin our studies . . ."

Octave Chanute himself died of pneumonia in November 1910, aged seventy-eight. Although his relationship with the Wrights became strained at times, the brothers never minimized the value of Chanute's inspiration and technical contribution.

Chanute had been attracted to aeronautics by the work of Francis Herbert Wenham, whose classic paper *Aerial Locomotion,* which he delivered at the first meeting of the Aeronautical Society of Great Britain in 1866, was hailed as a major milestone in aviation progress. (Also in 1866, Wenham patented the world's first biplane glider.) Wenham, regarded by the Wrights as "one of the ablest and most useful men who have labored in the cause of human flight," died in England at the age of eighty-four on August 11, 1908 — three days after Wilbur's first flight in Europe. The last of the great pioneers in aeronautical science in the preceding century, he lived to witness the realization of his principles.

In the early 1900s Chanute had become the chief conduit for aeronautical information between America and Europe, most of it information about the Wright brothers' achievements. Even so, the world did not know of their earlier successes until late in 1906. In fact, the first "official" details of their 1905 flights at Huffman Prairie were made public in March 1906 by Augustus Post, secretary of the then year-old Aero Club of America, whose lengthy report was circulated to the American press. Eventually, translations were carried abroad, the full text appearing as *Les Expériences des Frères Wright,* published in 1907 by Berger-Levrault of Paris.

Despite the news of the Wrights' accomplishments, many Europeans refused to believe "the impossible." A widespread feeling persisted, for example, that only the French were capable of discovering anything aeronautical; after all, the Montgolfier brothers, Joseph Michel and Jacques Etienne, had invented a man-lifting hot-air balloon in 1783!

Ironically, the first powered flights in Europe had been made in France, but not by a Frenchman. Alberto Santos-Dumont, the dashing, diminutive Brazilian who had gone to Paris to fulfill his boyhood dreams of flying, had succeeded in getting his awkward *14-bis* biplane off the ground at Bagatelle, France, on November 12, 1906. And because few Europeans would concede that the Wrights had actually flown, his brief flight was erroneously hailed by many as the world's first.

Santos-Dumont gave up flying in 1909, blamed only himself for the destructive role of the airplane in World War I, and died by his own hand in Brazil in 1932 at the age of fifty-nine. Today, Brazilian schools and monuments immortalize Santos-Dumont as a national hero, calling him the "Father of Aviation."

Until Wilbur's public flights in France and Orville's in America revolutionized aviation in 1908, technical progress on both sides of the Atlantic was relatively slow. In Europe, notably in France, aviation had been making an independent but wavering start, based mostly on secondhand acquaintance with the Wright gliders and the application of knowledge gained from Lawrence Hargrave's box kite, the recognized model for the first French airplanes, including Santos-Dumont's *14-bis*. Had the Wright machines been flown publicly in 1905, for instance, the evolution of the airplane would have been accelerated. But the blending of basic ideas, American and European, did not become general until 1909.

Gabriel Voisin and his brother Charles were the first to build airplanes in France on a commercial basis. But it was Gabriel who always maintained that the French aviation industry owed nothing to the Wrights; that it had evolved solely on the foundation of its own resources. In fact, he stated publicly that nobody had ever seen the Wrights fly before 1908.

Charles Voisin was killed in an automobile accident in 1912. Gabriel, who in 1919 had turned from the manufacture of airplanes to automobiles, retired in 1936. He lived in France until 1973, still harboring a strong bias against the Wright influence in early aviation development. He also outlived the famous Farman brothers, Henri and Maurice, with whom he had long feuded over who had contributed the most to European aviation.

In 1907, Henri Deutsch de la Meurthe, who was to become a business associate of the Wrights, and Ernest Archdeacon, the affluent Paris lawyer determined to send a French-built flying machine into the air, posted a prize of 50,000 francs for the first closed circuit flight of one kilometer in the air over Europe. On January 13, 1908, at Issy-les-Moulineaux, Henri Farman flew a Voisin-Farman biplane 500 meters in a straight line, turned, and came back to his starting point, winning the money and the plaudits of all Europe.

Actually, the Farmans were sons of a prominent British journalist living in France (a third brother, Richard, operated a successful automobile agency). Henri, a painter who raced cars, turned to flying in 1905, following a narrow escape in an auto race. He started with gliders, then moved to powered airplanes. After he won the 10,000-franc Jules Armengaud prize awarded for a 15-minute flight on July 6, 1908, also at Issy, Henri challenged the Wrights to a contest of speed and distance.

Fortunately for Farman, who would have surely lost, the Wrights declined; it was their policy not to engage in publicity stunts. Henri brought his Voisin biplane to New York anyway and, between July 31 and August 8, 1908, he tried flying the machine at Brighton Beach racetrack. Although the exhibitions were unsuccessful, Henri Farman had at least become the first French aviator to attempt public flights in America.

By this time, Henri had split with Voisin and had decided to build his own biplane, which he flew in April 1909. Demonstrating qualities far superior to its Voisin predecessors, the new Henri Farman design soon became the most popular biplane in Europe.

In 1912, Henri and Maurice, who until then had worked independently, combined their resources. Together, they produced 300 airplanes the following year. Maurice's designs differed somewhat from Henri's, but the distinction was slight. Maurice, last survivor of the three brothers, actively flew airplanes for 50 years, although he never had a pilot's license. He died in 1964 at the age of eighty-seven, in Paris. With characteristic modesty, he had requested that his funeral go unreported.

Louis Ferdinand Ferber, the French artillery captain who had opened negotiations for the purchase of a Wright airplane as early as 1905, was killed in a freak accident at Boulogne-sur-Mer in September 1909. He had just landed safely when the wheels of his Voisin biplane struck a ditch. The shock dislodged the engine, which toppled on Ferber and inflicted fatal injuries.

Léon Delagrange, the French pioneer who, after watching Wilbur Wright fly at Le Mans in 1908, declared to his fellow aviators, "We are beaten," was also killed in a crash. Flying a new Blériot monoplane at Bordeaux in January 1910, he fell to his death when a wing buckled. On July 8, 1908, Delagrange, himself a talented sculptor, had taken Mme. Thérèse Peltier, a noted French sculptress, for a short hop of about 650 feet at Turin, Italy. She thus became the first woman to "go up" in an airplane.

However, the distinction of being the first woman to make a *real flight* anywhere in the world belongs to Mrs. Hart O. Berg, wife of the Wrights' agent in Europe. Wilbur carried Mrs. Berg aloft at Le Mans on October 7, 1908, in a flight that lasted over two minutes.

Louis Blériot, one of the few persons to witness Wilbur Wright's first flight at Le Mans on August 8, 1908, soon earned fame in his own right by becoming the first pilot in history to cross the English Channel in an airplane. On July 25, 1909, he spanned the 25 miles from Calais to Dover in 37 minutes, winning the *London Daily Mail* prize of $5000.

Blériot, born in Cambrai, France, in 1872, had turned from manufacturing automobile headlamps to experimenting with powered flight in the early 1900s. He formed a partnership with Gabriel Voisin that lasted two years. Blériot favored monoplanes; Voisin, biplanes. As a result, in 1906 the two men went their separate ways. But Blériot's defection from the biplane school had already provoked a barrage of arguments pro and con.

Having survived numerous mishaps, he crashed into a house in Constantinople in December 1909. Seriously injured, Blériot flew no more, devoting his talents exclusively to the manufacture of the planes bearing his name. He died of heart failure in Paris in 1936.

Robert Esnault-Pelterie, another French experimenter whose work paralleled Blériot's, was credited with using ailerons (actually they were rather crude elevons) for the first time in history. In 1904, he built a glider patterned after the Wright machine of 1902. But instead of warping wings for lateral control, which he believed to be structurally dangerous, he substituted two horizontal "rudders" at each end of his wing. These were connected to a "steering" device that he could operate from his position in the glider.

A visionary who wrote about space travel, even predicting a rocket trip to the moon, Esnault-Pelterie in 1907 built the world's first airplane with a completely enclosed fuselage. Constructed of metal tubing and covered with red muslin, the monoplane was named *R.E.P.*, the designer's initials. In a letter to Orville dated June 3, 1908, Wilbur stated: "The Esnault-Pelterie machine infringes on our patent, but I see no danger that he will produce a machine of any practical value." Although the *R.E.P.* didn't fly successfully until 1910, it represented a type well ahead of its time. After suffering painful injuries in a 1908 crash, Esnault-Pelterie left the piloting to others and concentrated on development.

Meanwhile, back in the States, Glenn Hammond Curtiss, a builder and racer of motorcycles, had already developed an engine that could be used in airplanes. This had attracted the attention of Alexander Graham Bell, who formed the Aerial Experiment Association (A.E.A.), the purpose of which was to "build a practical aeroplane which will carry a man and be driven through the air on its own power."

Bell organized the A.E.A. in 1907 at his home in Nova Scotia, but moved operations to the Curtiss workshop in Hammondsport, New York, in January 1908. Besides Curtiss, who served as chief executive officer, his associates included Frederick W. Baldwin, chief engineer; J. A. D. McCurdy, treasurer; and Lieutenant Thomas F. Selfridge, secretary. (Selfridge was the first to go up in Bell's monstrous man-lifting tetrahedral kite; he had been temporarily assigned to the A.E.A. by authority of President Theodore Roosevelt.)

Under A.E.A. auspices, Curtiss built the *June Bug*, which he flew on July 4, 1908, in the first "officially observed" heavier-than-air flight in the United States. For this feat he won the *Scientific American* magazine's first air trophy, awarded to the first pilot who "publicly" flew one kilometer (about five eighths of a mile) in a straight line. But the honor of being the first Bell associate to fly went to Fred Baldwin, who flew the A.E.A.'s first airplane, the *Red Wing*, which Selfridge had designed, on March 12, 1908. *

During the association's brief lifetime, its members each designed an airplane, although they pooled their ideas and worked together in constructing each machine, including the *Red Wing, June Bug, White Wing, Silver Dart*, and a float plane called the *Loon*.

Perhaps it should be noted that neither Curtiss nor Baldwin could claim the distinction of being the next to fly after the Wright brothers. They followed Dr. William Whitney Christmas, of Washington, D.C., little known but long recognized as the third man in America to make a flight in an airplane. On March 8, 1908, four days before the first flight of the *Red Wing*, Christmas flew a biplane of his own design and construction a short distance at Fairfax Courthouse, Virginia.

Reportedly, the Christmas design was the first American airplane equipped with interconnected ailerons for lateral control. In 1914, amid conflicting claims of infringement, Christmas received a patent for his "recessed aileron," which nine years later the U.S. Government agreed to buy for $100,000. He lived to be ninety-four, dying in 1960.

At the time of his death, in July 1930, Curtiss had dissociated himself from aviation almost completely. He had spent his later years as a real estate developer, principally in Florida. And he had no active part in the amalgamation of the Curtiss Aeroplane and Motor Company interests and the Wright Aeronautical Corporation in the summer of 1929. But the fact that his name was given precedence in the title of the new organization — the Curtiss-Wright Corporation — seemed yet another insult to the Wright family.

However, the part Curtiss played in attempting to prove the airworthiness of Langley's *Aerodrome* in 1914, which lingers to this day, probably concerned the Wrights more than anything else. In the eyes of some historians, its degree of offensiveness eclipsed all the court fights put together.

Augustus M. Herring, the perennial thorn in the budding aviation industry's side, who once assisted Octave Chanute and had also worked

* But by this time the Wrights had been flying four and a half years — and, two and a half years before, had made circling flights of 24 miles in 38 minutes.

briefly for Professor Langley at the Smithsonian, resurrected the bankrupt Herring-Curtiss Company in 1918 and became its president. He then sued "Glenn Curtiss and others" for $5 million, charging that the bankruptcy had been contrived to ruin him. During the litigation Herring claimed he had built machines that flew "before the Wrights ever commenced to experiment."

In 1923 the court decided for the defendants, but Herring appealed. He died of a stroke, while the appeal was pending, in July 1926, the same year the State of New York finally dissolved the Herring-Curtiss Company. Herring's heirs carried on the case, however, and on March 14, 1928, the appellate division of the New York State Supreme Court reversed the lower court's decision against several defendants, including Curtiss.

Fourteen years earlier, on January 13, 1914, the U.S. Circuit Court of Appeals of New York had found in favor of the Wright Company in its suit — begun in 1909 — against the Herring-Curtiss Company and Glenn H. Curtiss, recognizing the Wright patent as a "pioneer patent." All told, the Wrights engaged in a dozen lawsuits in the U.S., France, and Germany, and of those not dropped, the Wrights won every suit.

Léon Bollée, the cheerful, goateed manufacturer of automobiles who had arranged for the use of the racecourse at Hunaudières and had lent Wilbur the convenience of his factory, followed Wilbur Wright in death by some 18 months. In his will he bequeathed to the museum at Le Mans the first engine used by Wilbur in his flights at Hunaudières in 1908.

The eldest son of Amédée Bollée, a French industrialist, Léon had joined his father in the automobile field, then developed his own designs in the 1890s. His models included a few steamers, but the gasoline-powered three-wheelers, known as the Léon Bollée Tandem Tricars, made him a fairly wealthy young man by 1900. When he died, in December 1913, at the age of forty-two, the firm continued under the management of his widow. Finally, in 1924, Mme. Bollée, who was to visit Orville Wright in Dayton four years later, sold out to W. R. Morris of England. The cars bearing the Bollée name were finally discontinued in 1927.

Hart O. Berg, a graduate engineer who represented the Wrights in Europe and helped guide their foreign business interests, died in New York on December 9, 1941, at the age of seventy-six. Although his chief work was the introduction of American products abroad, he also pioneered in the manufacture of machine guns, automobiles, and — in association with Simon Lake — submarines.

Despite their expanding international interests, the Wrights were directly involved in aircraft manufacturing for only a relatively short period. There is no evidence that they enjoyed the experience; they much preferred experimenting with new ideas or training pilots.

Moreover, the firms organized to manufacture and market Wright planes abroad were also comparatively short-lived, mainly because of mismanagement and the continuing disputes over patent infringement. The French and German Wright companies were formed first — in 1908 and 1909, respectively. But the British Wright Company did not come into being until 1913 (although as early as March 1909 Short Brothers, of Battersea, England, contracted to build six Wright machines).

Back home, in 1909, the Wrights sold their patents (for $100,000 in cash) to a group of New York financiers, then helped organize the first Wright Company in America — in which they received 40 percent of the stock and a 10 percent royalty on every machine built. Wilbur was the new company's first president; Orville, vice president. On Wilbur's death, in 1912, Orville became president, remaining in that capacity until the company was sold, in 1915.

Meanwhile, in January 1911, the Wright Company entered into an agreement with the Burgess Company, making Burgess the first licensed aircraft manufacturer in the United States.

When the Wright Company was sold to another syndicate in October 1915, Orville stayed on as a consulting engineer at an annual salary of $25,000. However, this arrangement terminated in August 1916 with the merger of the Wright and Glenn L. Martin companies as the Wright-Martin Aircraft Corporation. The following year, Glenn Martin re-established his own company, and Wright-Martin subsequently evolved into the Wright Aeronautical Corporation, which in 1929 merged with the Curtiss interests.

The original Wright Company plant in Dayton finally closed its doors in March 1917. By this time Orville had established his Wright Aeronautical Laboratory. (During World War I he served as an engineering consultant to the U.S. Government and to private concerns involved in aeronautical development.) He had also continued active flying, testing experimental aircraft and new safety devices, and teaching others to fly.

Orville Wright made his last flight as a pilot on May 13, 1918. On that day he flew an early model 1911 Wright biplane alongside the first American-built DeHavilland DH-4. The DH-4 had been produced by the then year-old Dayton-Wright Airplane Company, which had arranged a special airshow to celebrate the milestone.

Although Orville was listed as one of the organizers, the Dayton-Wright Airplane Company, formed in April 1917 to turn out the famous Liberty engine, Curtiss Jennies, and British DH-4s, had no direct connection with other Wright interests. (A major factor in America's wartime buildup of a rapidly mobilizing air service, the company delivered more than 3500 airplanes in 1918 alone.) Eventually absorbed by General Motors, Dayton-Wright ceased aviation activities in June 1923, selling its designs to a newcomer in the manufacturing ranks, Consolidated Aircraft.

Perhaps the most perplexing question in the whole Wright saga is why the brothers, once they had proved the airplane's practicability, allowed others to race ahead in what by then had become a rapidly advancing technology. True, the Wrights made significant improvements to the airplane in later years, but many important developments that were well within their power (tractor — as opposed to pusher — propulsion, closed-in cockpits, wheeled undercarriages, the perfection of float planes, and the like) were left to other innovators.

Marvin W. McFarland, chief of the aeronautics division of the Library of Congress, writes that the "explanation seems to lie with their over-riding concern for what they had already achieved." McFarland suggests we be content with the Wrights as they were, and then adds: "We are always asking of genius more than genius is ready and willing to perform. It is a privilege that is not necessarily ours. The immortality of the Wrights is assured. They designed, built, and flew the first airplane. They discovered and established on a scientific basis the principles of human flight. They taught themselves and the rest of mankind to fly. They developed the airplane to a point of high practical success and demonstrated its capabilities to the world . . ."

William J. Tate, the postmaster at Kitty Hawk who acted as the Wrights' host until their camp was ready in 1900, never quite got over the fact he missed witnessing aviation's greatest event — the first pow-ered flight in history. Bill Tate had thought it too windy for flying that chilly December day in 1903, so he had stayed home. The five *official* witnesses, certified by Tate for the National Aeronautic Association in 1928, were John T. Daniels, W. S. Dough, and A. D. Etheridge, all of the Kill Devil Hill Life Saving Station; and W. C. Brinkley, of Manteo, and Johnny Moore, of Nags Head. (Captain S. J. Payne, chief of the Kitty Hawk Life Saving Station, and Robert Wescott, on duty at the Kill Devil Hill station, watched the proceedings through telescopes.)

Over the years, Tate, who had assisted the brothers in their early gliding experiments, became very close to the Wright family. He also participated in a number of national and local activities periodically commemorating the historic achievement of his two good friends. His last great wish was to be present at Kill Devil Hill memorial on Decem-ber 17, 1953, for ceremonies observing the first flight's fiftieth anniver-sary. Unfortunately, Bill Tate died that year on June 8, six months short of his goal. He was eighty-four.

Charles W. Furnas, the Wright mechanic who became the first pas-senger ever carried in an airplane, died at the age of sixty-one, on October 16, 1941, in the National Soldiers Home (now the Veterans Administra-tion Hospital) at Dayton, near the lake where Wilbur Wright had been injured. On May 14, 1908, at Kitty Hawk, Wilbur had taken Furnas up on his historic "first flight," a short one that lasted less than 30 seconds. Later the same day, Orville, with Charley aboard, remained airborne for over three minutes, proving the new Wright *Flyer* was capable of carrying two persons, which the U.S. Army had specified.

Charley Furnas wanted to be a pilot, but he abandoned the notion after Lieutenant Selfridge was killed and Orville seriously injured in the 1908 crash at Fort Myer. He soon left the Wrights and opened a garage in West Milton, Ohio, near Dayton. In later years he also operated a motion picture theater there.

Charles E. Taylor, the "unsung hero" of man's conquest of the skies, died on January 30, 1956, at the age of eighty-eight. He was the principal employee and intimate associate of the Wrights in those early, critical years. It was Charlie Taylor who, without precedent or fanfare, built the engines for the first airplanes of Wright design, including the *Kitty Hawk Flyer*.

In 1937 Henry Ford wanted to hire Taylor to help restore the original Wright home and shop when he moved the buildings to his Greenfield Village museum at Dearborn, Michigan. Not knowing Taylor's whereabouts, Ford commissioned William W. Mounts, his former chief pilot, to find him. Mounts located Taylor quietly running a lathe for North American Aviation in Los Angeles, and eventually persuaded Charlie to join Ford. Taylor remained at the museum until 1941, when he returned to California for health reasons.

When Mounts first contacted Taylor in 1937, no one at the aircraft company where Charlie worked knew who he really was. At the time, Taylor was making 37.5 cents an hour — roughly 7 cents more than the Wrights had paid him in 1903. After learning Charlie's true identity, North American's J. H. "Dutch" Kindelberger raised his pay to 48.5 cents.

Tragically, at the time of his death, Taylor was destitute. His only income was the $800 a year he received from a fund left by Orville.

On December 17, 1948 — exactly forty-five years to the day after its first flight in 1903 — the *Kitty Hawk Flyer* was formally presented to the Smithsonian Institution, where it now proudly occupies a place of honor in the National Air and Space Museum.

Unfortunately, Orville Wright wasn't there to see it. He had died eleven months earlier.

Appendix B

The high level and extraordinary quality of the Wrights' scientific achievement is very well illustrated by the caliber of discussions that were carried on in their correspondence with Octave Chanute. In a letter of February 19, 1902 to Chanute, Wilbur analyzed the information that had been sent to him by Chanute in previous correspondence. The letter illustrates the point.

As I understand it the object of your formulae is to provide methods of applying the Lilienthal tables to surfaces moved horizontally with a positive angle of incidence. As power machines will at first seek the stillest possible wind, it is a question whether it is advisable in this handbook to complicate the matter by the introduction of α and β. Would it not be sufficient to use i (the angle of chord with the horizon) in all cases? The formulae would then become:

(1) $L = KFV^2 \alpha \cos i$ or $\alpha = \dfrac{W}{KFV^2 \cos i}$ (Computed *vertically*).

(2) $T = KFV^2 \theta\alpha \cos i$ (When the tangential is computed horizontally).

(3) $D = KFV^2 \alpha \sin i$ or W tang. i (Computed *horizontally*).

(4) $H = KV^2E$

(5) $A = D + H \pm T$

I cannot quite make out your meaning in regard to your last formula $A = W$ tang. α. I suppose that is a slip, and that you really mean the *angle of descent.* Then the total resistance of a surface flying as a kite in horizontal wind, or moved horizontally in still air, would be approximately equal to the weight of the surface multiplied by the tangent of its angle of descent in gliding. There is, however, a very small difference resulting from the fact that in gliding downward η is nearer vertical, and θ nearer horizontal, than when the surface is moved horizontally or held as a kite.

Meanwhile, Chanute on the same day was replying to previous correspondence from Wilbur, which indicates how the old gentleman played the part of a co-analyzer of the Wright brothers' data.

> I was going on next to compute the *resultant pressure* but I have struck a snag. You say "to find the resultant pressure when lift is known, divide the lift by the cosine of the angle found by adding the tangential to the angle of incidence. Example — Find the resultant pressure of #9 at 10°. Lift at 10° = 0.839. Cos 10° + (−3°) or 7° = 0.992."
>
> Now the tangential of #9 at 10° is (−3¾°) so that the resultant pressure = 0.839 ÷ 0.944 [0.994] = 0.844 instead of 0.845 as you have it.
>
> The difference is, of course, trifling but raises the question whether the error is in the rule or in the taking the wrong coefficient in the example. I feel pretty sure that it is in the latter, but thought best to ask.

It will be noted that this information quoted by Chanute is derived from a system of tables presented on the following pages, which the Wrights computed in the process of their wind tunnel tests: Table I: Rectangular Pressures; Table II: Tangentials, Gliding Angles, Drag: Lift Ratios; Table III: Resultant Pressures. To show how effective these tables were and how easy it was to calculate performance of any given airfoil or of a complete machine from these data, we merely have to follow the process of reasoning that Octave Chanute used in his quotation above; for instance, where he says: "Example — Find the resultant pressure of #9 at 10°." This refers, of course, to the airfoil #9, whose performance had been tested in a series of wind tunnel experiments made between November 22 and December 7, 1901. Each airfoil was numbered from 1 to 48 and was presented at angles of attack to the flow of air through the wind tunnel at intervals ranging from 0°, 2½°, 5°, 7½°, 10°, 12½°, 15°, 17½°, 20°, 25°, 30° to 45°. These are all shown in the tables.

To follow the line of reasoning, we merely have to take Octave Chanute's quotation of the formula by Wilbur Wright in previous correspondence. Quote: "To find the resultant pressure when lift is known, divide the lift by the cosine of the angle found by adding the tangential to the angle of incidence." Sounds tough, but it is really simple if we use the tables.

For instance, we find in Table I, entitled Rectangular Pressures, which is the Wrights' term for lift, that the lift coefficient of airfoil #9, when presented at a 10° angle of attack to the airstream flowing through the wind tunnel, was .839. Therefore, we do as Chanute did; we insert the

TABLE I. RECTANGULAR PRESSURES

Lift coefficients in terms of pressure normal to a square plane of equivalent area

Row 1:	Angle indicated by lift balance, in degrees
Row 2:	Rectangular pressure

Rectangular pressure = sine of indicated angle $\times \dfrac{8 \text{ (area of normal plane)}}{\text{area of surface tested}}$

Surface no.:	8	⑨	10	11	12	13
Lift begins at:	−2¾°	−2¾°	−3°	−2¾°	−2½°	−4°
α						
0°	8 / .185	8 / .185	7⅞ / .183	7 / .162	6¼ / .145	8¼ / .191
2½°	17½ / .401	15¾ / .361	18¼ / .417	16¼ / .373	13½ / .311	15 / .345
5°	23½ / .531	22½ / .510	26½ / .595	25 / .563	22¾ / .515	22¼ / .505
7½°	29½ / .656	27¾ / .621	33½ / .736	32 / .706	32 / .706	27¾ / .621
⑩°	39 / .839	39 / ⑧⑨ .839	36 / .784	37 / .802	39 / .839	29¼ / .656
12½°	49¾ / 1.017	46½ / .967	36½ / .793	37 / .802	44 / .926	30½ / .676
15°	55½ / 1.098	50½ / 1.029	38 / .821	38¾ / .834	46½ / .967	32½ / .716
17½°	56¼ / 1.108	51 / 1.036	39 / .839	41⅞ / .890	45½ / .951	34¼ / .750
20°	52 / 1.050	48¾ / 1.002	41 / .875	42 / .892	44 / .926	35½ / .774
25°	47½ / .983	44 / .926	44½ / .935	41½ / .883	41½ / .883	36 / .784
30°	44 / .926	41½ / .883	41 / .875	39¼ / .843	39¼ / .843	37½ / .812
35°	42¼ / .896	40¾ / .870	39¾ / .852	38¾ / .834	38½ / .830	
40°	41 / .875	40 / .857	39 / .839	38¼ / .825	38 / .821	
45°	39¼ / .843	38¼ / .825	38¼ / .825	37 / .802	36½ / .793	30½ / .677

Chanute source for lift coefficient used in this equation for determining the resultant pressure — letter of February 19, 1902.

figure .839 into the beginning of Wilbur's equation for the computation of rectangular pressures.

We stated that lift at 10° equals .839. Chanute then determined that the "cosine of the angle [is] found by adding the tangential to the angle of incidence" by referring to Table II: Tangentials; Gliding Angles; Drag: Lift Ratios.

Now, if we look for the performance of airfoil #9 at a 10° angle of attack, we find that in row 2, column 1 of Table II, the cosine of the gliding angle is .994. Therefore, as Chanute said, if we divide the lift, or lift coefficient .839, by .994 (the cosine of the gliding angle), we then find that we have the figure .844, which is the resultant pressure.

He pointed out that Wilbur's error had been in computing the cosine of the gliding angle found by adding the tangential to the angle of incidence or attack. It can be seen, of course, that the angle of attack is 10°. That is the figure we have used all along. And the tangential is $-3\frac{3}{4}°$, which is precisely what Chanute said. Therefore, the algebraic sum of the angle of incidence, or attack of 10° that we have been using for airfoil #9, plus the tangential angle of $-3\frac{3}{4}°$ for airfoil #9, as indicated by the Wrights' drift balance used in the tunnel, is $6\frac{1}{4}°$. This then becomes the gliding angle, and the figure .994 becomes the cosine of this gliding angle.

Chanute, with his very engineering-oriented mind, saw immediately that the figure Wilbur had used and quoted in his correspondence to Chanute was in error.

It is quite obvious that what Wilbur did was inadvertently to transpose the tangential of airfoil #8, at 10° angle of attack, with the tangential of airfoil #9. Airfoil #8, as will be seen by the table, shows the tangential as $-3°$, which results in the cosine of the gliding angle being the algebraic sum of $10° - 3°$, or 7°. Now, the cosine of this gliding angle, according to the tables, would be .9925, but here again, Wilbur apparently made another transposition, because he used the cosine for airfoil #8 at $7\frac{1}{2}°$ instead of airfoil #9 at 10°. The cosine of airfoil #8 in his tables at $7\frac{1}{2}°$ angle of attack is .992, which apparently he used in solving his equation. This resulted in his dividing the coefficient of lift .839 by his selection of the cosine of the gliding angle .992, which gave the resultant pressure as .845, off by $\frac{1}{1000}$. As Chanute so astutely pointed out, "the difference is of course trifling, but raises the question whether the error is in the rule or in the taking the wrong coefficient in the example. I feel pretty sure that it is the latter, but thought best to ask."

The difference, or error, was indeed trifling. *The point was not.* It was as Chanute said: if the error is in the coefficient, that is one thing; but if the error is in the table, that's quite another. Any errors in the table used to design aircraft, when finally multiplied out to their end use, will result in grave variations in the performance of the machine.

Wilbur immediately answered, on February 25, "I have yours of 19th and am very much at a loss to understand how I could have made such

TABLE II. TANGENTIALS; GLIDING ANGLES; DRAG: LIFT RATIOS

	Column 1	Column 2
Row 1	Tangential (angle indicated by drag: lift balance, in degrees)	Gliding angle (α + tangential, in degrees)*
Row 2	Cosine of gliding angle (for use in Table III)	Tangent of gliding angle (drag: lift ratio)

* Minimum gliding angles in bold-face type.

Surface no.:	8		9		10	
α						
0°	12¾ .9753	12¾ .2263	11 .9816	11 .1944	17½ .9537	17½ .3153
2½°	5½ .9903	8 .1405	4 .9936	6½ .1139	6¾ .9870	9¼ .1628
5°	2 .9925	**7** .1228	1 .9945	**6** .1051	2¾ .9908	**7¾** .1361
7½°	−¼ .9920	7¼ .1272	−1⅛ .9938	6⅜ .1110	1 .9890	8½ .1404
10°	−3 .9925	7 .1228	−3¾ .9940	6¼ .1095	0 .9848	10 .1763
12½°	−4⅞ .9912	7⅝ .1338	−5 .9914	7½ .1316	−½ .9781	12 .2125
15°	−5½ .9963	9½ .1673	−5 .9848	10 .1763	−1⅛ .9708	13⅞ .2470
17½°	−4⅞ .9758	12⅝ .2340	−4 .9723	13½ .2400	−1⅞ .9631	15⅝ .2796
20°	−3¾ .9600	16¼ .2915	−3 .9563	17 .3057	−2¼ .9523	17¾ .3201
25°	−2 .9205	23 .4245	−1¾ .9188	23¼ .4296	−3 .9272	22 .4040
30°	−1½ .8788	28½ .5429	−1¼ .8767	28¾ .5486	−2 .8829	28 .5317
45°	−1⅛ .7209	43⅞ .9614	−1 .7193	44 .9957	−1⅔ .7301	43⅓ .9434

① ② ③ ④

Wilbur used these two transpositions in error for ① cosine of gliding angle, ② tangential — thus giving wrong gliding angle.

Chanute used these correct numbers for ③ cosine of gliding angle, and ④ gliding angle.*

* *Editor's note:* The number .9940 given in this table for ③ is correct. The author made the correction after discovering that Chanute had written the number incorrectly as .944 in his letter to Wilbur dated February 19, 1902.

TABLE III. RESULTANT PRESSURES

$$\text{Resultant pressure} = \frac{\text{Rectangular pressure (from Table I)}}{\text{Cosine of gliding angle (from Table II)}}$$

Surface no.:	8	⑨	10	11	12	13
α						
0°	.189	.188	.191	.168	.150	.197
2½°	.404	.363	.422	.377	.313	.351
5°	.535	.512	.600	.566	.517	.512
7½°	.661	.624	.744	.711	.710	.632
⑩°	.845	.844	.796	.810	.844	.673
12½°	1.026	.975	.810	.815	.934	.698
15°	1.102	1.044	.845	.854	.982	.745
17½°	1.135	1.065	.871	.919	.980	.789
20°	1.093	1.047	.918	.934	.972	.823
25°	1.067	1.007	1.008	.960	.965	.853
30°	1.053	1.007	.991	.959	.963	.915
45°	1.169	1.147	1.129	1.114	1.104	.933

Proof in tables that the solution for the equation to find resultant pressure, as offered by Chanute in letter to Wilbur (dated February 19, 1902), was correct and that the wind tunnel data verified this.

a blunder in giving the example for computing *resultant pressure*. The correct tangential of #9 at 10° is [−] 3¾°, and the *resultant pressure* is .844 as you have it."

Thus it was that Wilbur acknowledged immediately the problems involved in referring to the tables too casually or failing to cross-check his references. Of course, Wilbur went a step further by showing his extreme confidence in the tables when used correctly. A cross-check will show that under Table III, the resultant pressure for airfoil #9 at 10° angle of attack is .844, which is, of course, the result obtained in the equation as submitted by Wilbur and corrected by Chanute. This is a good example of how Wilbur and Orville — particularly Wilbur — used Chanute as a backup and check for their calculations. They recognized Chanute's high degree of engineering proficiency and found in correspondence with him that a great many of their problems could be hashed out and put in better perspective.

Appendix C

When the Wrights first tested their 1900 glider on Big Kill Devil Hill, they had observed their calculations to be in error. Actually, the glider, to their bitter disappointment, produced about one half of the computed lift. Very naturally, this was not only confusing, but most disheartening.

They had observed that the drag, or resistance of the total frame when it was carrying no weight and was therefore flown at a very flat angle of attack, was very much less than they had anticipated, perhaps more than half less.

At first, the Wrights did not associate these two factors with having any interrelated significance. They attributed the disappointing lift to one of two things. Either they were using incorrect wing curvatures (was the camber too small or too great?) or their mistake lay in using the arc of a circle instead of parabolic form. On the other hand, after a lot of thought they attributed the drag reduction to the high quality of their design of the interplane struts and of the leading edge of their wing structure.

Of course, at that moment in 1900, they were well aware that their glider had given them many other problems to solve, not the least of which were those involving the maintenance of equilibrium with the erratic center-of-pressure travel on curved surfaces. In addition, they were still faced with severe problems of three-dimensional control. Therefore, it is not surprising that they didn't arrive at an immediate solution to the problems of reduced drag and reduced lift.

It was obvious by the spring of 1901 that, because of the small lift available, they would have to build a much larger glider if they expected to have a satisfactory man-carrier. Consequently, they increased the size of their wing area from the 165 square feet of the 1900 glider to 290 square feet in the 1901 glider. This new machine *did* show the capability of greater lift, but it evidenced certain erratic characteristics, which they soon found attributable to their excessive wing curve of 1-in-12. They later reduced this curve to 1-in-22, which immeasurably improved the characteristics of the glider but left them with the same basic problem. True, they got more lift out of 290 square feet and, consequently, more carrying capacity, but the glider's performance was disappointing in that it did not produce the lift it was calculated to develop.

Here again the same problems arose, like dragons guarding a cave. The lift was about half that indicated by the formulas developed from Lilienthal's tables of tangential pressures, and the drag could be measured to be only about *half* that anticipated. The Wrights even disassembled the glider and flew each panel separately. The results were the same, but in this way they were able to observe the peculiar action of curved surfaces at different wind velocities, as shown by the diagram on page 369. In addition, as can be seen in the diagram showing the action of curved surfaces at varying wind speeds, they were able to measure exactly the straight pull of a given air surface in a given wind velocity.

The results proved, without a doubt, that Lilienthal's tables. of air pressures were seriously in error. By the time Wilbur had prepared his talk to be delivered before the Western Society of Engineers on September 18, 1901, the two brothers had agreed that they should make some calculations of their own and perhaps submit these in place of Lilienthal's. But Wilbur's first draft of this presentation seemed so severe that they hesitated.

Orville suggested that perhaps they should not attack the great Lilienthal's principles quite so drastically until they had further proof. No doubt for this reason Wilbur toned down the criticism in his presentation, and, in the end, made only gentle reference to those discrepancies which the brothers believed their experiments had revealed. This hesitation to express their opinions or convictions *before* they had made adequate tests to back up their theories stimulated their eventual extensive program with respect to the wind tunnel operation.

Immediately after Wilbur returned from Chicago in late September of 1901, the brothers set about the various kinds of experiments that have been described.

In addition to performing these, the brothers made some astute calculations along theoretical lines to answer some of their questions. They developed a formula for lift, which they employed to determine the all-important question as to whether *any* machine they could build would have the capacity to carry the weight of a man. Then they asked their formula the same question, but added the weight of an engine, fuel, and all the necessary controls and systems for activating the aerodynamic mechanisms for three-dimensional equilibrium.

They also devised a formula for power-to-weight ratio and propeller efficiency that would answer whether or not they could supply to the propellers the power necessary to deliver the thrust to maintain flight. In other words, the brothers asked themselves, "After we build the

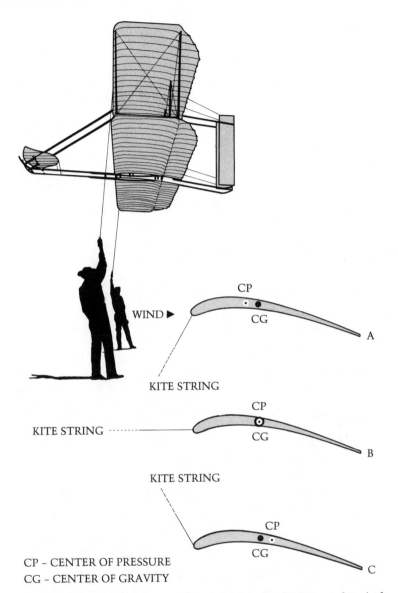

CP - CENTER OF PRESSURE
CG - CENTER OF GRAVITY

Wind tests: By flying glider as a kite (top sketch of 1902 machine), the brothers were able to study action of curved surfaces at varying wind speeds. As wind velocity increases (diagram at lower right) from A to B to C, the wing's center of pressure (CP) moves rearward, changing the kite string's pull direction from overhead (A) to straight downwind (B) and finally to a downward angle (C). In B the center of pressure and center of gravity coincide.

machine, how can we be sure that it will truly fly and sustain the weight of a man?"

The first formula was designed to determine the lifting capacity of the apparatus at a given relative wind velocity (that is, the velocity in which the machine could be driven through the air) and to ascertain whether that lift was equal to or greater than the total weight of the machine with the operator.

This formula, they concluded, showed that the lift generated by forcing the machine through the air at a given speed would be equal to the pressure of the air at the moment that the flying activity took place, times the total area of the lifting surface of the wings and horizontal rudder, times the square of the velocity of the relative wind, times the coefficient of lift of their particular airfoils (as taken from their tables).

The formula was expressed in terms of:

$$L = k \times S \times V^2 \times C_l$$

Where:

$L =$ lift generated
$k =$ coefficient of air pressure
$S =$ area in sq. ft. of the lifting surfaces
$V =$ relative velocity of the wind
$C_l =$ coefficient of lift

The coefficient of lift was, of course, that factor which we find in the first table of observations, in the second row under the heading "Rectangular Pressure."

From the examination of this formula, it can be seen that all factors on the right-hand side of the equation express the capacity of the machine to lift weight in pounds in fairly simple agreement with known facts. For instance, if we took the specifications of the *Kitty Hawk Flyer*, we would know that S (the area of the wing surface) was, from the plan form of the aircraft, 512 square feet. To determine the second factor, namely, the relative wind velocity, we can refer to Orville Wright's diary of December 17, 1903, in which he says wind was blowing at "27 miles according to the government anemometer at Kitty Hawk."

On that first flight, Orville covered 120 feet in 12 seconds, or 10 feet per second, for a ground speed of 6.8 miles per hour. This, added to 27 miles per hour of blowing wind, gives a total relative air speed of 33.8 miles per hour. One can enter this figure, then, into the equation for wind velocity.

We assume that during the flight the aircraft flew at a wing angle of attack to the relative wind of approximately 5°, which seems reasonable. The wing curve used in the *Kitty Hawk Flyer* was close to the configuration defined as number 12 in the three tables of tabulated wind tunnel tests. We then merely have to refer to the rectangular pressure coefficient for airfoil #12 in the first table. This figure is shown in the second row of the coordinate between airfoil #12 and the 5° angle of attack, and is tabulated as .515. If we enter this into the equation, then

TABLE I. RECTANGULAR PRESSURES

Lift coefficients in terms of pressure normal to a square plane of equivalent area

Row 1:	Angle indicated by lift balance, in degrees
Row 2:	Rectangular pressure

Rectangular pressure = sine of indicated angle $\times \dfrac{8 \text{ (area of normal plane)}}{\text{area of surface tested}}$

Surface no.:	8	9	10	11	⑫	13
Lift begins at:	$-2\frac{3}{4}°$	$-2\frac{3}{4}°$	$-3°$	$-2\frac{3}{4}°$	$-2\frac{1}{2}°$	$-4°$
α						
0°	8 .185	8 .185	7⅞ .183	7 .162	6¼ .145	8¼ .191
2½°	17½ .401	15¾ .361	18¼ .417	16¼ .373	13½ .311	15 .345
⑤°	23½ .531	22½ .510	26½ .595	25 .563	22¾ .515	22¼ .505
7½°	29½ .656	27¾ .621	33½ .736	32 .706	32 .706	27¾ .621
10°	39 .839	39 .839	36 .784	37 .802	39 .839	29¼ .656
12½°	49¾ 1.017	46½ .967	36½ .793	37 .802	44 .926	30½ .676
15°	55½ 1.098	50½ 1.029	38 .821	38¾ .834	46½ .967	32½ .716
17½°	56¼ 1.108	51 1.036	39 .839	41⅞ .890	45½ .951	34¼ .750
20°	52 1.050	48¾ 1.002	41 .875	42 .892	44 .926	35½ .774
25°	47½ .983	44 .926	44½ .935	41½ .883	41½ .883	36 .784
30°	44 .926	41½ .883	41 .875	39¼ .843	39¼ .843	37½ .812
35°	42¼ .896	40¾ .870	39¾ .852	38¾ .834	38½ .830	
40°	41 .875	40 .857	39 .839	38¼ .825	38 .821	
45°	39¼ .843	38¼ .825	38¼ .825	37 .802	36½ .793	30½ .677

Lift coefficient used by Wilbur and Orville to calculate total lifting capacity of the *Kitty Hawk Flyer*.

solve for L (by multiplying all of these factors in accordance with the dictates of the equation), we end up with a solution for lift of 994.1 pounds.

The *Kitty Hawk Flyer*, according to specifications, weighed 605 pounds without the operator. Orville Wright weighed approximately 140 pounds, so the machine and operator weighed 745 pounds.

It is obvious from the solution to the equation that the value of L, or lift, is greater than the combined weight of the machine and the operator. Therefore, the apparatus *will* fly, providing that it has the correct *power-to-weight ratio*, which means an engine powerful enough to overcome the head resistance of the machine when being driven against a wind of 33.8 miles per hour.

Now, the brothers asked this of their second equation: Is there enough power in the engine to produce a thrust adequate to overcome the drag of the total frame of the apparatus fighting a 33.8 mile relative wind, after taking into consideration the loss of power through the chain drives and the loss through propeller efficiency?

To determine that, the Wrights developed the equation for drag. According to the Wrights, a formula for determining the amount of drag is equal to the pressure coefficient of the air, times the area of the square surface of the apparatus, times the square of the velocity of the wind, times the coefficient of drag.

The formula expressed is:

$$D = k \times S \times V^2 \times C_d$$

Where:

$D =$ drag
$k =$ pressure coefficient of the air
$S =$ area of the wings of the aircraft
$V =$ velocity of the relative wind
$C_d =$ coefficient of drag

If the Wrights developed all of their information from the tables they compiled as the result of their experiments with airfoils in their wind tunnel, we can do the same. To determine the coefficient of drag we merely need to obtain from the tables the tangent of the gliding angle, which is shown at 5° angle of attack for airfoil #12 and appears in column 2, row 2 of Table II, of the tabulated intercept and has a value of .1051. This is multiplied by the coefficient of lift, which we have seen before in the formula for lift; it was the figure (.515) that was obtained from Table I. We arrive at a coefficient of drag value of .0541. Therefore, if we enter these into the equation, we can determine drag of the machine expressed in pounds.

This expression will tell us the minimum amount of thrust necessary to drive that machine through the air at the required speed of 33.8 miles an hour, relative to the wind, in order to sustain it in flight.

This is the calculation that the Wrights had to make to know that the

Table II. TANGENTIALS; GLIDING ANGLES; DRAG:
LIFT RATIOS

	Column 1	Column 2
Row 1	Tangential (angle indicated by drag: lift balance, in degrees)	Gliding angle (α + tangential, in degrees)*
Row 2	Cosine of gliding angle (for use in Table III)	Tangent of gliding angle (drag: lift ratio)

* Minimum gliding angles in bold-face type.

Surface no.:	11		⑫		13	
α						
0°	15½	15½	14¾	14¾	14½	14½
	.9636	.2773	.9640	.2633	.9681	.2586
2½°	6	8½	5⅓	7⅚	8¼	10¾
	.9890	.1494	.9908	.1376	.9824	.1898
⑤°	1¾	6¾	1	6	5	**10**
	.9930	.1183	.9945	(.1051)	.9848	.1763
7½°	−¼	7¼	−1⅓	6⅙	3½	11
	.9920	.1272	.9942	.1080	.9816	.1943
10°	−1⅞	8⅛	−3¼	6¾	3	13
	.9899	.1427	.9930	.1183	.9744	.2309
12½°	−2⅛	10⅜	−4⅞	7⅝	2	14½
	.9836	.1830	.9912	.1338	.9681	.2586
15°	−2½	12½	−4¾	10¼	1¼	16¼
	.9763	.2217	.9840	.1808	.9600	.2915
17½°	−3	14½	−3⅓	14⅙	⅞	18⅜
	.9681	.2586	.9696	.2524	.9489	.3321
20°	−2¾	17¼	−2¼	17¾	−⅛	19⅞
	.9550	.3105	.9524	.3201	.9404	.3615
25°	−1⅞	23⅛	−1⅛	23⅞	−1¾	23¼
	.9197	.4270	.9144	.4219	.9188	.4296
30°	−1½	28½	−1	29	−2½	27½
	.8788	.5429	.8746	.5543	.8870	.5205
45°	−1	44	−⅞	44⅛	−1½	43½
	.7193	.9957	.7179	.9698	.7254	.9489

Tangent of gliding angle, which, when multiplied by the coefficient of lift, gave the coefficient of drag used in the equation to determine total drag of the *Kitty Hawk Flyer*.

Kitty Hawk Flyer would really fly. It can readily be seen that all of the factors in these equations for drag and for lift are well known and comprise the square footage of the aircraft involved, which is easy enough to figure. The speed of the wind, taken from the anemometers at Kitty Hawk, plus the estimated speed of the aircraft over the ground, gives the relative total wind velocity. The derivation of the factors for the coefficient of lift or coefficient of drag can be taken from the tables as explained and as obtained through wind tunnel tests.

The one factor that was critical in the whole solution of these equations was the value of k, or the pressure of air on a flat plane of any given size and at any given wind speed. This was the key to the whole show, and it was the Wrights' ingenuity, genius, and perception that solved it very accurately and satisfactorily.

At the time that Wilbur made his address before the Western Society of Engineers on September 18, 1901, he referred to the fact that all of his calculations for lift and drag had been made with the well-known so-called Smeaton coefficient for pressures — namely, $.005 \times V^2$. It meant that you could multiply the square of the velocity of the wind in miles per hour (mph) by the factor of .005 to arrive at pressures in pounds per square inch of any given surface. The Smeaton factor was named after John Smeaton, who in 1759 submitted to the British Royal Society a table of wind pressures based on experiments with mechanically driven windmills.

The value of k in the Smeaton table was .00492 rounded off to .005 for convenience in making calculations. The table, which was quoted for years in textbooks, was used by Lilienthal, but after the units in the Smeaton table were converted to metric (the measurement system used in Germany and other European countries as far back as the 1890s), another small inaccuracy was apparently added to the Smeaton coefficient, to derive the value of .0055. The Wrights were convinced that this figure was seriously in error, so they measured the pull in pounds on various parts of their aircraft, including the pull on each of the wings of the biplane in level position in known wind velocities, together with the computed drag caused by a man lying in the prone position. These last measurements were taken from their bicycle experiments.

Thus, with the known total pounds of drag (D) and with the coefficient of drag developed from computations (C_d), times the square of the known velocity of the wind (V^2), times the area of their aircraft (S), they could calculate k, the pressure coefficient of the air. They came up with the remarkably accurate figure of .0033 as that coefficient. Incidentally, this is very close to the figure of .003289, now used in the design of modern high-speed aircraft. It is a truly remarkable achievement for their time, education, and technology.

During the process of entering into these calculations, the interrelationship between the disappointing loss of *lift* performance of their 1900 glider and its rather surprising low *drag* factor, which they were able to measure, became readily apparent. If the Smeaton factor was off by the difference between Lilienthal's .0055 and the Wright brothers' measurement of .0033 (in other words, a figure only about 60 percent as great as that used by Lilienthal for air pressure), then, indeed, not only would the aircraft show much less drag, but, at the same time, quite obviously, much less lift — and the mystery of their interrelationship had been solved.

Now, if we enter this factor of .0033, derived by reversing the equation for drag into the equation for lift, we have all of the factors necessary to determine with great confidence whether the *Kitty Hawk Flyer* had enough wing area and enough power to lift itself from the ground and to sustain flight. However, the Wrights knew that it was necessary to assure themselves that their estimate of loss from propeller efficiency was correct. This question launched the brothers on their greatest theoretical adventure, namely, their calculations to determine design efficiency in their propeller.

Bibliography

Books

Chanute, Octave. *Progress in Flying Machines*. New York: Forney Company, 1894.

Charnley, Mitchell V. *The Boys Life of the Wright Brothers*. New York: Harper and Brothers, 1928.

Crowther, J. G. *Six Great Inventors*. London: Hamish Hamilton Ltd., 1954.

Da Costa, Fernando H. *Alberto Santos-Dumont, the Father of Aviation*. Brazil: Ministry of Aeronautics, 1973.

East, Omega G. *The Wright Brothers*. Washington, D.C.: U.S. Government Printing Office, 1961.

Freudenthal, Elsbeth E. *Flight Into History*. Norman: University of Oklahoma Press, 1949.

Gibbs-Smith, Charles Harvard. *Aviation*. London: Her Majesty's Stationery Office, 1970 (based on author's *The Aeroplane: an Historical Survey*, also published in London: Science Museum, 1962).

————. *Flight Through the Ages*. New York: Thomas Y. Crowell Company, Inc., 1974.

————. *A History of Flying*. New York: Frederick A. Praeger, New York, 1954 (originally published in London: Batsford, 1953).

————. *The Rebirth of European Aviation*. London: Her Majesty's Stationery Office, London, 1974.

————. *The World's First Aeroplane Flights*. London: Science Museum, 1963.

————. *The Wright Brothers*. London: Science Museum, 1963.

Glines, Carroll V. *The Wright Brothers — Pioneers of Power Flight*. New York: Franklin Watts, Inc., 1968.

Hallion, Richard P., ed. *The Wright Brothers: Heirs of Prometheus*. Washington, D.C.: National Air and Space Museum, Smithsonian Institution, 1978.

Harrison, Michael. *Airborne at Kitty Hawk.* London: Cassell and Company Ltd., 1953.

Hayward, Charles B. *Practical Aviation.* Chicago: American Technical Society, 1912.

Jackman, W. J., and Thomas H. Russell. *Flying Machines: Construction and Operation.* Chicago: The Charles C. Thompson Co., 1910.

Kelly, Fred C. *Miracle at Kitty Hawk.* New York: Farrar, Straus and Young, 1951.

———. *The Wright Brothers.* New York: Harcourt, Brace and Company, 1943.

McFarland, Marvin W., ed. *The Papers of Wilbur and Orville Wright* (2 volumes). New York: McGraw-Hill Book Company, Inc., 1953.

McMahon, John R. *The Wright Brothers — Fathers of Flight.* Boston: Little Brown and Company, 1930 (originally published as a series of articles in *Popular Science Monthly,* 1929).

Miller, Francis Trevelyan. *The World In the Air* (2 volumes). New York: G. P. Putnam's Sons, 1930.

Miller, Ivonette Wright. *Wright Reminiscences.* Private printing, 1978.

Mouillard, L. P. *The Empire of the Air: An Ornithological Essay on the Flight of Birds.* Paris: Octavo, 1881.

Peyrey, François. *Les premiers hommes-oiseaux: Wilbur et Orville Wright.* Paris: H. Guiton, 1908.

Renstrom, Arthur G. *Wilbur and Orville Wright — A Bibliography.* Washington, D.C.: Library of Congress, 1968.

———. *Wilbur and Orville Wright — A Chronology.* Washington, D.C.: Library of Congress, 1975.

Reynolds, Quentin. *The Wright Brothers — Pioneers of American Aviation.* New York: Random House, 1950.

Ritchie, Malcolm L. *The Research and Development Methods of Wilbur and Orville Wright.* Dayton, Ohio: Wright State University, 1976.

Roseberry, C. R. *Glenn Curtiss: Pioneer of Flight.* New York: Doubleday and Company, Inc., 1972.

Villard, Henry Serrano. *Contact!.* New York: Bonanza Books, Crown Publishers, 1968.

Walsh, John E. *One Day At Kitty Hawk.* New York: Thomas Y. Crowell Company, 1975.

Wherry, Joseph H. *Automobiles of the World.* Philadelphia: Chilton Book Company, 1968.

Wright, Orville. *How We Invented the Aeroplane.* New York: David McKay, 1953.

Articles

Anderton, David A. "Wings — 75 Years of Powered Flight," *Popular Mechanics,* December 1978.

Anonymous. "The Wright Aeroplane and Its Performance," *Scientific American,* April 7, 1906.

Baker, M. P. "Wright Brothers," *Aero Digest,* July 1953.

Buist, H. Massac. "The Human Side of Flying," *Flight,* March 6, 1909.

Casson, H. N. "At Last We Can Fly," *American Magazine,* April 1907.

Comley, Roland W. "I Saw It Fly," *Army,* December 1978.

Courtney, W. B. "Twelve Seconds That Shrank the Earth," *Collier's,* December 25, 1948.

Crouch, Tom. "December: Diamond Anniversary of Man's Propulsion Skyward," *Smithsonian,* December 1978.

Dwyer, Tom. "Getting the Military Off the Ground," *Air Line Pilot,* December 1978.

Gardner, Lester D. "The World the Kitty Hawk Made," *Collier's,* December 25, 1948.

Gibbs-Smith, Charles H. "The Wright Brothers: The Family Background of the American Pioneers in Aviation," *History Today,* February 1974 (London).

Glines, C. V. "The Wrights in Europe: Struggle for Recognition," *Air Line Pilot,* December 1978.

Hooven, Frederick J. "The Wright Brothers' Control System," *Scientific American,* November 1978.

Horgan, James J. "Aeronautics at the World's Fair of 1904," *Missouri Historical Society Bulletin,* April 1968.

Jerram, Mike. "Gentleman Adventurer," *Wings,* vol. 5, part 74, 1978.

Langewiesche, W. "What the Wrights Really Invented," *Harper's* magazine, June 1950.

Langley, Samuel Pierpont. "Experiments in Aerodynamics," *Smithsonian Institution Report,* 1902.

———. "The Story of Experiments in Mechanical Flight," *Aeronautical Annual,* 1897.

Lilienthal, Otto. "The Problem of Flying," *Prometheus,* no. 205, vol. 4, 1893.

MacCracken, W. P. "Wilbur Wright Memorial Lecture," *Journal of the Royal Aeronautical Society,* 1929.

McClarren, Robert. "Wright Flyer," *Aero Digest,* July 1953.

McFarland, M. W. "The Gentlemen and the Press," *Boeing* magazine, December 1953.

Parke, Robert B. "1903, When People Began to Fly," *Flying,* December 1978.

Pritchard, J. Laurence. "The Dawn of Aerodynamics," *Journal of the Royal Aeronautical Society,* March 1957.

Roth, Mickey. "Orville Who?" *AOPA Pilot,* December 1978.

Snyder, Jim. "Lifetimes of Invention," *Air Line Pilot,* December 1978.

Taylor, Charles E. "My Story of the Wright Brothers," as told to Robert S. Ball, *Collier's,* December 25, 1948.

Weiner, Philip. "America's Forgotten Daedalus," *Aerospace Historian,* Autumn 1968.

Wright, Orville. "Diary of the First Flight," *Collier's,* December 25, 1948.

———. "How We Made The First Flight," *Flying,* December 1913.

Wright, O. and W. "The Wright Brothers' Aeroplane," *The Century Magazine,* September 1908.

Zahm, A. F. "Octave Chanute — His Work and Influence on Aeronautics," *Scientific American,* May 13, 1911.

Index